Letters from a War Bird

Letters from a War Bird

THE WORLD WAR I CORRESPONDENCE of Elliott White Springs

Edited by David K. Vaughan

The University of South Carolina Press

© 2012 University of South Carolina

Published by the University of South Carolina Press
Columbia, South Carolina 29208

www.sc.edu/uscpress

Manufactured in the United States of America

21 20 19 18 17 16 15 14 13 12   10 9 8 7 6 5 4 3 2 1

Library of Congress Cataloging-in-Publication Data
Springs, Elliott White.
  Letters from a war bird : the World War I letters of Elliott White Springs /
edited by David K. Vaughan.
      p. cm.
  Includes bibliographical references and index.
  ISBN 978-1-61117-040-5 (cloth : alk. paper)
  1. Springs, Elliott White—Correspondence. 2. World War, 1914–1918—Aerial
operations, American. 3. World War, 1914–1918—Personal narratives, American.
4. World War, 1914–1918—Campaigns—France. 5. Fighter pilots—United
States—Correspondence. 6. United States. Army. Air Service. Aero Squadron,
148th. I. Vaughan, David Kirk. II. Title.
  D606.S63 2011
  940.4'1273092—dc23
  [B]

                                        2011031534

Contents

Illustrations

Preface

At the time of his death in 1959, Elliott White Springs was one of the wealthiest men in South Carolina and one of its most colorful characters. With his flamboyant management style and often outrageous advertising campaigns, he made the Springs Mills textile plant one of the most productive of its kind in the United States. However, his innovative and unpredictable management style was not developed after he assumed management responsibilities for the Springs Mills upon the death of his father; in his approach to management he displayed the same characteristics as when he faced the challenges of being a combat pilot in World War I: energy, determination, and creativity. Running a million-dollar textile company was a task no less daunting than surviving as a pilot of an obsolescent biplane, the Sopwith Camel, in the face of unpleasant odds in a dogfight against more modern German fighter aircraft.

When he was still at Princeton in 1917, Springs determined to join the U.S. Army Air Service (over the objections of his father). After completing his Princeton training, he sailed with 150 other aviation cadets across the Atlantic to England, where they continued their training at Oxford University and then at other training bases. He eventually flew as a combat pilot in France, first with William "Billy" Bishop's Royal Air Force 85 Squadron and then with the American 148th Aero Squadron, which was assigned to support the British, not the American, army. Shot down and badly injured in late June 1918, he nevertheless recovered and continued to fly until the armistice ended the war. He flew in some of the most intense aerial combats of the war, especially during the Allied drive of August and September, and was lucky to survive.

If the world knows anything about Elliott Springs's career as a pilot in World War I, it is probably as a result of the continuing popularity of *War Birds: Diary of an Unknown Aviator,* which was published in 1926, eight years after the war ended, and in which he (or to be exact, his character) figures prominently. The main character in the book is an "unknown" aviator who dies in the late summer of 1918. However, the unknown aviator was soon identified as one of Springs's two best friends, John McGavock "Mac" Grider; the other member of the trio was Larry Callahan. These three men had made a name for themselves as inveterate partygoers in

London in the spring of 1918 and then as stalwart aviators in Canadian ace Billy Bishop's 85 Squadron, which left for France at the end of May 1918.

Recognition of these two aspects of Springs's life prior to his becoming a textile magnate—his career as a fighter pilot and his postwar efforts as a writer—indicates the importance of the letters Elliott Springs wrote home to members of his family while he was in flight training and while he was assigned to two combat flying units in France. Reading these letters provides several valuable insights into Springs as a man. They reveal first the actual path that Springs followed through training to combat, a path that was, not surprisingly, similar to that described in *War Birds*. Second, the letters describe both the technical and emotional aspects of Springs's experiences in the aircraft he flew; they reveal his developing confidence in himself as a pilot (a confidence achieved in spite of, or perhaps because of, his numerous accidents and crash landings). Third, they indicate, sometimes in a disturbing manner, the dynamics of his family relationships, especially between him and his strong-minded father and to a lesser degree with his stepmother, Lena. Fourth, the letters clearly demonstrate Springs's unmistakable style, a unique combination of cleverness and a hard-edged wit, mixed with many references to the popular culture of the time as well as to classical literature and mythology. Springs's manner of writing is intended for insiders, those who have somehow achieved a perspective of the world similar to his—detached, occasionally cynical, certainly fatalistic (as long as there is a war to fight), worldly wise, and intellectually engaged. His often elliptical style frequently frustrated the best intentions of his father (and modern readers) to understand the meaning of the letters.

In reading Springs's letters (and his associated documents, including his 1918 diary and his flight log), we can begin to understand how he used the various elements and documents of his war-time experiences to assemble *War Birds*. This discussion is found in a separate section following the letters.

This project has been many years in the making, and I am thankful to many who helped along the way. First and foremost my gratitude goes to Mr. Henry Fulmer and his staff at the South Caroliniana Library of the University of South Carolina for their cheerful and prompt responses to my requests, primarily making copies of the Elliott Springs letters and other materials available to me during the course of my academic travels.

An equally important source of materials was the Springs Close Family Archives, located at the White Homestead, Fort Mill, South Carolina, which provided additional World War I letters written by Elliott Springs and photographs showing Springs and his fellow aviation students at Princeton University and Oxford University, England, many of which are included here. Ann Y. Evans, archivist and curator of the Springs Close Family Archives, was wonderfully helpful in bringing to my attention not only letters and photos but also other artifacts dating from the period, including a map that Elliott Springs used to orient himself as he flew along the front lines in the hazardous months of August and September 1918. The opportunity to visit the White Homestead, an impressive residence originally built before the Civil War and home to Elliott Springs and his family after World War I, was invaluable in giving me a more complete sense of the cultural heritage of the Springs and White families; I thank Anne Springs Close, Elliott Springs's daughter, as well as Ann Evans for the opportunity to experience true southern hospitality.

The staff members of the Seeley G. Mudd Manuscript Library at Princeton, New Jersey, have been especially helpful in providing copies of various documents found in their Elliott Springs files. Their prompt response to my requests for assistance was invaluable.

I would also like to thank Alexander Moore of the University Press of South Carolina for his friendly and enthusiastic assistance. Without his collegial and editorial efforts, this book would not have been as complete or as informative as I hope it now is.

My heartfelt thanks go to you all.

Introduction

Elliott Springs was a determined individual who distinguished himself in three separate careers: war pilot, writer, and businessman. As a pilot flying SE-5 and Sopwith Camel aircraft in France during World War I, he was credited officially with twelve German aircraft destroyed, placing him among the top five American aces of the war.[1] A novice pilot when he flew with William "Billy" Bishop's 85 Squadron in June 1918, he was a flight commander in the 148th Aero Squadron from July through September and would have been assigned as a squadron commander had the war not ended in November. As a writer after the war, he specialized in stories of air combat, producing nine books; *War Birds: Diary of an Unknown Aviator* is the best known of the nine. As a businessman, he became owner of the Springs Mills, located in Lancaster and Fort Mill, South Carolina, after the death of his father in 1931. Springs increased the productivity and profitability of the company significantly, primarily through a creative and aggressive advertising campaign with controversial but attention-getting full-color advertisements that featured double-entendre texts and women in risqué poses.

In the first two activities (flying and writing) he achieved success through personal preference and desire; the third (business) he came to through inheritance. According to his own statements, he was much happier in the first two areas than he was in the third, though his work as a businessman occupied him for the greatest period of his life. As a military pilot flying in France for less than six months in 1918, he accumulated a store of experiences that he recalled throughout his life, and which he put to good use as a writer of war-related stories. He also was able to establish some distance between himself and his overly protective, controlling father and to begin to develop his own personality away from his father's direct influence. He achieved this distance physically, by traveling across the Atlantic Ocean and eventually flying in France, as well as emotionally, though, as we see in his letters home, his father's concerns continued to affect his outlook, even in the intensity of aerial combat.

In the letters that he wrote home while he was in training—first at Princeton, then in England, and finally flying in combat in France during World War I—we can see his attitude toward his parents changing and his

Elliott Springs at Princeton University, date unknown. Courtesy of the Springs Close Family Archives, the White Homestead, Fort Mill, South Carolina.

sense of self-definition developing during the year and a half of his armed forces odyssey. His war-time letters reveal a clever, witty, and occasionally harsh intelligence at work as he attempted to report on his success as a member of the armed forces while at the same time maintaining an emotional separation from his parents. While it was a common pattern, especially among the officers and men away from the United States and serving in France, to communicate on a regular basis with their families at home, recording in letters and diaries their experiences in training and under fire in a distant land, Springs's letters are notable for their vigorous and perceptive analysis of events occurring around him. For that aspect alone they would be valuable in their own right, but because he produced, after the war, one of the most important and influential narratives of the air war, *War Birds: Diary of an Unknown Aviator*, the letters are especially valuable as they relate to and illuminate the descriptions included in that book.

Family Background

Elliott Springs, born in 1896, was the only child of Leroy and Grace Allison White Springs. Elliott's father was, according to one biographer, "an acquisitive, irascible entrepreneur" who worked hard to establish the family fortune in the making of cotton fabric and had, as a result, little time to devote to his son.[2] Leroy Springs was an ambitious, aggressive businessman who made up in nerve what he may have lacked in analytical skills. He was born in 1861, near Fort Mill, South Carolina, less than a year before the onset of the American Civil War. His father, A. Baxter Springs, was a lawyer and a planter with an interest in railroads. In 1884 he began his own business, Leroy Springs and Company, in Lancaster, South Carolina. His entrepreneurial success increased, and in 1891 he married Grace Allison White of Fort Mill. Elliott Springs was born five years later.

Elliott's mother came from a distinguished southern family; her father, Samuel White, had fought on the Confederate side during the Civil War and had been wounded more than once. Samuel White figured large in Elliott's imagination because of his military background and fondness for storytelling, and he served in many ways as Springs's preferred role model. His mother, Grace Springs, was educated, gracious, and caring. His two parents were of strongly contrasting natures. Unfortunately, Grace passed away in 1907 at the young age of thirty-three, when Elliott was only ten. Elliott's maternal grandmother had passed away four years earlier, when Elliott was seven; the shock of his grandmother's passing was especially traumatic for Elliott, as he was the one who first found her lifeless body when he entered the White residence to look for her.[3]

In 1908 Leroy sent Elliott to Asheville School in North Carolina, where Elliott was effectively removed from any immediate family support. While he was at Asheville, Elliott received letters from his father urging him to do better in his schoolwork and to avoid participating in sports activities, such as football, that might cause physical harm. Even at this early stage, Elliott was beginning to recognize and resist the strong and insistent will of his father, expressed in his letters, as his father attempted to control Elliott's behavior. In response Elliott began to develop methods of deflecting his father's requests and working around his father's desires, a mode of responding that continued until Leroy Springs's death in 1931.

In 1911, four years after his mother died, Elliott's maternal grandfather, Samuel White, passed away; Elliott was fourteen. Thus before Elliott had completed his childhood, the most important members of his mother's family were gone; his father, Leroy, was the sole source of financial and emotional support for his son. Providing financial support was no problem

Leroy Springs. Courtesy of the Springs Close Family Archives, the White Homestead, Fort Mill, South Carolina.

for Leroy; providing the necessary emotional support, however, was more challenging, as Leroy's brusque nature and efficiency-oriented manner of thinking made it difficult for the two to be comfortable with one another.

The loss of so many family members in such a relatively short period of time must have affected Elliott's outlook and emotional state. It probably did not help the relationship that Leroy decided to send his son to school at another distant location, Culver Military Academy in Indiana, where he remained for two years, from 1911 to 1913. At Culver he distinguished himself in his military activities, especially as an equestrian. He also developed an interest in writing stories, and this continued for many years.

Perhaps to help him raise his young son, Leroy courted and soon married another distinguished southern woman, Lena Jones Wade, a widow who was head of the English department at Queen's College in Charlotte, North Carolina. Leroy and Lena married in 1913, six years after Grace Springs had died. Lena Springs did not withdraw from active involvement in the world as a result of her marriage to Leroy. On the contrary she seemed to thrive in the energetic force field generated by her husband. She

Lena Springs.
Courtesy of the
Springs Close
Family Archives,
the White Home-
stead, Fort Mill,
South Carolina.

clearly saw her role as the wife of one of South Carolina's wealthiest and most influential men as providing leadership to the community in a variety of areas. During World War I, for instance, she was head of the South Carolina Red Cross effort, and she was also involved in providing support for Liberty Bond campaigns in the state. In 1924 she became the first woman to be nominated for the vice presidency of the United States on the Democratic ticket. Doubtless she was as determined in her outlook as she was charming in her personal demeanor.

It seems evident that Elliott did not immediately, if ever, accept Lena as an appropriate substitute for his dead mother. Self-confident and politically active in women's issues, Lena apparently did not worry excessively about winning the favor of the reluctant Elliott. She probably recognized that it would be futile to force Elliott's affections. As can be seen in the letters Elliott wrote home during the war, Elliott did not hesitate to complain about certain aspects of her home-front behavior as often as he did about his father's behavior.

When Elliott completed his schooling at Culver, his father ensured that Elliott's education continued, this time at Princeton University. At Princeton, Springs enrolled in literature classes taught by such distinguished professors as E. C. McDonald and Alfred Noyes, and yet he was unable to convince either of them of his abilities as a writer. Springs's Princeton classmates included two future major literary figures, F. Scott Fitzgerald and John Peale Bishop, whom Springs must have known but with whom he did not form any significant friendships.[4] Springs undoubtedly was hurt when he was refused membership, early in his college career, in the Quadrangle Club, whose members specialized in literary studies. Possibly Springs was rejected because his classmates believed that Springs's vigorous southern humor did not fit in with the more polished East Coast sense of sophistication. Perhaps as a reaction Springs apparently focused his energies off campus more than on, as he increasingly frequented the clubs and entertainment spots in New York City, a short train ride away. During his junior year at Princeton, Springs became increasingly distracted by the events of the war in Europe, but it was not until his senior year that the war fully engaged his attention (as it did that of many of his classmates).

Aviation Training

After the United States officially entered the war in Europe, on 6 April 1917, almost every young man of suitable age thought about entering one of the military services, and Elliott was no exception. As had occurred at Yale University, an aviation training program was developed at Princeton in the spring of 1917. While the Yale program was designed to provide potential aviators for naval aviation, however, the goal of the Princeton program was to provide aviation candidates for the U.S. Army. Springs participated in the Princeton program enthusiastically and quickly displayed his aptitude for flying and for military discipline. During the spring semester of his senior year, he was belatedly offered membership in the Quadrangle Club. Though he was pleased to have been considered, he declined, preferring to concentrate his energies in the newly developing Princeton flight training program. He quickly became one of the stalwart performers in the program, and after graduating from Princeton in June 1917, he was continued in the regular army flight training program.

In July and August, Springs was a flying cadet in the United States Army. He effectively completed his ground training while at Princeton, taking classes in a program similar to those being offered at a number of other universities across the United States, including Massachusetts Institute of Technology, Georgia Institute of Technology, the University of Illinois, and California Institute of Technology. When that program was complete, near the end of August, he and several other cadets from Princeton were transferred to the U.S. Army Air Service flying field at Mineola, New York, where he continued his flight training for a brief period. The standard training program for most U.S. aviators was to complete ground school first and then proceed to flight training. However, because Princeton offered flight training in aircraft provided by Princetonian benefactors, Springs was familiar with basic flight concepts and procedures prior to the official conclusion of ground school. His nonstandard pattern of flight training, begun at Princeton, continued throughout his training period in the United States and then in England. While most U.S. aviators were trained at newly created flying fields in Ohio, Illinois, Tennessee, and especially Texas, Springs and a group of specially designated flying cadets found themselves embarking on a unique and unusual program of instruction conducted on behalf of the U.S. Air Service by the men of the Royal Flying Corps in England, which later, in 1918, became the Royal Air Force.

By the middle of September he was on board the SS *Carmania,* accompanied by 150 other aviation cadets, on his way, he thought, to Italy, where under the leadership of Fiorello LaGuardia they expected to continue their training. When they arrived in England, however, they learned that their orders had been changed and they would be remaining in England to complete their aviation training program. After a short stay at Oxford University, where they were given some additional ground training, they were then divided into two groups and sent to a variety of basic and then advanced flight training airfields.

After completing their ground school at Oxford, Springs and several others were sent first to Stamford, England, and then briefly to London Colney, a flying field just outside London. From there he was sent to aerial gunnery school first in Turnberry and then in Ayr, Scotland, to engage in aerial combat school. The standard pattern for most American pilots was to complete their basic flight training in the United States and then proceed to France, where at special training fields established at Tours in 1917 and Issoudun in 1918 they completed the more advanced phases of the flying training program, including aerial combat, using specially mounted cameras that recorded images of opposing aircraft during simulated combat maneuvers. Practice in actual gunnery was conducted at French fields as well, first at Cazeaux and then at St Jean de Monts, on the French coast south of Marseille.[5] Springs and his fellow aviators were trained in the

British fashion, which provided gunnery practice first followed by aerial combat simulation. Once gunnery school and aerial combat phases were complete, the American aviators were ready to be assigned to flying units in France.

While the American aviators were normally assigned to American aero squadrons after the completion of their gunnery school, Springs and the other aviators in England were assigned to British squadrons. There were two reasons for this unusual routing. The first was that because the pilots had been trained to fly according to the British system, it was logical that they should be assigned to fly with British units, as the new pilots would have received the latest advice on aerial tactics from seasoned British veteran pilots and would understand the procedures and practices of the British flying squadrons. In addition, because British pilots had trained the men, they could be considered (at least for a while) as British resources. Many British squadrons included pilots from other countries: Canadians, Australians, New Zealanders, and even some from India. An additional, ultimately more convincing argument was this: although the American pilots were trained and ready to fly, there were not (at least in the spring of 1918) sufficient American squadrons in existence to accommodate the pilots. Pilots could be trained much more quickly than squadrons (with the appropriate enlisted men, aircraft, and support equipment) could be prepared. Rather than have these freshly trained pilots wait indefinitely for the Americans to find a use for them, the decision was made to allow them to fly with the British, who after all needed replacements, as they had been fighting an intense air war for nearly four years before the Americans decided to join the war effort.

Combat Assignments

Through a combination of luck and coinciding training schedules, Springs and two of his best friends, Larry Callahan and John McGavock "Mac" Grider, who had formed a formidable social alliance, were recruited into the 85 Squadron of the British Royal Flying Corps, newly formed under the leadership of Canadian flying ace William "Billy" Bishop. Flying powerful and sturdy SE-5 aircraft, the squadron flew en masse from England to France late in May 1918 and was soon involved in operational flying along the front lines of France. The squadron was assigned the task of supporting the British army in the area east of Dunkirk, and Springs, Grider, and Callahan flew their first combat missions doing line patrols and escorting British bombers of 211 and 206 Squadrons.

Springs remained with the squadron for about one month, until the combination of a serious aircraft accident and the needs of the U.S. Air Service combined to remove him from 85 Squadron. Early in July he was relocated into the 148th Aero Squadron as a flight commander. Although initially Springs resisted this move, he was in no position to argue with the U.S. authorities, who were bringing many new American aero squadrons into operation throughout the summer of 1918 and needed to fill the leadership positions in these squadrons with experienced American pilots. Although Springs was now in an American aero squadron, he was still in a way a British resource, because the squadron to which he was assigned was given the task of supporting units of the British army; the 17th Aero Squadron, with which his Princeton classmate George Vaughn Jr. was flying, was similarly assigned. The reason for this arrangement was as much logistical as political: the Americans were short of combat aircraft, which the British could provide; in this case the 148th was provided with the Sopwith Camel, an obsolescent, underpowered, but very maneuverable aircraft. Springs flew with the 148th Aero Squadron for the next four months, flying from fields in the vicinity of 85 Squadron, until late October, when the squadron received notice that it would be returning to American control and would be giving up its Sopwith Camel aircraft for newer aircraft. At this time Springs was notified that he would be given command of a new American aero squadron and would probably be assigned the more powerful and combat-tested SPAD XIII aircraft. However, the armistice on 11 November brought the end of fighting; no new squadrons were formed, and in fact most existing aero squadrons were soon disbanded. Springs returned home in February 1919.

During the six months he flew in combat with the British and American forces, he was involved in several aerial combats, was credited with twelve (or more, depending on the authority) victories, and crash-landed at least twice.[6] Like all pilots who had flown in combat and survived the war, he was lucky to be alive. He had seen several of his best friends, including Mac Grider, disappear during combat. Some of his fellow pilots were killed, and some became prisoners of war. Grider's death affected Springs deeply as he held himself responsible for not paying greater attention to Grider's situation during the flight from which he failed to return. Springs had suffered the stresses of combat typical of all operational pilots. Twenty-two years old at the end of the war, he had aged mentally and even physically. As did many other pilots, he suffered a mild breakdown as the war ended.

The Phases of Springs's Correspondence

Springs's letters to his parents can be divided into eight periods. The first consists of his training at Princeton University and his subsequent training with the U.S. Army Air Service prior to departure for England, from April to September 1917. In letters from this period Springs describes his growing interest in flying, his entry into Princeton's flight training program, and his transition into the U.S. Air Service. In this correspondence we can see Springs's verbal sparring with his father (at times bordering on something like whining) and the gradual shift in his attention from his educational and family concerns to his growing enthusiasm about flying.

During the second period (September to November 1917), he was the ranking cadet officer in charge of the flying cadets in training at Oxford, England. Springs's commanding officer in the United States and on the *Carmania* during the passage across the Atlantic, Maj. Leslie MacDill, was apparently so impressed with Springs's natural leadership abilities (no doubt based on Springs's irrepressible sense of brash self-confidence) that he recommended he be placed in charge of the cadets (not as an officer but as a cadet noncommissioned officer) during their stay at Oxford.[7] While Springs continued to enjoy a healthy social life at Oxford, it is evident that he also developed a sense of responsibility and determined, to the best of his ability, to maintain order and discipline among his fellow cadets, which, given the loose military structure under which they were operating and his own fondness for social activities, presented a significant challenge. As revealed in his letters home, he clearly was proud of his ability to maintain discipline in a difficult situation.

During the third period, from November 1917 to February 1918, Springs was involved in the continuation and completion of his flying training program in England. His letters home during this period show him becoming more confident in his ability to fly the various kinds of aircraft that he was encountering in his training program. They also reveal a growing fatalistic outlook—partly bravado to impress and persuade his parents to more sympathetic viewpoints, but also partly realistic, as he recorded death after death among his fellow flying students.[8]

In the fourth period, from March to May 1918, he completed gunnery school in Scotland, where in addition to practicing his ability to shoot at fixed and moving targets from aircraft in flight, he also learned something of the ways of the Scots, including their social and cultural habits. After leaving Scotland he was reassigned to a base near London, where the scope of his socialization activities increased dramatically, especially after he reestablished his special relationship with Larry Callahan and Mac Grider, the other two of the group that their eventual squadron commander, Col. Billy Bishop, termed the "Three Musketeers." In company with Callahan and Grider, Springs undertook a program of London partying that was as strenuous as any segment of his flight training. During this period he no longer had any supervisory responsibilities and was free to enjoy opportunities for socialization, and his letters to his parents describe many such events, intended as much to shock as to educate or entertain his (no doubt disapproving) father.

Letters from the fifth period, from May through June 1918, cover the time Springs flew with Billy Bishop's 85 Squadron, from its initial formation, to its departure for France at the end of May, to its first combat patrols along the northern segment of the front lines. These letters home are filled with the excitement of flying in combat for the first time and his awed response to the seemingly effortless success his squadron commander, Billy Bishop, was having in downing enemy aircraft. Although Springs makes it appear as if the whole exercise of going after enemy aircraft is the equivalent of a Princeton athletic event, we can detect between the lines something of Springs's nervousness arising from his increasing awareness of the profound hazards of aerial combat, especially as he begins to record the failures of several members of his unit to return from missions, including his friend John McGavock Grider. This section ends with Springs's own failure to return safely from a mission, as his engine was disabled during aerial combat and he crash-landed just inside the Allied front lines, suffering relatively severe injuries to his face and head.

Letters from the next period, from the end of June through the first week of August 1918, describe Springs's recovery from injuries received in his crash, his reassignment to the 148th Aero Squadron, and his combat (and occasional leave) experiences for the first six weeks of the squadron's combat flying. During this time Springs was B Flight commander, responsible for leading members of his flight on their patrols over or behind the lines. Along with Bennett "Bim" Oliver and Henry Clay, the original commanders of A and C flights respectively, Springs was one of the leaders of the squadron, and he soon built a reputation for aggressive, nearly ruthless determination to attack enemy formations, for which the price often paid by his wingmen was to be shot down.

Letters from the seventh period, from the second week of August until the end of September 1918, cover the days of the most intense aerial combat by members of the squadron as they flew against the strength of the German air force. They often faced superior odds as the German leadership attempted to defeat the efforts of the Allies in the air as on the ground, hoping to stop the Allied advance that was forcing them to retreat constantly, a retreat which eventually ended with the armistice. In these hard days of flying and fighting, it was rare for patrols to return to the home field without the loss of at least one man. On one mission Springs was the only one of his flight to return. His letters home during this period show a mixture of exhilaration and weariness as he recounts the details of his numerous aerial combats.

The final period of his letters home is from October 1918 through January 1919, during which time he effectively ceased his operational flying, attempted to recover his health, and awaited orders to return to the United States. Poor flying weather in October and the news that he was to become a commander of his own squadron combined in the final six weeks of the war to offer Springs a respite from combat. While his body and spirit badly needed the rest, his mind continued to engage in aerial combat, and he suffered a series of mental and physical breakdowns, first in October and then, after the armistice, in November. His letters home show the results of combat stress, in their disconnectedness and their desperate efforts to display the wit and gaiety of an earlier time.

During this final period Springs attempted to adjust to the end of the war. He was simultaneously relieved to be liberated from the stresses of flying combat and genuinely distressed that this period of nearly superhuman achievement had ended. Clearly he would have liked to lead a squadron of his own, but that opportunity was denied him. During this period he wrote an undated letter home, free from satire or rebuke, that describes as eloquently as any passage written about the war in the air the sensations and impressions of a pilot who spent hundreds of hours flying over, along, and behind the front lines.[9] The absence of letters home during this period tells us as much about his mental state as any information contained in the existing letters. The end of the fighting brought to Springs, as to many other aerial crew members, combined feelings of release and letdown to which there was no simple adjustment.

The Letters

The Elliott Springs Collection in the South Caroliniana Library Special Collections Division at the University of South Carolina consists of several boxes of materials. The Springs World War I materials are found in five of these boxes. Most of the World War I letters are retyped copies of the handwritten letters Springs sent home. It is not clear who retyped the letters or even when they were retyped; it is likely that they were retyped by someone in the Springs Mills offices for easy reference when Springs was preparing *War Birds* for publication, for he used much of the material in his letters home in *War Birds*. These retyped letters contain few errors of grammar or content and appear to be accurate transcriptions of the originals. Unfortunately few original copies are in the World War I files, and comparing style and content of the retyped copies with the original versions is not possible. Most of the letters written by Springs to his parents dating between April 1917 and January 1919 are in this collection. An additional fifteen letters are contained in the Springs Close Family Archives in the White Homestead at Fort Mill, South Carolina. These are original letters in Springs's handwriting, and they date from his days at Princeton University to the final months of the war.

In addition to the letters written by Elliott, a number written by his father, Leroy, to his son are included in the Springs files at the Caroliniana Library, with some duplicates at the White Homestead. The letters from Leroy Springs that are included in the collection are copies of originals, probably dictated to and typed by his secretary; Leroy Springs seems to have sent multiple copies of his letters to more than one address in Europe because he knew his son was moving from location to location during his training and combat assignments, and he wanted to ensure that at least one of his letters reached his son. He also kept copies of what seem to be these letters in his office files. Excerpts from several of these letters have been included here in order to indicate the business and community issues with which the senior Springs was involved during the war, to illustrate the style of writing and the content of the letters written by Leroy, and especially to give a sense of the kind of parental commentary to which Springs frequently responded (and often objected) in his letters home.

While the letters of Leroy Springs frequently suggest the overly cautious concerns of a father who has a plan that he wishes his recalcitrant son would follow, they also display the legitimate caring concern of a loving parent, allowing us to recognize the often unfair assessment Elliott frequently makes of his father's comments. In reading the letters of the two individuals together from a period of eighteen months, we can see that Elliott had developed a fairly elaborate and consistent rhetorical pattern that he used repeatedly to complain about supposedly offensive or silly behaviors displayed by his father and stepmother. Even after he had faced hazards in combat that his father could never fully grasp, and after Elliott had grown and developed through profoundly life-changing experiences, Elliott was still unable to set aside these defensive rhetorical mechanisms used to distance himself from his father. Unfortunately no letters from his stepmother, Lena Springs, can be found in the South Caroliniana collection or in the Springs Close Family Archives, so it is not possible to compare her comments with Elliott Springs's reaction to them; she probably wrote these by hand and did not make copies. However, it seems probable that if such a comparison could be made, we would find an often unfair assessment of Lena's comments similar to those made in response to correspondence from his father.

In his letters home three issues constantly recur: Springs's apparently desperate need for sweets, especially Page and Shaw's candy; his need for additional funds; and his complaints about the quality and quantity of the letters written to him by his parents. Springs's requests for candy from home appear almost as soon as he reaches England, and they increase as he moves into his flying training program and into his operational combat assignments. In one letter he states that he needs more candy because his new squadron commander, Billy Bishop, has consumed what was left of his latest package. Once in France, Springs added sugar to his requests, writing that he needed it as an important ingredient in the drinks he was now preparing for the other members of the squadron.

Almost as often as he requests candy from home, Springs asks for additional funds, usually justifying his requests by noting the need for new equipment or expenses related to his constant relocation or, in London, expenses associated with the upscale lifestyle needed for his social activities. In an obvious but unstated effort to reinforce this need, he repeatedly requests that his parents (especially his father) write to him in care of the local bank, not to any military address or in care of the American Embassy. His father initially acquiesced to Springs's requests for money, but then as the requests continued, he pointed out that other soldiers he knew who had been assigned to France were not only living well within their army salaries but were in fact sending money home to their families.

In his letters home Elliott Springs largely ignores these comments, saying that he is the best judge of his monetary needs and adding, in increasingly fatalistic terms, not-so-subtle hints that the kind of military activities in which he is engaging may soon lead to his eventual demise. After he received what appeared to him to be a wholly unreasonable request from Elliott to honor a bank draft from one of his friends, Leroy wrote his son an unusually long and fully articulated letter (excerpted here) in which he details the personal and professional failings of someone who is a "spendthrift" and cannot live within his economic means. His target here was clearly his son. Although the occasion for the letter arose from a misunderstanding, and Leroy eventually admitted that he overreacted, it seems clear that the incident gave Leroy the opportunity he must have long desired to express his feelings about Elliott Springs's assumption that his father would always provide the funds he requested. When Elliott received the letter containing these comments from his father, in the fall of 1918, Elliott's response was uncharacteristically subdued. However, at that point his spirit and energy were flagging as a result of the stress of aerial combat, and he probably was anticipating the end of the war. One of Elliott Springs's underlying, unstated arguments was that his father should not complain about sending money to him since Elliott would in all likelihood (or so Elliott truly believed) eventually become a fatality. By October 1918 it seemed clear that the war would end soon, and Elliott could no longer use that argument as justification for his requests.

The third, and most annoying, issue, certainly for readers of these letters as well as it must have been for the recipients, is Elliott Springs's often-expressed antagonistic attitude toward his parents about the superficial content of the letters they were writing and the fact that they were not writing as often as Springs thought they should. The substantial number of letters from Leroy Springs in the files shows that he wrote once a week, on average; undoubtedly some parents wrote their sons more often than this, but once a week seems like a reasonable schedule, especially for someone as busy as Leroy must have been during these months, running a company that was supplying necessary goods for the military services. Though no correspondence from Lena survives, Springs's responses to her letters seem to suggest that she wrote about as often. For two busy individuals heavily involved in the production of textiles for the war (as Leroy Springs was) and Red Cross and fund-raising efforts for the war (as Lena was) and with significant demands on their time, a one-letter-a-week schedule would seem entirely appropriate. Elliott Springs, however, did not appear to be at all sympathetic with their war-related activities; he complained often of the style of his father's letters, which he said read as if they had been written by a machine on a machine (Leroy Springs undoubtedly dictated his letters to his secretary, who then typed them; it is true that Leroy's letters occasionally read uncomfortably like business letters, lacking the personal touch). He objected to two main themes that his father repeatedly mentioned: the first was that Elliott appeared to make important career and life decisions without consulting his father; the second was Elliott's repeated requests for money. Both of these issues are illustrated in the excerpts from Leroy's letters included here; most readers are likely to sympathize (or at least empathize) with Leroy rather than Elliott. It does seem at times that Elliott is complaining unfairly about his father's concerns. However, for Elliott, these might have been symptoms of a larger problem not specifically articulated by either the father or the son: long-term involvement (Elliott might have said meddling) of the father in the son's right to make important decisions for himself.

This larger issue is presented, interestingly, in some detail in *War Birds,* the novelized memoir of his war-time experiences that Elliott published eight years after the war ended. Although the book purportedly describes the experiences of another, "unknown" aviator, Springs's relationship with his father is described at some length in the book. An extended sample from the book is given here because it is so revealing of the forces at work in the relationship between father and son. In the book the unknown aviator relates that

> Springs is all right until he gets mail from home, then he gets into a terrible rage and wants to fight the wide, wide world. He and his father seem to carry on a feud at long range. He's got so now he doesn't open any letters until he's had a few drinks and some of them he doesn't open at all. His father writes him full details and instructions in triplicate about how to do everything and finds fault with everything he does. Springs is no saint but he isn't nearly that bad. . . . He worries about everything his father says and takes all his criticism to heart, tho why he should worry over it when he's three thousand miles away is beyond me. . . . He must be awfully fond of his father to care what he thinks about things he doesn't know anything about.[10]

In an incident described in *War Birds,* the unknown aviator and Springs find themselves taking shelter during a night-time attack by a German bomber, and they have some time to themselves before the attack ends. The nameless aviator says:

> We got to talking about home. He said he had to get killed because he couldn't go home. He said if he got killed, his father would have a hero for a son and he could spend all his time and money building monuments to him and make himself very happy and proud. But if he lives thru it and goes home, he says his father will fight with him for the rest of his life. No matter what he does, his father will say it's wrong and worry about it. I told him he was crazy but he was quite serious about it. He says it's a family trait. . . .
>
> He says if he lives thru it, his father is determined to make him go down in a cotton mill and work five years as a day laborer and live in the mill village. Some sort of foolishness about starting in at the bottom and working up. And the slightest mistake he makes will break his father's heart. . . . I asked him what he wanted to do. He said he wanted to write [books and stories] but his father is determined to make a horny-handed hardboiled superintendent out of him.[11]

When Springs included these passages in *War Birds,* published in 1926, he must have known his father would read them. If he expected any sympathetic reaction from his father, he was seriously disappointed, for Leroy responded with a letter of "outrage" at the description: "I literally staggered under the attack," he wrote, seeing it as a "bitter denunciation" from his own son, which would be read "in every city, town, and precinct in

America."[12] The frequent unkind comments to his father in his letters home represent the tip of a large iceberg of father-son antagonism that must have been building for many years.[13]

If Elliott Springs's comments to his father were unkind, his comments to his stepmother Lena were equally so, if not worse. He repeatedly ridiculed Lena's Red Cross volunteer work, suggesting that such activity did not count in comparison to the actual fighting of the war carried on by the soldiers and airmen, and that the women of the South (personified in Lena) saw the war primarily as an excuse for adding new events to the social agendas of the day, alongside matrimonial notices in the newspaper about women marrying men in the service or notices about men joining such (less important) military organizations as the Quartermaster Corps.

While we might understand why there was a pattern of ongoing tension between father and son, which must have begun many years earlier, there is no evident reason why Springs was so antagonistic, so hostile, so ungenerous in his comments about his stepmother's truly significant contributions to the war efforts at home. Even though he alternately addressed his letters home to individual parents, Elliott must have known that a letter written to one parent would have been read by both. Leroy might have been willing to overlook harsh comments from his son addressed to him, but he could not ignore Elliott's unkind remarks to his stepmother; beginning in letters written to Elliott midway through his training in England, Leroy repeatedly requests that his son cease using "frivolous" language in letters to Lena. In spite of his father's requests, Elliott continued to make fun of her war-related activities, relying increasingly on humor to cover his attacks. Some of Elliott's harshest comments about Lena's work appear in letters written home while he was involved in some of the most difficult flying experiences of the war. While we might at first think that the stress of war flying would cause Elliott to soften his tone in his letters home, such does not appear to have been the case. In fact his comments to his stepmother became more caustic, not less, as the war progressed. Leroy repeatedly cautioned his son that his letters home were being read by censors who might not understand the point of the comments in the letters. The censors, of course, would have been concerned about military, not family, secrets, but Leroy's point was that other, nonfamily members were reading the letters. Leroy pointed out that even though Lena was closer in age to Elliott than she was to Leroy (in 1918 Lena was thirty-five years old, Leroy was fifty-six, and Elliott was twenty-two), Elliott's "frivolous" language was not appropriate. Leroy's comments could indicate another source of tension between father and son; even at Princeton, Elliott prided himself on being a "ladies' man," and he certainly continued in that manner while he was in training in England. Perhaps he was upset that his attractive, talented stepmother preferred his father to him.

Springs assumed that his readers (his father and stepmother initially and now more modern readers) would recognize every reference he makes in his letters, whether the references are to military people and events or to popular cultural events and entertainers. He seldom troubled himself to explain who these people were or what relevance the reference had to his current situation. For instance he refers to other aviators sometimes by their last names and at other times by their first names; seldom does he include both first and last names. It would have been nearly impossible for Leroy or Lena to know who these individuals were. The only names they were familiar with were those from their immediate South Carolina vicinity and perhaps those of a few men they might have met when they visited Elliott at Princeton. Certainly after Elliott left the United States and arrived in England, they would have had very little information to help them identify the names and references that Elliott tossed out so casually in his letters home.

It is clear that Leroy read widely in the newspapers and other journals of his day to become informed of the kinds of activities that American aviators were experiencing in the war. At one point he seems to have learned more about what his son was doing from the newspapers than from the letters Elliott was writing home. For example, it took Leroy several weeks to understand fully that the new commander of Elliott's 85 Squadron was one of the most famous British aces in the war, William "Billy" Bishop. In his letters home written in April and May, Elliott alludes indirectly to the fact that his new squadron commander is someone famous, but he never makes it as clear as he might have. It is as if Elliott were intentionally trying to keep his father in the dark about his military activities, occasionally suggesting that censorship rules were forcing him to be unclear about specific details. In one of his letters to his son in France, Leroy complains about his son's lack of clarifying details, requesting once again that he substitute factual information about his activities in place of the "frivolous" comments about his parents. There can be little doubt that Springs knew exactly what effect his obscure style would have on his parents, and especially on his father. On one hand, he was doing his duty by communicating with his father (and doing so on a regular basis); on the other hand, he was withholding information essential to gaining a complete understanding of his actions, an effect that Elliott must have intended.

In spite of these annoyances, however, Elliott Springs's World War I letters offer rich rewards for readers today. They are especially significant for the insights they offer in three areas: the training and combat experiences

of a select group of American aviators during World War I; an understanding of the mental process and personal adjustments of the man as he dealt
with the pressures of war; and valuable information about Springs's postwar fiction. First, they illustrate in detail one of the many routes followed
by a significant group of American aviators during World War I. Although
their aviation training program was not typical for most American aviators trained during the war, the two hundred Oxford cadets were unusual
and noteworthy for the challenges they faced and the role they played in
fighting the war once they entered active flying service, as most of them—
such as Springs and his two closest companions, Larry Callahan and John
McGavock Grider—flew with British squadrons in support of elements of
the British army. Second, the letters offer detailed accounts of the strate-
gies and tactics of Springs and the other flight commanders as they devised
methods to outwit and overcome the challenges presented by opposing
German aviators, especially in the intense months of August and September, when Allied advances forced the German army to retreat. Third, they
illustrate the progress from enthusiastic novice to battle-weary veteran
typical of all participants in war but especially of the aviators, who had to
force themselves to continue to fly in spite of known hazards and the
deaths and disappearances of so many of their companions.

The letters are also useful because they give us insight into the workings
of the mind of Elliott Springs, one of the most aggressive and creative individuals to survive the war. We can see how Springs, taking advantage of his
family's privileged economic status, developed compensation mechanisms
for the pressures of war even before he entered World War I, by living a
sophisticated lifestyle in London for a few brief months before departing
for France. His letters are filled with references to the popular shows and
entertainers of his day and provide a thorough indoctrination into the popular cultural life of London in the last year of the war. Through footnoted
commentary attempts are made to clarify the references and to show how
Springs not only acknowledged these entertainment events but also incorporated them into meaningful illustrations of his intellectual processes.

In addition the letters provide a basis for understanding the fictional
works that Springs wrote in the years following his return to the United
States. They are most important for illustrating the design of and motiva-
tion for the creation of *War Birds: Diary of an Unknown Aviator,* his most
important and best-known work about the war in the air, and for illumi-
nating the creative process that brought the book to fruition. The letters
also describe the events that are included in Springs's other war works,
including *Nocturne Militaire, Above the Bright Blue Sky, Contact, Leave
Me with a Smile,* and *The Rise and Fall of Carol Banks.* The relation of

the letters to *War Birds* is discussed in a separate section at the end of the book.

For the most part the letters included here are exactly as written. The relatively small number of grammar, punctuation, typographic, and spelling errors they contain have been silently corrected. Occasionally a few passages pertaining to family members have been silently deleted when relatively unimportant family matters were being discussed or references were made to obscure or unknown individuals. The overriding concern is to maintain the wonderfully vigorous style that Springs displays in his letters and their often irreverent and even occasionally confrontational tone of voice. Especially in the letters he wrote during the hectic weeks when he was flying over the front on a daily basis, Springs's style demonstrates an incomparably breathless, nervous energy that reflects the mental state of one living a hazardous life.

Additional information about people and events has been included primarily in footnotes, where background information could be amplified as necessary without distracting attention from the text. In some cases brief clarifications have been provided directly in the letters, to avoid requiring the reader to refer unnecessarily to footnotes too frequently; these clarifications (and other editorial modifications in the text) are indicated by brackets. The names of military aviators who were part of the complement of aviation cadets and who accompanied Springs in his training programs at Princeton and in England are listed in Appendix A. The bibliography includes the titles of valuable reference works that can provide additional insight into or information about Springs's training and combat experiences.

In addition to Springs's letters, other supplementary information has been included in the text. This includes entries from Elliott Springs's 1918 diary, Elliott Springs's flight log, relevant information from the 148th Aero Squadron history,[14] and some comments by Springs that describe his flying activities in the 148th Aero Squadron at some date well after the end of the war. A few comments describing these sources may be helpful.

Elliott Springs apparently kept only one diary during his World War I career; diary entries began on 1 January 1918 and ended on 1 January 1919, with a four-month break from the end of June until the end of October 1918 (unfortunately this was the period of his most intense combat flying activity). Unlike the detailed entries in the more complete (and controversial) diary kept by his fellow aviator John McGavock Grider, the entries in Springs's diary are terse, informal, and often incomplete and difficult to decipher. It is evident that maintaining a complete and detailed diary was not one of Springs's priorities. He seems to have written the entries almost as afterthoughts, and there are suggestions that he occasionally backfilled them on occasion, thus dating some activities erroneously and describing some events incompletely. Given that Springs wrote detailed (if sometimes unclear) letters home, it is not surprising that he would not have wanted to write extensively in his diary also. However, his reactions to certain key events are recorded there in a bare and open manner, thus giving a truthful representation of how he felt about some of the more important events of his military career. Chief among these are his reaction when Mac Grider failed to return from a flight over the German lines on June 1918, the loss of several of his men during a September dogfight with the Germans, and his own physical and emotional relapse after the November armistice.

Springs kept a log showing his flights from November 1917 through September 1918. A typical line in the flight log includes the date of the flight, the type of aircraft and its tail (identifying) number, the duration of the flight, the purpose of the flight, and remarks about the flight. The format of the log required that the information for each flight be entered in a limited amount of space, as its primary purpose was to demonstrate to higher authority the currency and proficiency of the pilot. The numbers indicating the duration and dates of specific flights give little indication of the traumatic experiences that may have accompanied them, even when Springs noted additional details, as he did on 27 August, for example, when he wrote "15 to 20 Fokkers got 1." The information from his flight log is especially helpful, for it helps to explain why there are intervals between letters home; we can see, for example, that especially in August and September he was occasionally too busy flying operational patrols to spare the time to write. The information in a flight log entry is often explained by subsequent comments in the next letter home, for example when Springs gave a detailed account of a particularly hazardous and hectic dogfight.

Taylor and Irvin's *History of the 148th Aero Squadron* includes a narrative overview of the movements of the squadron, the arrivals and departures of its personnel, and forty-seven combat reports that were filed when pilots were successful in shooting down opposing German aircraft. Nine were attributed to Springs, and these are included to show the official version of the event to complement the necessarily more general account that Springs was forced to write in his letters home due to the actions of the censors, who would literally cut out specific details if they revealed military information of possible use to the Germans should the mails go astray. In addition to combat reports, the 148th kept reports of attacks on ground targets and straffing[15] actions (flying low and firing machine guns into enemy troops and supply columns on the roads).

The final supplementary source is an undated short narrative, included in the Springs World War I files in the South Caroliniana Library, that

Springs wrote sometime after the war had ended, probably well after the war had ended, perhaps as remarks to be given at one of the 148th Squadron reunions held in the 1950s. Though relatively brief, this narrative offers an informative account of Springs's activities, and excerpts are inserted into the text at the appropriate places.

The general pattern of the text is to begin each of the eight sections of letters with a brief introduction, which provides necessary background information, followed by the texts of the letters (and supplementary sources) as appropriate. Because most of the supplementary sources bear on the combat flying of Springs, especially in the 148th Aero Squadron, these materials do not appear until the latter part of the book.

Letters from a War Bird

Capt. Elliott Springs, U.S. Air Service. This picture, taken after the armistice, shows Springs wearing the rank of captain. Courtesy of National Museum of the United States Air Force.

Princeton and Mineola

March to August 1917

The letters in this section begin in March 1917, as Elliott Springs and his Princeton University classmates are beginning to think about joining some branch of the military or volunteer service to participate in the war in Europe. The early letters included here show how his concerns with his social life at Princeton University are gradually displaced by his desire to become a part of the aviation training program established at Princeton. A number of Princeton University graduates desired to implement an aviation training program similar to that established at Yale University in the summer of 1917. The program at Yale had been supported by wealthy and influential Yale graduates, who were able to persuade the Yale faculty to institute an aviation training program for aircraft on floats and were able to purchase several training aircraft and the services of an instructor.[1] The Yale program was well under way by the time the United States declared war on Germany on 6 April 1917.

A plan for privately financing an aviation program at Princeton was developed by James Barnes, an 1891 Princeton graduate, and was accepted by the university's Committee on Military Instruction. A flying field of sixty acres was established on the farm of William Schenk, also a Princeton graduate, where a hangar and an office were built.[2] Eventually four planes were used in the program, and the first flight occurred on 22 April. Approximately thirty-five students participated in the Princeton Aviation School training program. Springs had to pass a physical examination before he was officially accepted into the program early in May. He continued in the training program until he graduated from Princeton. He was sworn in to active duty in the U.S. Army on 29 June and continued his training, now under army administrative control, on 5 July. He and the other Princeton men in the program completed their training on 25 August, when they were transferred from Princeton to an army training field at Mineola, Long Island, New York. Those Princetonians whose names appear most often in Springs's letters and subsequent writings include George A. Vaughn Jr., John H. Raftery, B. H. Bostick, Harold K. Bulkley, and Arthur R. Taber.[3] In his letters Springs provided some details about his training program, indicating that he was flying as often as he could.

One of Springs's Princeton classmates, Arthur Richmond Taber, documented their training program in some detail in letters he wrote to his parents. Like Springs, Taber participated in the Princeton aviation training program, flying on a regular basis from April through June. Upon completing the training program following graduation from Princeton, Taber was accepted as a flying cadet on 29 June. In July instruction in the ground school of the U.S. Military School of Aeronautics at Princeton began in earnest with classes in flying theory, wireless communication, drill, military law, aircraft design and construction, and machine gun familiarization. Springs's schedule was essentially the same as the one Taber described.[4]

Just before graduation from aviation ground school, Taber wrote his father that a sign-up list had been posted for all men who wished to go to Italy for their flight instruction, and he decided to accept the opportunity.[5] Springs also enthusiastically signed up for the "Italian detachment," as it came to be called. After the cadets graduated from school, they were briefly assigned to the military camp at Mineola, near Garden City, New York, where they awaited final preparations before sailing to Europe. Several other detachments of cadets from other schools, such as Cornell and the University of Illinois, arrived at Mineola in the last days of August, swelling the numbers of men who knew that they would be shipping out soon to continue their flying training but not in the United States. They believed that they were all going to Italy.

Springs's letters to his father describe his progress through the Princeton aviation training program, his successful transition into the army, and his increasing involvement in the administration of the army's flying training program. His supervising officer, Maj. Leslie MacDill, evidently relied on Springs's assistance, a reliance caused in part, apparently, by the availability of Springs's Stutz Bearcat, which according to Springs served as the unit's unofficial administrative vehicle. Springs's enthusiasm for the flying

Elliott Springs at Princeton University, sitting in his Stutz Bearcat. Pilot's wings and the initials "E W S" are painted on the side of the door. This picture was probably taken in May or June 1917. Courtesy of the Springs Close Family Archives, the White Homestead, Fort Mill, South Carolina.

training program at Princeton is clearly evident in his letters. Excerpts from four letters from his father, Leroy, to Springs are included to show his father's unhappy reaction to Elliott's decision to join the U.S. Air Service and to give an indication of the efforts of Leroy Springs to influence (usually unsuccessfully) his son's actions and especially his spending habits. We can also see in these early letters how Springs played upon his father's sympathies to provide his two most important needs at this time: a Stutz automobile and money to support his lifestyle.

It is evident, even in this early period, that although Springs sparred verbally with his father over the issues of an army career and the need for money, it was important for Springs to maintain continuous contact with his father, as he wrote letters home often. Though he might disagree with his father on a broad range of issues, it was important that communication occur on a regular basis, and contact with his son was important to Leroy. Although Springs left the Stutz behind without any hesitation when he left the United States to continue his training abroad, he never ceased to work on his father's sympathies to provide money.

The first letter included here was written early in March, before the United States officially entered the war on 6 April; no mention of any kind of military activity appears in it, as Springs seems to have been occupied with defending his interest in women to his father and his upcoming graduation from Princeton.[6] This first section ends with a telegram that Springs sent to his father telling him of his imminent departure for England. Elliott Springs along with 150 other flying cadets sailed out of New York harbor on 18 September 1917 bound for England and eventually, so they believed, a flying training program in Italy.

Princeton University, Princeton, New Jersey
March 3 1917

Dear Father:

Your letter of the 1st arrived this morning and was quite a gloom. I quite agree with you, however, that women are a nuisance in the first place and an expensive nuisance in the second place. Not that I am at all cynical or trying to appear prodigiously sophisticated, but I wish to make a clean breast of everything and confess that I am well aware of the fact that the three causes for masculine failures are first, girls; second, girls; and third, girls. However I appreciate your numerous warnings but there's hardly any use in continuing them further: I could write a little on the subject myself.

But there's another side to the proposition. Somehow I enjoy the Theatre more in New York if I have some expensive nuisance along with me: and when I dance, I much prefer something fluffy though expensive, and after all, you know, "a thing of beauty is a joy forever" as Keats says. I don't know why I should feel that way about it but I just do. It's just in me that's all, possibly I get it by inheritance.

And allow me to say that if I can possibly get away with it, you, Lena, and Aunt Addie[7] will be my only guests at commencement. I will stir and get some rooms. But I warn you not to come. The affair lasts five days and you'll probably see me from a distance every other day. I think you would have a much better time if you stayed in New York and came down whenever there was anything special going on. However—

. . . . . . I am enclosing a bill from the University Store, the Book Store here, hoping you can find it consistent with the dictates of your conscience to pay it for me. Of course I know that I ought to pay it out of my allowance as I have done heretofore but the money I am expecting daily from you is all dated up and my last month's allowance is all worn out. It's mostly for books, stationery, etc. And if you can't pay it for me, please return it to me right away and I'll manage to pay it somehow before the 10th. You can send the check either to me or to the Store direct.

We cleaned up on the University of Pennsylvania 32 to 17 in water polo last night. Yale's getting nervous and doesn't want to play us.[8]

With a heartful of love to you and Lena I am

Your devoted son, Elliott

The following letter was written immediately after the entry of the United States into World War I. Springs had apparently left Princeton the day before the official announcement was made by President Woodrow Wilson on 6 April. Springs had traveled to White Sulphur Springs to enjoy the Easter holidays with some of his Princeton friends. The letter shows his concern about his ability to enter the aviation training program at Princeton, as the news of the declaration of war undoubtedly stimulated the thoughts of Springs's classmates about entering war service as soon as possible.

The Greenbrier, White Sulphur Springs, West Virginia
Undated, Sunday [8?] April

Dear Father,

I received the letter from Senator Tillman and sent it in at once. . . . I hope it didn't cause you too much trouble. I am writing to him to thank him for it. They say that there are several thousand applicants for the Aviation Corps so I'm not sure I can get in. I'd appreciate it very much if you'd use your influence to get me in. In the meantime I am going to apply for a commission in the Infantry and will probably take an examination in the next two or three weeks and will start drilling tomorrow when I get back to Princeton.

I ran down here Thursday as there was nothing I could do at Princeton. Am going back tonight and will get there at eight in the morning. I've had a delightful time. There are a lot of people here I know but have spent most of my time down at the Kahlo's. They ask to be remembered to you. The Princeton Glee Club was here Friday and Saturday on their Spring trip and a dance was given in their honor. Also there are ten or fifteen Princeton men down here for Easter. Your friend Mr. Cohn[9] and his two boys are here also. He talks of you continuously and says he wishes he had the money you are making.

I rather expect that class work will be suspended at college and we'll devote all of our time to drilling.[10] The senior class will graduate as usual, of course. I enjoyed seeing you all in New York very much. You were very good to me and I appreciate it very much. Also many thanks for bothering about the letter from Senator Tillman for me.

With a heartful of love to you and Lena, I am your devoted son, Elliott

In this excerpt from a letter to Elliott dated 6 April 1918, the day the United States officially entered the war on the side of the Allies, Leroy Springs expresses his concerns about Elliott's desire to enter aviation training.

I . . . have been constantly thinking about you in connection with your enlisting in the aviation corps. It has been a source of constant worry and anxiety.

You do not consult with me or take me in your confidence as you should and, my dear boy, you have no idea how much it worries me and what a source of regret it is. You should try to school yourself to consult with me on all things and to weigh matters of this kind well before taking any steps. There is hardly anyone who really gives my judgment and ideas less consideration than you, whether you are conscious of it or not. . . .

In regard to the aviation business, I wish to impress upon you further (it is my duty regardless of your being my son) that it is a very serious step you are taking. The aviation business is perhaps the most dangerous and hazardous of any part of the army in the first place and you should not enter it unless you have a thorough taste for that kind of work and unless everything should be right for it. . . . The mortality from accidents on account of engines or machinery getting out of order in some way is anywhere from 25% to 50%. . . .

This war, as I told you, is going to be no child's play. It is going to be a very serious matter and, as you are entering the service, I much prefer that you enter the service that you are suited for. You have had good military training. Consequently, I would much prefer that you go into the navy or army. With your training, you would perhaps be of greater value and better suited to the navy where you would get active service. No doubt, I could arrange for you to stand the examination for either army or navy by which you could enlist as a captain or lieutenant. . . .

Whatever you go into, even if it is in aviation, I do not want you to go into it half-hearted. I want you to go into it with your whole heart . . . . Now, before you go too far, please carefully consider this enlisting in the aviation corps and everything connected with it. . . .

Trusting you will consider this matter carefully and with love and best wishes, I am

Your affectionate father

P.S. The more I think about it, the more I am opposed to your joining the aviation corps and I do not feel that I should give my consent to it.

Princeton University
Wednesday, April 11 1917

Dear Father:

I received your letter of the 6th and was delighted to hear from you. I do try to consult you on all matters, Father, but you won't let me. I spoke to you last year about the Ambulance work. "I don't care to discuss it" was all the satisfaction you gave me. I spoke to you Christmas about the Aviation Corps. "It's ridiculous, don't annoy me," you said. So what could I do. I tried to discuss several matters with you in New York. You went to sleep the first time I tried and the second time you got mad about something or other and told me you didn't care what I did and that I was abnormal anyway.

I try to take you into my confidence but you don't seem to want my confidence. You think I am nothing but a machine and that a Father's only duty is to force his son to study. As a matter of fact I have never had to be forced to study and if I was as well developed on other lines as on Academic you might have reason to be proud of me. I only say this because you feel that I don't consult with you. But I do try to consult with you but every time I ask your advice I get no advice at all but blame instead, for something I'm supposed to have done long ago. I tried to consult you about everything but after several failures I just go ahead and do what I think best.

For instance I wanted a new machine [automobile] here in the spring. You wouldn't discuss the matter with me at all at first. Then you said I couldn't have it because I was going abroad. Then you said I couldn't have it at all because it cost too much and finally you said I could have it but not until after commencement. In other words, I can't have it until it's too late, when it will mean nothing to me as I will be at work then and will have little use for it. When I wanted it was now here at Princeton this spring until I graduate so I could enjoy commencement. Every one else has a machine here. But now I suppose it's too late and I'll just have to wait until I can get one for myself. But that's not having it here this spring. Of course it will give me a great deal of pleasure but if that's your only objection I have nothing more to say. And besides I may not be here until June.

Please don't think I am going into this Aviation Corps half-heartedly. I mean to do it thoroughly. I've enlisted and done everything possible to get in at once. But the Department can take only a very limited number of men and they are swamped with applications. If I don't get in [the Princeton aviation training program] within the next two weeks, Bob[11] and I are going to enlist in the Hydroplane or Flying Boat Corps as they have several vacancies and we can get in at once. I see no use in finishing out the year here as I will get my diploma just the same and half the college is leaving anyway. My [university] work is practically all done anyway and I will miss very little.[12]

But the Flying Boat training will probably entail some expense and I want to know if I can depend on you to furnish me the necessary money. Otherwise I will have to enlist for three years, war or no war. They've organized an Aeroplane Corps here but they have only three machines and about a hundred have signed up so I don't think there's any use in going into it. Only about five can be trained on one machine and they [would] probably all be smashed before I'd ever have a chance to get near one.

I took a physical exam and am perfectly sound and healthy so you needn't be worried about my not being physically fit. I'm in perfect condition and can pass all the requirements for the service. I have given the matter a good deal of consideration and am determined to go into the Aviation Corps at once if possible. You are right when you say this war is no child's play and I might as well get ready. My work here is practically over and I see no reason for staying any longer. Even if there had been no war I intended going in the Aviation Corps as I told you before but you paid no attention to me.

I am enclosing a couple of bills. One for shoes and one for a suit which I would like to get paid.

With a heartful of love to you and to Lena, I am,

Your devoted son, Elliott W. Springs

The following is an excerpt from a letter dated 10 April from Leroy to Elliott.

Now, my dear son, I wrote you frankly what I thought regarding your entering the aviation corps but, if you have made up your mind to enter, you have my consent, but, as I wrote you, I much prefer your entering the navy. However, you should make up your mind at once and not vacillate. . . . I regret exceedingly that you, my only son, should be subjected to the dangers of war. At the same time, I appreciate that in this time of defense of our country there should be no discriminations as to who shall go and who shall not go. If you are going to enlist in the aviation corps, you should do so at once.

The following is an excerpt from a letter from Leroy to Elliott dated 14 April.

My dear son: Your long letter [of 11 April] received and contents noted. I regret the tone of same. You state that I do not pay attention to you when you want to discuss things with me. The trouble is you want to discuss abnormal unreasonable things for a young man your age. The whole trouble is you want to start everything at the top instead of the bottom and go to extremes.

Naturally, as you are my only son and I am your father, I did not wish to consider you in the aviation business—certainly not for pleasure—and I think there are plenty of men better equipped for war duty in this business than you and you should take other people into consideration besides yourself. Please bear in mind that you are all I have and it distresses your Aunt Addie very much to be considering you in any such proposition. . . . In case anything should happen to me, you would be absolutely helpless as regards my estate and also that of your grandfather and mother. You know nothing about it and would not be fitted in any way to take charge of it.

It is no pleasure to me to be constantly taking issue with you. If I consulted my own pleasure, I would simply turn you loose, let you have all the money you wished, and all the good times you wished, but this would simply ruin your life and unfit you for anything you should do. I think the sensible thing for you to have done, would have been to have applied for a commission, as your military training fitted you for this. As regards your leaving Princeton, I do not wish you to leave under any circumstances unless compelled to until you get your diploma. . . .

As regards your car, it is not a question of the car but I do not see what use you would have for it, as you will leave Princeton as soon as you graduate and, if you enlist in the army, the car would have to be sent here. If, however, you are bent on having a car at college before you leave, send me a description of the car you want and I will see if I cannot get you one for early delivery and also save commission on it. I feel like this will be like all your other cars, you never stop until you get what you want and then when you get it, you care very little for it. . . . I want to indulge you in everything reasonable but it is not for your good for you not to realize that you have duties to perform in this world and you will not be happy unless you perform them well and faithfully. . . .

With love and best wishes, I am always, Your affectionate father

Princeton University
April 17, 1917

Dear Father:

I received your letter [of 14 April] and was more than delighted to hear from you. The glad tidings about the car were the greatest news I've had since the doctors at the Johns Hopkins told me I'd pull through.[13] Please get me a Stutz "Bearcat" by all means, and I think I'd like a yellow one. However if the thought of a yellow car displeases you, make it a red one.

I don't think I'll be able to get one anywhere except through the New York agency. It is a very popular car and they are pretty well sold out. However the New York branch told me they could deliver one by the 18th of May provided the order was placed at once. Whatever you do, please order it at once, or let me know and I'll order it myself through the New York branch. I certainly am tickled all over at the prospect and you have no idea how much pleasure it is going to give me.

The chances are that unless I leave here within the next ten days, I'll be here until the 1st of July or even later. I have heard nothing from Washington as yet so am drilling here in the infantry in the meantime. I am an officer, though no special ranks have been given any of us.[14]

You see yourself that we have no discussion when you consider everything I want to discuss "abnormal unreasonable things." I am always condemned unheard by that idea. That was all I meant. If you agree with me beforehand, for instance in fact that I don't need anything, there's no discussion necessary, if you don't agree with me then I'm abnormal and unreasonable. You'll have to admit that those are pretty heavy odds for me to struggle against.

I'm sorry to have to bother you about my [W]hite [S]ulphur [Springs] bill[15] and I couldn't pay it very conveniently myself and I didn't want to ask you for money.

I'm still curious about your business affairs, particularly the L&C.[16] But you only remind me that I can't at present run anything and refuse to tell me anything. I regret exceedingly that I don't know more about business but I flatter myself that I know a good deal more than some people give me credit for. You know I wanted to work when I left Culver[17] but you insisted on my going to college. I wanted to go to college but I wanted to go to work. You even wanted me to take another year at prep-school [to] make me ready for work in 1918. I am graduating in 1917 and will be ready for work shortly, a [year] ahead of your schedule and am very anxious to get to work but still you jump on me about it.

I am doing my best and am the youngest man in my class which ought to mean something. I'm sorry you aren't pleased. Some other people have even been so foolish as to compliment me. I don't think there's any danger of any Springs becoming conceited so I'm not afraid to say it. And I'm an A.B. too at your request. I'm glad of it, too, and I think you were right, but please don't jump on me about [it]. In spite of the fact I am very anxious to get to work and will endeavor to prove it to your satisfaction later. How much later depends on the war.

Please don't delay about ordering the Stutz "Bearcat" or letting me order it in New York. Many thanks to you and Lena, I am with a heartful of love your devoted son

Elliott W. Springs

Princeton University
22 April 1917

Dear Father,

I went up to New York yesterday to place an order for a car and finally got the Stutz agency to make out a contract to suit me. But they won't accept the order without a deposit of $500 so I am enclosing the contract and if you will please sign both of them and return them to me at once with a check . . . I will make the final arrangements. Also could you please write to them and direct them to draw on you for the balance when the car is delivered. . . .

I suppose you've read in the paper that we may graduate on May 15th. It's not at all settled yet, but the faculty are considering it. . . .[18]

Many many thanks Father, I shall certainly enjoy it.

With a heartful of love to you and Lena I am your devoted son, Elliott

Princeton University
April 26 1917

Dear Father,

Mr. Rice[19] wired me he had forwarded you my letter in Atlanta so I know the reason for the delay in the answer. The reason for my haste is that the Stutz people are overflowing with orders but I figured that an offer of cash and a refusal to take the car after the 10th might bear fruit. I know for a fact that they can't get me a car before the 1st of June but I am figuring on them giving me someone else's car on the 10th and making them wait.

When I get your letter and contract I shall call them up on the phone and cancel the order saying that I'm getting a Marmon. If they promise me a delivery in a week I'll send them the contract, if not, I'll send it to them anyway but I have an idea that I'll get that car in a few days. The Marmon is a wonderful car but as I said before $500 more than the Stutz. However I am awaiting your letter and will be governed by what you have to say. I suppose it will be here in the morning. And Thanks a Thousand times, Father.

I am still a lieutenant in the infantry here[20] and waiting to hear from the government. I am going to take my final physical exam Monday [29 April] and if I pass it I will transfer directly into the Aviation Corps.[21] We have an Aviation Corps here but 240 have applied for it and they can take only 20 so my chance of getting into it is not too good. They are going to take the 20 most physically fit. I'm in fine condition right now but so are a lot of others.

I suppose you've read in the papers how the War Department gloomed on these Reserve Officers. They have to serve three months or more in a training camp before they will commission them and at that they will only take a certain percentage. If I can't get into the Aviation Corps I'll probably go [to] France with the Princeton Ambulance Corps which sails on the 26th of May. In which case I graduate at once and can come home for a couple of weeks before sailing. But I still have hopes that the War Department will accept me. . . .

The University will probably close in a couple of weeks.[22] 175 have already left and 320 more are going this week—mostly seniors and juniors. With my next allowance could you please send me $20 for class assessment and $20 for a uniform and $25 for a license for the car and license plates as it will have to be licensed in the state of New Jersey and must be applied for in advance. I hate to bother [you] about these things, particularly after you've just given me a car but it simply has to be done.

The graduating class each year has a lot of expenses, programs, invitations, dances, favors, erection of platform stands, and the printing of the class book. They add up the total and divide by the number in the class. This year each man has to pay $20. And whether we're here at commencement or not we have to pay it just the same.

With a heartful of love and many thanks again for the car, I am

Your devoted son, Elliott

P.S. I will get either a Marmon or a Stutz as your letter says. I can't go wrong on either. EWS

Princeton University
April 28 1917

Dear Father,

I can't tell you what a wonderful car the Stutz is. It's the finest car I've ever driven and many many thanks. Jimmie [Latham] and I went up to New York yesterday and got it and brought it down. The Stutz people were very unaccommodating and insisted on having cash but I finally talked them into taking the $500 and drawing on you for the rest. I am contemplating staying here in Princeton in the Aviation Corps instead of going into the Government school. If I can get in here I'll begin work Monday and will notify you at once if I do anything. Please send some money as I am hard pressed. The Stutz is not too easy on gasoline. I am also going to have it insured here at once as soon as I get some money.

With a heartful of love to you and Lena I am,

Your devoted son

Elliott

Princeton University
May 1st 1917

Dear Father,

I took my preliminary equilibrium tests Sunday and passed them easily and will take the rest tomorrow or the next day. They are very particular about whom they take for the Aviation Corps and examine us very minutely. It's the most exacting examination the Army gives. They spin you around on a stool, make you balance blindfolded, fire pistols behind you and all sorts of things like that. I'll notify you when I pass the test. If I do get through it will mean that I am physically perfect and will start flying at once. I'm worried about my eyes as they only allow a small percentage of variations from normal and I am only two degrees out in my left eye. They allow two and a quarter I believe.[23]

I got an invitation to join the club yesterday that I wanted to join in the beginning.[24] Of course I declined, but it was very flattering and makes me feel much better, especially after I understood the reason why I was not invited before. It was the second time I was ever put up in this club and my election was unanimous. I have some very good friends down there and they have always been very nice to me. A week has not passed since sophomore year that I haven't had an invitation to eat down there. I would like very much to join but don't see how I can now. Not that it makes very much difference one way or another as I think the clubs have had their day and clubs have nothing to do with friendship but it was quite a compliment as it is very unusual to invite a man to join after his sophomore year. This makes the fifth invitation I've had since sophomore year.

I am enclosing you Dr. Fordyce's bill. My complexion has cleared up completely and I think the $75 well spent. The Stutz is running like a top and I am very proud of it. I've gotten a terrible drag with my Profs by taking them home after classes every day. Papa Fixe[25] positively beamed at me during his lecture this morning. He even offered me a cigarette after it and invited me down to his house.

It's awfully hard on gasoline though and is quite a wear and tear on the pocket book. Please send me some money or I shall have to put it in storage and ruin the tires. When are you and Lena coming to New York? I am very anxious to see you all again.

With a heartful of love to you both I am

Your devoted son, Elliott

The following letter from Leroy Springs dated 8 May illustrates his concern about decisions that his son had been making without consulting his father.

My dear Son: I received your letter and was glad to hear from you but, as I wired you, am very much distressed to think of your going into the aviation corps. As I have written you several times, I seriously object to your having anything to do with aviation machines even in peace, as I regard it such a hazardous undertaking and so dangerous. I have been very much worried over it, in fact ever since you have insisted on going into the aviation corps. However, I congratulate you on your successful examination.

I also am proud of the fact that you graduated at Princeton with honor and will have a diploma from that institution which you will be proud of all your life.[26] I can only hope for the best and sincerely trust that everything will turn out best for you but I shall be constantly uneasy and worried about you until this terrible war is over. I am still in hopes that something will happen in Germany that will put an end to the war before so many young men like you will have to hazard their lives in the defense of the country and civilization.

I would not have you think that I do not want you to fight for your country but, as you are my only son, I preferred that you go in less hazardous service. Since you have gone into it, I feel sure that you will avoid all danger possible and that you will not experiment with the machine and try to do any fancy stunts. I want you to be careful and considerate and you must remember that being in the air is very different from being on the ground and, if anything should get wrong with the machine and you should attempt to do any unusual feat with it, it would perhaps dash you to the ground and be your death. I cannot urge upon you too strongly to be careful and considerate in the study of your machine and, my son, please do not take any hazardous risks that you can avoid.

I am enclosing check for $150, additional, which I trust will meet your additional requirements. Of course, you should not waste your money and should have something to show for it. I do not wish to be stinted [stingy?] but wish you to have what you need and, if you need additional money, do not go into debt but write and let me know how much you need and I will send it to you.

With love and best wishes and trusting that everything will turn out for the best, I am always

Your affectionate father

Princeton University
May 15 1917

Dear Father,
You will probably be very pleased to hear that I arise every morning at 5 o'clock including Sundays and am out at the Field ready to fly twenty minutes later. We get breakfast out there and are pretty busy until eight or nine at night. And so far I haven't been late though I have had to [stay] up pretty late some nights.

Also the Stutz is the official Emergency Car and when anything goes wrong you see the Stutz tearing madly across the country registering much speed and anguish. I had to plow up a wheat field yesterday to rush some tools to a sick plane and whatever such trips I run errands for the Corps when not flying.

I can't begin to tell you the wonderful fascination of flying and I enjoy it more every time I go up. I had control of the plane yesterday for twenty minutes at an altitude of 4000 feet and I don't know when I enjoyed anything more. I'm afraid I'll never be happy on land again.

I saw with regret the article in the *Lancaster News* and it made me feel very badly. Please instruct and request the Editor to mention my name no more. I would like to write to you what I am doing and made the mistake for the first time in some years of doing so with the result that the news gets all broken out with incoherency and the final chapter of Little Lord Fauntleroy.[27] No matter what happens I shall be afraid to write to you about it now. All my letters are written for the consumption of the person to whom

Aviation ground school instruction, Princeton University. The instructor is describing airplane components in an upper room of a Princeton building. Elliott Springs, wearing a light shirt, is seated on the sawhorse at left. This photograph was probably taken in April or May 1917. Courtesy of the Springs Close Family Archives, the White Homestead, Fort Mill, South Carolina.

I address them and I had no idea that the General Public was to be included in confidence. If so I should not have written and am very sorry I did.

By all means come up Sunday. We will probably be flying all day and you can watch me take a cloud bath. You can leave Washington late Saturday night and get a sleeper to Philadelphia. Then you can catch a local into Phila[delphia] at 8:03 which will put you at Princeton Junction at 9:24 where I will meet you with the Stutz. Please wire me what you expect to do.

Sidney Brewster has been trying to get into the Aviation Corps but was turned down on his first exam.[28] He's trying again though. I'm sorry you are worrying about me and I assure you there is no cause for it.

With a heartful of love to you and Lena I am your devoted son, Elliott

Princeton University
June 5 1917

Dear Father:

I was out at the field from 4:45 this morning until eight tonight so am very tired and can't write much. I am in receipt of your letter of the 2nd with the instructions to buy a Liberty Loan Bond stamped across the envelope. Not sarcasm I hope. It will probably be some time before I will be able to get to New York before eight in the evening so I don't see how I'll be able to get a picture taken.

I am renting a professor's house for Commencement Week and am now looking about to hire a cook for you. But why not bring Aunt Carrie[29] up with you? You'll have to have a cook. I will expect you, Lena, and Aunt Addie on the 15th when the festivities begin. Please wire me at once if these arrangements suit you.

The Stutz continues to run like a left handed sewing machine and outside of its proclivities for picking up nails is in excellent shape. My creditors show no signs of uneasiness but I would like very much to get some bills paid. I hold each letter to the light anxiously.

With a heartful of love I am your devoted son, Elliott

[P.S.] Tell Lena if I ever get over this tired feeling I'll write to her. I suppose her red and cross activities keep her in a constant state of exhaustion. EWS

Princeton Aviation School
June 8 1917

Dear Father:

I have rented a Professor's house for you for Commencement Week and have a cook coming on Thursday the 14th so everything will be in shape. The Prof was leaving today so I gave him a check for $150.00 on the Bank of Lancaster. I have an account there so please just have $150 deposited to my credit there and all will be well. Better have it done at once as the check will be there the day after this letter. I wrote Aunt Addie that I would expect her also, so I will expect you three next Friday. I am awaiting some cash anxiously and need it badly. The flying progresses nicely and I have not been up this morning. Please be sure to deposit the $150 to my credit and I am with a heartful of love to you and Lena, your devoted son,

Elliott W. Springs

Princeton University held its commencement exercises on the weekend of 16–17 June 1917. In acknowledgment of the impact of the war on university life, a special military drill exhibition in which units of the student battalion and the flight of the Aviation Corps were to participate was scheduled for Saturday afternoon. Springs, as a member of the Princeton Aviation Corps, would have participated. The commencement exercises were held Sunday morning at 11:00 in Alexander Hall, and his father and stepmother must have attended. Springs's name is listed in the commencement program as a candidate for the degree of bachelor of arts. According to his Princeton academic record, he was a philosophy major and completed eleven philosophy courses, seven English courses, four history courses, six ancient language (Latin and Greek) courses, five modern language (French, German, and Spanish) courses, five science and mathematics courses, and one economics course. He graduated with a gentlemanly C+ average but was nevertheless ranked in the top half of his class (thirty-eighth of one hundred).[30]

Princeton University
June 26 1917

Dear Father,

I am enclosing you the bills which I have paid and for which I drew checks. I also drew a check for $200 to deposit to my credit here. Also I drew a check for $25 to the Aviation Corps and $35.19 for insurance to Augustus Dohen, Agent. I am enclosing the Stutz bill for $143.85 which is OK. Please send them a check.

I've been flying about three times a day for the past two weeks and have been getting along very well. I took my preliminary military test Thursday and passed it so got my pilot's license and hope to be flying alone in a week. I can do it now but I'm going to be on the safe side and wait a little while.

The government takes us over Monday and from the schedule they have mapped out for us it seems that we are going to be pretty busy. We have to learn to operate an aeroplane machine gun, a moving picture camera with a telescope lens, to drop bombs, to draw maps, to send at least eight words a minute by wireless while operating a plane at full speed, and to direct artillery fire from an altitude of 5000 feet. It's going to be no child's play. We're to be sworn in Monday morning and begin at once.[31]

The next time you come up I'll be able to take you up for a ride myself if you care to go. You may have to indemnify the machine but I hardly think it will be necessary. With a heartful of love to you and Lena I am your devoted son,

Elliott

Aircraft instruction at Princeton University. Elliott Springs is second from left. Captain Stanton, wearing helmet and goggles, is instructing students, others of whom are not identified. Judging by the heavy clothing, this picture was probably taken in April 1917. Courtesy of David K. Vaughan.

Princeton University
[July] 2 1917[32]
Dear Father,

My new camera arrived and I am enclosing some of the pictures I got with it. It's a very complicated machine and I don't know much about working it as yet so the first bunch aren't too good but I enclose them to let you see what a good camera can do. The planes are going about 70 miles an hour—one landing and one going off the ground and it takes a fine camera to catch [them] in the air.

[A portion of the letter is missing] . . . landing and when he came to rest was in the position depicted. That's one of the reasons they make us practice landings so much.

I'm all through with my instruction now and hereafter will go up alone. Planes are scarce though and they aren't going to let me do very much solo flying until they get some more of them as two have been smashed already.

I was sworn in last Friday and am now in gov't service. For the next eight weeks I'll spend most of my time learning bomb-dropping, wireless etc. The man standing beside the Stutz in the picture is the Australian Instructor.[33] He and 24 others are all that are left of a regiment that fought through the Gallipoli campaign. He was discharged because trench foot left him unfit for further service and he took up flying over here. He's a wonderful instructor though he's only 22. They pay him about $1500 a month.

With a heartful of love to you and Lena I am your devoted son

Elliott

Princeton University

[no date, but probably written during the first week of July]

Dear Aunt Addie:

I should have written to you long ago but I have been so busy lately that I just haven't had a chance. I'm out at the Aviation Field from six in the morning until seven at night and when I get back I'm too tired to do anything but go to bed. I am now a graduate of Princeton University and in the U.S. Aviation Corps with the provisional rank of 1st Lieutenant.[34] We have four planes here and two instructors and 22 of us are trying to learn to fly as quickly as possible. It's a great sport and I am enjoying it very much. It's like riding on a huge beetle which you can control just like an automobile, only you can do so much more with it. I had to stand a very rigid exam to get in and was very much pleased and surprised to find that I was in perfect physical condition. Three doctors tried for two days to find something wrong with me.

Father very kindly gave me a car and it is quite the joy of my life. The field is four miles away where we fly and it's very handy to have some way to get out there besides the street car. I'm in the Army now so my movements from now on will be rather uncertain. I'll let you know if I am transferred anywhere else.

With a heartful of love I am

Your devoted nephew

Elliott

Elliott Springs in the cockpit of a Curtiss JN-4 "Jenny" aircraft. This photograph was probably taken in May or June 1917. Courtesy of the Springs Close Family Archives, the White Homestead, Fort Mill, South Carolina.

Aviation students cleaning a Curtiss JN-4 training aircraft, Princeton University, June or July 1917. Many hands make light work. Elliott Springs, in a light shirt, is on the left. Courtesy of the Springs Close Family Archives, the White Homestead, Fort Mill, South Carolina.

Aviation students in front of a Curtiss JN-4 "Jenny" aircraft. All students are in an especially jovial mood; apparently someone has just made a clever remark. Elliott Springs, in the second row, second from the right in a billed cap, is especially amused. This photograph was probably taken in June or July 1917. Courtesy of the Springs Close Family Archives, the White Homestead, Fort Mill, South Carolina.

Princeton University
July 6 1917 9:30 PM

Dear Father,

Just have time for a line. They've moved us into Patten Hall or Barracks and we have nothing down there but army cots and I sneaked up to my old room for a minute to write this. Must hurry back as I'm supposed to be in bed. The Government has got us and is working the life out of us. 5:30 AM–9 PM drill and study. Five hours of drill a day and then we have to sleep on a cot that makes marble feel soft in comparison. We won't have much flying for the next two or three weeks. I hope to get a little flying [in] before 5:30 in the morning and after supper at night. Weather's been bad ever since Saturday.

Sorry to hear about your carbuncle. Hope it's well by this time. Would like to see you very much but am afraid I couldn't see much of you if you came now. Be sure and wire me a day ahead or you won't be able to see me at all. [I] get Sunday off though but have to stay here.

With a heartful of love to you and Lena

Your devoted son, Elliott

Princeton University
July 31 1917

Dear Father,

I've had no chance for two days to get up to my room where there is paper and ink so will have to write to you on this in pencil if I am to write at all. Please excuse as it can't be helped.

I want to congratulate you on the fact that your only son has at last reached his 21st birthday—without ever having been in jail, married, or completely hors de combat. I also congratulate you on his splendid record of which I fear you have not been correctly informed. May the returns of the day, if many, be happy for you.

Twenty-one years is a long time, I suppose, to have to prune the vine so constantly; particularly when the vine is rather a fungus growth and persists in growing again in the same place but you can now contemplate the results of your labor and I hope you will not regret the trouble I caused you. Uncle Sam is now my official pater familias and I can only hope that he is as good a provider as you have been. Outside of that I don't see that the situation is very much altered.

As yet we have no official instruction as to when we will sail. There is a rumor that some of us will go next week but I'm afraid there's nothing in it. My own personal opinion is that we will sail about the 28th of August or possibly a week sooner. The middle of September ought to see us on the other side at the latest.

I dined with Mrs Gummere [an acquaintance of Leroy Springs] Saturday and Sunday. The food was excellent. She spoke affectionately of you and regretted not seeing you when you were here. She has a charming daughter. I felt that I could become very much interested [but] just at present I haven't a moment to spare for such things. So I thanked Mrs Gummere in your name for her hospitality and promised to show up again next Sunday afternoon. But now I find that I can't as I am Officer of the Day next Sunday and will have to remain here. She has the $ mark engraved all over her, the house, and daughter but even the latter is not sufficient to lure me from the pursuit of wireless and the correct method for forwarding ammunition to the Germans [machine gun practice].

As soon as I get my orders I'll wire you. We ought to know at least 48 hours before we sail.

With a heartful of love to you and Lena, I am

Your devoted son, Elliott W. Springs

Princeton Aviation School
Tuesday [No date, but probably late July or early August]

Dear Father,

I wired you from Washington because I needed some money and wanted you to wire it to me. I didn't want to worry you or have you getting anyone to come around to the hotel. What I needed was money, not influence. Nothing much happened in Washington except we were detailed back here and had to wait around Washington until they had some new blanks printed for us to sign.

Just at present I'm long on liabilities and short on assets. I'm not stone broke; I have about thirty dollars but I have quite a large garage bill and have some other bills I'd like to pay. I can use quite a bit of cash currently.

The flying is progressing nicely. I get up nearly every day and am getting so I am pretty much at ease in the air. Will write again shortly; have to help fill the machine with gas now. With a heartful of love to you and Lena, I am

Your devoted son, Elliott

P.S. Will do as you request in your letter. If I work all week from 5 A.M. to 8 P.M. you can't blame me for going to New York for a good meal though. That is if I can get off. Don't forget to send me some cash. EWS

Later [written at top of letter]—Just came down. Very good ride though pretty windy. EWS

Princeton University
August 15 1917

Dear Father,

I sent you the papers yesterday and suppose you have received them by this time. There has been no official information yet as to when we are to sail but I suppose it will be sometime within the next three weeks. We have received instructions though that when we do get our orders we are not to spread the news about but keep it quiet. So if I wire you to meet me at the Vanderbilt[35] as soon as possible you'll know what's going on. The names of those picked to go went in to Washington last week but the Major won't tell us who they are.

As I owe the Aviation School about $160 now and the garage $132 besides the Nassau Inn[36] and the telephone company, I'll have to draw some more money and will draw a check as soon as can get uptown to the bank.

Aviation cadets, in-ranks inspection, Princeton University. The military officer in charge, Capt. Adlia Gilkerson, is standing at the left; Elliott Springs, one of two cadet leaders, is second from the left; the other cadet leader is Paul Nelson. This photograph was probably taken in August 1917. Courtesy of the Springs Close Family Archives, the White Homestead, Fort Mill, South Carolina.

There's another rumor about that some of us will get a chance to fly at the Front instead of coming back as Instructors. If so it may not be so bad.

Please send me a "Bank of Lancaster" Check Book as I have run out of checks. The Stutz came back Sunday night with a busted self starter. The mechanics tried to get it fixed before bringing it back hence the delay.

I am hoping to get in a couple more solo flights this week. I feel like quite an avigator now; it's just like driving the car. The Major gave me some extra time to drill the Squadron Monday and Tuesday and they are doing much better. I had to quell mutiny and sedition when the announcement was made but finally they decided to take their medicine. I was in charge of the Battalion yesterday and nearly ruined my throat on them.

The Fifth Squadron rebelled yesterday and went over in a body to tell the Major what they thought of him. They were joined by all except my squadron and they had a merry time of it. Ten of them resigned and a lot more say they are going to. The Major is threatening to let up on us a little as two men fainted yesterday from overwork and several others looked pretty green.

You certainly spoiled my drag with the Major. He thought I had been doing solo for the last six weeks. He also thought that all I knew about drilling I had picked up here in six weeks. Consequently he thought I was pretty bright. Now—

All I have time for now.

With a heartful of love

Devotedly, Elliott

Immediately after completing the ground school program at Princeton on 25 August, Springs and a number of his fellow Princetonians were transferred to the army flying field at Mineola, New York. Springs did not write about this un-expected development, perhaps because he visited with his father in New York City about this time, but the excitement of the sudden move is captured in a letter[37] that Arthur Richmond Taber wrote to his mother shortly after the move:

Mineola, New York
August 28, 1917

Dear [Mother]:

Yesterday afternoon about five o'clock, about half my squadron includ-ing myself were suddenly ordered to report for duty at Mineola immediately. You can imagine with what a thunderclap this struck me, just as I was hoping that word would come from Washington granting me a leave of absence for a few days, since I had just finished the ground-school course and am expecting to go to Italy. It was a very keen disappointment indeed; the commandant had applied for leaves of absence for us and had given us to understand that they would be granted by the War Department; however, I had not allowed my hopes to rise too high, for I know some-thing of the way in which army orders are issued—just when you expect them least.

Upon being ordered to go, I had to work like mad for several hours. I removed all my surplus outfit from the barracks . . . [and] packed away my remaining civilian clothes. . . .

From what I can gather we shall fly here [at Mineola] until sent to Italy. This seems to be a concentration point for the men who are going to Italy; to-day a batch came in from Cornell; they are a clean-cut, military-looking lot, and I am rather heartened by their appearance. . . .

While at Mineola, Springs continued his flight instruction. He flew on 6, 7, 11, 12, 14, and 15 September, accumulating three hours and thirty-nine minutes of flight time, of which twenty-two minutes were solo time.[38] After training at Mineola for approximately two and a half weeks, Springs and the other members of the detachment of cadets were confined to Mineola, pending orders to sail to Europe. On 17 September they were told to make their final preparations for sailing.

First graduating class, School of Military Aeronautics, Princeton University. Front row, from left to right: William Kelly, George Vaughn Jr., Edward Cronin, Wistar Morris, Frank Sidler, Paul King, Hagood Bostick. Second row, left to right: John Raftery, Meredith Pyne, Newton Bevin, Fairfax Burger, William Neely, unidentified, Edmond Keenan, Frank Newbury. Standing, left to right: Elliott Springs, Allen Bevin, Harold Bulkley, George Bond, John Bohmfalk, Frank Dixon, Walter Knox, Capt. Adlia Gilkerson, Charles Brown, Sydney Brewster, Percy Pyne, Lansing Holden, Arthur Taber, Paul Nelson. This picture was probably taken in August 1917. Courtesy of the Springs Close Family Archives, the White Homestead, Fort Mill, South Carolina.

Western Union Telegram
September 17 1917

To Leroy Springs, Lancaster SC (Collect)

Leaving Stutz with Wm Parkinson Motor Car Co who are Stutz agents to be overhauled. Running fine but needs general overhauling. Did eighty five yesterday but rattles at times. You can write there about disposition of it. Suggest you trade it in for new 1918 model with same motor but four passenger body. Everything has worked out so beautifully that I'm afraid I'm dreaming. Forty men who were picked for France got special permission to join us last week to fill vacancies. We go 150 strong. Have been flying regularly and had my last flight at Mineola this morning. By drawing on you frequently through the Vanderbilt [Hotel] I have secured an outfit fit only for a king. Be sure and pay my bill here even though it may seem a bit exorbitant to you it was worth it. Love to you and Mother. Elliott 8:15 AM

Across the Atlantic to Oxford University, England

September to November 1917

On 17 September Elliott Springs and approximately 150 other flying cadets boarded a train at Mineola that took them to the docks in Hoboken, New Jersey, to board the *Carmania,*[1] which departed on 18 September. After a brief stop in Halifax, Canada, where she joined a convoy of ships, the *Carmania* sailed across the Atlantic and docked in Liverpool on 2 October. On board with Springs were the two cadets with whom he would develop strong friendships in the next ten months, John McGavock (Mac) Grider and Lawrence (Larry) Callahan. Because he had demonstrated distinctive leadership abilities during his training at Princeton and Mineola Field, Springs had been invested with a modicum of power as cadet sergeant in charge of the Italian contingent. His leadership abilities probably resulted from his special combination of his personal drive to succeed in aviation and his personal habit of getting what he wanted. Having learned how to get his way with his authoritative and strong-minded father, he must have adapted his interpersonal skills to advantage in his interactions with his superior officers. His background of wealth and privilege certainly must have helped him, and he was not reluctant to use those qualities as leverage when the situation required. He expected to get his way, and he usually got it. It is evident, however, that he also worked hard to achieve and maintain whatever advantages he could gather.

When they debarked in Liverpool, the cadets in the Italian detachment were astounded to learn that they would not be proceeding to Italy but would be remaining in England to continue their aviation training. The officer in charge, Maj. Leslie MacDill, was ordered to proceed to London and left Elliott Springs in charge, telling him to ensure that the cadets arrived safely at Oxford, where their training program would continue. At Oxford the cadets were split into two groups, one located in Christ Church College, with Springs in charge, and the other group assigned to Queen's College, where another of Springs's friends, Bennett "Bim" Oliver, was placed in charge. For the next three weeks they adjusted to life in England and attended military training classes, covering material the Princeton cadets had already learned. About 21 October both groups, those in Christ Church and those in Queen's College, were merged into one group in Exeter College. According to Springs's account, the merger was the result of the English officers' efforts to keep a tighter rein on the off-duty actions of the American cadets.

His first letters, mailed after the *Carmania* docked in England, record his activities on board the ship and indicate his developing relationships with his fellow cadets and superior officers. Subsequent letters describe his challenges as the acting cadet in charge of one half of the Oxford detachment, and he comments repeatedly on the irony of his being placed in charge, an inveterate partygoer trying to keep his party-going fellow cadets in line. His letters in this section are among his best, filled with information and insights, exuding the energy of a young man in a foreign country for the first time, and filled with optimism and high spirits.

On board the [censored (*Carmania*)]

Dear Father,

As this epistle is going to be carefully censored I don't suppose there's much use in giving any details at all but I would like to give you some idea of the trip. And as this letter won't be mailed until we arrive in [censored (Liverpool)], there's no use dating it and I'll just write it in diary form from time to time.

Tuesday September 18

We're off. We passed the Statue of Liberty at 1:00 PM and are now quite alone. We've been instructed for the past week not to mention anything to our families relative to our sailing date and I've been too busy to write anyway. I really have. Try acting as commander in chief, quartermaster sergeant, mess sergeant, sergeant major, officer of the day, corporal of the guard, and headwaiter to 150 avigators on the verge of departure and see how much time you have to yourself. Then in your off hours make two or three flights and play chauffeur to the Major and you're busy, yes, unquestionably busy.

The first intimation I had was last Thursday [13 September] when the Major [Leslie MacDill] handed me a big envelope and said, "That's the sailing orders. Jump in your red devil and hand them to the Embarkation Officer at Hoboken as quickly as possible and report to me by telephone." Thirty minutes later I was at 42nd street and in 30 minutes more I had crossed on the ferry and in one hour and six minutes from the time I had left Mineola I was talking to the Major [on the phone]. How's that for speed. All the cops along that road have seen me driving the Major around so much that they think the Stutz is an official car and me the chauffeur so they never stop me.

The next day I drove the Major over to Hoboken in 1.10 and then we ferried down to the Battery and went down to lower Pearl Street. Of course I got lost on the way up and after circling around the Cotton Exchange for half an hour and bumping into the piers of all the bridges we finally came out at 14th Street and the Bowery. If you ever saw truck driving, that was the time—on those narrow streets—full of street cars and children and peddlers' cars, I was in my zenith. We lunched and then I took the Major 85 [miles per hour] on the way back. Then I got an hour of flying and was ready to go to bed when I had to go to New York on another errand. I got back at two and was flying again at five in the morning.

And speaking of flying I worked a great graft at Mineola. I wasn't supposed to fly but the Officer in Charge was a Princeton man and I got the Major to telephone down to Washington and get permission for [Bonham] Bostick, [Harold] Bulkley, and myself to fly so they gave us a plane and told us to go to it.[2] Everything went fine except I had a little crack-up the second day. Didn't get hurt at all—not a scratch but it was sheer luck. I had a new kind of machine, one I had never seen before and I didn't know much about landing it. I got off all right and circled around the field several times and then came down. I was all set for a pretty landing but I was landing with a strong side wind and the machine had a big dihedral angle so the wind got under it when I was about five feet off the ground. I had lost flying speed by that time so my controls were dead and all I could do was yank her level but couldn't straighten out. The result was that I landed on one wing and one wheel sideways. You can imagine what that meant at 55 miles an hour—the thing just spun around in one spot on one wheel and then started backwards. The damage wasn't much though—a smashed aileron, wing skid and control wires. As a matter of fact the instructor came out and we flew it back to the hangars. The next day I got one of the old ones without the dihedral—like the ones I had been flying at Princeton—and it was all right.[3] Had no more trouble at all—except from the wind which is always bad at Mineola.

The last day I was there, they gave me an old machine and told me to run along and play. I did and I had the time of my life. I stayed up nearly three hours and made ten or fifteen landings. You can't imagine how it feels to be up over Long Island, flying about at will. I flew over Camp Mills[4] several times. It was a wonderful sight—just a brown patch from a great height and then when you dived at it, the camp would divide itself up into streets and alleys and then you could see each tent with the smoke curling out of every tenth one where they were cooking. I don't think I ever enjoyed anything more. I'd have stayed up all day if my gasoline hadn't given out. By the way our Major is quite a trick flyer—looped the loop eleven times one day out there while joy riding.

Sunday the Major told everyone to get rid of their cars, except me and told me to place sentinels around the barracks to keep anyone from leaving even for a few moments. Then we went to New York to arrange the final details. Monday he tipped me off to get rid of the car and I drove it into New York and left it at the Blue Sprocket garage with instructions for it to be sent up to the Stutz place. Then I drew some more money, wired you, got a good dinner, left the wrist watch for you at the Vanderbilt, got a bath (a soldier's greatest luxury), and returned about 2 AM to find special orders waiting on me to have breakfast at 4:30 and be ready to break up camp at 6:30. Camp was broken promptly at 6:30 and we were on a train at 7:00 bound for Long Island City. Our trunks had been on the boat for a week and a tugboat took us from Long Island City [censored] to the docks at [censored] and at 12 we began to move. We got the best passenger ship in service at present and we're in luck. There're 150 of us and about 75 other officers—mostly infantry—and about a dozen passengers traveling 1st Class and the rest of the ship is filled up with troops 3rd Class and steerage, but we rarely see them except from the upper decks. I'm certainly in luck personally—being in command next to the Major I get the best stateroom in the bunch, that is of the aviators, and my responsibilities for the present are over. No more roll calls—no more drills until we land. . . .

I certainly bought an equipment worthy of a Cadet Major before I left, you can probably see by the Vanderbilt [Hotel] bill how much it cost. I got a wonderful pair of field boots ($45) and a wrist stop watch ($55) and two pair of shoes and gloves and a leather outfit and 2000 cigarettes and several boxes of cigars and soap and pipe tobacco and various other things which I found I needed. Being broke I just drew cash on my Vanderbilt bill. Also I paid out quite a bit for gas and oil.

Wednesday 19 September

All is well but I don't suppose I'd be allowed to say much about the trip. They say the censorship is very strict about such matters. Our only duties on shipboard are Calisthenics which I have to give at 11:30 and boat drill in the afternoon. At other times we play bridge up in the smoking room.

Saturday. And later.

You ought to see me playing bridge with two majors and an English lieutenant commander. Not only that but removing sheckles from them in large quantities. Our Major is a prince and quite a good bridge player. He said he didn't want any gambling for high stakes among the men and I'm supposed to watch out and handle it. Also he directed me to look after the drinking so any man that I see taking too much I kick out [of] the smoking room. And I thought all my worries were over! But what do you think of me as a Vigilance Committee and protector of public morals? And I certainly have the eagle eye. I can tell at four tables distance how much of [Jim] Stokes' glass is water and how much is highball. He's from Nashville and I'll probably catch him putting some water in his highball yet. I can also smell a crap game all the way across the boat and if I don't win all the money I stop it. As yet however I haven't had to stop any. I've broken up several though. The Major certainly has turned everything over to me. I only see him across the card table now. He's probably the most efficient man I ever saw but at the same time never makes you uncomfortable and never appears to be struggling himself. He's treated us like gentlemen but at the same time nobody slips anything over on him.

We're starting Italian classes now. We have plenty of Italian books but are rather shy on instructors. As usual I'm the goat and am now a full fledged Italian instructor. It's very easy too. Knowing something of Spanish, French, and Latin as I do it's not so hard to teach. My accent they say is a wee touch off but that won't hurt anything.

We are getting into the submarine zone now and wear our life belts all the time. There's a rumor that a boat was sunk by a submarine 12 miles away.

I'm getting fat as a pig. The food is great—never seen better—and all we do is stuff ourselves and then get behind a big cigar and bid ourselves into a stupor.

We have a wonderful bunch of men. 150 picked men from all the ground schools. All college men too. There's a Shaw from Sumter in the bunch [Ervin Shaw], a Fry from Columbia, Tennessee [Clarence Fry], and Jim Stokes from Nashville, a Griffiths from Georgia [Edward Griffiths]. Maybe you or Lena know some of them. One of our cooks is from Yorkville. And my boon companion is none other than Albert Spalding, the famous violinist, who is one of our enlisted men but when I found out who he was I got the Major to move him up from steerage to a vacant stateroom.[5]

There are about 40 Red Cross nurses on board and some of the men get desperate and walk around the deck with them but as yet I have been faithful and true. It hasn't been very hard to forswear their company—it's like declining an invitation to a party with the Hippodrome chorus.

I don't know when you're going to get this, not for several weeks anyway and by that time I'll probably be flying again in a strange land—the Promised Land—full of spaghetti, garlic, chianti, opera, and wops. It will certainly be interesting, if not exciting. But regardless of the place we land, there will never be a dull moment as long as these 150 avigators are together and able to wiggle. Of course an onslaught of Titian blondes may split us up somewhat and divide us and cause dissention and consternation in our ranks, but nothing else ever will—certainly not lead.

I'll try and write again from somewhere en route and until then Goodbye.

A heartful of love

your devoted son, Elliott

P.S. I left the Stutz for a general overhauling but it was running fine that last trip. Did 85 for three miles at a stretch.

On board the *Carmania*

Dear Mother,

Gee, it's great to be alive and you can't imagine how rosy existence has become. I feel like a prince now and every day a new opportunity seems to open itself to me. Why I wouldn't swap jobs with a Colonel of Infantry! And you wouldn't know me now. Why I'm just death on efficiency and discipline. Bismark's Blood and Iron has nothing on me now.[6]

So far it's been more like a sightseeing trip than a military expedition. We have the best accommodations the world can furnish and we will have a couple of days off in London and a couple off in Paris. What more could I ask. And as for this Italian proposition—well, all the boys that were going to France tried to get to go with us and as we lost 40 of our men by a mistake in orders, 40 of them came over from Fort [Leonard] Wood the last couple of days and joined. None of the Princeton men got a chance to as they were on leave but I understand all of them tried to.[7]

Another thing—one day at Mineola a man reported to me as being assigned to duty there. He looked like a gentleman, well groomed and well set up, about 24 or 25 I should say but I need men to wash dishes, "so," says I, "run in the kitchen and report to the mess corporal for duty and get a uniform this afternoon." Very well says he. But wait, says I, give me your service record first. He does and I look at it. Albert Spalding is the name—occupation musician. I nearly fainted. As you were, says I, have you got your violin with you? Yes sir, he says, it's outside. Then stay away from that kitchen; you will dine with me (great honor) and from that time forth he and I have been boon companions. Have you ever heard him play? Well, if you haven't, you have something to live for. And he's the prince of gentlemen, a good bridge player, a good cocktail architect, and speaks six languages—quite an asset. He's not really one of us—not a flyer—just a regular $30 per month private, sent along with us because he can speak Italian and wash dishes.

And you know War is not so bad after all. So far I've enjoyed myself immensely and think it will be even better at the front. My nerves have never weakened for a moment. It's 14 days since we sailed and no more homesickness than seasickness and I've not yet missed one of the five meals a day that we eat. I hate to say it but it's true. But life has become so pleasant and so potent with possibilities that I'm afraid I don't want to relinquish my share. It's not the flesh pots of Egypt that I crave, it's the possibilities of what I myself can do that appeals to me. I feel now that I can make good and all I want is a chance to do it. I have gotten away with this so far and it's given me unbounded confidence in myself that it will take a lot to shake. So far there hasn't been the slightest thing to mar my administration. And I know that I can fly a plane—I did it to my own satisfaction at least at Mineola.

But rest assured—I'm going to finish this thing in the proper style and I'll be in at the death but just at this moment I feel that I would like a little more time—not to enjoy life or to get ready—but to develop a little further. It might be an interesting experiment. This idea, however, vanishes like thin air when I get my hands on the controls and start up. I just begin to live then. I think if I knew my next flight would be my last one—was sure of it—I'd still go up, and I'd get to the plane on the run. That's how it takes hold of you. Well, I've got no kick coming—I'm ready—the Gods have been kind to me—very kind lately—and I promise you, my indulgent parents, that when I sight a Boche I'll not weaken.

I'll probably see Pabst [Goodrich][8] in Paris next week and if I get a chance I'll write to you from there.

A heartful of love

Always your devoted son, Elliott

P.S. Address: Maj MacDill, American Embassy, Rome, Italy. Also I left a suitcase at the Vanderbilt which you may want to use. Lost the check.

Christ Church College, Oxford, England
October 7 1917

Dear Father,

You aren't half as surprised to hear that I am now quartered at Christ Church [College] as I am to be here. It was certainly a bolt out of a clear sky.

We landed about eight o'clock in the morning and were all ready to rush through England to Italy. The Major told me to get the men and baggage off the ship and form up on the dock. I did and then we waited for an hour with our packs on our backs and suitcases in hand. It was certainly my moment of triumph—at the head of an American detachment of officers in England![9] And the sun came out and the people gave us a cheer every now and then and all was well. Then the blow fell. The Major called me off to one side and I knew something was wrong.

"Springs," says he, "we're not going to Italy. You're to stay here and train in England and Captain LaGuardia and myself and the doctors and enlisted men are ordered to report to Paris. I'm sorry. I'm going to London in about five minutes and try to get it changed. You take the men on to Oxford."

He was so sorry to leave us he couldn't go on but rushed off to his train. He tried to tell the men goodbye but couldn't. Then my troubles began. A Debarking Official found us and showed us the way and about eleven we piled into a queer little train and started for Oxford.

The men simply went wild when I told them what was happening. The swearing must have been heard in Berlin! No Italy! Where's the Major? Where's LaGuardia? Where's Spalding? Where're we going? What the h— are we going to do with all this Italian money? All my mail's gone to Roma! I've been studying this damn Dago lingo for two weeks! They all but lynched me. And then we landed here [at Oxford] about dusk and the English Authorities weren't expecting us. I felt like I imagine a Roman dictator must have felt. A nice army to be in command of—but what'll I do with them? No one seemed to know. And I had to hold the men at attention all the time to keep them from deafening me with questions. Finally an

American aviation cadets marching to ground school classes, Oxford University, England. Elliott Springs is on the left. This photograph was probably taken in October 1917. Courtesy of the Springs Close Family Archives, the White Homestead, Fort Mill, South Carolina.

English Major arrived and guided us through the most picturesque streets I've ever seen to the old quadrangle of Exeter College, Oxford. Imagine it: 150 Americans marching in a column of fours through Oxford! I nearly got the whole bunch run over by not keeping on the left hand side of the street.

Our trunks had gone on through on the way to Italy, so I had to run and see about stopping them. An American first lieutenant sent down from the Embassy at London was the only thing that saved us from complete disintegration and then we finally got assigned to rooms and passed out. I had to leave five men on the boat to look after our freight and they haven't shown up yet. Am afraid they're lost in the shuffle—and they were good men too. They may show up yet though—it was only five days ago.

What's going to happen to us nobody knows. There're 150 of us here with no Regular Commissioned Officer in charge; so I've been having a pretty busy time. I don't know what my rank is—but I'm supreme around here and that's enough. There're 50 Americans quartered over in Queens College and they have a First Lieutenant in charge [probably Geoff Dwyer] who helps me out some by doing all the talking with the English officials. We've gotten some of our Italian money changed—though at a great loss and things could be a great deal worse.

Since we've been here we've done nothing but eat excellent food and lots of it and go sight-seeing and watch the English drill. It's a great life. They treat us like their own officers and last night I went to see a show entitled "Baby Mine."[10] Ever see it in New York?

The men have gotten over their disappointment somewhat and are beginning to really enjoy themselves. It's delightful here, really. I haven't had much time to enjoy it yet as I've been pretty busy but hope to before long in spite of the way I feel now. You see I have the Detachment "Office" with me to look after which consists of three trucks of papers relative to the men and supplies so I'm Officer boy-in-chief in addition to my other duties. Everyone has ordered huge supplies of English uniforms and big English high boots and if we stay here long enough we will certainly be a spiffy-looking crew—the Beau Brummels[11] of the Army!

I'll write you more about Oxford when I get a chance to see more of it. Yesterday I went in to church in a cathedral the foundations of which were laid in 750 I believe and the whole edifice was completed in 1004 and remodeled in 1340 or thereabouts. Enjoyed it very much. In [our] mess hall I look about and on the walls [they] have several Gainsboroughs, a Reynolds or so, and a half dozen Romneys so I don't feel bad about things.[12]

However, you can appreciate how keenly we felt our disappointment when we first arrived—particularly losing the Major. But more later—I want to get this off now. With a heartful of love to you and Lena I am

your devoted son, Elliott

Christ Church College, Oxford, England
October 17 1917

Dear Mother,

Well, you've heard of Moses and the children of Israel getting lost in the park haven't you? Well, Moses had a non-flying commission compared with this little job of mine. One more week of this and they put me in the dry-dock for repairs. I'm a nervous wreck. After guiding these 150 would-be Dagos all over England, somebody somewhere orders us here and leaves me in charge of them. That was two weeks ago and my life hasn't been worth living or worth two cents. We're waiting here to be assigned to English squadrons where we will be trained before going to the front. And every time I go to someone to get them to take these neophytes all they do is keep on giving me unlimited authority, something more to be responsible for—but no assistance! So all I do is go back and line them up and give them what for and tell them that General so-and-so will have them shot at

Mail call, Oxford University, England. Elliott Springs is calling names and handing out mail. This picture was probably taken in October 1917. Courtesy of the Springs Close Family Archives, the White Homestead, Fort Mill, South Carolina.

sunrise if they don't quit asking questions. It's a great life. There's a lieutenant from the Embassy who gives me the gossip from London every now and then and outside of that I deal exclusively with the English authorities, who by the way, have treated us like Princes. We expect to be assigned in three or four days and then I hope my troubles will be over as we are to be split up. Some of us may go to Scotland, some to Egypt, and some to France. Nobody knows.

Our Italian bubble certainly burst with a thud. We had it all figured out so nicely too. We could just picture ourselves sitting on the banks of the Tiber teaching blue-eyed Titian blondes and ox-eyed Junos how to pronounce *camouflage*. Instead we are learning to speak English at Oxford. And Oxford by the way is magna cum laude and per ardua ad astra.[13] I can't begin to describe it to you. The next time you're in New York go to the Public Library and get a book on the subject and read up about Christ Church. The building I am quartered in was built about 1500 and everybody from Watt Tyler[14] to Capt Ball[15] has been here and has their initial on the walls. I positively feel sanctified. And the food—well, I weigh 172.

These English people are wonderful. Everybody in uniform—even the women—but everybody cheerful. There was a little lieutenant here last week—looked about 17 and I was kidding him about trying to hide his new commission by making his Sam Brown belt look old. "Oh that," says he, "not a bit. The belt was my brother's. He went West last month. An Albatross got him." And he showed me a stain on the belt. Just a kid and he's off to France now—smiling. And they are all sportsmen, through and through. I've had tea at several estates nearby and the women all seem to have the same attitude. And they'll certainly never quit until there's nobody to fight with. I wish I'd gotten into it sooner.

I haven't heard what happened to the Major and our enlisted men. He went on to Paris with the doctors and Captain LaGuardia and that's the last we heard of them. The last thing he said to me was that as soon as he got settled somewhere he was going to get me transferred to his command but I guess he's been sent back to the States to bring over another bunch. He was certainly a wonder. The men hated to lose him worse than anything else. And if it's possible I know he'll get me transferred. He told me one day that he knew I was working too hard but it was my own fault—I was too damn efficient. Biggest compliment I ever had paid me. Forgive me for telling you about it but I have confidence that you won't let anyone read this but Father so I guess it's all right. And maybe Father won't think I'm such a bum.

And you ought to see me in my new role of Major Domus and wet nurse. The Spartan Generals had nothing on me. Knowing me as you do, what do you think of me as the righteous representative of Law and Order? Can you imagine me restricting a man to his room for a week for getting tight? And giving him a good lecture besides? And with a straight face? Of course they all plead not guilty, so remembering Solomon and the questionable baby, I have prepared a system of judging them. I ask them what they had to drink. If they can remember, I let them off. Otherwise—bing, on goes the lid. And the men have certainly behaved wonderfully. Otherwise I could never get away with this at all. And the funny thing is, the dire punishment I threaten them with is to have them sent over to France. And it works too.

But the hard part of it is that I have to be so careful. I hardly dare to take a drink because then I can't hold down the others. And I have to always be the first one at formations, otherwise there ain't no formation. And my shoes and leggins have to glisten like mirrors, otherwise I can't have inspection. My room has to be spotless and oh well—I'm just miserable I'm such a model soldier. And you know my real inclinations! If I ever get out of this job I certainly will never let anyone pass the buck to me again. Life's too short.

We had our pictures taken the other day with the English cadets here at Christ Church. I'm having one of them sent to you. Also one of the whole [bunch]. I didn't mean to hog the camera—it just turned out I was told to sit where I did in each picture.

British and American cadets at Christ Church College, Oxford University, Oxford, England, October 1917. Elliott Springs is in the second row, just left of center, eleventh from the left end. Courtesy of the Springs Close Family Archives, the White Homestead, Fort Mill, South Carolina.

And by the way, we are now wearing the little aviation caps like the English officers. Just got them yesterday. You ought to see me in one—I look like Happy Hooligan.[16] When I first put it on I had to call off drill because the men couldn't keep a straight face at all. However, they're very convenient. I guess you've seen the aviators at home wearing [them] though.

We're really in luck, getting sent here. We'd have had a better time maybe in Italy but I believe we'll make better progress here. And we'll certainly get to the Front a lot sooner. Please write to me—American Aviation Detachment c/o American Embassy London and they'll forward it to me wherever I am. By the time you get this I'll probably be in Egypt, France, or Italy, so don't be surprised at my next one.

By the way, [the poet John] Masefield[17] lives about 5 miles from here. I was over there Sunday. And why did you stick in a volume of Lawrence Hope[18] with the Dago literature? You evidently haven't read any of it. Do so!

Someone got a postcard this morning from Sydney Brewster and the other crowd. They are down at Southampton and hope to sail for France in a few days. Nothing doing over there yet, though, I heard.

I am trusting you as per your agreement not to show this letter around. The George stuff is for your benefit only. Later if you want to use [it] for your own glorification all right. But be sure there's no chance of my returning.

A heartful of love to you and Father. Devotedly, Elliott

Exeter College, Oxford, England
November 1 1917

Dear Mother,

If I ever do come home I'm afraid I'll be too thoroughly obnoxious for polite society. I'm getting so conceited that there's no living with me. And I've been an absolute monarch so long that I'm afraid I'll be a bad actor when I'm dethroned. But as yet they just keep on shoving it to me faster than I can take it—I no sooner finish one job than they give me a bigger one. And thanks to the philosophy [of] objectivity which I cultivated at Princeton via Psychology and Ethics I've gotten away with it. I haven't gotten near enough to Germany to commit any murder but I'm certainly getting away with it.

Remember this letter is strictly confidential or I wouldn't tell you about it. It is not [to] be read aloud or passed around!!! I don't know how strictly this will be censored but I'd better not say anything about affairs military anyway.

Yes, I owe a lot to Psychology and Philosophy. Father will tell you that it is all due to my Culver training; but he's wrong. There's six Culver men and two former West Pointers in the detachment that are worthless and my job has not been that of a drill master. I'm doctor, minister, diplomat, bouncer, steward, and bartender as well as cashier to the avigators and I certainly will be happy when this part is over and we are split up into smaller detachments. I even had to inspect the new uniforms last week and pass on the fit and design. Really they've surely worked me to death. I suppose I do take it too seriously but when I have to pick out men to act as officers in various capacities and discipline others I feel the responsibility in spite of my sense of humor which has become highly developed.

I've enjoyed my stay here immensely and have learned a lot, not technically perhaps but certainly in other ways. And the principal thing that I've learned is the value of education. Impractical practical education. And

I'm not going to say that I wish now that I had more of it and had studied harder at college etc. Not on your life. I certainly consider myself well educated. And I've proved it. Only this morning we were studying aerial photography and I was the only one including the instructor who knew anything about binocular vision or Berkeley's Theory of Distance.[19] Score two for Psychology.

I lunched today with the Dean and had a most delightful time. He has only eight undergraduates now so has time to discuss Philosophy with me. And once in a while I get a chance to attend one of the university lectures on Descartes or Idealism. By the way I sent you some books. I hardly know what they are—I just wandered into a bookstore and picked them out at random.

I made a terrible mistake the other day. A lady invited the whole detachment to tea on Saturday and I misread the note and thought it was Sunday.[20] Consequently there was no one to eat the food on Saturday and no food to be eaten on Sunday. But when the lady understood how much else I had to do she readily forgave me and recommended a nerve tonic to me.

I received your letter from Columbia yesterday. It was the first news from home. Please write often. There are times when I reflect upon my peaceful existence in Lancaster with a certain degree of pleasure. Lots of soap and water and the only thing to be afraid of—indigestion. And now—well, I won't describe it. I know this letter is considerably overdue but I have been too busy. I've been trying to find time to write to Aunt Addie too but it looks as if I never will. I saw in the paper where poor Bob Lamont [Springs's fellow Princetonian who went into the ambulance service] got all shot up in France. No details and the paper was dated Sept 27.[21]

We had quite a bit of excitement last Saturday. There was another detachment here, fifty of them that had come over at the same time Walker Ellis[22] did and they were leaving on Monday. Also one of my men had a birthday and hence a party. Well these others were throwing a farewell party and so we merged the two. It was a regular riot. About ten I decided that I had better leave as the party was on the Q.T. and it would never do for the Sanctified Seneschal and Right Royal guardian of the Sacred American Reputation to be seen in such company so I sneaked and beat it back to quarters instructing the more rational members of my detachment to come in a side way. So I returned and sent the corporal on guard to bed and took his place. Well I got my men in safely but not so the others. They were bent on making it an occasion. About that time the Commanding Officer, an English Colonel, showed up and with the exclamation, "The

Americans have broken loose," he proceeded to disperse the party. They dispersed peacefully via an alley being directed by some English officers who had joined the melee. But it seems that some English troops were also on a rampage and the C.O. went wild. The next thing that occurred was a formation at 12:30 [at night] of all men quartered in a certain college. The colonel had them yanked out of bed to find out which of his English troops were mixed up in it.

Well they say that there will never be another formation like it. Those that saw it still have hysterics and those that were in it have not yet recovered. They tried to get six different men to take charge and then had to give it up. It looked like a snake dance. The next morning the air was blue. The C.O. called me up and complimented me on the fact that my detachment was so well behaved—was pleased that I had them so well in hand. And no one knows now who started the riot. And I'll never tell. But there are three English officers that tip me the wink every time I salute them because they were there. But needless to say they aren't telling anyone because they were the ones whom the C.O. was looking for. They are anxious for me to organize another one but I decided that Americans are famous enough here and put my foot on it.

I'm getting along fine with these English officers. Particularly so since we have 360 lbs of sugar which we brought over with us. And everybody in Oxford is after it. A major took me up to his rooms the other night and gave me some port which came from Noah's private supply and I dined last week with a captain. They both have designs on our sugar but I'm guarding it very carefully and we use it only for coffee at breakfast. I heard that cotton was 30 cents a pound. I almost bought a Rolls Royce on the spot. Suppose you've ordered gold butter plates and three Wintons.[23] Go ahead. I'd like to hear of you showing 5th Ave how it's done. And it is considerable savings to have me in the Army in a country where you can't buy gasoline. By the way we had a Zep[pelin] scare last week. They passed only 30 miles from here.

A Press Photographer came up from London yesterday and took some pictures of us. If you see me staring you in the face some day labeled "Australian mechanician sighs for home in Egypt" don't be surprised. We had a big boxing contest last week. All the RFC men and the Americans. I went in and to my surprise was put in the heavyweight class, drew a 190-pounder the first crack. I got by for several nights and then lost out in the semi-finals. However I won a trip to London out of it—three days leave— but I couldn't take it—had to stay here to look after things. However, I am entitled to leave any time I want it so will go next week.

If you are in New York any time soon, please stop in and tell a certain person that I'm still alive and write me how she looks. Please—I mean it.

A heartful of love to you and Father.

Your devoted son, Elliott

P.S. I am dining tomorrow night with Sir Gilbert Murray[24] who as you know is the grand old man of the Classics. Probably the most respected scholar in England—head of the Classical Dept here. EWS

Flight Training in England

November 1917 to February 1918

Early in November, soon after the two cadet groups were merged in Exeter College, they were told to prepare for another move. Twenty cadets were to be sent to a training field to begin their flight instruction at Stamford, England, and Springs was tasked to select the twenty who would attend. The other men were to report to gunnery ground school at Grantham. Springs apparently selected the twenty (including himself) to attend flight training based on previous flying experience, which simplified his task, as not many men had received much actual flight instruction before they left the United States. Springs, of course, had received some intensive instruction at Princeton and then at Mineola, so he was ideally situated to attend the British flight school, and it seems evident that he selected some of his Princeton classmates as well, for Arthur Taber wrote to his father of his good luck in having been selected to be included in flight training: "It was my very good luck to be one of the twenty chosen (largely because I had already done some flying). I was delighted with the prospect of flying at last, but it was not entirely without regrets that I prepared for the flying-school, for it meant leaving the rest of the bunch, and some mighty fine and admirable fellows among them with whom I have developed close friendships. This was the parting of the ways."[1]

Springs was still in charge of the men who were sent to Stamford, although his administrative duties were much reduced in the training school, and he felt a great sense of relief. Once at Stamford, Springs no longer was required to behave in a manner appropriate to someone in a supervisory position, and he was able to enjoy his off-duty hours with greater enthusiasm and less concern for decorum. After Springs completed his training at

Stamford in December, he was sent to London Colney, where he remained for one month from the middle of January through the middle of February.

Springs did not select two of his best friends, Mac Grider and Larry Callahan, to attend flight training at Stamford, most likely because they had not yet flown many hours in an aircraft, and they proceeded to Grantham to begin aerial gunnery ground training. However, approximately two weeks later, on 19 November, they and the rest of the men in their group were sent from Grantham to Thetford, where they began their flight training. Their program at Thetford continued until early January, when they were transferred to another flying training field, London Colney, near London, where Springs arrived to join them on 13 January. From this time on, the three of them began to develop their socializing skills in earnest, soon earning for themselves the name "Three Musketeers." According to Springs's flying log, he graduated from his flying training program at London Colney on 27 January 1918. He remained there until 13 February, when he was transferred to Turnberry, in Ayrshire, Scotland, to attend aerial gunnery school, while Grider and Callahan remained at London Colney to complete their flight training.

During four months of training, Springs accumulated over fifty hours of flying time, operating a variety of training and operational aircraft, and gaining competence and confidence in his flying skills. He also survived a number of forced landings and near crashes without injury. In this regard he was much more fortunate than many of his fellow cadets, for at least five of them died in flying accidents.

No. 1 Training Depot Station
Stamford, Lincolnshire, England
November 6, 1917

Dear Father,

Well the Italian Detachment is no more. Saturday the noble organization ceased. One hundred and thirty [men] were sent up to Grantham for a course in Aerial Gunnery and twenty of us were picked to come up here [to Stamford] to this Flying Squadron of the RFC. I'll probably be here about three weeks and then I get a Sopwith Biplane [Camel] which they say does 160 miles per hour and drinks [fuel] like a rocket. It was rather hard to say goodbye to the 130. We've worked hard together and they've worked hard for me.

Just before they started [to leave] the three platoons presented me with a gold knife, a silver match box, and a silver canteen. It was just before they started and it is probably the one moment in my life I will always remember and I'll never feel quite the same again. I'll certainly never be the same again. Even though I should some day get to be a major I would not have the authority, influence, or responsibility that I've had for the past two months. However, I'm glad it's over—I should have gone mad in another week. I don't think I'm sane as it is. You can't imagine the strain I've been under and the thousands of little things I've had to worry me.

Now I'm relieved of all official duty. I'm still in charge of these twenty here but we live where we please, and eat where we please, and dress pretty much as we please, and there're no formations. It's quite a relief and I can relax myself now. I've had to be on the job and up to scratch myself for so long that it certainly is a luxury. Because if I hadn't been okay myself down at Oxford I could never have handled the others.

And it is certainly glorious to feel that your work is done. And whether it was well done or not—it was done satisfactorily and to the best I had in me. Anyway it's done and I've got a rest coming to me. And it's never again for me. I didn't mind the work but when you're in command there's a question of ethics arising every day that is absolutely tormenting.

For instance, all 150 men were wild to come here. And I had to choose the twenty from them. How was I to do it? There was no one to help me.[2] Naturally I wanted to bring along my best friends and those who had helped me the most. But could I do it conscientiously? Every one would raise a howl no matter whom I chose and say that it was favoritism. And all my best friends expected me to put them on the list. I had twenty-four hours to do it and I certainly spent them in agony. I guess I did take it much too seriously, but I wanted to be fair and even though I may never see the others again I simply couldn't do it any other way. So I finally closed my eyes to friendship and prejudice and picked them. I didn't even put my two roommates on the list though another might have done so in all fairness. It certainly hurt me to do it for it would have been wonderful for twenty of us—congenial and sworn friends—to have been together it may be for the rest of the war. When the list was announced some of them took the disappointment rather hard but they've proved before that they're men and they certainly did it again. It was after that they decided to give me something so I feel a lot better about it.

It's things like that which make a commander's position trying. I never want to be in the position again. I believe in sticking by one's friends but if you're in authority you can't, even though you can do so much more for them. If I am capable I will manage your mills some day with great delight and welcome the responsibility, but deliver me from authority over my fellow man. You know, I've changed a lot since I left America. I'm beginning to take Life seriously—though why I don't know. Imagine anyone in the Flying Corps taking Life seriously! It's ridiculous. The English Pilots certainly wouldn't consider it for a moment.

Please whatever you do, consider this letter as strictly confidential—just between you and me—a son to his Father. If you want to brag about your son—wait and I'll do my best to supply the data when I get a chance. I may not get the chance but in case I don't, I want you to know that your son isn't the worthless bum you've always considered me. At least I want you to know that I've gotten away with my first big job—probably the biggest I'll ever have.

But enough of that.

I had my first big crack up yesterday. I was awfully lucky and hardly got a scratch. Ruined my brand new uniform though. Handsewn whipcord it was and just paid for.

I was talking to an English officer and he told me that he was going to go up in a new Curtiss which had just come. "I've never flown one," he said, "and never flown from a Dep[erdussin] control.[3] What are they like?" I told him. "How do they loop?" "All right; also, they spin." "Well, watch me, I looped an old soap box this morning. Want to go?" Sure I did—he'd been six months at the front and was the first man to loop a "soapbox." "All right, come on."

So we got in and taxied down the field. He whipped around and after inquiring about how it flew, we started up. About 25 feet up a puff hit us and almost upset us but he got it level and we were climbing fine when the thing stalled about 75 or 100 feet up and went into a slide slip. Of course, 'twas all over. And remembering Stanton[4] at Princeton I doubled up and ducked down into the cockpit and waited. She landed wing first—crumpled it—and stuck her nose in the ground, driving the landing gear through the fuselage (body) and smashing all to pieces. To my surprise I was able to wiggle out and the officer crawled out too. We lit our cigarettes and dismissed the ambulance which had started out while we were still up in the air. He didn't even get bruised and I got both knees bruised up and my trousers and coat ripped. But you should see the machine—kindling wood. I missed my flight for the day but I'm not sorry—'twas easily worth it. But a certain young lady will have to knit me another helmet.[5]

Was too cloudy to fly today but I'll be at it again tomorrow in a brand new Curtiss with stick control—which is better by the way than the Dep.

Remember this letter is for you only.

A heartful of love to you and Lena. Your devoted son, Elliott

The following is from a letter by Leroy Springs dated 10 October 1917. An extensive excerpt is given here to establish the context of the family environment that Springs would have had in mind as he wrote his letters home. The details Leroy Springs includes in this letter provide some idea of the issues and topics that were important in the United States at this time, especially as they involved the South Carolina area.

My dear Son: It is certainly a great relief to know of your safe arrival, as I have been thinking about you constantly and was very much relieved to receive your cablegram. I think you should have written me a letter from New York the day you left giving some intimation of what you were doing. You did not have to give me all the details but you could have given me some idea as to when you would leave etc. . . .

I have been very busy since you left, as usual, doing so much building, enlarging the mills at Fort Mill, rebuilding the [railroad] depot here which was burned, and building Waddy Thomson a warehouse and storage place for his textile business. I am also building an addition to the store. I have been able to buy a new bridge for [across] the river. It was built for the C&NW[6] and they were not able to pay for it and I bought it at a reasonable price and am now building new piers for the river to put it over. One of the old piers was washed away and these piers were too far apart so I will have to build all new except one, which will be very costly but it is the only thing to do.

The war, of course, is the general topic of conversation. The cantonments at Charlotte, Spartanburg, Greenville, and Columbia, are nearing completion and they expect to concentrate 30,000 to 40,000 troops at each place. Charlotte and Columbia are literally jammed with soldiers and everything is very much demoralized. The government has been paying all kinds of prices for labor and consequently has demoralized everything. It looks as if our government is going to have the best trained army in the course of a year that was ever known and I think they will begin sending them to Europe in two months from the different cantonments. All the Lancaster boys are now in Columbia and they are now sending negro troops there also from North Carolina, South Carolina, Georgia, and Florida. . . .

Cotton is very late and bringing very high prices. It has gone up to 27 and ½ cents and farmers, of course, are very happy over the fact. It looks as if Germany and Austria are getting tired of the war and are anxious to make peace but I hardly think there is any prospect of it, as I do not believe the Allies should or will agree to anything short of unconditional surrender and I certainly hope they will not, though I would like very much to see this horrible war ended but I believe the Germans should be made to pay for all the damages and outrages they have committed.

Did you get any promotion after you left or are you still sergeant in charge of your corps? I understood you went over with 150 young men. Are they all with you yet? Write me as much of your plans as you can, as I am very much interested, and let me know how you are getting along flying. I will be looking for a letter from you daily from now on. I hope you wrote us while you were on the ship. I sincerely hope you will devote your time and attention to making yourself perfect. As I have repeatedly told you, you will be all the better equipped to take care of yourself and to serve your country ably and efficiently by making yourself efficient in every way in the aviation service and being an able and efficient aviator, which I am sure you will do. . . .

I have done nothing about your Stutz car that you left in New York but am waiting until I go there again. They have offered to swap a four seated car at $800, to boot but I do not think I will trade, as I think they are asking too much. They state, however, that they have overhauled your car and it is ready for shipment.

Now, my dear boy, I hope you will be very careful and considerate of yourself and do not take any undue risks and do not do any special stunts in the air. What you want is to be a competent aviator but there is nothing to be gained by fast flying and that is where most men get killed in the air, just like reckless driving in an automobile.

Please write me regularly. Rest assured I am thinking about you all the time and I am not contemplating anything else but your safe return and that we shall have a good account of you and I feel sure you will be faithful in the discharge of your every duty and in serving your country in the best way possible.

With love and best wishes, I am always, Your affectionate father

Stamford, England
November 12 1917

Dear Mother,

Well, for the moment I'm a regular gentleman of leisure. All I have to do is tell the batman which boots to shine and fly every day that the weather permits. Of course I have to monkey around a bit with machine guns and bombs but I don't miss as much sleep as I did at Oxford. There are twenty of us here and the 130 others are up at Grantham 25 miles away. A couple of us are planning to fly up for Thanksgiving dinner if the weather permits and we don't crack up all the planes before then. We got so we rather liked Oxford and hated to leave, but it's a big step forward and after one more shift we ought to be off to the Front.

Stamford, I suppose you know, is the second oldest town in England. The hotel is still standing where Hadrian[7] stopped when he was here and there's an old road that Julius Caesar ordered repaired in 46 B.C. However, we're very comfortable and as Noyes[8] would say, "It's not so far from London."

I think we left a very good impression in Oxford. The English Commanding Officers were very complimentary before we left and they have a new impression of Americans. So maybe my vigilance in guarding the Sacred American Reputation was not in vain. And the men made me feel pretty good about the whole thing. Before we broke up finally they decided to get me something. Well, the committee consisted of several pretty good friends of mine and the result was that the presentation was more like a pounding [a roast]. It was about a half an hour before the 130 were to leave and I had them all drawn up and was giving them holy thunder for not having their baggage ready. From that I passed on to their other shortcomings and then appointed the men to take charge and run things up at Grantham.

All of a sudden one man walked up and everybody relaxed. I was just about to blow their heads off for not standing at attention when someone yelled "speech" and someone [else] proceeded to present me with a box. I nearly fainted—it being the first time in my life anything like that ever happened to me. And here I was face to face with 149 of them. I wanted to run. I didn't know what to say. So I said a few words that meant nothing and turned over the detachment to the new officers and they marched on down to the station. When I opened the box I found a gold pencil, a silver match box, and a silver canteen. I certainly did hate to see the fellows go. And my best friends were in the bunch that went, too. We stayed at Oxford three days longer with nothing to do and managed to keep out of trouble.

Funny thing—I knew all along that something funny was going on. The gates were always locked at 11 every night but no one came in at that time. However, I didn't look for trouble and only went after it when it was under my nose or when it was apt to cause a general disturbance, so I didn't try to stop it. And it meant fewer passes for me to look after.

Well, the last night at Oxford three of us wandered over to Abingdon [a town about eight miles south of Oxford] and didn't come back until pretty late. So one of them guided us around through an alley to the college wall. It was 12 feet high but there was a tree on the inside and by standing on my shoulders he grabbed a big limb. Then he sat on it to hold it down for me. I jumped, got it, and got my feet around it. But alas for English Cuisine the blooming limb broke and limb Kelly [Robert Kelly] and all landed right on my belt buckle. Funny? We couldn't move for half an hour and then we had to build a sort of ladder out of the broken limb to get in. When we came in we found the English officer in charge sitting in my room finishing up some port. "What ho," he said, "how'd you get in." "Well," I said, "you needn't worry. None of your Englishmen will come in that way now. We broke the limb." "The hell you did, how am I going to get in now," he growled. I thought I would never get over laughing—particularly so as I had heard him jumping down all the Englishmen's throats all afternoon. He's been two years at the Front too. Been shot down twice.

Another funny thing. What do you suppose I spend my spare time doing? Reading? Yes. What? Greek tragedy. Yes, I turned back to the classics for comfort and enjoy them more than ever. I got away with a short story the other day but haven't had a chance to revise it suitably. You should see me sitting over on a crack-up waiting to go up, reading Euripides. Also Prof Gilbert Murray[9] autographed a couple of his classic tragedies and translations for me.

You all have certainly been very negligent about writing. So far I have received two letters from you and one from Father and that is all the mail I have received. I expect there's a lot piled up at the Embassy but it ought to be through shortly unless I'm completely forgotten. I saw a *New York Times* not long ago. Dated October 3. But it did look good. I cabled yesterday to Father for some Page and Shaw's.[10] Please have some sent to me every now and then. You can't get any decent candy in England.

Our Government certainly is looking out for us well. The last thing they pulled off was to make all get new whipcord uniforms and a complete camp outfit, boots, and Sam Brown belts. That and a trench coat cost me just two months' pay. When we travel now you'd think we were a circus. Each man has his own bed, mattress, pillow, blankets, wash basin, bucket, bath tub, and chair in addition to the 200 lbs of baggage we brought with us and the junk we collected at Oxford. Also now we have a complete flying equipment from fleece-lined boots to fur helmet and chamois face mask. If I ever have to move my own baggage myself I'll pass out. But we certainly look like a million dollars. The London papers even printed our pictures last week.

Also I wired Father to swap the Stutz in for a new four-passenger one. The two-passenger one won't do you all any good and is built for speed only. And there's no use keeping it there for me. By the time I get back autos will be out of style. It's rather a futile idea anyway. And the four-passenger is a wonder and is the very thing you need. I saw one of them just before I left. I certainly hated to leave mine behind. The Sunday before I sailed I drove it 230 miles about, and she never missed once. And we were traveling at quite a rate of speed. I got arrested twice and went through a wire fence at 70 but I stalled off the cops and didn't do any damage except to her nerves. So if anyone says that I left it in bad condition—laugh at them. It was full of carbon and rattles a bit and the paint was none too good, but it certainly would go forward.

Don't bother to send me any Xmas presents. I'd probably never get them anyway. No telling where I'll be then anyway. Speaking of beds I have one of the collapsible affairs and this morning I awoke on the floor. Complete collapse. So now have it propped up on two trunks. Great life in the army! It's six weeks since I've been between sheets.

I trust you and Father are considering my letters strictly confidential. If I find out otherwise I'll quit writing. Also I'm expecting to find the trunk intact on my return. Every time I write a letter I hesitate about posting it. And Father's [recent] letter shows that his attitude towards me hasn't changed. I am in constant fear of the worst. . . . Heard from the Major [MacDill] the other day. He's in France and writes that he's unable to get me transferred to his command. Capt La Guardia is in Italy now and can't get me transferred either. Just as well, I suppose.

Did you do as I requested and stop in when you were in New York? If not please do. Pabst is in Paris but as yet have been unable to get in communication with him.

With a heartful of love to you and Father, Your devoted son, Elliott

At Stamford, Springs began to fly with English instructors, mostly pilots from the Royal Flying Corps who had previously served at the front. Entries from his flight log are included to indicate types of aircraft flown and the nature of individual flights.

FLIGHT LOG: 12 November: Flight with Capt. Blayne: 25 minutes in a
   JN4B, #1946. 800 meters. Practiced landings. Back seat 15 m[inutes.]
FLIGHT LOG: 12 November: Solo flight: 15 minutes in #1946. 700 meters.
   Two landings; one good.
FLIGHT LOG: 13 November: Solo flight: 1 hour, 15 minutes in #1948.
   4000 meters. Over Stamford. Stalls and vertical banks.
FLIGHT LOG: 13 November: Solo flight: 1 hour, 35 minutes in #1948.
   1500 meters. 24 landings.
FLIGHT LOG: 14 November: Solo flight: 1 hour, 40 minutes in #1948.

FLIGHT LOG: 14 November: Solo flight: 1 hour, 10 minutes in #1948.

FLIGHT LOG: 15 November: Solo flight: 35 minutes in #5164.

FLIGHT LOG: 15 November: Solo flight: 55 minutes in #1923.

FLIGHT LOG: 16 November: Solo flight: 35 minutes in #1932.

FLIGHT LOG: 16 November: Solo flight: 20 minutes in #5164. Forced landing (2)

FLIGHT LOG: 16 November: Solo flight: 1 hour, 20 minutes in #5163. Oil pump went west [broken]

FLIGHT LOG: 16 November: Solo flight: 5 minutes in #5164. Motor gave out—got back.

FLIGHT LOG: 16 November: Solo flight: 10 minutes in #5164. Engine dud. Got back.

FLIGHT LOG: 17 November: Solo flight: 1 hour, 5 minutes in #5164. Over Stamford. Motor turning up only 1300 [RPM].

FLIGHT LOG: 17 November: Solo flight: 35 minutes in #1932. Over Stamford. Center section strayed [broken?].

FLIGHT LOG: 18 November: Solo flight: 30 minutes in #1259. Over Stamford. Excellent weather.

FLIGHT LOG: 18 November: Solo flight: 1 hour, 55 minutes in #5164. 3000 meters. Spiddlegate. Weather good.

FLIGHT LOG: 18 November: Solo flight: 1 hour, 15 minutes in #1909. 2000 meters. Followed railroad. Landed [at] Spiddlegate.

FLIGHT LOG: 18 November: Solo flight: 1 hour, 15 minutes in #1909. 1500 meters. Return. Fog—got lost—found railroad.

FLIGHT LOG: 19 November: Solo flight: 1 hour, 15 minutes in #1936. 2000 meters. Railroad to tunnel. Formation.

FLIGHT LOG: 20 November: Solo flight: 45 minutes in #5163. 2000 meters. Stamford. Very bumpy. Bus unstable.

FLIGHT LOG: 20 November: Solo flight: 55 minutes in #5164. 8100 feet. Altitude test. Stalled at 8100.

FLIGHT LOG: 20 November: Solo flight: 1 hour, 15 minutes in #5164. 2000 feet. Grantham. Narrow escape at Grantham.

Stamford, England
November 19 [20?] 1917

Dear Mother—

Well, the dance is on. 'Tis Pluto's ball and the ballroom lies between the Styx and Lethe. Pluto and Proserpine are leading the grand march and the Three Fates are the Belles of the Ball (I wish I could remember their names).[11] Venus and Bacchus have been dancing and carrying on in a scandalous manner and are thus far unreproved and Calliope[12] is a wall-flower. The decorations are knives and pruning scythes in honor of the Three Fates and the sport of the evening consists in stealing one as a souvenir. Minerva wasn't even invited and Mars is outside arguing with the Pacifists who want the ball called off. It's a mad revel but I am beginning to enjoy it. I don't know how I am going to get home though. There are only two paths. One leads to Lethe and plunges you into its oblivious waters. The other leads to Styx and Achillean immortality but no one here knows which is which. Many try to tempt the Fates to show them—others wander out blindly.

I just found this piece of paper in my pocket and thought I would fill in the time writing to you. You see I am out in the middle of a beet field about eight miles from the aerodrome and am waiting for them to send me out a new mechanic and a new magneto. I was on my way back from Grantham, flying at about 3000 [feet] when she started spluttering and died on me. This looked like a nice field so I pancaked her without doing any damage to anything but the beets. Everything is okay except the mag[neto] so I found an intelligent-looking youth with a bicycle and sent him off to a telephone with the message. In the meantime I sit here and write to you in peace and comfort. I have my trench coat in the front seat and in it happened to be a flask, some chocolate, and some cigarettes, so it might be worse. Have been carrying this paper for several days to write to you on anyway.

I was just up at Grantham and had lunch with the fellows. Was awfully glad to see them again and they received me quite royally. Found a nice landing ground up there. Don't know how I am going to get out of this field. Will have to get out with the wind at my back and it's not too big with some trees at the other end. Nice prospect! I have a good bus, though it's pretty ancient—one of Noah's original two I think. But it flies well—I even looped it last week. Should hate to crack it up getting out of this place.

I've been working pretty hard lately. Have lost all the weight I gained on the boat and at Oxford. Was in the air five hours yesterday—total of twenty-three for the week. Not bad considering that the weather's been bad—foggy every day. Somebody getting lost all the time. Got lost myself this morning. Landed at Peterborough, got my bearings, and followed the railroad back. If it's clear Wednesday three of us are going to fly down to London and spend the night.

I'm practically through here. Hope to pass on to the fast scouts next week. Then it won't be long before I'll be ready. You have no idea how much there is to learn about this game. I've still got my night flying to do.

There're about six of us ready for it. Myself and five from the first detachment who came over a month before we did. The English Officers certainly win the game hands down. They're fine fellows every one of them, and if they ever have a serious thought nine to one it's about their digestion. One of them hit a tree yesterday and cracked up. In a half an hour he was up looping in another plane. All the paper I have with me. Will finish later—if Igetoutofhere.

Later.

Well I got back all right and am up at the mess waiting for dinner. Pretty tired after my day's labor. Got four hours [of flying time] to my credit in spite of the delay at the [beet] field. It was the mag[neto] after all and the bus went fine with the new one. Only casualty was the loss of my wrist stop-watch. Must have dropped it messing about in the field. However, we get paid on the first and I'll invest my pay in a new one.

We have very nice quarters here. Two of us are living over a little millinery shop on High Street. My roommate is a prince. Three years ago he went out to Arizona to die with consumption. He's now the healthiest specimen you ever saw. I call him Morituri.

'Tis certainly a masculine world I've chosen to live in. You know I haven't spoken to a woman socially since I left Oxford. And I haven't spoken to a woman under thirty socially since I left New York. Haven't had a single tete-a-tete since I sailed. And I certainly like it. I haven't missed the feminine touch, at all. Strange, isn't it? My landlady looks after me excellently, thank you, and I court disaster daily at the aerodrome—what more can be desired? However I'm e pluribus unum. The rest of the outfit go flapper hunting all the time.

Get a copy of Horace will you and read over the 12th Ode for me please. I've been trying to recall it for weeks and can't. I think it's the 12th: "What fates have the gods in store for thee Lucae and what for me" etc.[13]

Did I tell you about christening my silver canteen? No? Well I took it up with me and went to 7000 feet and put the joy stick between my knees and drank a toast to Pegasus and Bellerophon and another to Daedalus. Then spiraled all the way down. Enough this time. More later.

A heartful of love to you and Father. Devotedly, Elliott

FLIGHT LOG: 20 November: Solo flight: 15 minutes in #1259. 1500 feet. Stamford. Very bumpy. Foggy. No good.
FLIGHT LOG: 21 November: Solo flight: 30 minutes in #1259. 2000 feet. Toward Grantham.

FLIGHT LOG: 21 November: Solo flight: 45 minutes in #1259. 2500 feet. Formation flying.

Waldorf Hotel, London
November [23/24] 1917[14]

Dear Father—

London—Waldorf [Hotel]—what do think of me? Anyway, don't write me about the perils of the city and how it demoralizes you, please. There's certainly nothing demoralizing around here. It happened this way. My Squadron Commander, an English officer, came up to me yesterday and says, "Springs, you'll kill yourself." "Why?" says I. "Did you see me side-slipping this morning?" "No, not flying," he says, "you're too lucky, but you're working too hard. You can't go without food or sleep much longer. You're out here every morning at daybreak and you don't stop flying long enough to eat. You've got to quit it."

"Oh," says I, "but I always take up some chocolate with me and sleeping is a bad habit—Father says so."

"Well, you stop now. I'll see that you get 48 hours leave tomorrow. Somebody just ran my bus into a tree so take off those Eskimo BVDs and come on in town and we'll get something to cure my cold."

So I got 48 hours leave. What we are all struggling for here is to get recommended for scout squadrons—that is, the small fast fighters. Only the best of us are to be recommended. Well, when I went in next day to get my leave, the Adjutant says to me, "You're posted to a Scout Squadron. You're through here. Captain —— recommended you yesterday."

So after 48 hours here I'm to proceed to my new squadron, 20 miles away, at London Colney, St. Albans. Great things are coming my way! So far only two of us have been posted. The other fellow is one of the detachment that came over four weeks before I did and we are the only two Americans to go to higher squadrons yet. So I rushed down to the bank and drew some money and packed my things and arrived here about ten like a soldier from the front—bed, blankets, and all.

But a city is rather a lonesome place when you don't know a soul there so I'm going around in the morning and try and buy some Xmas presents and go to a matinee and then go on to my new squadron and try my luck at Scouts. The next week will be pretty critical. The machines have only one seat so you can't get any instruction on them. You just get in and go up and take your chances. They do about 120 miles per hour and will do anything. I may not get by with it, but I'll certainly go up once and that once is going to be *some* ride.

I had quite a nice time at Stamford last week. The weather was good and I managed to get ahold of the fastest machine in the place. Managed to get in three to four hours of flying a day by flying during lunch hour. That's pretty good considering the fog and one hour in the air for a machine usually means two on the ground. Used to be able to go up and circle around the other machines while they were at full speed. Once though it was rather bad. We were doing formation flying and I had a terrible time keeping in place with it. All the planes were slow planes and mine wouldn't fly that slow.

Be sure and put U.S. Aviation Corps on my letters.

Love to you and Lena, Devotedly, Elliott

No. 74 Squadron , Royal Flying Corps
London Colney, Herts., England
November 25 1917

Dear Mother,

Behold—I have moved again—regular Cook's Tour[15] I'm on. I spent one night in London and then came on here to get some advance information on how to fly these new planes. I went out to the hangars and told the Flight Commander that I was to fly a _____ tomorrow. He asked the names and addresses of my nearest relatives and which cable was the best to use. Rather encouraging isn't it. But I'll fool them yet. The sergeant growled about being short of machines anyway and asked if I had been disappointed in love or was I a consumptive. I fled to the bar in horror but hope to spring a surprise tomorrow if the weather isn't too bad and my safety belt holds.

And by the way I want you to do something for me. I was unable to do any shopping in London due to the exportation rules so I want you to have five pounds of Page and Shaws sent to Frances [Robertson] and Olive from me for Christmas. You know Olive's address—Olive Kahlo, White Sulfur Springs, West Virginia. Just have the enclosed cards put in please.[16]

'Tis bitter cold here, snowing a little now. I've been flying in a fur-lined suit though and chamois face mask so don't mind it up in the air. But down on the ground I freeze. Up about 12000 feet let me remark that it is chilly.

I've been trying to write some but have had very little time to myself and the Muse has entirely forsaken me. Besides, I still retain my opinion of the hoi polloi so why put my ideas on paper. Funny thing about this war business—all my convictions have been strengthened, if 't'were possible, and I've become absurdly sure of myself. All my theories have worked out beautifully. And I've certainly proved my psychology sound. . . .

But 'tis funny how my theories and convictions have proved themselves. I'm getting more and more conceited. Last week I had considerable opportunity to think over things. I was distinctly morituri and had a minute or two to review my past and future while I was waiting for the crash to come. I didn't think I had a chance to avoid it but luck was with me and I got it practically under control about ten feet off the ground. But in those few moments I thought a lot. Rather a pleasant sensation it was—no regrets— and I thought to myself: better now than later when I may have regrets. I think I enjoyed it. But then followed a twenty minute battle with the elements which nearly ruined me. A regular gale was blowing and I expected any minute to crash but finally I got back to the aerodrome and made a lucky landing without hurting a thing—and there were two machines upside down on the field!

Did you get my suitcases and silk hat at the Vanderbilt? Better do so.

And please have my shot gun cleaned and oiled. I'm afraid the barrel might get a little rusty. Perhaps Mr. Robbins[17] would like to use it. Tell him I saw a man fly over a field to stir up rabbits and then shoot them with his machine gun. Absolutely straight, too, no kidding. Must admit, I'm not that good yet.

I'm going to try and fly up to Grantham for Thanksgiving dinner with the fellows. Will drop you a post card from up there.

A heartful of love to you and Father. Your devoted son, Elliott

Stamford, England
[no date; late November]

Dear Aunt Addie,

Just a line to tell you I am well and getting along fine under the circumstances. I'm still having to work as hard as ever but the work is most interesting, and flying will never be boring I don't think. We have wonderful planes to fly—the very latest things in speed scouts and fighters and you can do anything in the world with them.

Yesterday was Thanksgiving so four of us went in and had a big Turkey dinner at the Savoy. We are only about 25 miles from London and we can go in to the Theatre any time we wish. I shall be ready to go to the Front in three weeks so am hoping to eat my Christmas dinner in Paris.

It's colder than blueblazes over here now but these English don't seem to mind it at all. It's such a damp cold is the trouble. I spend all my money buying warmer garments of various sorts. I have several fur and leather outfits so am not suffering any.

London is full of American Officers. I ran into 15 or 20 of them yesterday at different times. Met a couple of classmates from Princeton and one from Culver. Felt as if I were back in New York again.

A heartful of love, as always, your devoted nephew, Elliott

No 1 Training Depot
Stamford, Lincolnshire, England
3 December 1917

Dear Father—

Yes, I'm back here for a few days. Cause? General mix-up which I can't tell you anything about. However, I'll only be here a few days and will cable you where I am going long before you get this.

I received your letter written from the Vanderbilt and am sorry to see that you are worrying about me again. Don't do it. In the first place it's unnecessary and in the second place it's useless. Please write me in your own hand hereafter. The letters you dictate and those you write [yourself] are like letters from different persons. Those dictated sound like "Letters from a Half-made Merchant to his Idiot Son," only they lack the humor of the originals.

You needn't worry about me being antiseptic if not good though. You remember that you used to say that you were too busy to be sick. Well, if it's any comfort to you, I'm too busy to be tempted. Also I'm in the Army but not of the Army as yet. Just because I have a uniform on is no reason for you to have nightmares. I claim no halo; I strike no pose; but let me remark that I came over here looking for Germans—and that's all I'm on the lookout for. However if you can't give me credit for either singleness of purpose or strength of mind permit me to assure you that everywhere we go the medical officers give us a special lecture and I know more formulas than a chemist. But I appreciate your anxiety and were it necessary would be guided accordingly.

I drew some money on that letter of credit. I wasn't short myself but I was in London and ran into some of the fellows who came over with me. They were dead broke and wanted to see the town so I went down to Cooks and drew L30 for them. I had plenty myself but didn't want to get caught short as I was once before several weeks ago. I saw a couple of good shows in London and ran into numerous Americans. Walker Ellis is somewhere here in England I heard but haven't any direct news of him.

I ought to have my commission any day now. But there's no telling when I'll get it. The requirements and examinations for it over here are about three times what they are at home. The censorship won't permit me to give my opinion of the way we've been handled in that respect. I completed my last qualification for it several weeks ago but nothing's been done about it as yet.

I'm enclosing the menu of the Thanksgiving party in Grantham. You will notice the quotation on the front page. That was one of my favorite commands because I had to rearrange the Detachment almost daily and that was the way I did it. They used to kid me about it all the time. "At ease, attention here" was the only one but they kidded me about it so much I had to quit using it.

I am sending Lena some pictures which were taken at Oxford for the press. A lot of them were published in the English papers. My address is c/o U.S. Air Service, Hotel Goring—London.[18]

A heartful of love to you and Lena,

Devotedly, Elliott

No 1 Training Depot Station
Stamford, Lincolnshire
December [4] 1917[19]

Dear Father—

I hear that you passed on one of my letters to Mr. Brewster and he passed it around generally. The last thing I asked you before I left was please not to pass my letters around. I also wrote you asking you not to pass them around. Evidently my wishes are absolutely ignored. Very well, I know you will continue to use my letters as advertising material for the Springs family, but you'll never get another letter from me to use that way. This is the last letter you will get from me. I'd like to continue writing to Lena but I don't dare. However, you needn't be worried about me. If anything happens to me you will be notified by cable so you need have no anxiety. Besides I'm too lucky.

I just want to explain why you aren't going to hear from me anymore. I told you in New York that if I found out you were showing my letters around I wouldn't write any more. I also got some papers yesterday. In one of them was my picture. I hardly think I need comment. I am very sorry I sent Lena those pictures the other day. Hope none of them get by the censor. Anyway, they are copyrighted, and anyone who publishes them will get sued. Hate to be nasty, Father, but you don't leave me any choice in the matter. Goodbye.

A heartful of love to you and Lena. I'm sorry I wrote at all. Your devoted son, Elliott

Stamford, England
December 5 1917

Dear Mother—

Word has reached my ears that my confidence has been betrayed and that my letters have been generally passed around. One in particular reached Mr. Brewster [father of Sidney Brewster] and was further passed around by him. I don't know whether you were particeps criminis[20] or not but you certainly could have done something to prevent it. Also I am rather disappointed that you didn't use your influence to prevent Father from getting the Columbia Record to publish my picture which stared at me like Banquo's ghost.[21] You remember what I said in New York. And the Brewsters of all people. I feel worse than betrayed. I shall take jolly good care that it doesn't happen again. But if my own Father betrays my confidence, who am I to trust? I know that he reads your letters so I won't dare write you what's going on, at the same time I hate to disappear as far as home is concerned. If you cable me that no one, not even Father, will read the letters I write to you perhaps I'll let you know from time to time where I am and the state of my digestion—otherwise this is positively the last.

It was all my fault, though, I suppose. I certainly shouldn't have tried to write interesting letters home or send any pictures. I forgot for the moment that I was Leroy Springs' son that he might meet some other Father and rub it in on him at my expense. And just incidentally, while I'm in a nasty humor—you seem to have time to run the Red Cross, suffering league etc but no time to write to me. And when you do, you might take more than 15 minutes to do it. Other people seem to find time to write to me.

Now that that's off my mind I feel better.

Did you read an account of our stay at Mineola in the Literary Section of the *New York Times*? 'Twas rather good—Oct 7 I think it came out.

I wanted to send some things home for Christmas but the exportation laws are so queer and strict that I had to give it up. Then I had some pictures taken but Father's little stunt [sending Springs's picture to the *Columbia Record*] vetoed that so I'm afraid Merry Christmas is the best I can do.

I've been out at the field all day joy-riding about in any old plane that no one is using for the moment. Lots of fun watching the crashes too. There were seven crack-ups today and they are always more comic than tragic. For instance one fellow went up on his first solo. He got up all right and circled about and tried to land. He hit the ground at about eighty [mph] and bounced about forty feet into the air. So he put his motor on and went around again. We had the ambulance ready for we knew he'd never get down right. Well, he did the same thing six times—each time a little worse, and the seventh his motor didn't catch and he simply pancaked. The ambulance was halfway down the field but his undercarriage held and all that he did was blow out a tire. The machine started to circle of course with one side low and there were about ten other machines about. He dodged about and was so rattled that he forgot to cut off his motor and he chased all over the field until we sent two mechanics down who caught him and cut his motor. The plane was a complete wreck by that time. Extremely humorous.

My roommate was starting up and his motor went dead at the other end of the field. Instead of waiting for an Ac Emma [AM—aircraft mechanic] to come down and crank it up, he set his switch and jumped out and spun it [the propeller]. So far, so good—she started and he ran around to the seat. But the throttle jarred open and away went the plane—poor Jim [Stokes] chasing along behind. He caught up and grabbed a wing but it threw him and started off faster than ever in the opposite direction. We nearly died laughing as poor Jim chased it all over the 'drome. Finally it hit a ditch and turned a somersault just as he caught the tail. Almost tossed him up in the air.

I was out in a field with a dud motor and looked up to see a motor blow up and a plane wobbling overhead. The field was small but the pilot dove for it. I rushed over just in time to see him disappear in a thicket and mud and saplings come flying out. A moment later the pilot appeared covered with mud. I offered him a ride back as I had gotten my bus fixed up but he said no, he'd stay there with the wreck. So I flew back and told them to send for him. They told me he'd already telephoned in and this was his message: "Forced landing, dud motor, broke prop, lost both wings and tail unit, cracked fuselage, and motor in mud. Awfully afraid I can't fly it back." Can you beat it?

I was out yesterday and there was a heavy fog so I managed to get a bus and go up. Remembering the fellow who looked up to see the ground I went up to six thousand feet and looped. I give you my word for twenty seconds I didn't have the slightest idea where the ground was. Finally located it by the help of the instruments and the wind in my face to be beyond my left wing. 'Twas great sport. I looped nine times then and my controls jammed while I was on my back. But luck was with me and I got her straightened out and came down to where I could see the ground—but it was strange ground. Took me 20 minutes to get back to the drome without any ailerons. Can hardly say I've been bored very much while flying.

I hope Father isn't unduly worried about stunting. Funny—over here we're sent up and told to do certain stunts. That is unless we're doing them of our own accord. We're taught stunting, if it's necessary, just as we're taught flying. You've no idea what can be done with a fast scout—almost defy the Laws of Gravitation. When I get to the Front I shall have a little bit of a machine hardly bigger than the Stutz fairly bristling with machine guns that will do anything—about the fastest thing made, too.

Over here you know they have girls driving the motor transports. Someone suggested that the way to win the war was to get Mr. Ziegfeld[22] to organize an Emma Loe corps.[23]

About fifteen of us gave a dinner party to the RFC staff officers last week and night before last they gave us a return party. I've been on parties and parties but those two as yet win the brown derby. I wish I could tell you about it but I dare not trust the details to paper. But Americans will long be famous in Stamford. I was sitting between the CO and the Adjutant and I could have sworn they were born in Kentucky. And the beauty of England is that no one disturbs you unless you burn the town hall or show a light at a window or sprinkle cigarette ashes in the butter. Oh, it's no ordinary war. And just incidentally Sherman[24] was all wrong and so are people who think that New York is the capitol of the Land of the Midnight Bun and the Home of the Thirsty and Free.

Guess I'd better close this farewell letter before I include any advertising matter. You might show your appreciation for letters I've written you by writing to me occasionally. Oh I forgot—you're running the Red Cross now. They sent us some 1915 *Saturday Evening Posts* not long ago.

A heartful of love to you and Father. Devotedly, Elliott

FLIGHT LOG: 7 December: Solo flight: 50 minutes in #5164. Around aerodrome. Bad wind.

FLIGHT LOG: 8 December: Solo flight: 40 minutes in #1914. Around aerodrome. Foggy.

FLIGHT LOG: 8 December: Solo flight: 30 minutes in #1259. Around aerodrome. Looped 10 times.

FLIGHT LOG: 10 December: Solo flight: 20 minutes in #1909. Around aerodrome. Rotten bus.

FLIGHT LOG: 11 December: Solo flight: 1 hour in #5994. Around aerodrome. Stalls. Wouldn't spin.

FLIGHT LOG: 11 December: Solo flight: 40 minutes in #1942. Around aerodrome. About six spins.

FLIGHT LOG: 13 December: Solo flight: 40 minutes in #5163. Cloud chasing. Lost prop in spin. Dud.

The following is an excerpt from a letter by Leroy Springs written 28 November 1917.

My dear Son: I am in receipt of your letter of November 6th written from Stamford and was delighted to hear from you again. It is a great gratification to get your letters. You are developing into a good and interesting letter writer. I am very proud of the record you have made since you started in aviation and I felt sure you would make good. You are very much mistaken if you think I did not think you could make good at anything you undertake. It is only a question of application. I am sure when you come home you can help me a great deal in running the cotton mills and will measure up to it as soon as you have a reasonable amount of experience. . . .

Do not take any unnecessary chances. You should not go up in any machine that you do not know yourself is all right. You and the Englishman evidently had a very close call in the old machine so do not be risky like that again. As I have told you before, there is nothing to be gained by your taking chances with your life unnecessarily. . . .

Business is about as usual. Cotton is still going up and is now 30 cents a pound and looks like it is going higher and goods are going up proportionately. We are running Lancaster almost entirely on government contracts. The Fort Mill mills I have almost rebuilt and they are a fine piece of property.

Lena is still very busy with her Red Cross work. She gets up at seven thirty every morning and is at the Red Cross room by nine and works there until six thirty or seven every night. All the people here are very much interested in the Red Cross work and are trying to do their part.

I am very much disappointed at the attitude of the Russians. I believe if they had stuck to their job in dead earnest, the Germans would be almost ready to quit by this time but, with the Russians out of it and Italy having such a bad backset, I am afraid it will prolong the war one to two years. I am still very much in hopes that the Germans will come to their senses and realize that they had best sue for peace on almost any terms they can get and that they will discontinue their brutal methods, which will make it all the harder for them in the end. . . .

With love and best wishes and trusting you will take the best care of yourself, I am always, Your affectionate father

Savoy Hotel
London, England
Christmas Day 1917

Dear Mother—

This is no ordinary war. Please send me some cigarettes and candy and the *Christian Observer*[25]—don't forget the *Christian Observers* with love—

'Tis Christmas morning, Mother dear, and I am so completely at peace with the world that I thought I'd just drop you a line while I am waiting to meet some fellers and assure you that all was well.

Three of us got 4 days leave and came down yesterday morning. I was rather glad to get away as Stamford has been rather a gloomy place lately. We've been averaging about six crashes a day and three men killed in four days. Too bad. You remember I wrote about having a very fast machine which I could do anything with. Well another fellow took it up and looped it and the wings collapsed at 4000 feet—just over the center of the aerodrome. He was an awfully nice fellow—Harold Ainsworth from Swarthmore, Pa. Good flyer too.

So far, Christmas has been most joyous. We ran into five or six Americans we knew, Princeton and Culver men. The hotel is full of them. I won't tell you where we gather but it's the second one I've seen in England with a brass rail. We combined forces and went over to Simpson's[26] for dinner last night. Simpson's is something like Sherry's[27] or Delmonico's.[28] In there were about 15 Canadian Officers just back from this recent battle. Well when Americans and Canadians meet it's just like the Governor of North Carolina and the Governor of South Carolina. So we joined them and bought the place. The manager came up after a little to throw us out but after a little elbow exercise he joined us and made more noise than anyone else. Then we proceeded to Murray's night club[29] picking up two majors more on the way. One of them had just lost a lung from gas and was most entertaining. Imagine a public dance at Sherry's and you have Murray's. There we found three or four instructors from Stamford. To relieve your mind let me assure you that 'twas distinctly a stag party.

A Scotch Captain joined us and said he was going to New York in three weeks. He was a prince and everybody at once took out their address book and gave him addresses of people to look up there and take around. God help him if he uses that list. Every chorine and movie queen in Greater New York (meaning thereby all those who from time to time sojourn between 23rd and 72nd). Mr. Ziegfeld would do well to get him to provide the chorus for the next Follies.

Thus did we spend Christmas Eve. I don't know what happened to the others but I ended up by teaching a London policeman how to roll his own. In return for which he escorted me to the hotel as I was completely lost due to darkness on account of the [Zeppelin air] raid. A very good Bobby he was too—has a brother who's a cop in Pittsburgh.

Here come a gang of Americans—more later.

December 27

All has been well. Alex Matthews[30] and myself ate our Christmas dinner with Sir Charles Lyall, father-in-law of "Tee-Hee" Fleet, once my Greek prof at Culver. Alex Mathews was one of those with me on that famous party on the Frolics[31] when your unworthy son so disgraced himself—or shall I say—was disgraced. You know I never have forgiven you for all that.

We had a delightful dinner, each falling in love with a daughter apiece—not seriously—just for the duration as they say over here. We got by without disgracing ourselves—didn't use the wrong tools or drink out of the wrong glass at the wrong time.

Then we left and joined a supper party in the Canadians' suites which was followed by a large crap game at which the Americans easily excelled. The party again grew noisy and the manager came up to stop the party but we persuaded him to join us and 'twas all right, he won too.

There was one poor avigator up there on crutches. "Smash up?" says I. "Yes." "Huns or Scotch?" "Neither," says he, "too much camouflage. My engine conked out and I lit in a field. Scrambled out and saw 'twas a pasture. I was dressed completely in leather and before I got my helmet off a whole herd started after me. One of the bulls tossed me over the fence. Hereafter I fly in fleece coats." I wonder what the bull thought he was.

Yesterday I lunched with a couple of officers from HQ and saw a couple of shows dining at Frascatti's.[32] Today I've been investing Father's most welcome Christmas present in furs—not as he might have done it—but in furs for myself. I am now provided with fur from the bottom of my feet to the crown of my head. It took a big wad but I've got to have it—I was frozen stiff the other day at only 7000 feet. And yet these Scots fly in kilts.

Which calls my attention to something. I read in the papers of the girls always organizing something. I wish someone would organize a Flapper's Brigade and get one of these Scots to instruct them. You know the kind of flapper I mean—the variety that every time she sits down spends five minutes adjusting her skirts and thereafter every two minutes glances at her—well, that portion of her anatomy which in nine cases out of ten ought to be covered up; and readjusts her skirts. This being done largely to attract attention. And usually they manage to lift them instead of lowering them. Well, these Scots could certainly drill them to perfection. They have to be experts or they get arrested. One awkward movement and all is lost.

Harken a moment. Thus far I have received from you two letters and two notes. Well if you ever expect another line from me you want to work up a bad case of writer's cramp. And don't think that swilling tea at the Red Cross HQ is an excuse. You waste more time plastering on beauty spots than I have to myself in a month. I really think you and Father have treated me outrageously. And when I do hear from you, there's no news. I don't know yet what's happened to the Stutz or whether you've been in Rickson's lately.

I haven't gotten any packages yet. Think you'd better try the American Express next time. Please send me a lot of Page & Shaw's as candy is very warming before flying and you can't get it over here and some Hershey nut bars. Also some Egyptian Deities cigarettes and some "Barking Dog" tobacco.[33] Another thing—we find that the warmest combination is silk under wool under leather. I wonder if you could have me a helmet knitted out of heavy silk—closely knitted with only a small opening for the eyes. I could also use some silk socks. I have everything else I think.

I have become quite used to 4 o'clock tea now. I never wrap myself around any tea but its an excuse to eat. It's a sacred institution in the British Army though. Lot of people over here didn't know there was a war on until there was a shortage of tea. I've seen Ack Emmas go out supperless to guard a machine all night in some tree or hedge and do it cheerfully and then grouse for a week because they missed tea. The Germans ought to have their air raids at 4 PM and nobody would bother them. No anti-aircraft gunner (commonly known as Archie) would leave his tea for all the Germans in Heathendom.

Say is everybody at home getting married? Every day I get another announcement. Poor fools. If people knew what I know about these neophyte husbands, these repent-at-leisure birds when they get over here—well there'd either be less of this catch-as-catch-can stuff or more Battalions of Death. The same birds who ruined my nerves at Mineola trying to get into New York to tell their brides-of-a-day farewell gave me nervous prostration at Oxford trying to keep dates. Tell them to quit it will you, please, and vice versa, getting married before going to war is like taking a ham sandwich to a banquet. And the dear sweet blushing things—why do they want bichloride in the cocktails, or arsenic with the hors d'oevres [*sic*]? One sweet thing ("priceless old thing" as the English say) told me she thought black becoming to her. Well that's different. All right, said I, but won't you be in wrong if I get transferred to the Quartermaster Corps or get flat feet! Have you heard the American National Password? "Has she a friend?"

That and "What ho, Major, the Americans have broken loose!" have become famous over here already. Only now we've educated them sufficiently so that the majors invariably reply, "That's so? Well let's hurry up and join them."

Pabst [Goodrich] I have been unable to locate. Last I heard from him he was going to Russia or Italy to drive an ambulance. Nothing more from Ernest [Mount].

I appreciate your anxiety about the American Army. The percentage [of losses] will unquestionably be pretty high but don't waste any valuable time worrying about me. If you can't give me any credit for being good, at least don't imagine that I'm a fool. If that gives you no comfort permit me to call to your attention the fact that I'm at least discriminating.

The next time you're in New York I wish you'd get me a pair of Triplex goggles [special goggles designed for flying in open cockpits]. Can't get any over here. If you can't get Triplex get a pair of auto goggles from Meyerowitz.[34] They're shaped like this—[sketch]—and have a rubber fitting.

This being the Xmas season I relented sufficiently to have a picture taken which I enclose. But it is to repose in the privacy of the bedroom and not to be passed around. I suppose I'm foolish to trust you but I'm feeling very charitable today.

I hear that everybody in Charlotte is taking unto themselves something for no worse than possible [getting married]. You might cheer them up by reading them a paragraph of my sentiments. And you might cheer them up by telling them that the German idea of a second wife is being taken almost seriously all over Europe. You suffragettes. I suppose we'll have a parade advocating vice versa and picket the White House. Or hadn't you better picket a training camp.

After all—it's no ordinary war.

And this Siege of London is quite the fiercest battle I've ever fought in. I've been gassed repeatedly. New York in its balmiest days was like Monteagle[35] at Christmas compared to this. The only campaign that ever approached this was the advance on Milwaukee and the Retreat from Boston in '16.

I saw a very clever take off on the 13th Chair[36] last night in "Here and There."[37] Instead of searching for the dagger they lost the body. By the way you ought to subscribe for the *Bystander, Sphere, London Illustrated News* or *Graphic* and keep up with me.[38] I suppose Father can keep up with me all right by watching my signatures arrive at the Hanover National.

But as they say in the trenches (and hockshops) "no advance without security." *Per ardua ad astra* "if you're chasing stars you must have rocks." And England's motto should be "status quo ante diluvium" or evil to him who thinks fast.

A heartful of love to you and Father.

Devotedly, Elliott

Elliott Springs started to make diary entries on 1 January 1918, but he was inconsistent; most days in January and February have entries, but in March and April he made fewer. In May and June he wrote in his diary fairly regularly, especially after he became a member of Billy Bishop's 85 Squadron. For some reason he ceased to make entries for a four-month period after his accident on 27 June; this four-month period exactly matches the time that he was a member of the 148th Aero Squadron. He resumed writing in his diary on 28 October 1918 and made sporadic entries until 1 January 1919. His diary entries are included to provide additional insight into Springs's activities and frame of mind.

DIARY ENTRY: 1 January 1918: I began the New Year in the most approved manner. At the stroke of 12 [Robert] Kelly and I were lying most socially in the gutter being very binged. 1918, may you bring me at least an honorable demise.

DIARY ENTRY: January 2: Kelly and I are still wrecks. We see things at night—horrible things. It looks as if I'm going to have to swear off. Much hell being raised about the party last night. We have to be in at 10 now and do patrol duty. Great sport. Buss, Hodges, [William] Tipton and [Samuel] Walker hung thundermugs [chamber pots] on all the steeples and posts in town. Riot at Cadis, out of bounds now.

DIARY ENTRY: January 4: I go out to the field and Capt Reeves gives me a DH-6 to fly. Go up and do everything possible to it. Had a pupil but he disappeared. Kelly and I still seeing things.

DIARY ENTRY: January 5: Kelly and [James] Roth are both posted [sent to a new training field]. I go out to the field and get a job on a DH6. Take [John] Raftery up for 40 min. instructions. Got lost twice. Go to bed absolutely sober for the first time since I've been over here.

London Colney, England
January 5 1918

Dear Mother—
'Twas snowing last night
Raining the night before
And it's goin' to be dud tonight
If it's never dud any more
But when it's dud, I'm as happy as can be
For I am instructing
In the R.F.C.

Well it happened this way. As we were lined up before the bar last night, in walks Capt _____ of C Squadron. Says he to me, "Cheery Oh, old binge, I thought you were in France by this time. Give it a name." "Oh no," says I, "I'm here for duration or until my constitution gives out. It's pretty dud already." "Why don't you fly?" "I have, everything they've given me. But they ordered me not to loop, spin or roll and I'm tired of cloud chasing." "Well, I've got a machine over at my drydock you haven't flown, I'll bet. Come out in the morning and try it." "But what if I crash?" "Then I'll buy you a dinner and charge it up to the mess account."

So I went out in the morning and sure enough he had it ready for me. I rather expected him to take me up dual but instead—"Want to instruct?" says he. "Why not?" "Well," says he, "here's a pupil that crashed me yesterday and it may have been personal prejudice. Take him up and find out whether he's malicious or ignorant."

I looked at the pupil and shuddered—for him. Then I looked at the machine and "—" both of us.

"Suppose," says I to him, "that I take this up solo first and find out whether I can fly it or not."

So up I went and I could close my eyes and imagine I was in 5 ton truck. Put a pair of folding doors on the Winton[39] and you have it—or stream line a bath tub. Well, it was fun at that and I spun it and side-slipped and stalled and tail slid and then spiralled down for my pupil. But no pupil. When last seen he was breaking all records towards town.

But out of the crowd of spectators stepped a young Englishman—2nd Lt at 19—and asked if he could be my pupil. So I took him up for an hour and I instructed him to the best of my ability. But by that time a heavy fog had come up and it took me some time to find the 'drome. Somehow between us we made a good landing. So now I'm a bona fida instructor in the R.F.C.

And after dinner tonight my own Squadron Commander offered me a job instructing in my own squadron. So until my orders come I have a job here and have several requests for instructions. Even old morituris Kelly wants to go up with me tomorrow. Wants me to teach him how to loop. Oh, it's no ordinary war.

Latest reports from London are that the battle is still raging at the Savoy and that the Canadians have brought up reinforcements in large numbers. However there was considerable action here New Year's Eve. Kelly won the Double Cross and two are reported missing. 'Tis rumored that they started for Dublin where they said they had friends.

The woolen goods arrived—also the box from Cross.' Many many thanks. Also please thank the Red Cross for me personally. But as yet nothing else. Your letter of the 13th of December arrived; also Father's of the 1st. I had about decided not to write any more but I'm beginning to relent. But mum's the word in regard to me and my letters. If the Germans knew I had gone to war—! Or if any of the Generals at H.Q. knew that I was enjoying myself and flying about in streamlined bathtubs—!

Another thing you can do for me. Next time you're in New York go to Stern Brothers, or Tiffany's,[40] or somewhere and get me two pairs of R.M.A. wings (Reserve Military Aviator) as these we get over here are rotten. Also a pair of M.A. wings. I'm only an R.M.A. now but hope to be an M.A. in a couple of weeks as soon as I pass my final tests on the new 'planes. . . .

Say—did you see my picture in the N.Y. Sun of Dec 5. Some spiffy. Did they ever send you those pictures from Oxford? Anyway I paid for them. Have a heart and drop me a few lines—a real letter every now and then. You've treated me disgracefully.

A heartful of love to you and Father. Devotedly, Elliott

DIARY ENTRY: January 6: Go out to the drome and Capt Reeves gives me a pupil. Great stuff. I'm beginning to feel like a regular guy. Wrote a letter to Frances [Robertson] which made me feel funny.

Thetford, Norfolk
January 6, 1918[41]

Dear Mother—

Behold—I'm a Ferry Pilot! It all happened this way. This morning at Stamford I was joyriding my prize pupil in a snowstorm and having great sport. It stopped snowing so we landed—not without some difficulty—and the C.O. walks over to us. "Springs," says he, "you lazy loafer, lay off putting the wind up my best flyers and go over to Thetford this afternoon on the train and fly back a new bus from over there for us. Get a chit and cash from the Adjutant. Better catch the 1.55 and I'll have them give you a map." So with those meager directions I arrived here about seven and commandeered an RFC Ford to bring me out here. It's a god-forsaken place, cold as Greenland, but I'll get away early in the morning.

After reporting to everybody in the place I finally found the right man and he told me the bus was ready—full of everything—and that if I was exceedingly lucky I'd be able to make the 80 miles to Stamford on one load of gas. I was rather disappointed to find that it wasn't a new bus—'tis an old one built up from numerous crashes—however, with the grace of God and a long-handled toothbrush I may make it by sundown. I follow railways some of the way, a canal for ten miles, another railway, a river, and make the last 14 miles by compass. That is, if I'm lucky.

It's always considered good form over here when visiting another aerodrome to do some stunts when you're leaving, out of courtesy, sort of, "Thank you for the petrol," you know. But what's bothering me is what in thunder I'm going to do with this ice wagon in the morning. If I loop I'll lose my tail. If I spin I'll lose my wings. And she won't roll at all, they say. Probably have to content myself with diving at the hangars and zooming into a stall or try to steal the flag or something like that. I'd hate to smash one of John Bull's busses.

They are pretty crowded here, so they told me I could sleep in the hospital—isolation room—great sport. I ought to catch something out of it. I'll wait and mail this when I get back to Stamford so you'll know if I got back safely.

Strange as it may seem, the muse has been with me lately and I've been tearing off short stories and essays by the yard. And in all modesty I must say that my last two stories have been exceptionally fine. I'm really proud of them. But it's funny—I can't write anything but optimistic tragedy—moriturus—you know—life is great but death is glorious—sort of stuff. I believe I'll get by with them too.

Every now and then I write sort of an essay to you but I have presence of mind enough to tear them up. I wish I felt free to write to you as I feel. I hate to think of leaving this world with all my ideas and impressions unrevealed. However, you may find some interesting stuff among my papers.

I awoke the other morning and couldn't figure out where I was. I didn't try to recall my position very hard but just lay there and tried to figure out where I'd like to be and what sort of a day I'd like to have before me. Thus inspired, I jumped up, started a fire, and, wrapped in blankets, began to write. The result was sort of a mixture of Peter Pan, Alice in Wonderland, and Spoon River Anthology.[42] I think maybe I can rewrite it into something.

January 11. Well, I'm still stuck here. It has been snowing constantly and so have been unable to get away. There are about six or seven other Ferry Pilots here waiting to fly machines away and so we all join forces and have had a glorious time. I wired [Robert] Kelly and he came over from Harling Road [a few miles east of Thetford] where he has been sent, bringing along a couple of cronies of his. This place being rather slow, we all wandered up to Norwich for a day and night and over to Ely for an afternoon and then I went over to Harling Road with Kelly. At Ely there is the most wonderful cathedral I've ever viewed. Built in 700AD—1200AD—1500AD respectively and partially destroyed by Cromwell.

These Ferry Pilots are a wonderful lot. All of them [have] been overseas since Mons[43] and [are] simply covered with medals and wound stripes. But they won't tell you anything about their experiences at all. You are talking to one of them and you ask him how he got his MC.[44] He looks at you in amazement and has an important engagement elsewhere. But Kelly and I have got a system by which we separate them from their pasts. Get a bunch together in a quiet spot, put a glass in their hands, keep their glasses filled and then get in the background.

The conversation may be about blondes or mint juleps but after a while, one of them says, "Yes, she was some beauty. Say, old thing, did you ever know Thompson of the 39th? He was thumbs up with her."

Says the other, "Sure I knew him. We used to fly together. I saw him killed."

"How did it happen?"

"Well, we were at 10,000 when we ran into seven Huns and he. . . ."

Then for the next couple of hours our hair stays on end. None of them would ever think of talking alone but when they get started reminiscing and comparing notes and discussing mutual friends—well, it's worth a whole week's maneuvering. Kelly and I have an infallible system. We go into the bar and spot our meat. We pick out a couple with a lot of medals and as high rank as possible. He takes a couple and I take a couple and then we slowly herd them together and then sit back and wait until they get beyond the Blonde and Brunette stages and get their back teeth floating. Usually they've never seen each other before which makes it all the better.

If the weather is dud tomorrow we're all going down to London. It ought to be a pretty good party.

I hope you and Father aren't worrying over me unduly. I have a mental picture of you sitting in front of the fire and all of a sudden Father has a fit. "What's the matter?" you ask. "Ah, woe is me," says Father. "I fear me our long lost son may even tonight be wrapped around a glass of English ale. And he is so young and cannot stand it." Then you gurgle and it begins to rain. Ring down the curtain! Let us speak no more of Bacchanalian Revels in my letters lest you get really worried.

But hearken to Stevenson. Once there was a man with a pocket full of gold on a journey on a rough road. He knew that the highwaymen were waiting for him and sooner or later would hold him up. So he stopped at every inn and ate and drank heartily. When the highwaymen fell upon him and killed him, they found his pockets empty and a smile upon his face. And greater prudence than this hath no man.[45]

But even at that I've followed the straight and narrow path pretty closely. For one thing, I've been pretty busy, and for another I still have my good taste and the supply of $C_3H_5(ON)$[46] is very low. However, I have seen the handwriting on the wall several times and have had no need of an interpreter.

A heartful of love to you both,

Devotedly, Elliott

DIARY ENTRY: January 7: Take Raftery up in a DH-6 and disconnect him [disconnect his controls], then zoom him and do an Immelman. Give my other pupil 40 minutes. This place is certainly gloomy.

DIARY ENTRY: January 8: Capt Reeves, Lt Price and I do a little formation flying. Capt Blaney [probably an instructor] sends me over to Thetford [to ferry an aircraft back to Stamford]. Arrive about 6. Dine and get awfully tight with two Scotchmen—Weir and Aiken.

DIARY ENTRY: January 9: DH-6 not ready and weather dud so go in to Thetford and wire for Kelly, who is at Harbury Road. He comes over at 8 and we drink until I pass away. Then he does so in peace.

DIARY ENTRY: January 10: Kelly and I go up to Norwich where we run into 6 ferry pilots[47] and we have a regular party.

DIARY ENTRY: January 11: Leave Kelly and return to Thetford. Weather still rotten. Call up Capt Ryan and he says come on back. So I do arriving at Stamford at 7.

DIARY ENTRY: January 12: Pack up and start for London [Springs was reassigned to the training field at London Colney]. Tear off a moderate party with Jim Stokes and run into two RFC captains at Savoy which calls for a great and glorious party.

DIARY ENTRY: January 13: Go out to London Colney and report. Deep gloom here. Only two Avros. Grider and Callahan here. Great wind up here. Must go to machine gun [school] and can't swear at the waitresses.

FLIGHT LOG: 13 January 1918: Dual flight: 30 minutes in Avro #4401 with Lt Piggot. Around drome. First ride in Avro.

DIARY ENTRY: January 14: Weather bad so no flying. I kid Piggot into putting me on his list for instruction. He's at least 17 but seems to be a good flyer.

DIARY ENTRY: January 15: Piggot takes me up and I find an Avro remarkably easy to fly and land. To hell with having an instructor up with you though. Mac gives a big party at St. Albans. . . . [The remainder of the entry is unclear.]

FLIGHT LOG: 15 January: Dual flight: 15 minutes with Capt Horn[48] in #4401. Around drome. Turns left okay.

FLIGHT LOG: 15 January: Dual flight: 30 minutes with Capt Horn in #4401. Around drome. Turns, 2 landings.

FLIGHT LOG: 15 January: Solo flight: 40 minutes in #4401. Around drome. 1 stall, 7 landings.

DIARY ENTRY: January 16: Capt Horn takes me up and then lets me go solo in an Avro. Have a great time. Now for London. Mac, Cal, Kelly, Weir, Fuller and myself endeavor to wreck the Savoy.[49]

DIARY ENTRY: January 17: A Handley Page is a great machine. We start out again and all is well. I draw the first real blank since I've been in England. But I certainly put that Scotsman [Weir?] under.

DIARY ENTRY: January 18: Much tattered and torn [Thomas] Herbert and I get back at 3 to find we're in for a big strafe. So we make a last night of it and go up to Stamford. Cal and Mac arrive from London.

DIARY ENTRY: January 19: The C.O. gives us hell but no CB [not "confined to barracks"]. Hoorah. I get in 1 hour in a machine which had been condemned. Christ I'm lucky. And I certainly was doing some splitassing.

FLIGHT LOG: 19 January: Solo flight: 1 hour 5 minutes in Avro #4473. Around drome. Vertical banks.

DIARY ENTRY: January 20: I get in two hours solo. I can loop, spin, and Immelman with great gusto but I find vertical banks very difficult.

No. 56 Training Squadron,
Royal Flying Corps
January 20, 1918

Dear Father:

Well I guess blood is thinker than ink but please have some consideration for me. There are many good reasons why you should consider my letters absolutely confidential beside the fact that I especially requested it. Headquarters has been raising hell and threatening court martials about us writing home about what's going on over here. Why, I don't know, but we're warned not to mention military affairs in letters. You can write to me c/o London City and Midland Bank, 5 Threadneedle Street, London. I've arranged with them to forward all parcels and letters to me. I opened an account there with the $200 and had them transfer the remainder of my letter of credit to it. Many thanks for the cash. I wasn't broke at all but I feel a lot more comfortable with some cash where I can get to it quickly. I invested a slice of it in furs and a new uniform and a dinner party.

My finances are in very good condition but not nearly as good as they ought to be. I've all sorts of money coming from the government. I should have been getting $100 a month from June 2 and my First Lieutenant's pay dates from November 13th. I don't suppose I'll ever be able to collect any of it but I'm certainly going to put in for it someday. I've certainly got it coming to me, anyway.

I've had a lot of delay and disappointment but am getting on nicely now and another week ought to see me finished with my advanced training. I've got four days' graduation leave coming as it is. Think I'll run up to Edinburgh for a couple of days. It ought not be so long before I get in on the fireworks [that is, he is assigned to an operational squadron].

I'm enjoying the best of health—weigh about 160 and have a constitution and digestive system like a nail-fed goat. I can fly upside down without getting dizzy and if you can do that, there's nothing the matter with you. I haven't been near a doctor since I enlisted except to have a drink with him. Such is the life. If anyone had told me about this a year ago I would have laughed at him and then shot myself because I had to wait so long for it to begin. Beat it?—you can't even crack the shell.

I'm going on a little trip in a couple of days. I'm going to fly up to Stamford for lunch and then over to Harbury Road and Norwich to spend the night with Kelly and then back here next day. I have a wonderful machine to do it in—the worst thing I have to fear is getting lost. I'll probably double the mileage before I get back. A heartful of love to you and Lena.

Your devoted son, Elliott

FLIGHT LOG: 21 January: Solo flight: 1 hour 25 minutes in Avro #4473. Around drome. Loops spins and banks.

FLIGHT LOG: 21 January: Solo flight: 55 minutes in Avro #4401. Around drome. Loops spins and banks.

FLIGHT LOG: 22 January: Solo flight: 30 minutes in Avro #4401. Around drome. Vertical banks.

FLIGHT LOG: 22 January: Dual flight: 35 minutes in Avro #4401 with Capt Horn. Around drome. Everything possible.

DIARY ENTRY: January 21 [22]: Capt Horn takes me up for a little stunt instruction and then turns me loose on a Pup. Great stuff. I get away with it but bend an axle.

FLIGHT LOG: 22 January: Solo flight: 20 minutes in Sopwith Pup #2233. Around drome. Very foggy. Turns.

FLIGHT LOG: 22 January: Solo flight: 45 minutes in Sopwith Pup #5386. Around drome. Stunting.

DIARY ENTRY: January 22: More Pup riding. I loop, spin, roll, have a forced landing, and nearly crash but luck is with me. No damage.

FLIGHT LOG: 23 January: Solo flight: 1 hour in a Sopwith Pup #6006. Around aerodrome. Stunting—roofs.

FLIGHT LOG: 27 January: Solo flight: 1 hour in Sopwith Pup #6236. Around aerodrome. Stunting upside down.

FLIGHT LOG: 27 January: Solo flight: 1 hour 10 minutes in Sopwith Pup #6239. Around aerodrome. 6 landings.

FLIGHT LOG: 27 January: Solo flight: 15 minutes in Sopwith Pup #6006. Around aerodrome. Photography. Graduated 27 January 1918.

FLIGHT LOG: 28 January: Solo flight: 45 minutes in Sopwith Pup #2233. Around drome. Stunts.

FLIGHT LOG: 28 January: Solo flight: 40 minutes in Sopwith Pup #6066. Around drome. Stunts.

56 Training Squadron R.F.C.
London Colney, Hertfordshire
February 1, 1918

Dear Father—

Your letter of the 5th [January, probably] written yourself, arrived yesterday and was very welcome. If you'd rather dictate them, go ahead—I know it's hard for you to write yourself—but when you dictate them—please remember it's your son you're writing to and not your military representative so to speak. And you waste an awful lot of paper with the same cautions and health directions. Would you appreciate my letters if I neglected to mention anything but business advice and health instructions? And I know just as much about your business as you do about mine. The "Self Made Business Man" who wrote those celebrated letters to his wayward son at least had a sense of humor when he told said son to tread lightly on the Primrose Path and use salt with his dalliance.

I suppose you and Lena are very busy but it does seem strange that you all can't ever find time to write more than a few hurried lines to me every two weeks. But at that I'd rather you'd not write at all than the sort I've been getting thus far. Why I sacrifice my precious sleep to write you all and in return I get tabloid directions for becoming a general and the most uninteresting news. I naturally do not feel stirred to respond with startling literary efforts. Other people seem to appreciate my letters and accordingly write me letters that I enjoy. You can tell Lena also that her last letter was a complete failure and I don't know whether I shall write to her again or not. However, I'm in a good humor today and I don't care to think of the way my family has neglected me.

The weather has been very bad this past week and I've done little flying. I've been to two dances in neighboring towns and dined in St. Albans one night with some charming people—the Drakes—you've heard of Sir Francis? Callahan and I were playing troubadour, as O. Henry would say.[50] He makes the piano get up and walk around the room and if we get a good dinner I fly over the next morning and entertain my hostess with some "stunting." Don't be alarmed—I've got a machine I can turn inside out with perfect safety.

I finally declined my graduation leave. I'll get to the front that much sooner. The C.O. and Adjutant here nearly fainted. It was entirely without precedent. I looked sober and after I repeated it they got worried. Then they offered to lend me money or postpone it until I got some. They're still rather puzzled about it as they can't accuse me of doing it for effect because they see me flying every day during lunch and tea, any sort of bus in any sort of weather. I think I'm going to get a job testing out some new machines in a few days. It ought to be good fun.

What happened to the Stutz? Why the secrecy? I still suggest that you swap it in for a 4-passenger Stutz or sell it. Don't contemplate saving it for me. Even if I came back I wouldn't want it. It can't go fast enough. I think I'm spoiled for motoring anyway, it's too dangerous. No joking. I wouldn't trust myself to drive a car now. I'd get killed in ten minutes. I'd probably see something ahead and speed up and try to jump it. And I couldn't keep from speeding up for the turns.

A heartful of love to you and mother,

Your devoted son, Elliott

56 Training [Squadron] R.F.C.
London Colney, Hertfordshire, England
February 4 1918

Dear Aunt Addie—

The fruitcake arrived last week and the whole squadron joins me in thanking you for it many many times. It arrived in perfect condition and was immensely enjoyed by everyone who was lucky enough to get a slice of it. 'Twas the best thing that ever passed my lips in solid form that I can remember of.

Certainly I never enjoyed anything more. Food is plentiful enough over here but delicacies and sweets are very rare. No chocolate about, for instance, and no cake. Sugar is almost unobtainable except in the Officers' Mess where we always have a plenty. I have nothing to complain of at all but I certainly do crave sweets more than ever (don't tell Father though) and that Fruit Cake just went to the spot.

The weather has been pretty bad lately—cold and foggy so I haven't done much flying. Two more clear days and I'll be leaving here. England is a delightful country—I'm enjoying my little visit immensely. Wouldn't have missed it for anything. It's been a wonderful opportunity for us over here. When we do get to the Front shortly we will probably be the best trained men in any branch of the service in any army.

Many thanks again for the cake. A heartful of love always from

Your devoted nephew, Elliott

FLIGHT LOG: 5 February: Solo flight: 30 minutes in Sopwith Pup #2233. Around drome. Stunts.

FLIGHT LOG: 5 February: Solo flight: 30 minutes in Sopwith Pup #5942. Around drome. Landings.

FLIGHT LOG: 5 February: Solo flight: 10 minutes in SPAD #9100. Around drome. Engine dud.

FLIGHT LOG: 5 February: Solo flight: 1 hour 10 minutes in SPAD #8795. Around drome. First solo. Ground straffing.

FLIGHT LOG: 6 February: Solo flight: 1 hour 5 minutes in SPAD #9137. Around drome. Stunts mostly spins.

FLIGHT LOG: 6 February: Solo flight: 1 hour 35 minutes in SPAD #9137. London and St Albans. Formation.

FLIGHT LOG: 6 February: Solo flight: 15 minutes in SPAD #9131. Target [practice]. Gun jammed.

56 Training Squadron R.F.C.
London Colney, Hertfordshire, England
February 6 1918

Dear Mother—

To say that I am furious is putting it very mildly.

In the first place you needn't write at all. This is my last effort. You all must care a lot about me at home. Not enough to write to me anyway, and you haven't enough pride to take any trouble to write a decent letter. In the second place I received a note telling me that Father had been showing those pictures I sent you to everyone in the state who was polite enough to look at them.

I boil, I seethe, I spit fire.

I suppose the bold bad man took them away from you by force and locked you in your room while he spread them around. Now I sent those pictures to *you* and that can be your only excuse. Et tu Brute again.

All right—you all think that because I'm 4000 miles away you can give yourselves a boost at my expense. Well it can't be done. I had some new photographs taken the other day in my new whipcord but I don't dare send you one. But I've sent them to two other people that you all know with a special request that they show them to no one, and I'll bet you two bits to a Canadian dime that you and Father never see them. Just to show you how other people treat my requests.

But enough, I'm not feeling that way today. Every thing has been going well lately. Except they've got me drilling a bunch of American Air Mechanics or Ack Emmas, as they're called, and I've about lost my voice on them. But I've got them bluffed and they drill for me like fiends. And I'm feeling like a gentleman again. All the clerks and waiters at the Savoy know me just like a few at the Vanderbilt used to. They even cash checks for me and tell Kelly where he can find me. Makes me quite homesick for the Vanderbilt where I used to feel I was appreciated.

I happened to see a picture in the N.Y. Times of a Stutz closed car—16 valve—which was a beauty. If the old man's got any spare cash about make him get it for you. If he won't, go buy it and charge it to me. My credit's good up there.

The weather's been better lately and I've gotten in 8 hours in three days—on a new machine—most difficult thing made to fly—and it keeps me in a cold sweat all the time [probably the Sopwith Pup]. And just by the way you might tell Father again to quit worrying about my stunting. It saved my life yesterday. I got into a nose spin at 300 feet. I thought all was over but I've practiced spinning so much that it's just like skidding in the Stutz so instinctively I did the right thing and got her out with about 25 feet to spare. Roy Garver was killed that way last week but I suppose you read about it in the papers. He evidently hadn't practiced spinning enough. Long live "Stunting." I feel about as much at home upside down now as any other way.

I was up this morning and got caught in a storm ten miles away. Had a nice time getting back with the wind behind me. Coupled with the fact that I saw two men killed right on the 'drome a half hour before I went up I was rather glad to get in out of the wet with no damage done. Terrible accident it was. We saw them collide at 2000 feet and burst into flames.

You know, one thing that strikes me about this country is the policemen. Nothing in the world like a London Bobby. I was on awfully bad terms with the New Jersey and New York cops and they were always very impolite. But not so over here. 'Tis more thus. My taxi stops somewhere that there's no doorman and if there's a Bobby about he politely opens the door for me and touches his hat. I return in a moment—we pass the time of day—he opens the door for me—tells the taxi driver where to go and I'm off. Beat it? You can't break the shell. If he's not busy he may have a drink with you. I'm getting so I like this country and hate to be leaving shortly.

Great thing about these people is they insist on having their play with their work. The American idea of work hard and then tire yourself out some more playing is totally foreign. We do our work as well as possible but manage to have a lot of fun at the same time. For instance yesterday I was told to go up for two hours and stunt. Fine, but why make work out of it? I go over to another 'drome twenty miles away where I'll have an audience and then I land and have lunch with them. Found some of the Italian Detachment there and enjoyed myself immensely. Then I went up and outdid myself on fancy stuff and returned. Great sport. . . .

Which reminds me—I see in the papers much discussion of snobbishness and I am impressed by the fact that many people commenting upon it know nothing about it. Consider the British Army for a moment. It is a court martial offense for an officer to associate with an enlisted man socially. But there's no snobbery about it. Discipline is discipline is all. When we were privates first class in the U.S. Army some of the best parties we had were with English officers—as high as Majors and Colonels. The best party we had was turned into a riot by a couple of Colonels. That's how much they cared for rank. And one of them had a title too. At the same time such would have been impossible had they been in the U.S. Army or we in the British. Incidentally the fact that I was a social companion of all the men at Oxford seriously affected the discipline and made it infinitely harder for me. If they hadn't been the fine type of men they were it couldn't have been done. And military rank does not make for social attractiveness. Only last week Mac stole a girl from a Colonel and he's still a Private First Class getting 23 a month.

As usual, though, I should hate for many people to agree with me. Would make me think I was wrong.

And again in the papers I see that Prohibition has come to stay—real Prohibition, too. Makes me think of that film "Intolerance."[51] One half of the world has always been trying to "high tone" the other half. "Orthodoxy is my doxy and heterodoxy is your doxy" has always been the moving spirit. Of course it will make the U.S.A. a cleaner, more wholesome, efficient and decent place to live in. Imagine a fanatic of the 15th Century saying to another—"If we can only kill off a few of their leaders and force the others to join our church or kill them, too, Europe will be saved and the kingdom of God exalted. For the sake of civilization and future generations—load your blunderbus and set fire to the church." O welfare-of-others, what crimes are committed in thy name!

Not that it makes any difference to me. By the time it goes into effect I'll be yelling for Gunga Din[52] and complaining of the draft.

A heartful of love to you and Father,

Your devoted son, Elliott

P.S. Send some Page and Shaw's

FLIGHT LOG: 8 February: Solo flight: 1 hour in SPAD #9137. Stunting and firing.
FLIGHT LOG: 8 February: Solo flight: 1 hour in SPAD #9137. Landed at Northolt.

London Colney, England
February 9 1918

Dear Mother—

Well, the Three Musketeers have extinguished themselves again in high society. Yes we went raspazassin again the other night—Callahan, Grider, and myself—and not since the days of Oxford did we burst forth with such glory. I'll have to tell you about it. Yes, 'twas a real raspazas affair—but possibly you are not familiar with that sport. No, probably not, it's a new invention.

Well you are familiar with snaking in its unadulterated form. You know—a kind lady invites you to dinner, in return for which you entertain

The "Three Musketeers":
Larry Callahan (left), Elliott
Springs (center), and John
McGavock Grider (right).
This picture was probably
taken in London in April
or May 1918. Courtesy of
the Springs Close Family
Archives, the White Home-
stead, Fort Mill, South
Carolina.

her to the best of your ability—you tell her all about flying and why it isn't like riding in an elevator—and you praise her cooking and flatter her daughter. Result—you get another free meal and if you're good at it you sort of get to be a member of the family and drop in without invitation. We got to be awfully good at that: Callahan is a wizard on the piano, Grider can sing the blues like a Tennessee Native, and I am interlocutor and campaign manager. And, of course we've all developed one of the smoothest lives in existence—each different. Result—there're at least twenty delightful homes in England where the three of us don't bother to call up to let them know we're coming. That's snaking.

But raspazassing is different. Say we're out snaking and our hostess has Lady Agatha to dinner and Lady Agatha takes a fancy to us and invites us to dine with her next Thursday at a state dinner at eight and will send her car for us. Lord and Lady _____ will be there as will the Hon Bertie and the honorable Alice etc. No entertainment is expected of us—nor will be tolerated. For once the Americans will be overawed. Well, that is raspazassing.

Such was the affair we were slated for, but it never came off. To be brief, we arrived at eight and three or four butlers worried us for a moment but we got our color back and were announced and introduced without breaking anything.

It looked like the House of Lords and General Staff were on a holiday and were assembled there. All the men were covered with medals and all the ladies were quietly dressed showing that they didn't have to depend on that to attract the men. Dinner went off all right but was very stiff and the Three Musketeers did a bit of listening and watched the hostess for the proper tools and the host for the proper glass.

After innumerable courses we arose and the ladies left us. We refilled our glasses and, as the Lancaster [South Carolina] News would say, "delightful conversation was enjoyed by all." We laughed at each other's jokes without getting the point at all and Grider got very sacreligious trying to get the titles straightened out. Evidently our host had not been to see "Turn to the Right," for he didn't say "Suppose we join the ladies" at all. We stayed there as long as we could because everybody dreaded the boredom to follow. We did join [the ladies] finally and everybody made themselves uncomfortable and prepared for the worst.

But over in the corner was an opera grand [piano] and I lazed over to our hostess and told her that Cal could play some native American music. So she asked him to and he made for the piano and sort of fingered it tenderly for a moment. Then he dug down into the insides of that instrument and extracted a rag such as has never been heard before. The piano roared and swayed like a dozen Jazz bands and everybody began to look up and wiggle.

"Do show me how you Americans dance," says my hostess, "I'm not very good but if you don't mind we'll try it once." With that we started and Grider grabbed a sweet young thing and we were off. Well, that lady could dance—no mistaking it—but we'd certainly have been put off the floor of any dance hall in New York. She sure shook a wicked foot.

The honorable somebody-or-other got a partner and stepped forth. He certainly betrayed himself. It was quite clear that when he was on that mission to America he did something else besides inspect munitions factories.

Then came a break and I wandered over and whispered to our host that Cal could never really do things to a piano while his throat was dry and if he really wanted to see his Steinway tortured. . . . Well in a moment he had two flunkeys working in relays and Irving Berlin would have torn his hair if he'd heard Cal making "Nearer My God to Thee" sound like "Turkey in the Straw." I'd never heard anything in my life to touch it and it's a lead pipe cinch that no one else there ever had.

All the ladies demanded that they be taught "Those American Dances" and the party became a regular cabaret. One of the Englishmen did a burlesque drill with a German musket (captured at Ypres (or Wipers as they call it)) and Mac had to sing the Blues four times before they'd let him stop. Somebody played the piccolo and the flunkeys simply panted from their labors.

Cal then committed murder on that piano but stopped short when he saw me doing the giant swing with an honorable flapper and heard Mac reproving his partner for moving her feet and someone else played while he dusted the room with the hostess. Needless to say the cars had to wait about three hours for us and we left with a bang.

But next morning! Mac told me at breakfast that I had disgraced him in high society and Cal and I argued that Mac's party manners would make a great hit in a nice polite livery stable. It was also clear that Cal had missed his calling and should be the professor of a shining upright in a Bowery Saloon. But one thing is clear to us—we disgraced ourselves and belong not in high society. No more raspazassing for us. If any other kind lady wants to high tone us she'll have to take us singly.

We don't know whether to call up and apologize or write her we've been killed or just do nothing. I compromised by flying over there and chasing the children into the house. Thus has our career in high society ended.

A heartful of love to you and Father.

Your devoted son, Elliott

FLIGHT LOG: 11 February: Solo flight: 45 minutes in SPAD #9132. Engine cut out.

FLIGHT LOG: 11 February: Solo flight: 15 minutes in SPAD #8795. Firing.

FLIGHT LOG: 11 February: Solo flight: 40 minutes in SPAD #8867. Firing and low stunting.

FLIGHT LOG: 13 February: Solo flight: 1 hour 45 minutes in Sopwith Pup #2233. Forced landing.

FLIGHT LOG: 13 February: Solo flight: 45 minutes in SPAD #9131. Ground straffing.

DIARY ENTRY: February 13: Go ground straffing on Pup and Spad. Dam fool wonder I'm not dead. One forced landing, roll my wheels at 114 MPH.

DIARY ENTRY: February 14: Am going to Turnberry. Finish up here and go to town at 4. Grider and I stage a party. I get Arlette but she gets [entry unclear]. So take her home. Barry shows up.

Preparing for
Operational Flying in England

February to May 1918

From February through March 1918 Springs completed his flying training program under Royal Flying Corps (RFC) instruction. From the middle of February until the end of March he attended aerial gunnery school, located at Turnberry,[1] and the aerial combat school at Ayr on the west coast of Scotland, where he practiced shooting at fixed and moving targets from an airplane. Temporarily separated from Larry Callahan and Mac Grider, he remained in close contact with them, and on 25 March, after he learned that Grider had been assigned to a squadron in France, Springs made a hurried trip to London, where he met Grider and Callahan; he was concerned that the three of them might be separated. Good fortune intervened in the person of Canadian RFC flying ace William "Billy" Bishop. Springs's instructor at London Colney, Capt. Spencer Horn, had been selected by Bishop to become a flight commander in 85 Squadron RFC, which was in the process of being prepared for combat in France. Horn apparently had been impressed with Springs's flying skills and nerve, and he recommended him, along with Callahan and Grider, to Bishop, who was selecting men for his squadron. Bishop, with his stature as one of the top-scoring aces in the RFC, had been given the authority to hand-pick the men he wanted, and after meeting with all three on 25 or 26 March, he decided that he liked them and wanted them in his unit.

According to Springs's diary entries, Bishop's first attempt to enlist Springs, Grider, and Callahan in his squadron, on 27 March, failed. However, five days later, on 1 April, Springs noted with great excitement that Bishop's efforts had finally been successful. He, Grider, and Callahan were transferred to the military flying field at Hounslow to become part of 85

Squadron. Although the American authorities had initially resisted Bishop's request, the imminent transfer of the three to other squadrons was delayed by a report from RFC authorities stating that the three were deficient in essential flying skills and were required to stay in England for further training. This ruse, perpetrated by Bishop, was made possible with the conniving assistance of some of the lower-ranking American officers, apparently including Lt. Geoffrey Dwyer.

During the months of April and May, Springs, Grider, and Callahan flew frequently from Hounslow. Because the flying field at Hounslow was only about ten miles west of the heart of London, they rented a house in that city, where they hosted many parties while they waited for the squadron to move to France. During this time Elliott Springs flew a variety of aircraft (the Sopwith Pup, Avro, and Dolphin, as well as the SE-5, the aircraft that the squadron flew in France) to two other locations (Maidenhead, farther west, and Eastbourne, on the southern coast of England), as Bishop prepared his pilots to fly efficiently and competently prior to their entry into aerial combat. In addition to their flying activities, it is clear that Springs, Grider, and Callahan were also engaging in a full schedule of social activities with wholehearted, even desperate, energy, throwing party after party, accompanied by a variety of feminine companions: entertainers, singers, women whom they had met on their previous visits to London. Mac Grider apparently developed a serious relationship with one of them, Billie Carleton, the star of the then-popular musical *Fair and Warmer.*[2] They were often joined by a young Georgia girl, Hallie Whatley.

If Springs's diary entries are to be believed, he was often under the influence of alcohol, certainly during his off-duty hours, which may help to explain some of the tone of robust near-belligerency in his letters to his father and stepmother. Under the constraint of meeting the approval of the censor in writing his letters home, he avoided mentioning specific locations and dates of proposed activities and resorted to generalizations to indicate some of his experiences. In his letter of 26 March, he could not provide specific details, for example, of how close he had come to being assigned to Bishop's 85 Squadron. Instead he began that letter with a description that must have proved more confusing than enlightening to his readers at home.

Well, I've had my day of triumph and almost got away with something big. The third general who was consulted vetoed our little plan altogether and completely spoiled our party. But anyway triumph was mine and I feel like somebody again. And besides if I had gotten away with it, 'twould have been too good to be true. So I go overseas as an ordinary pilot instead of as a little tin angel with gilt wing tips as was almost the case. 'Twas quite a disappointment but Army life is full of them and then when it's a real general who does the glooming it's more of a boom than a kick. It's certainly the most complimentary thing that has yet happened to me.

A few days later, on 3 April, when the transfer to Bishop's squadron had finally been approved, his letter home conveyed his excitement in equally confusing terms.

Well, I finally got by with what I was trying to swing last week consequently my hat doesn't fit at all. I doubt if there's one in England big enough for me now. I thought I was going to the front yesterday but for some reason or other was held over and told to await orders today but as yet nothing has come through.

This section closes with a list of Springs's last flights in the vicinity of Hounslow before 85 Squadron left for France.

DIARY ENTRY: February 15: Off for Turnberry. We arrive at 9:30 and find Hash Gile, [Earl] Hammer, [Charles] Evans, [Wilbur] Davidson, and [Lloyd] Hamilton here.[3]

DIARY ENTRY: February 16: Not a bad place but everyone very snotty. We go down to Girvan [a nearby town south of Turnberry] and throw quite a party.

DIARY ENTRY: February 17: Very boring this machine gun stuff. Bridge relieves the monotony thank god.

DIARY ENTRY: February 18: Don't get enough to eat here. No place to get extra food either. Oh god for some Page & Shaws. My uniform arrives. [Rutledge] Barry puts up wings [attaches Springs's specially tailored wings].

DIARY ENTRY: February 19: [Reed] Landis arrives with the news that [Lindley] De Garmo, [Harold] Bulkley have been killed. [Henry] Frost, [Merton] Campbell and [Andy] Ortmeyer are with him.

DIARY ENTRY: February 20: Frost gets news that [Donald] Carlton has been killed in an RE-8. Capt Morton arrives and straightaway we all get pickled as is befitting.

DIARY ENTRY: February 21: Hash [Gile], Hamilton, [William] Armstrong and Capt Morton and I throw a rare party in Girvan. Never have I seen a bunch drunker. We spend night.

FLIGHT LOG: 22 February: Solo flight: 1 hour 35 minutes in BE2C #4963. [Over the Irish] Sea. Gunnery practice.

FLIGHT LOG: 22 February: Solo flight: 45 minutes in BE2C #4192. Sea. Gunnery practice.

DIARY ENTRY: February 22: Capt Morton and I do our best to celebrate Washington's birthday but I am terribly weak today and have to copy notes.

DIARY ENTRY: February 23: A letter from Arlette and Frances, two from Olive, Oh Christ. I get drunk with Cal.

DIARY ENTRY: February 24: Cap and I go down to Ayr and find it good to look upon. Alex [Mathews] and Hash [Gile] get us very tight and the cup passes [around until we pass (?)] out.

DIARY ENTRY: February 25: We return in a Ford very much the worse for wear and I get in trouble with everyone and everything. Pickled again at dinner.

DIARY ENTRY: February 26: Much drinking and nothing else.

The following is an excerpt from a letter by Leroy Springs dated 26 January.

My dear Son:

I have been intending to write you for several days but in the rush of business overlooked it, though you are constantly in my mind. . . . As I wrote you, there is no danger about my showing your letters any more. I only let Mr and Mrs Brewster read your second letter and I cannot see that any harm was done. I think Mr. Brewster was dissatisfied with the way Sidney was writing to him. It seems that he was not writing often and I think Mr Brewster wrote him rebuking him for not writing them more often and writing letters like you do. They appreciated very much my letting them see the letter. However, I will not show your letters in the future. . . .

No 2 Auxiliary School of Aerial Gunnery
Turnberry, Ayrshire, England
February 26 1918

Dear Mother—

Ulysses had nothing on me when it comes to variety of scenery, occupation, companionship, or disposition. Here I sit in a luxurious hotel looking out upon the Forth of Clyde and wondering idly whether the Scotch mist will ever lift enough for me to do some flying. My boon companion is a Scotch Captain who after spending three years in Flanders mud decided he'd rather fly. He's about six feet four, looks like Johnny Walker[4] himself, and insists on flying in his kilt because he says he has rheumatism in his knees and that's the only cure for it. Together we wander about Scotland and the combination of a kilt and an American hat opens every door. He has a temper like Sweet Annie Laurie[5] is popularly supposed to have had, and if all goes well we're going out [to the front] together.

I left London Colney in rather a hurry. I was out having a great time diving into the machine gun pit and landed to change machines so I could get further in when they yanked me into the office and sent me on up here. That was about ten days ago.

Our little raspazass[6] affair ended rather pleasantly. We had just decided that eternal disgrace was ours when our hostess called up and invited us all to another little affair which she was organizing for our special benefit. The other two members of the eternal triangle probably went but I left too soon. Also a couple of fellows came back from a dance somewhere and reported that they had met someone who was at the party and that we had "knocked them cold"—made a great hit in other words—and that Lady _____ was expecting to eclipse that party completely the next week and that three other ladies would shortly invite us to a raspazass in turn.

We'd just had three bad crashes when I left and everybody was sort of figuring on who was next. All the walls had handwriting on them. My roommate, DeGarmo of Florida, was killed in a machine that I had just been flying and Harold Bulkley was killed ground straffing. Carlton was killed spinning next day and [Clark] Nichol up at Stamford.

It was too bad about DeGarmo. He came over a month before I did but we were the first two Americans to qualify for our commissions over here and consequently have been together ever since. There's always been considerable competition between us and we've been neck and neck until just recently when he got lost one day and while he was away I got in about six hours flying on a new type of machine. We both looped for the first time on the same day—both spun for the first time on the same day, etc. As a matter of fact so did Bulkley (as you know he was with me at Princeton) but DeGarmo and myself got ahead of him when we went to London Colney.

I've given up ever trying to explain anything to Father. In his last letter he assures me that showing my letter to that potbellied old fool Brewster was all right because it did no harm and Sydney was not writing properly. In other words he doesn't care a rap about my wishes or requests and still doesn't. If he can get away with it he'll do it. Can you beat it? You don't seem to be much better yourself though. . . .

And don't write me any more cards! If you can't waste the time writing a letter, don't write at all. It's an insult. The color of socks [which Lena apparently offered to send] won't matter as they are worn underneath field boots you know and are never visible except to the laundrymen. . . .

My health continues to improve and I can't say that I am suffering for lack of anything. Candy is scarce—almost unobtainable and I would sell my soul for some glace nuts or salted roast almonds and peanuts or a Hershey nut bar. Funny, no one has mental energy enough to figure out just what a soldier over here would enjoy.

And just apropos, you might pass the word around to those who have friends over here that they had better put away their knitting needles and get out the old sauce pan and pen and paper. The angels above blush every time a soldier smacks his lips over a big juicy parcel from home and then opens it to find it contains sweaters, socks, and mufflers and eight bibles. We've had to invent a new kind of profanity to cover it. I venture to say that not a man in my detachment has less than ten of the aforementioned articles but gets few letters and still fewer boxes of food, tobacco, and up-to-date magazines. It's been ages since I've seen Puck or Life.[7] And what food they do send is usually of the perishable variety which never arrives in fit condition. Chocolates in tin boxes or wrapped in tin foil, such as nut bars, milk chocolate, fruit cake, glace nuts, Boullion cubes, stuffed dates, chocolate-covered molasses candy, peanut bars, Fudge, sea foam etc are the things.

Would it interest you to know that I have already received 11 sweaters? Unappreciative swine, says Father, but not so. I appreciate each and every one and every one of those sweaters is being worn by a soldier but I can't find anyone to read all my bibles. Another Page and Shaw's arrived— Allah be praised, and so say all of us.

A heartful of love to you and Father.

Devotedly, Elliott

DIARY ENTRY: Feb 27: Go to Ayr [about fifteen miles north of Turnberry, still on the coast]. We are all put in Wellington House.[8]

No 1 School of Aerial Fighting
Ayr, Scotland
February 27, 1918

Dear Father—
Your letter of January 27 received also your Cablegram last week. I wired reply which I suppose you received. I qualified for my commission on November 24, but due to various tie-ups in Headquarters I understand that my name didn't go to Washington until January 7. Ever since November 24 I've been expecting my actual commission daily but as yet nothing has arrived. Not that it makes much difference as we've been considered officers ever since November 2 and have been treated as such by the English.

I understand that no commissions have been issued at all over here, certainly none of the 200 here in England have gotten them. Walker Ellis got his commission but he got a non-flying commission. I understand, though, that he has been doing some flying since then unofficially as have the eleven others commissioned at the same time.

As you request I shall take out the insurance in your favor and you can do what you please with it. I would rather you wouldn't build a brewery with it, though. The hospital idea doesn't appeal either. You might endow a room at the Vanderbilt for the use of the Italian Detachment. My health is exceptionally good except that my imagination insists that I have a bad tooth and my financial condition is equally sound. Scotland is a delightful place and I'm enjoying it unusually. . . .

A heartful of love to you and Lena. Devotedly, Elliott

No 1 School of Aerial Fighting
Ayr, Scotland
March 1 1918

Dear Aunt Addie,
I received your letter of Jan 31st the other day and was delighted to hear from you. I have been up here in Scotland for the past two weeks getting the final polish and outside of excitement, which is always diverting, I have had rather a good time. It's been cold, all right, but I'm dressed like an Eskimo and it never bothers me. Of course, it's rather disconcerting to get your nose frozen and have it appear a beautiful bright red for several

days but as long as everybody understands where you got the blossom, it's all right.

And I've never flown over the sea before nor touched my wheels on the beach. It seems we never exhaust the possibilities of flying. I haven't run my wheels on the top of an express train yet either but I'm reserving that for the time when all else bores me. Nor have I looped off the ground so I have several things to look forward to.

And I like Scotland. You would too. It's just full of monuments and churches and family history. And the Presbyterians are aces-up everywhere. And only we heathens in the R.F.C. consider that Sunday is a day of the week. The Scots have a special calendar for it I think. It's like Sunday at home not Sunday in the Army. I'll write you more about it later as I shall be here a week longer and will doubtless know more about the country then and I shall probably have seen ten more monuments to Burns[9] by then.

A heartful of love. Your devoted nephew, Elliott

No 1 School of Aerial Fighting
Ayr, Scotland
March 1 1918

Dear Mother—

Tis an old belief that writing in its various phases requires a particular humor. I suppose 'tis true. Anyway, somehow or other I'm always in a rotten humor when I sit down to write a letter. Possibly it's because I always feel I have to write letters and never want to. Anyway, in such a humor do I find myself now. Particularly does it annoy me to have to write the kind of letters I do. Between the military sensor and the parental recipient, I feel my style considerably cramped.

But there's really no reason for my bad humor now and it applies only to correspondence. I say to myself "I am writing to narrow-minded ignorant people—hence I must write a letter correspondingly." Then why write? Yes indeed why write? I see no reason to. But to assure you all that the Page and Shaw's will be eaten by the proper person I'll keep it up.

No, there's no reason why I should feel so nasty—I have very little to worry me. And it's rather foolish to worry, anyway, when you're awaiting orders to go to the front. Over here an aviator never worries about anything unless it's vitally connected with his stomach and he doesn't worry much then. I met a fellow last night who was swearing goodnaturedly because one of his kidneys had been shot away and he said it interfered with his drinking.

Yes flying is the nearest thing to the Balm of Gilead I know. It's the only bona fida surcease, nepenthe, and Headache liniment. The other day, for instance, two of us went up to practice fighting. The other fellow was in a rotten humor and so was I. After an hour of missing each other by inches we came down and started back to the mess. "Ha ha," says he, "good joke. I got a letter this morning from H.Q. I owe the Gov't $3 on this month's pay." "How's that?" "Oh they found out I was married and are deducting $33 for three months back and $4 for my insurance, Ha ha." I never knew he was married and said so. "Oh," says he, "I was once but got a divorce and the funny thing is, they're docking my pay for her and she's married again. I hope they don't run out of sugar before we get there. Let's hurry— we're late." Poor fellow, he's in the hospital now. Can you beat it?

When I see someone dive into the ground and write themselves off it rather makes me feel bad. You know, sort of uncertain and sad. But I immediately get a bus and go up and turn the thing inside out and go ground straffing and hedge hopping and I come down feeling fine. We make it a rule to go up ourselves right away, if there's a bad crash. Particularly if he's killed stunting.

And it's wonderful what you can do with some of the busses. I read sometimes in the Flying magazines from the U.S. about somebody pulling off some stunt or other—looping 100 times, or something like that, and it makes you laugh. Over here no one pays any attention to you unless you dive on them and make them lie down flat for you. And if you crash no one takes any notice unless you spread the machine all over the field or do something comical like one fellow the other day. He hit a tree and knocked the motor out but the plane kept going and he landed beautifully in the field just as if nothing had happened. I didn't see it, but they say Capt ____ came into the hangars upside down, and went out and gave a new pupil a telling off for smashing a wing tip.

I understand that our commissions came through several weeks ago but by some chance they were 2nd Lts so were sent back to Washington to be changed to 1st. They were for twelve of us, but only nine of us are still here to get them. They'd better hurry up with the nine.

Another box of candy arrived as did some candied fruit from the Scotts. Glory be! How we did pitch into it. Either flying or the Scotch air has given us horrible appetites. Unless old ptomaine gets me shortly I'll be fat. Only weigh 178 now—due mainly to sitting around the Turnberry hotel playing bridge. Who said sweets made you fat. Nonsense! If you eat sweets it kills your appetite and you eat less. If there's nothing sweet about I eat more at tea than I used to at home in three days.

There are a lot of American mechanics here who were on the *Tuscania*.[10] They are attired for the most part in a mixture of British and American uniforms and present a most unusual appearance. I'm turning over what I can spare in the way of uniforms to them and so are a couple of other Americans who are here.

I see in the papers where Vernon Castle[11] was killed. Too bad. Capt [Spencer] Horn down in 56 [Squadron] was in the same squadron in France with him and says he was all O.K. One of the fellows here in the mess flew with him in Canada last year and said the same. Also his roommate was killed in a crash with Castle though he escaped. And the irony of it is that his departure only serves to bring Irene [Castle] into the limelight. I suppose all the papers will print her picture when they mention it. . . . And apropos I saw Irene last night at the movies. Tonight I shall see Mary Pickford[12] unless I can find something else to do.

When the war's over I'm going to join a Highland Regiment. I'll never be happy until I wear a kilt.

A heartful of love to you and Father.

Devotedly, Elliott

DIARY ENTRY: March 1: Ortmeyer and Landis arrive.
DIARY ENTRY: March 5: Dealy[13] and Ortmeyer killed on Camels.
DIARY ENTRY: March 7: Velie killed on Camels.
DIARY ENTRY: March 9: Two more Camel smashes.

Wellington House, Ayr
March 10, 1918

Dear Father,

Your cablegram was received the other day also one which the bank forwarded on to me in which you were inquiring for my address. But I haven't as yet gotten a letter from you since I left Turnberry though one came from Lena.

My commission hasn't arrived yet but HQ in London says they ought to be here any day now. It came through about a month ago but was for a 2nd [lieutenancy] instead of for a 1st so had to go back. I'm getting skeptical though and will probably fly over the lines as a sergeant yet. My seniority and pay will date from the time I get my commission. I don't suppose it makes much difference but it ought to date from November 24th 1917.

Outside of that everything has been getting along nicely and we've been getting quite a bit of flying and are now aerial aerobats of the first water. Four Americans were killed last week and two the week before, unfortunately—two of them here. One of our best Bridge players went yesterday. And it's strange but all of them were killed spinning.

A heartful of love to you and Lena,

Your devoted son, Elliott

Wellington House, Ayr, Scotland
March 11 1918

Dear Mother—

Gee, it's great to be alive. Anyway, that's how I feel this morning. I don't particularly crave longevity but I would like to get to the front first. They've been going fast this week. I suppose you have already heard about young Montgomery's death. I saw Ipers yesterday and he told me about it.[14] He put up an awfully good fight for his life, too. He was up as an observer and somehow or other he and the pilot were thrown out of their seats. The pilot fell but Montgomery caught the cowling and held himself on the fuselage. Then as the machine plunged, he scrambled and pulled himself up the fuselage until he got to the controls. Just too late! In another 100 feet he would have saved himself. Please convey my sympathy to his Mother and Father and tell them that he was generally considered one of the best of the whole bunch, a good pilot and a prince of a gentleman. Everyone feels his loss and the British are loud in their praise of the game fight he put up to save himself.

Also our best bridge player here went west last Friday. Andy Ortmeyer, of Chicago, one of the fellows who flew last winter at Memphis. A good pilot, a fine fellow, and liked by everyone. His roommate here is in despair. He's had three roommates killed in three weeks. Naturally no one will room with him now.

But let me say a few words lest anyone at home get the wind up and get the idea that there's something wrong because so many are going. There isn't. It's absolutely unavoidable. To teach men to fly fast planes you must expect to lose a fair percentage. Thus far we have lost only one on primary training machines like we were flying last spring. The training machines that they use for instance in the States are comparatively safe, almost foolproof—but when it comes to fast scouts and fighters—well, every time a man goes up he's flirting with the undertaker and every time he makes a landing he's kidding the three Fates about their scythes being dull.

Cal [Larry Callahan] had a narrow escape the other day. His controls jammed but he got them working again enough to land on a golf course. But unfortunately he hit a bunker. After looping over the ground several times he stopped upside down with his head just above the hole. Made it in bogey, as the players remarked as they pulled him out of the wreckage. He ruined a new machine and a good green but wasn't hurt himself.

I had rather a squeakest time myself some time ago. Lost my motor at about 300 feet over a wood. I thought I was done for, so I cut my switch so as not to catch fire and braced myself and waited. But I always was the luckiest man alive and by dodging trees and summer houses I ended up by landing in a sort of formal garden and didn't strain a wire. I was even so lucky that I got my motor started again and by dodging and zooming [over] summer houses and flower beds managed to fly out and back to the 'drome all right. I certainly cheated the ambulance driver that time.

Did I write you about my experience in a London air raid? No? Well, I'll tell you about it. Cal and I were down there one night when a raid came over and things suddenly became very lively during dinner. After dinner we went outside to see what we could see. Guns were making a bit of noise and shrapnel was falling all about in the streets. A bomb fell about six blocks away and when things quieted down a touch we strolled down to look the place over. A half an hour after we left, a bomb fell ten feet from where we had been standing. The guns started up again so we took shelter behind the scenes in the Shaftesbury Theatre.[15] After an impromptu dance there we went on down to the Savoy and a few minutes later a bomb fell just back of it and put the bar out of commission for several days. Horrible people these Germans.

The raids do little actual damage and frighten no one to speak of. It won't be long before I'll be taking a crack at the swine. I can't say that I'm particularly bloodthirsty, I'm not, but it's a wonderful game, this fighting in the air, and I'm anxious to start playing it.

I'm learning to like Scotland more and more. We're very comfortable here—have an exceptionally nice crowd of fellows and lots of diversion. And there's no hot air about this place. If it's cloudy or there's no flying we organize all sorts of expeditions. Glasgow is only an hour from here but is not much of a place. If the weather is good tomorrow we are going to fly over to Turnberry and bring Cal and Mac over here for dinner.

My Scotch Captain has departed. He was ordered overseas and departed night before last in a blaze of glory. We gave him a send off worthy of a Crusader off to the East.

[final page of letter missing]

FLIGHT LOG: 13 March: Dual flight: 25 minutes with Lt. Sheppard in
   Avro #7517. Near drome. Stunting.
FLIGHT LOG: 13 March: Solo flight: 20 minutes in Avro #7517. Near
   drome. Stunting.
FLIGHT LOG: 13 March: Solo flight: 1 hour in Avro #7517. Near drome.
   Two fights [practice dogfights], one victory.
FLIGHT LOG: 14 March: Solo flight: 30 minutes in Avro #182. Near
   drome. Three fights.
FLIGHT LOG: 15 March: Solo flight: 20 minutes in Avro #183. Near
   drome. Formation.
FLIGHT LOG: 15 March: Solo flight: 20 minutes in Avro #183. Near
   drome. Fighting.
FLIGHT LOG: 15 March: Solo flight: 15 minutes in Avro #7517. Near
   drome. Fighting with [Rutledge] Barry.
FLIGHT LOG: 15 March: Solo flight: 1 hour 25 minutes in SE-5 #3432.
   Near drome. Fought 3 Camels, one Avro.

Wellington House, Ayr, Scotland
March 18 1918

Dear Mother—

   We had a concert some time ago and the feature was an opera consist-
ing of parodies on popular and unpopular music. Some of them were very
clever and I thought you might like to have them. They were as follows:

Opening Chorus (Tune: Entrance of the Bing Boys)[16]

> We're the R.F.C.
> Bold bad airmen are we
> And we fly scouts and big battle planes
> We straff the Huns
> Dodge their Archie guns
> As they fire H.E. up in tons and tons
> We fly Spads, B.E.s
> S.E.5s and F.E.s
> Martynsides and the big DH[17]
> On the road to ruin
> There'll be something doing
> When we're through with this old war.

Enter some Air Mechanics (Tune: "365 Days")

Three hundred and sixty five wires
All go to make a Quirk[18]
Three hundred and sixty five wires
With which to make more work
But always remember
From January to December
The R.A.F.[19] we should worship and praise
We'll try to refine it—and then redesign it
Three hundred and sixty-five ways.

Enter a weary Flight Commander (Tune: "Murders," from *To-Night's the Night*)[20]

I have a few confessions which I think I ought to make
And I'll try to break them gently for everybody's sake
The first's about my rigger[21] who has left this world of strife
If you listen I shall tell you how he came to lose his life
I murdered him last Tuesday for I thought it would be right
And never never more will he perturb me in my flight
And now I'll get my Henris and F.E.s in one piece
For I slew him with my joy-stick;[22] it's a merciful release

2

A terrible bereavement did befall our family
My Henri[23] instructor has gone into eternity
He called me heavy-handed[24]—he won't do that again
He said my landings pained him—so I put him out of pain
I murdered him, that Henri man, I don't think I did wrong
He wasn't wanted in our flight, he'd been there far too long
He said I sideslipped outward so I sideslipped in instead
And now my poor instructor I regret to say is dead

3

I had a young observer who observed from out my Fee[25]
But now he'll never observe again for he has ceased to be
I sallied forth one evening when the light was growing dim
And I took up my machine gun and I pointed it at him
I shot that young observer for I thought his time was up
And never more will he throw things back through my prop[26]

And now he will not swear to me that Albert is Bapaume
For he's busy doing petit Bosche in his Eternal Home

4

A pilot one day joined the wing to teach us how to fight
He used to get above the clouds and dive on us at sight
He had a little Bristol Scout that brought sweat to my brow
He used to sit upon my tail—he doesn't do that now
I murdered him quite neatly for I crossed his controls around
And so whene'er he tried to zoom, he nosedived to the ground
The C.O. saw what I had done but said he wouldn't tell
But he gave me three days' C.B.[27] so I murdered him as well

5

Another notoriety has left this world full speed
And once again I must confess 'twas I who did the deed
It's a pilot I'm referring to, a most obnoxious lad,
If I'd let him live much longer I'd have soon gone raving mad.
'Twas on a summer's evening that the dreadful deed was done
No fuss or noise about it—it was just the Lewis gun
He couldn't even fly a Fee, he crashed a Bristol Scout
But when he stalled a Martynside 'twas time we put him out.

Enter a dud pilot (Tune: "A Broken Doll")[28]

I wonder why I fly the way I do
But now it seems the others have been wondering too
I thought I should be good in days gone by
But all that now has changed—somehow I wonder why
I learned to fly a year or two ago
I thought I knew all that there was to know
I soon learned what bumps were and sideslips too
So off I went one day in search of something new.
I landed on the drome one day down wind[29]
The C.O. said some pretty things to me
For when I came away, I'm sorry to say
I left behind a broken Fee.

Enter a dud pilot mournfully (Tune: "When You're all Dressed Up")[30]

When the flares shine bright o'er the 'drome at night
And there's petrol and oil and mud
Life is one delight if your landing's right

But it's hell if your landing's dud[31]
Though your soul may crave for the deeds called brave
And at times you would gladly die
'Tis a bitter cup when you're all dressed up
And have no bus to fly

Enter an harassed pupil (Tune: "Every Little While")[32]

I miss you so Henri when you're away
I find myself dreaming of you night and day
I'm losing my revs and I'm losing my height
I'd like to forget you awhile if I might—
But every little while I crash an Henri
Every little while I hit a tree
I'm always stalling, I'm always falling
Because I want an F.E. 2B
Every little while my engine's conking[33]
Every little while it catches fire
And from the time I turn the switch up
I know I'm going to bitch up
Every every every little while.

You'll have to get the music and play it before you can appreciate them.
The fellow who wrote most of it got killed last week and these are all I can
get now. Here's another.

(Tune: "Old Tarpaulin Jacket")

A young aviator lay dying
And as 'neath the wreckage he lay
To the A.M.[34] assembled around him
These last parting words he did say.
Take the cylinders out of my stomach
The connecting rod out of my brain
From the small of my back take the crankshaft
And assemble the engine again
[Additional lines—scratched out:
Take the joy stick out of my stomach
Take the cylinders out of my eye
In the back of my neck
You will find about a peck
Of rivets and washers galore

(Funeral March)

> Never mind about my pain
> But assemble the damn thing again]

Enter a weary Squadron Commander and disheveled pilot (Tune: "What Do You Want to Make Those Eyes at Me For?")[35]

> What did you want to go and crash like that for,
> It's the second one today
> You drive me mad
> The huns are glad
> But I'm glad you crashed a Rumpty 'stead of a brand new Spad[36]

(whisky tenor gets in some dirty work here)

> What do you want to fool around like that for
> You banked all right
> But then you slipped away
> You're all right
> You go up again tonight
> With a dozen bombs
> All loaded with dynamite
> And if you go and have a crash like that one
> Well, you won't draw any pay.

That just reminds me. About an hour ago my roommate got a big box. He had to pay ten shillings duty on it and it was big and heavy. He brought it in and we smacked our lips over it. No knitted goods this time—food! We opened the box and simply spluttered. We called the whole house in to help us swear. The box contained 6 cakes of Pears soap, 3 tubes of toothpaste, 2 tubes of shaving cream, a mirror, 2 large cartons of Wrigley's chewing gum, 5 pounds of indestructible peppermint candy (now one huge lump after three months' passage), and some unsmokeable tobacco. I'm afraid he wrote his family rather a nasty letter.

My Page and Shaw's always causes a riot as did the Deities, chocolate, and Barking Dog. Please always send plain tip cigarettes. We never smoke cork tips. So the next time anyone calls you up and asks my address, find out first what they're going to send and then tell them you don't know it.

The wings arrived—many thanks.

A heartful of love to you and Father.

Elliott

FLIGHT LOG: 19 March: Solo flight: 1 hour in Avro. Reconnaissance. Dud motor.

FLIGHT LOG: 19 March: Solo flight: 1 hour in SE-5 #3432. Near drome. Looking for [Thomas "Cush"] Nathan.

DIARY ENTRY: March 19: Cush Nathan killed. [Bennett "Bim"] Oliver, Winston, [Reed] Landis, [Rutledge] Barry and myself commissioned. Big celebration. Everyone drunk.

FLIGHT LOG: 20 March: Solo flight: 30 minutes in SE-5 #3432. Near drome. Disgraceful.

DIARY ENTRY: March 20: Cush's funeral—horrible.

Wellington House, Ayr, Scotland
March 21 1918

Dear Mother—

I'm getting fed-up with you and Father. No mail for two weeks from you. The papers and other things have been coming through so I presume you have been busy again. However, many thanks for the Deities and Peters and wings. All arrived safely and intact.

Could you please send some sugar. They judged me guilty the other day and sentenced me to make the Eggnog. I threw together a beauty but had nothing to sweeten it with. On the first round I tried condensed milk and saccharine on the second. I don't know which caused the greatest howl. They swore more at the first round though because it was somewhat of a surprise. So please send sugar ere I lose my reputation.

My commission has arrived but now that it's here I hardly know what to do about it. It makes absolutely no change in our status quo and all I had to do to wiggle out of the cocoon was to rearrange my collar gadgets and order some silver bars (my own design). I think I'll send you my Sergeant's Warrant and Flying Certificate as I'd hate to lose them. You can frame them with my two diplomas and hang them in the garage but they must not be on display in the house!!!!!

I've been doing quite a bit of flying lately but the greatest excitement has not been in flying so much as getting back on the ground, as I've been flying several new types of machines. And, you know, your first trip in a new machine beats anything else for excitement. Imagine telling a man who's never seen water before how to swim, let him watch you swim, and then push him in. That's what it's like the first time up and it's just luck if you land O.K. because you don't know the machine at all. The machine I was up in yesterday I think is about the 12th different one for me thus far so I know whereof I speak. I've got it systematized though. After I once get it off the ground I don't hesitate until I get to 2000 feet. Then I turn it inside out and study it. Then I fly with hands off to see its tendencies and play with the motor. Finally I go up higher and practice imaginary landings on the clouds. And I don't come down until I know that bus like I used to know the Stutz. Once I got fooled though. After five minutes up the engine cut out with me and I had to come down in a hurry and land blindly.

There's a lot in knowing your machine. You'd be surprised the accuracy necessary. For instance say you're up practicing firing on a ground target. That means you'll get above it at 1000 feet and dive straight on it. To get in the maximum shots you'll want to continue your dive as long as possible say to 100 feet. And then you must bring her out slowly or you'll tear your wings off. Now your speed will be somewhere between 150 and 250 miles per hour—say 180 for argument. That's 5280 feet in 20 seconds, or 100 feet in 2/5 of a second. So when you're diving with your eye to the sights, you've got to stop firing, judging your height in the meantime, make up your mind and start easing her out all in 2/5 of a second. And too little or too much pressure on the joy stick will cause no end of trouble. Two men went west last week at it. And that's only one of a thousand things that's got to be learned. They say that Major [William "Billy"] Bishop used to come back after shooting down a couple of huns and then practice firing for a while before lunch. A wonderful man is he—considered sort of a superman saint over here.

Fine weather here lately. Not very cold either. You'd be surprised at Scotch weather,—as well as Scotland generally. I'm sort of getting the hang of the language now too. My batman—

I'll have to explain. You see every officer in the British army has a servant—batman—and being attached to the R.F.C. we get one too, or rather several of us share one. I have a Scotch one and our conversation is ludicrous. Neither understands the other. This one aroused me this morning with a flow of Scotch. Unable to interpret, I started to get up. But my boots weren't shined so I howled for him and back he came. I explained and he spluttered and I snozzed some more. Again I started to get up but still no polished boots. I howled again and more spluttering. This time he refused to bother with me and I seethed. Much spluttering again. Finally he pointed triumphantly to the floor and held up two fingers. "Twa," says he, "twa, twa." He'd shined two pairs of my roommate's boots twice.

And Sunday it was raining so I slept. About three times he woke me. The fourth I was indignant and slid down further in my flea bag. "Ged oop, sah," says he, "live clock."

"Well and then what?" says I rather peeved.

"Gid oop, sah," says he, "I want ta mek oop yo bad."

It reminds me of Waddy[37] helping me with the broiled chicken by blocking its skidding with his thumb. But a good sort are these batmen. Usually the acme of service, always faithful, and very grateful for any attention. And they always take to Americans.

A heartful of love to you and Father. Always your devoted son,

Elliott

FLIGHT LOG: 23 March: Solo flight: 30 minutes in SE-5 #3432. Near drome. Mag drive broke.

FLIGHT LOG: 24 March: Solo flight: 20 minutes in SPAD #9141. Dud motor.

FLIGHT LOG: 24 March: Solo flight: 5 minutes in SPAD #9142. Write off. Hot wires.

FLIGHT LOG: 24 March: Solo flight: 5 minutes in SPAD #9141. Dud.

FLIGHT LOG: 24 March: Solo flight: 10 minutes in SPAD #9156.

Wellington House, Ayr
March 24, 1918

Dear Father—

Your letter from Palm Beach arrived as did two Cablegrams which I answered. My roommate here, Cushman Nathan, was killed Wednesday. It was too bad. He was a fine fellow, a very good friend of mine and an excellent pilot. If you care to, I wish you would write to his father, Frank M. Nathan, and express your sympathy. He was a very good friend of mine. That's two roommates I've lost in a month. Mac and Cal are here now and we're hoping to go out together.

I wish you and Lena would write oftener and when you do write tell me some news and quit filling up letters with advice. What's happened to the Stutz? Also I need some sugar badly.

Spring has arrived and I can't say that I'm at all sorry. I was flying today without goggles or helmet and it was great. My motor cut out, though, and I nearly froze coming down and traveled at a [great] rate of speed. Luck was with me and I didn't crash though I missed a fence by inches.

I'm going to London tomorrow night to arrange about Nathan's effects. May stay there a day or so as I have some leave coming to me whenever I want to take it. However I don't think I want much leave as this is the best place I [have] ever been except Milwaukee and my duties here are nil except for flying when I feel so inclined.

A heartful of love to you and mother,

Your devoted son, Elliott

DIARY ENTRY: March 25: Mac [Grider] gets orders to depart for overseas. I go down to London with him.

DIARY ENTRY: March 26: [Sam] Eckert throws a party. I see Bricktop [Springs's nickname for a London female acquaintance, probably a redhead] again and go to a dance.

Lt E. W. Springs
S. O. R. 35 Eaton Place
London, England
March 26 1918

Dear Mother—

Well, I've had my day of triumph and almost got away with something big. The third general who was consulted vetoed our little plan altogether and completely spoiled our party. But anyway triumph was mine and I feel like somebody again. And besides if I had gotten away with it, 'twould have been too good to be true. So I go overseas as an ordinary pilot instead of as a little tin angel with gilt wing tips as was almost the case. 'Twas quite a disappointment but Army life is full of them and then when it's a real general who does the glooming it's more of a boom than a kick. It's certainly the most complimentary thing that has yet happened to me. I'd like to tell you about [it]—for you know I'm not modest and never claimed to be—but I don't care to have Father howling it from the housetops.

Also another thing. Father is going to get me in trouble trying to find out where I am always. The same day that anything happens to me, he will be cabled. Isn't that enough. From now on you will never know where I am writing from and I don't want you all trying to find out. What [do] you think the censorship is for. And if your letters don't improve I shall cease to correspond with you all at all. Father's last effort was a disgrace. Where does he copy them from, "Lord Chesterfield's[38] 'weaker moments'" or a railway "Guide to Correspondence"? You didn't give a course in letter writing at Queen's[39] by any chance, did you? I'd much rather have you just mail me your manual. It might prove humorous at least.

I was in the photographer's the other day and saw something familiar on the wall.

"Et tu Brute," says I to him, "when were you in New York?"

"Never been there," says he.

"Well," says I, "why the picture of Mr. Ziegfeld's[40] top sergeant hanging thusly on your walls? Why worship you the famous Daisy Dewitt?" For 'twas she and no other.[41]

"Oh," says he, beaming, "that picture was sent me as an advertisement for some American paper. Isn't she charming?"

Can you beat it? That happened in the sedate devout village of Ayr, than which there is none such.

A heartful of love to you both.

Your devoted son, Elliott

The following is an excerpt from a letter by Leroy Springs dated 8 March 1918.

My dear Son:

I trust everything is well with you and that you are enjoying yourself. Lena had a letter from you this morning and you seemed to be being entertained a great deal. I think you forget the fact that all your letters are censored and, as they are written to your father and mother, I am afraid they would not make the right impression on the people who censor them and they might not understand them. I think if you would tone your letters down a little, they would be more dignified, if you will pardon me for making the suggestion. However, we enjoy all you write but you must not forget the fact that your letters are censored and frivolous letters written to your father and mother might not make the right impression, though we understand them. Do not think I am lecturing you. I am merely making the suggestion and you can take it for what it is worth. . . .

DIARY ENTRY: March 27: Start back to Ayr after spending a day trying to fix it up to go overseas with Bishop. It can't be done. He's certainly a Prince.

DIARY ENTRY: March 28: Arrive back and start an eggnog drink.

DIARY ENTRY: March 29: More eggnog—more punch.

Wellington House, Ayr
March 29, 1918

Dear Father,

I received your letter of the 9th [of March, probably] and was delighted to hear from you though I didn't hear much. I just got back from London this morning where I've been for the past three days arranging some things. When in London I called, as you instructed me, on Commander Arthur. They had never heard of him at Admiral Sims' office.[42] I've also been making final arrangements about Nathan's effects.

I've always heard that Scots were thrifty and I've also heard that they were very close. But it's not true. When I was settling Nathan's bills, every one refused to accept any money, which is quite unusual. I knew he had been going to a certain dentist so I went to settle up with him. The dentist expressed regret but refused to consider a payment. I asked him to look at my teeth and he found I had twelve holes that he could put all his instruments into. Several days later I was asking if he couldn't give me more time. But all his time was taken. A moment later he asked me what I had to do Sunday morning.

"Absolutely nothing, Doc," says I, thinking to myself that I was going to get all my teeth plugged.

"Then, no doubt, Mr. Springs," says he, "ye'll come and go to church with me and my wife." He considered the argument finished and dug at a tooth with renewed energy. I tried to explain but every time I tried to assure him that Sunday morning was a time for rest, he'd dig at a nerve with such vigor that I had to subside. The result was that I went to church with him but I displayed such ignorance in keeping up with the rest of the congregation in operating the various psalm books, hymn books, bibles and prayer books that I don't think he'll invite me again. He decided I was a heathen when he caught me trying to find Hebrews XI in the Old Testament. It was some queer variety of Scotch Congregational Presbyterian Church and they used a different book every time we stood up. But I made a good bluff at it and one of the elders invited me back again.

The doc is a brick, though. I missed an appointment with him at five because I had a crash and, after I did show up at six, though rather disheveled, he took a look at me and says, "I was a worrying for ye, I knew you'd had a mishap. I'm verra glad, 'tis no wuss. You didna disturb that new inlay, did ye?"

Fortunately I hadn't, but if I hadn't been infernally lucky [thinly lined out: they would probably have had to identify me by that inlay] you would be consulting an architect about that hospital.

A heartful of love, devotedly, Elliott

Three men of 85 Squadron. Left to right: Larry Callahan, Malcolm "Mac" MacGregor, and Thompson standing in front of a Sopwith Dolphin. This picture was probably taken at Hounslow in May 1918. The other individual is not identified. Courtesy of the Springs Close Family Archives, the White Homestead, Fort Mill, South Carolina.

DIARY ENTRY: March 30: Continue the party and pass Marshall[43] out.
DIARY ENTRY: March 31: I am going overseas on Dolphins or SPADs so
     start for London. Alex Mathews and [Reed] Landis also.
DIARY ENTRY: April 1: Maj Bishop intercedes [is successful in bringing
     Springs, Callahan, and Grider into 85 Squadron]. Capt Horn and I
     throw a big party. . . .
DIARY ENTRY: April 2: I meet Florence and we decide to have a big
     party immediately if not sooner.
FLIGHT LOG: 3 April: Solo flight: 15 minutes on Dolphin #3969. Around
     drome [Hounslow]. First solo.

Savoy Hill
London W.C. 2, England
April 3 1918

Dear Father—
     Well, I'm off and all is well. I've gotten by with murder and the Prince of
Pilsen[44] has nothing on me. I shall still use the London bank for my mailing

address and also for my banking as I shall be fighting for the next three or four months with the R.F.C. And just incidentally I have plenty of cash on hand at the moment but I think I'll draw some more through the Hanover and have it deposited there to my credit in case I need some cash in a hurry. I have thirty or forty pounds I think now but I'll probably spend that on equipment when I get to France. I'm thinking of doing some experimenting in parachutes also.

I borrowed a very tricky bus yesterday [a Sopwith Dolphin] and flew up to [London] Colney and had lunch with the old crew. I certainly did hightone them. They nearly passed out when they saw I was flying with spurs on.

Well, goodbye [and] a heartful of love to you and Mother.

Your devoted son, Elliott

P.S. If you want to help win the war send me some phonograph records (Victor)—Cigarettes (Deities plain tip, Fatimas)—Page & Shaws—Hershey's nut bars—Romeo Cigars—sugar—Guava jelly—Pickled peaches—Potted beef—Ripe Olives.

Page & Shaws weekly

I'm enclosing a kodak picture of myself and Cush Nathan taken just before he was killed.

E. W. Springs

1st Lt Sig[nal] R[eserve] C[orps] A[viation] S[ection]
S.O.S., U.S.A.
35 Eaton Place
London, England
April 3 1918

Dear Mother—,

Well, I finally got by with what I was trying to swing last week consequently my hat doesn't fit at all. I doubt if there's one in England big enough for me now. I thought I was going to the front yesterday but for some reason or other was held over and told to await orders today but as yet nothing has come through.

However having nothing else to do today I went out to a nearby 'drome and kidded an old friend of mine in charge out there into letting me take up his pet bus. 'Twas a new type that I hadn't flown before and a wonderful bus. I liked it so well that I stayed for lunch and went up again.

I am enclosing my [enlisted] discharge which you might keep as a souvenir.[45]

I certainly hated to leave Ayr. 'Tis a wonderful place and I'll never forget it. I had a better time there on the whole than any place I've ever been—'twas ideal. And I got a send off that made me regret leaving even more. I could stay there for [the] duration cheerfully.

I haven't had any Page & Shaws for some time but hope some is on the way.

And say—when you get the news about me I don't want any weeping and wailing. Just keep in your mind the fact that I went down happy and smiling and that the game has been worth the candle. The reason I say this is that another friend of mine since Nathan has been killed and it was my hard luck to have to break the news to his fiancee. Ten minutes later I was wishing that it was the other way 'round. So don't do it and don't let anybody else do it. I don't want anybody weeping over me or mourning for me. And don't you dare wear any black—unless you consider it becoming to you.

Yes, the game is worth the candle. I've lived a whole life time since I sailed. And what a glorious life, too. I've done more and had more fun than in several ordinary lifetimes. So I'm ready and waiting—

A heartful of love to you and Father. Devotedly, Elliott

FLIGHT LOG: 4 April: Solo flight: 30 minutes on Dolphin #3969. [To] London Colney. Mac [Grider] and I go over for lunch.

DIARY ENTRY: April 5: Larry arrives in time to upset my party.

FLIGHT LOG: 6 April: Solo flight: 40 minutes in Dolphin #3969. Return trip [from London Colney].

DIARY ENTRY: April 7: We take Lord Athlumney's house and have a big housewarming party. ["Billy"] Bishop, [Capt. Arthur] Benbow, Young, Capt [Spencer] Horn, Col Hastings, Hallye [Whatley], 4 Beard sisters [not identified] and Florence.

FLIGHT LOG: 8 April: Solo flight: 35 minutes in Sopwith Pup #1763. Around Hounslow. Joy ride.

DIARY ENTRY: April 8: Another party tho somewhat quieter.

FLIGHT LOG: 12 April: Solo flight: 1 hour in SE-5 #1942. Around Hounslow. Joy ride.

DIARY ENTRY: April 12: Publey wanders in with Alex Matthews and Mac and Alex fight over Sheila.

FLIGHT LOG: 14 April: Solo flight: 50 minutes in Dolphin #3969. Around Hounslow. Joy ride. Looped and rolled.

DIARY ENTRY: April 14: Big dance at Elysee Gardens.[46] Mac tries to kill an Englishman.

American Officers' Club
9 Chesterfield Gardens W.1
London, England
April 14 1918

Dear Mother—,

Still waiting around and things are going very nicely. I'm pinching my-self all the time for fear I'll wake up and find out it's all a dream. It's really too good to be true. Unless everything falls through I shall consider myself one of the most fortunate men alive. I wouldn't swap places with General Pershing[47] himself now.

Mac and Cal are with me now and we've gotten by with some great stuff. I was having lunch the other day with Lord Athlumney, the Provost Marshal of London, the other day, and of all funny things—well, I'll tell you about it some day.[48]

Yes, we've been doing a touch of raspazassing again. We dined the other night with a British General and a British Colonel. Can you beat it? The Colonel is a Prince—one of the finest I've met for a long time. We took a fancy to each other last week and have been chasing around together ever since.

The lump sugar arrived safely as did another box of Page & Shaws. Please keep it coming.

I saw a brief account of my career in the *Charlotte Observer* which aroused much wrath and ire. And after all I said on the subject! Don't you think you'd better save something for my obituary? I'm thankful I won't have to read what Father will get the papers to print about me. Anyway I'm ready now. I've lived long enough as it is.

A heartful of love to you and Father.

Your devoted son, Elliott

FLIGHT LOG: 15 April: Solo flight: 45 minutes in Sopwith Pup #1763. Around Hounslow. Joy ride.
FLIGHT LOG: 15 April: Solo flight: 50 minutes in SE-5 #1942. Around Hounslow. Forced landing in drome.

3 Charles Street
Berkeley Square, London
April 15 1918

Dear Father—

I regret to have to draw on you by cable but as my movements are so uncertain I thought I had better get the cash. I drew some checks in Scotland and some more down here and several days later dropped into the bank to inquire my balance. They told me but my account wasn't up to date so several days later instead of having a comfortable balance as I thought, my account was nil. Hence the cable so don't be alarmed—I haven't bought the Savoy or anything like that.

Everything proceeds nicely. Mac ran into a pole the other day and stepped out of the worst crash I ever saw—unscratched. The machine was matchwood and was strewn all over the field. 'Twas too bad, as it was a little beauty and had been turned over to the three of us to joy ride in. However we have another one promised us tomorrow. When it arrives I'm going to fly up to Oxford and see some old friends up there.

The bank will continue to be my address no matter where I go so write me there and send any thing you can think of that might be useful. I pulled a terrible bone the other day. I was talking to the Major and I remarked that I had some candy from home and I would send some around to Mrs. Bishop. "Fine," says he, "my car's outside and I'll take it around now." The box had been opened but hardly any taken out so without looking in it I got it and put it in the car. I doubt if I ever [will] hear the last of it. Mac and Cal had been at the candy and had left about two pieces which was all that greeted Mrs. Bishop's astonished eye. However, I took her some sugar yesterday and the Major took all [of] Mac's cigarettes so I think I'm forgiven.

A heartful of love to you and Mother, Your devoted son, Elliott

The following is an excerpt from a letter by Leroy Springs dated 27 March.

My dear Son:

I had a communication from the war department telling me that you had your commission which had been issued over there and they sent your engraved commission as First Lieutenant to me here, which I was very proud to receive. If you wish me to, I will send it to you, but they said it was not necessary. They stated your commission had been arranged by cablegram. I am very sorry it was held up. . . . In fact, it seems to me that you should have had a commission when you went over and had the responsibility of taking charge of the 150 men under you.

I am sorry to hear that some of your friends have met with such sad accidents. There have been a great many accidents in Texas—at Fort Worth, Houston, San Antonio, and several other places. I notice one of the men at Ayr met with an accident several days ago. I hope he was not one of your friends. I feel sure you will act on my advice and be careful to see that your machine is always in good order before going up in it. I am thinking about you, my dear boy, all the time, and wishing everything will come out for the best and I feel sure it will. . . .

I judge that you are taking practice in scout flying from your being located at Ayr, Scotland. As I understand it, that is where all the ships pass through going from America to England and France and it is a beautiful place and a manufacturing town. I notice a great many textile mills are located in that county. . . .

Everything is high in this country and we are doing everything we can to conserve food and encourage farmers to raise more. Almost anything is 300% higher than it was when you left. Common negro labor is bringing $2 a day, so you can readily understand what wages are. Other wages are in proportion and negroes are making more money than they know what to do with. . . .

Now, my dear son, your letters are frequently censored and I would suggest that you do not write such frivolous letters to Lena and me, as the people who censor your letters will not understand it and they are not the kind you should write us. We are glad to hear from you but think you should write us less frivolous letters. . . .

I would suggest . . . that if the government wishes to send you back to this country as an instructor that you do not hesitate to come, as you have been away from home so long that we would love to see you but, of course, you will have to go where the government decides for you to go but I am in hopes, if they wish you to come back to do instruction work, which I know you would be efficient in, that you would not object to same. However, I am sure you will want to serve your country in the capacity you feel best fitted to serve. I would suggest that you mark on the outside of your letters "Officers' Letters," as I understand they will not be censored if so marked. . . .

With love and best wishes for you always, I am

Your affectionate father

3 Charles Street
Berkeley Square W.
London, England
April 16 1918

Dear Mother—

Last night I dreamed I was back at the Vanderbilt. Bellhops rushed to greet me—the clerks nodded as they handed me the pen—three doormen guarded my car—upstairs were two beautiful bottles of Blue Ribbon in a tub of ice—dinner was waiting for me and the headwaiters knew what I wanted without being told—Canadian melon, green turtle, frogs' legs, alligator pear, strawberry ice cream, turkish coffee and a bottle of 102. And then like "Willie the Weeper"[49] I awoke.

And was I sorry 'twas only a dream? Not on your life. I looked out of the window into the dirty London fog and grinned from ear to ear. Much as I used to love New York I'm not at all sorry that it is to see me no more for many a moon. I'm feeling rather pleased with myself anyway and New York is a thing of the past. Fifth Avenue and Broadway have drowned themselves in the memory of their sordid associations.

But London—I can't describe it to you but it has little in common with the city of subways. 'Tis an overgrown town—big and old fashioned but—well, I like it. And I imagine you would too. But I'm leaving and leave regretfully. No, not regretfully because I'm more than anxious to get a shot at the Boche. I want to look the Three Sisters in the face and laugh at them.

Father's letter this morning of March 27 was rather a disappointment. I was hoping for some news. Nothing from you for a week. All right—maybe I'll write again. Tell Father to lay off the excellent advice and brief summaries of the situation at the front. He's all wrong anyway.

A heartful of love, Elliott

[In the margins:] Are you totally dead above the ears. When I send you an address I expect it to be used. Send my mail c/o the Bank and nowhere else. Thanks to your excellent idea of sending mail to wherever I was last month—all my mail at Turnberry-Ayr is lost.

FLIGHT LOG: 17 April: Solo flight: 30 minutes in Sopwith Pup #1763. Around Hounslow. Joy ride. Nearly crashed.

FLIGHT LOG: 19 April: Dual flight: 50 minutes with Capt Horn in Avro #4409. Brooklyns. Over to see [the] Snipe [a new aircraft built by Sopwith].

London, England
April 20 1918

Dear Aunt Addie—

I received your letter and was delighted to hear from you. Everything has been progressing nicely and things have been arranged far better than I dared hope at first. In other words I'm in great luck. I don't know whether it's your praying or my wire-pulling that did it—but something certainly has worked wonders.

The weather hasn't been too good for flying lately but I manage to get up an hour or so a day in some sort of a sky buggy and wander off somewhere for lunch or tea. I'm rather itching to get at the Boche though and hope to get a shot at one before very long. Almost got to go over two weeks ago. Censorship forbids me to say more.

A heartful of love always. Your devoted nephew, Elliott

3 Charles Street
Berkeley Square, W.
London, England
April 20 1918

Dear Mother—

Your letter written "Monday at Lancaster" received and it left much to be desired. You tell me Charlie has left but saying nothing as to the fate of the Stutz. Outside of that there's no comment to be made. Always write me c/o the Bank. When I give you an address please use it.

The weather has not been particularly good lately. Mac, Cal, and myself were up yesterday practicing formation flying and got caught in a snowstorm. Needless to say my face feels like it had been sandpapered. It cleared up and then I went up and did some ground staffing. My engine conked when I was about ten feet off the ground and [I] got quite a thrill. That's how Mac crashed last week but luck was with me and I managed to pancake in a swamp crosswind without doing much damage.

Most amusing thing happened the other night. Nat D. Ayer[50] was around—you've heard of him, haven't you? The famous composer of rag time. One of our flight commanders was here also and he's always very talkative—always recounting some affair. Well he started in—"Now over when I was in Malta, there was a little widow there—." Nat was sitting at the piano and immediately started in to accompany him improvising as he went. The result was a knockout. Do you remember "The Three Trees" from the "Spring Maid"?[51] 'Twas something like that only the speaker in this case was unconscious of the accompaniment. Wish I had a phonograph record of it. Nat is a prince—he invited the Colonel and myself out to his place for the weekend but we couldn't make it.

I'm expecting orders daily and things are going along nicely—.

A heartful of love to you and Father. Your devoted son, Elliott

FLIGHT LOG: 22 April: Solo flight: 40 minutes in Dolphin #3969. Around Hounslow. Formation.

3 Charles Street
Berkeley Square W.
London, England
April 24 1918

Dear Mother—

Still here and things improve daily. And again I'm glad to say I'm still alive. My motor cut out this morning as I was taking off and I was just over a town. I braced myself and decided to try and get between two buildings and thus break the force. Just as [I] was about to cut my switch so it wouldn't catch fire, my motor picked up a little and I managed to limp back into the 'drome before she coughed her last. Poor Tom Mooney[52] was killed that same way four days ago. Too bad—he was an A1 pilot and a fine fellow.

My friend the Colonel is going to be made a general very shortly. I wish I were going to be here when it comes through as it is something which should be celebrated.

These American Mechanics are making a name for themselves over here. For instance the other day, an American Captain was inquiring where he could get a check cashed. A private came up to him and offered to cash it. Cap thanked him and told him it was rather a large check, $300 in fact. "Oh, that's all right," says the Private. "I always carry several thousand around with me." Everyone passed out.

Another time we were on the top of a streetcar waiting in the square. I looked down and saw an American Mechanic talking to a girl. He seemed very serious and they were arguing. He looked up and saw me, pointed towards me, spoke to the girl, saluted, and grabbed the car as it started. He came up to me and saluted and breathing hard, says he, "Lootenant, I ain't got a cent but if you'll pay my way out to the barracks I'll get it there. But sir, I've just got to get away from that girl!" So I did. I'm still wondering what he told the girl—probably that I had beckoned to him.

By the way please send a lot of Page & Shaws. The Major swiped my last box and took it around to his wife. He says if I don't give him the next box, he'll put me under close arrest and make me dine with him while the cook is sick.

I can't write with Larry [Callahan] playing "Nearer My God to Thee" on the piano. Wish Irving Berlin could hear him.

A heartful of love to you and Father. Elliott

FLIGHT LOG: 26 April: Solo flight: 45 minutes in SE-5 #1960. Around Hounslow. Joy ride.

FLIGHT LOG: 28 April: Solo flight: 1 hour 30 minutes in Dolphin #3969. Around Hounslow. Joy ride.

FLIGHT LOG: 29 April: Solo flight: 40 minutes in SE-5 #1960. Around Hounslow. Rolled on top of loop.

3 Charles Street
Berkeley Square W.
London, England
April 30 1918

Dear Mother—

Your letter of the 9th from the Vanderbilt arrived and was a slight improvement on your usual style but leaves much to be desired. I am enclosing a request for a few articles approved by Major Bishop. His approval ought to be enough to move mountains. Also if you can get it through I wish you [would] send a box to Mrs. W. A. Bishop, 52 Portland Place, London, as she enjoyed some of the last box immensely.

Several nights ago Larry and myself were playing Bridge with two charming ladies—and strange to say they both played an excellent game— kept me on my toes—and in the midst of the game there was an air raid warning. And of all amusing things you should have seen us retiring to a subway station carrying with us two camp stools, some oranges, a cake, and a bottle. Imagine the procession!

Larry and myself unwilling to miss anything wandered out to see what we could see, but it was a false alarm so we returned and finished our game. Thank goodness I shall get a crack at the Hun before very long.

I suppose you saw in the papers that von Richthofen, the famous German pilot, has been killed. Everyone says it's too bad he couldn't have been taken prisoner. He's credited with eighty victories. That's the way they all go, a stray shot from some novice gets them. Guynemer, Ball, Boelke,

Immelmann, Pigoud, and the Mad Major have all gone—all supermen—
a startling combination of iron nerve, skill, and daring youth. That leaves
[alive] only two great names who have won the admiration of the world in
the air—Bishop and McCudden.[53]

I was strolling down Picadilly today and thinking of shoes and ships
and sealing wax.[54] I always salute British officers above the rank of Captain so when I saw two British Colonels all covered with red tabs and
medals I gave them my best salute still mentally straffing Huns. Imagine
my surprise when they both saluted me twice and dragged me into a restaurant. 'Twas none other than my friend the Colonel and another staff Colonel
I happen to know. I was still saluting when they got me inside. "Had lunch?"
"No sir." "Come on—sir." Away we go. Two more high officials there and
I began to get slightly nervous. Thought I was getting into a council of war.

However, I enjoyed my lunch and when we got outside some more red
tabs breezed up. They had me saluting with both hands and trying to shake
hands at the same time. Say, can you picture me driving about London in
a General's limousine? They then demanded that I, a Southern gentleman
(supposedly), should prove that I was from the South and show what I
could do to win the war. I pleaded lack of materials. Tut—why be in the
Army? Sugar is all that's lacking. Aha my mother has sent me some. Let
joy be unconfined.

Later they said my life had not been spent in vain and I do not regret
the time wasted in experimenting summer before last.

I sent you a couple of pictures today. Please don't pass them around.
The Colonel says not even a mother could love that face.

The Colonel wins the game easy. He went out at the beginning, has his
lungs full of shrapnel, has been gassed twice and has the M.C.[55] They were
arranging the disposal of his body when he came to the last time. I think
he's got the con[sumption] and won't be with us long.

A heartful of love to you and Father. Your devoted son, Elliott

FLIGHT LOG: 3 May: Solo flight: 45 minutes in Sopwith Pup #1763.
Around Hounslow. Joy ride.
DIARY ENTRY: May 6: To Eastbourne [on the south coast, east of
Brighton] we go.

Grand Hotel
Eastbourne, England
May 7 1918

Dear Mother—

Clarence Fry of Columbia, Tennessee, was killed Saturday and I wish you would send a letter of sympathy to his people. He was a particularly good friend of mine and an exceptionally fine fellow—clever, amusing, and with the heart of a lion. The whole Italian Detachment mourns his loss—particularly the Three Musketeers.

No one has been able to figure out why Larry and myself weren't killed Tuesday but luck again intervened. Mac, who was watching it, said later with tears in his eyes "The only reason you fools are alive is that hell is already packed with aviators." Poor old Mac—he couldn't enjoy it as we did because he was watching it—and I know how he felt because I had to watch him last week doing a spinning tail slide.

I've got a new stunt now. First I loop but instead of completing the circle when I get to the top and am on my back, do a full roll ending on my back again and then dive out of it. It's a very pretty stunt though you wouldn't believe it possible until you've seen it done. Also I have succeeded in looping off the ground at last. I had a pretty stunt some time ago. Do an upward roll, a roll level, and spin out of it. Another fellow tried it though and it cost me five shillings for flowers.

I went down to the hospital the other day to see an Australian friend and who should I run into but young [Bonham] Bostick.[56] Poor kid he's all smashed up. He had just been sent back from France and was just regaining consciousness. I did what I could for him—strawberries, mushrooms, oranges, peaches, flowers, but there wasn't much I could do as his jaw is broken and one eye bruised. The doctor tells me that he will recover and will only have some scars on his face to show for it where it was mashed between the machine guns.

He's a plucky kid, lying there all smashed up talking about going back in a month with a broad grin on his face. I've spoken to several ladies I know who are going around to see him and my batman goes around daily. He's very comfortable now and is getting the best of care. You might write his mother in Switzerland, S.C. that you heard he was all right. Funny my running into him. I told him goodbye three weeks ago when I started over. I was held up on a special job and he went on over. Last I heard of him.

Chick [Chester] Pudrith, once captain of the Dartmouth football team was killed last week. Funny thing—I am the only one that entered that

Boxing Contest at Oxford who hasn't been smashed up. [John] Fulford, [Walter] Stahl, [Elwood] Stanberry, [Donald?] Wilson, and [Burr] Leyson have all gotten it.[57] Chick was the champion, too. One of the best. One consolation—there's some mighty fine fellows waiting on me.

Certainly hightoned the Squadron the other day. We were all out on the tarmac watching some idiot who was up but who couldn't get down again, and up drove Uncle in his new car with a couple more Colonels and a Major or so all resplendent in brass hats and red tabs. We had a flip or so and then I piled into the car and drove away with them. Can you beat it? The Squadron was certainly hightoned and some of the mouths aren't closed yet. This hightoning is great sport.

A heartful of love to you and Father. Devotedly, Elliott

[P.S.] Send me Page and Shaws constantly or forever cease to consider me one of the family. Send it c/o the Bank!!! Why do you think I give you an address. The Major says if you don't hasten it along he'll cross my controls. EWS

DIARY ENTRY: May 10: We return and go to Maidenhead [west of London].

Maidenhead, London, England
May 10 1918

Dear Mother—

Were it not for the Censorship rules I should have a lot to tell you but such being the case you'll have to be content with the knowledge that before you get this I shall be popping away at the Hun with all guns.

No mail from home this past week but am looking for a lot any day now. The pictures in the papers from home never fail to amuse us. For instance today I saw a pictorial section and next to a picture of a French General was a large photo of Miss Lue Moments "who has been very active in Red Cross Work this past winter." We wondered what the General did to have his photo published.

Another large photo was there. At the top "Engaged in the Great Adventure"—and at the bottom—"2nd Lt ____ is a son of Mrs. ____ and a grandson of Mr. ____. Lt ____ is now in the Ordnance Dept somewhere in Kansas but hopes shortly to transfer to Aviation." According to the society papers every man in the Quartermaster, Ordnance or Hospital Corps has "applied for transfer to Aviation." Well as long as they don't do it seriously, we won't bother about it. It almost would seem that putting in an application for "Aviation," as they say, is equivalent to getting your name in the Social Register. I wonder why?

Please tell the Q.M. to lay off it anyway. How do they expect us to develop any esprit de Corps. Well that's the way I feel about it anyway because I just had a fight with one of these Quartermaster Lts and he irritated me considerably.

A heartful of love to you and Father. Your devoted son, Elliott

P.S. In every letter Father tells me how easily he could have gotten me my commission last November. All he had to do was to send someone in Washington a postcard. And yet I got a cablegram from him saying that he was unable to arrange to send me any Page & Shaws!

FLIGHT LOG: 11 May: Solo flight: 1 hour 25 minutes in Dolphin #3969. Around Hounslow. Close formation.

FLIGHT LOG: 11 May: Solo flight: 1 hour ten minutes in Dolphin #3969. Around Hounslow. Close formation.

85 Squadron, Royal Air Force
Hounslow, England
May 12th 1918

Dear Father—

Have been very busy lately but will take this opportunity to assure you that all is well. My new machine came several days ago and I have been a child with a new toy ever since—just like I used to be with a new car—and I've done nothing but tinker with it ever since. It's a beauty and the best part is that it's mine—no one else will ever fly it and no one else has ever flown it. I've been cleaning and oiling my machine guns, tuning up the motor, and testing the rigging continually. Then I got up to test it out in the air. I put her level about two feet off the ground this morning but the motor was new and stiff and I cut off when I got up to 120. Then I went up high and did a spinning tail slide. Nothing broke so I have perfect confidence in it. It cost about $12,000. 'Tis painted green so I have named it the Mint Julep and am having one painted on the side.

Larry has had some trouble with his motor and is beginning to lose sleep about it. Mac had hard luck with his. A Ferry Pilot was bringing his from the works [factory] and ran into the wires as he was landing. The machine was a total wreck and Mac won't get another until tomorrow.

This afternoon I've got to synchronize my gun gears, set my sights, and adjust my compass—then I'm ready. You ought to see the gadgets on it. The cockpit looks more like an engine cab than anything else. Compass, air speed indicator, radiator thermometer, oil pressure gauge, two gas pressure gauges, tachometer, compensator, two gun trigger controls, synchronized gear reservoir handle, hand pump, two switches, pressure control, wheel altimeter, gas pipe shut-off cocks, shutter control, thermometer, two cocking handles for the guns, booster magneto, spare ammunition drums, map case, throttle, joystick, and rudder bar. How's that for something to keep your eye on? Possibly you can understand why flying requires concentration.

Of course, I can't resist the temptation to add a few devices of my own and have also put in a cupboard and shelf for spare goggles, machine gun tools, map, cigarettes, chewing gum, etc. You know when you're in the air for two or three hours at a time you get awfully bored.

Do you remember "Fair and Warmer" that was such a success in New York two years ago? It opened in London last night with quite a famous cast. The leading lady [Billie Carleton] sent us some tickets so we went. 'Twas quite amusing—the English audience always laughed at the wrong time and their idea of American slang was simply weird. Which reminds me that while at Eastborne I went to a show and they sang "Over There" with the chorus dressed in kilts. Can you beat it? George M. Cohan should certainly be shot or hung for writing that song. It's gotten to be like a red flag to a bull to us. He has done more to give Europeans a contempt for Americans than any other thousand men in the country. Tell him so for me will you please.

Yet you'd be surprised to see how well Americans are getting along over here, much better than I expected. We were about the first American troops in England and I foresaw numerous difficulties which seem to have been overcome very well.

Do you remember at the Hanover National Bank when we were getting Italian money a young fellow came in to get some who later joined me at Mineola? A very fine fellow he was, too. He was killed yesterday firing at a ground target. He never came out of his dive.

Please send me Page & Shaw's regularly. If you have so much influence at Washington now is your time to use it. Besides I don't believe that ruling applies to me as I shan't be fighting with the American Army for some time. Also you might send anything else that you care to.

I should also appreciate it if no mention was made in the papers of me at all at any time. If anybody trying to kid you along asks where I am, just tell them "France" and let it go at that.

Well, goodbye—a heartful of love to you and Lena—I'll do my best. Your devoted son, Elliott

FLIGHT LOG: 14 May: Solo flight: 1 hour 20 minutes in SE-5 #6030. Around Hounslow. My new service bus [wrecked].

FLIGHT LOG: 14 May: Solo flight: 20 minutes in Avro #4407. Brooklyns. Over to ferry back 1885—new bus.

FLIGHT LOG: 14 May: Solo flight: 25 minutes in SE-5 #1885. Brooklyns. New bus.

3 Charles Street
Berkeley Square, W.
London, England
May 14 1918

Dear Mother—

Your letter from Hot Springs fanned me to a white heat and confirmed my opinion of all women. Of course it would be ridiculous to expect you to stay at home with Father and miss hearing a paper on "The Relation of Literature to War." The women at home certainly are backing us up!

I had a beautiful new plane the other day and what should I do but go up and smash it all to pieces. However the Major didn't think it was my fault so all is well and I got a new one an hour later and as a matter of fact it proved a much better one and I soon got my guns synchronized and my sights harmonized.

Larry and I were working on our busses the other day when Mrs Bishop and another lady strolled out on the tarmac. We were both very dirty, khaki breeches smeared with grease, golf socks, and shirt (no undershirt) as 'twas warm. But we knocked off for a few moments and went over and spoke to them. The lady with her was most agreeable but we didn't pay much attention to her. Mrs Bishop invited us to tea but we declined owing to our state but she insisted we come along as we were and we did—still in shirt sleeves.

During tea the lady mentioned the fact that she didn't know how to get to town. She said she expected to take the subway in. So I explained to her how she got to it and asked her where she was going. Buckingham Palace she said. After they had gone I asked the Major who she was wandering into Buckingham Palace afoot so nonchalantly and speaking so familiarly about the King. "Oh," says he, "that was Princess Mary Louise."[58] No one fainted but it was quite a surprise to say the least. Mrs Bishop told me later that we made a great hit with her though God knows why.

I wish you would tell Father and Aunt Addie to quit worrying so much about my soul and give my stomach a little more thought. That's the organ that needs careful attention.

I've got a beautiful egg on top of my head from my smash but it's gradually going away now and I can resume social intercourse without explanations.

I am sending you under separate cover a couple of souvenirs of the great war. Someone gave us a farewell dinner the other night and that's the menu with the signatures of some of the guests. Keep it; there are some famous names there.

A heartful of love to you and Father—It's "just before the battle—mother"—again. Devotedly, Elliott

P.S. . . . I got fifteen letters today. Most of them upset me very much. Father doesn't seem to like my letters. You might tell him that I can't say that I enjoy his. Your efforts aren't particularly exciting either. Get busy. E.W.S.

FLIGHT LOG: 15 May: Solo flight: 1 hour 10 minutes in SE-5 #6030. Close formation.

FLIGHT LOG: 15 May: Solo flight: 1 hour 25 minutes in SE-5 #6030. Close formation.

FLIGHT LOG: 16 May: Solo flight: 1 hour 15 minutes in SE-5 #6030. Formation—crashed.

FLIGHT LOG: 16 May: Solo flight: 25 minutes in SE-5 #1885. Testing new service bus.

FLIGHT LOG: 17 May: Solo flight: 1 hour 50 minutes in SE-5 #1885. Close formation.

FLIGHT LOG: 18 May: Solo flight: 1 hour 40 minutes in SE-5 #1885. Close formation.

With 85 Squadron RFC in France

May to June 1918

The first squadron with which Springs flew in combat was 85 Squadron, Royal Flying Corps, led by the famous Canadian ace William "Billy" Bishop. The squadron was initially formed on 1 August 1917 at the flying field at Upavon, at that time the home field for the Royal Flying Corps Central Flying School. The squadron was then moved to Mousehold Heath, near Norwich. Following the pattern of newly established squadrons, its first commanding officer, Maj. R. A. Archer, was given the task of developing a corps of enlisted men to provide maintenance, supply, and basic house-keeping tasks necessary to support an operational unit. In November the squadron moved again, to Hounslow, on the west side of London, and in March 1918 command of the squadron was officially given to Bishop, the officer designated to take the squadron across the English Channel and into combat. On 1 April the squadron was transferred into the newly estab-lished Royal Air Force.[1] At Hounslow, Bishop filled the ranks of pilots with men of his own choosing, a special honor accorded Bishop due to his sta-tus at that time as the second-highest-scoring ace in the RAF, second at that time only to James McCudden.[2]

Bishop chose a number of pilots he knew in the RAF, but he also selected three Americans to join his unit: John McGavock "Mac" Grider, Larry Callahan, and Elliott Springs. Bishop's fondness for Americans may well have come from his upbringing on the Canadian-American border. He was first assigned to 60 Squadron, the first unit with which he flew in com-bat, where he earned his reputation as a tenacious air fighter. In the late summer of 1917 he was reassigned to Canada, to help encourage Canadian efforts to assist the war in Europe, and he was then assigned to the British war mission in Washington, D.C., where he worked with American authorities to develop the U.S. Air Service. He undoubtedly brought increased sympathy for Americans when he returned to England for his next flying assignment.

Although the American military officials in London were initially reluctant to release Americans for service with the British, the fact that Bishop had requested them and the fact that the British training schools had, after all, provided flying and gunnery training for a number of Americans probably combined to persuade the Americans to release the three pilots to 85 Squadron. American authorities released other American pilots to other RAF squadrons as well, especially 84 Squadron, commanded by Sholto Douglas. It is indicative of the kind of support Bishop received from the highest levels of the British government that, when the squadron left Hounslow for France, Crown Princess Mary Louise was present, along with a number of American and British army personnel. It is evident in Springs's letters home that he was excited at the prospect of joining Bishop's squadron and, though he does not say so explicitly, must have adopted Bishop as a model of the kind of scout pilot he wanted to be. Bishop preferred to hunt for enemy aircraft by himself and was not hesitant to attack them, maneuvering for an advantageous position before doing so. Although historians later questioned some of Bishop's claims of aircraft shot down since there was no independent verification, neither Springs nor any other members of 85 Squadron ever doubted the victory claims of their squadron commander.

As the squadron prepared at Hounslow for the war, the pilots first flew Sopwith Dolphins, newly developed aircraft. However, Bishop must have expressed a desire for a more tried and trusted aircraft, and the squadron was soon equipped with the SE-5a, which Bishop had flown in his final weeks with 60 Squadron the previous summer. Reliable and rugged, the SE-5a was praised by all who flew it. Equipped and manned, the squadron departed Hounslow on 22 May and proceeded across the English Channel to Petit Synthe Aerodrome near Dunkirk. Three of the pilots, including Larry Callahan, failed to arrive in France due to accidents or engine problems, but all eventually crossed successfully. For the next ten days the men flew familiarization flights and practiced their aerial gunnery techniques in preparation for being placed on active combat status on 1 June. The squadron commander, Billy Bishop, could not wait for the official start date and, flying on his own, flew across the lines and shot down a German aircraft; by the beginning of June he had shot down a total of five aircraft. Springs, eager to shoot down a "Hun," or German aircraft, decided to fly by himself into France on 31 May and was almost shot down as he narrowly escaped from a group of six German aircraft. Eventually, however, he was successful, as he shot down his first German aircraft the following day.

The squadron moved to a new field, St. Omer, about twenty miles south of Petit Synthe, on 11 June, and there Springs's luck improved: on 17 June he and Grider shared the credit for shooting down a two-seater German observation aircraft, and on the next day he shot down another. However, Springs's normally optimistic spirits were seriously dampened when Grider failed to return from a mission that Springs led on 18 June. As flight leader, Springs felt responsible for the loss of his wingman (his diary entry for that day reads "Mac missing. Oh Christ. Am I to blame"). To add to Springs's feelings of despair, Billy Bishop was recalled to England on 20 June, after only three weeks as squadron commander. Bishop had continued to shoot down German aircraft in great numbers, and on 18 June, concerned that Bishop would be killed or taken prisoner, the British government ordered him to return to London. Bishop was "furious" at having been recalled so soon after he was sent out. To show his displeasure, he shot down several more German aircraft before he left for England three days later. Springs wrote that Bishop shot down twenty-five aircraft during the time that Bishop commanded the squadron in France. However, both the Canadian and British governments believed that he was, by now, more valuable as an inspirational leader than as a fighter pilot. As a squadron commander, he was supposed to direct his pilots to shoot down German aircraft, not shoot them down himself.

Bishop's replacement was an equally famous ace, Edward "Mick" Mannock, who officially reported as squadron commander on 21 June. Unlike Bishop, who believed in flying alone or with one or two wingmen, Mannock believed in flying in larger formations led by the flight commanders, and he quickly put this policy into effect. However, Mannock was shot down and killed on 18 July, less than a month after he had arrived in 85 Squadron. By this date Elliott Springs had long since left the squadron, partly as a result of injuries received on a flight on 27 June, less than a week after Mannock had arrived; his aircraft disabled during a dogfight, Springs crashed near the Nieppe woods, where he received a serious wound to the face when his head smashed into his machine gun during the crash, and he was transferred to the Duchess of Sutherland Hospital at St. Omer. While he was in the hospital, Springs learned that he had been reassigned to the 148th Aero Squadron effective 1 July. Springs had been credited with three and a half aircraft shot down while Bishop was in command of the squadron. Springs had flown with 85 Squadron for only a month, but he had learned much about the war in the air. The next commander of 85 Squadron, Maj. J. O. Leach, led the men until after the conclusion of the war, and because the squadron to which Springs was assigned, the 148th Aero Squadron, supported the British army, Springs was able to visit 85 Squadron frequently afterward.

DIARY ENTRY: May 20: Everything ready [for departure for France] at Hounslow. Run into a bunch at Murray's[3] and we have a party.

DIARY ENTRY: May 21: Make all last final arrangements and then run into Billy Roller at Criterion.[4] Can you beat it—the woman is in love with me? What'll I do? Answer I don't.

FLIGHT LOG: 22 May: Solo flight: 50 minutes in SE-5 #1885. Hounslow to Lympne. All off for France!

FLIGHT LOG: 22 May: Solo flight: 35 minutes in SE-5 #1885. Lympne to Marquise. France!

FLIGHT LOG: 22 May: Solo flight: 30 minutes in SE-5 #1885. Marquise to Dunkirk. 4 machines short.

DIARY ENTRY: May 22: Off for France. Billie Carleton, Babs Helm, Dora and Lillian, Army [personnel:] [Lt. Geoff] Dwyer, [Col. Joseph] Morrow, [Colonel?] Mitchell, to see us off. Larry crashes at Croydon, McDonald at Lympne, Cunningham-Reid at Marquise. The rest of us arrive at Dunkirk, Petit Synthe aerodrome.[5]

85 Squadron
Petit Synthe, France
May 23, 1918

Dear Mother—

Well, England breathed a sigh of relief as we pushed our throttles forward and took the air. Then we turned and dove on the people who had come to see us off and then pointed our noses towards the Promised Land. It was probably the finest day I ever spent. England, a mile below, raced by us all covered with flowers and trees and tiny postcard-like golf courses.

Then the Channel all covered with tiny boats and finally—France. I shouted for joy. Of course there was no one within 100 yards of me but I yelled anyway. Both guns were loaded and I had a life preserver on so felt as safe as in bed in London. Only one thing bothered me, Larry had engine trouble and went down about twenty minutes after we started. He hasn't turned up yet and we're beginning to get worried about him.

I don't think there ever was a squadron that got the send off we did. Two princesses, a couple of generals, several colonels and majors and the 'drome was simply covered with pink parasols. Though there were only three Americans going—Larry, Mac, and myself—two U.S. Colonels [Morrow and Mitchell] and a couple of majors breezed out to see us off—not to see us off but just to be present at the departure. I decorated Mrs Bishop with orchids. She's a wonder—had a stiff upper lip all the time though she knows what she's up against. Princess Mary Louise conveyed the royal Godspeed and a general made a very touching speech. Then goodbye everybody and we hopped in our machines and away we go.

We're very well fixed over here, comfortable huts, nice bomb proof dugout, plenty to eat, and a canal just behind the huts where we can swim. Not bad at all. And last night we had dinner in a nearby French town which made me forget London for a moment.

I hate to tell you, but if home is where the heart is, my permanent residence is No. 3 Charles Street, Berkeley Square, and you will always find me at the Criterion for dinner. If you don't find me there just ask for Ferraro or Luigi and they'll tell you what time I'll be in. I'm homesick for London already and my old cook positively wept when I left. Mac is writing to his sister, Mrs Jacobs of Washington to write to you. But as all women are natural enemies I myself hesitate to make a recommendation to you in regard to the matter. She was originally from Arkansas.

A heartful of love to you and Father. Your devoted son, Elliott

DIARY ENTRY: May 23: Nothing doing and we go up to Dunkirk for
   lunch and pray for [aircraft] mechanics [to arrive] in afternoon.
DIARY ENTRY: May 24: Mechanics arrive and we go to Ft Mardyck for
   a swim.
DIARY ENTRY: May 25: Transport arrives and I am made O/C Drinks so
   go to Dunkirk after a load. We have a big party around 6 gallons of
   eggnog and entertain 88 and 211 Sq.

The following is an excerpt from a letter by Leroy Springs dated 15 April 1918.

My dear Son:

I want to say to you that I appreciate very much the postal cards and letters you write to us. It is very good of you to write to us regularly. Both Lena and I appreciate it very much and are very much interested in your letters. . . . You have been very thoughtful in this respect and your letters are most interesting, except, my dear boy, I wish you would not write frivolous letters and skeptical things to Lena. I do not think you realize that the letters are all censored and the parties who censor your letters will not understand that Lena is only your step-mother and very little older than you and you write to her just as you would some girl of your own age and then it hurts me for you to write skeptical frivolous things. What Lena and I both enjoy is for you to write about what you are doing and your friends. We do not like to receive the letters where you are writing poetry, skepticisms, and frivolous things about life.

I know I have not done my duty in every respect but, my dear boy, I wish you would go to church regularly and would pick up your Bible occasionally and read it. I think you would find it a source of comfort to you and would be what your sainted mother would wish you to do. Do not forget what a life she led and what she would want you to be and think what a comfort it would be to her, if she were living, to know that you went to church at least once a Sunday and that you would read a chapter in your Bible at least once a day. Do this for her sake and remember what a wonderful example she set us in her Christian fortitude and in her absolute faith in what the future would be and bring forth.

I do not like to write you this way but I feel it is my duty and I hope you will give it serious thought, as it will be a great help to you in helping to win this war and you will find it will be a bulwark of strength for you to follow her example. Think what a wonderful thing it is to have faith and to believe and it will be a wonderful help instead of a hindrance to you in your fight for your country and in preserving your life.

Now I do not want to lecture you but I beg that you do not write us frivolous skeptical things but write us more about yourself, your friends, and your duties. . . .

Your affectionate father

85 Squadron
Petit Synthe, France
May 25, 1918

Dear Father—

Well, I'm feeling exceptionally good tonight. I had a nice swim in a canal followed by a glass of eggnog—made with real cream—and I can smell a good dinner cooking and I just got some mail—none from the States, just from England. So I am at peace with the world. We bought a piano today and have a big Victrola[6] so the mess is very cheery and excellently equipped.

I wired you from London to send me 200 pounds more as my account was getting low again and don't want to get caught short again on this side [of] the water. Even in No Man's Land you can make yourself very comfortable with a certain amount of cash and I intend to live in luxury to the last if such is possible.

I can't begin to tell you how glad I am to get out here. I am at last going to fight and earn my salt. And then again I'd rather be out here for other reasons. It's peaceful—everybody is in a good humor and we have a wonderful bunch of fellows or bunch of kids I should say. But we're about the keenest bunch of fighters that's been gotten together for some time. We're all very congenial—get along together fine.

The Major [Bishop] just blew in raising —— because he picked up the wrong tube and used cold cream for tooth paste.

And then again there're no women over here to bother with. Over in England you never could have a real cheery mess because everybody was chasing away every other evening to see some skirt or other and a lot of them had wives in the offing who cramped their style. Over here though there are no skirts on our clothes line and there is no chance that any will darken our horizon for some time to come.

And you know it's a great relief to be sure that it will be at least six months before you're going to see a woman again, that is anything eligible. I don't expect anybody at home to understand what I mean. Some one told me we were fighting for the women and children but just the same I'm not fighting to see any of them soon. I suppose I'll feel differently about it in three or four months but just at present I feel as if I had won the game by default and some one had arranged a big party just for me.

You should see the difference in the Squadron in France and in England. In England the chief consideration is feminine as in the States and the fellowship is somewhat neglected. Over here the detraction and distraction is removed and you can see what a man's world is really like. And strange to say, our social graces improve. We don't lapse into a state of degenerate coma as is the popular supposition. Woman's refining influence is not missed at all. I'm waiting to see the actual effect it will have on us and will write you more on the subject later, though I don't suppose you are at all interested in anything but my promotion and church attendance. Sorry I told you about my Scotch dentist. You seem to have taken it seriously.

A heartful of love to you and Lena. Your devoted son, Elliott

85 Squadron, Royal Air Force
British Expeditionary Force
Petit Synthe, France
May 26 1918

Dear Mother—

I'm still pinching myself to make sure I'm awake but there seems to be no doubt about it. Larry Callahan arrived yesterday and all is well.

Mac [Grider] pulled a good one yesterday. He went up late to practice shooting and he was told there was a ground target in an aerodrome nearby so he went over and fired several hundred rounds at it. A few moments later a voice over the telephone made the air blue. 'Twas the C.O. of the other aerodrome and he said one of our pilots had been over shooting up his wind vane [wind direction indicator] and chasing his mechanics into dugouts and he wanted it stopped because several other machines had seen him doing it and thought it was a grand target and now they were all firing at it. Naturally we've been kidding the life out of Mac.

For mascots we have four woolly little puppies, so fat they can't walk and most comical little beggars you've ever seen. Their mother was a chow and father unknown. The Major [Billy Bishop], Capt Horn, Capt Carruthers, and Mac claim them and spend most of their time trying to tell them apart and torturing them.

By the way the Major has written a book called "Winged Warfare"[7] which will be on sale shortly. I'll send you an autographed copy as soon as I get one. If you run across it in the meanwhile get it. I think it's already on sale over there. The Major says it's rotten but you might find something interesting in it.

We're much relieved to be out here. Mac was about to get married and Larry and myself were rather worried about it. Not that we weren't both in love with the lady ourselves but still we didn't care to have the Three Musketeers mixed up in matrimony.[8] Mac even went so far as to get a license but the lady had the good sense to refuse at the last moment. She was really quite charming and I think Mac was the most cordially hated and envied

John McGavock Grider.
This picture was probably
taken in April or May 1918.
Courtesy of the Springs
Close Family Archives, the
White Homestead, Fort
Mill, South Carolina.

man in London as the lady neglected many admirers for him. She certainly was a wonder.

Must tell you about the stunt Larry and I pulled. We decided that as long as we were going to the Front it would be greatly to our advantage to have someone in London send us things and do any errands for us, order uniforms or equipment, and send us tinned stuff etc. But who could we trust to do this for us? All our masculine friends were not only unreliable but might be leaving any day. So it must be some lady. But naturally you can't ask some casual acquaintance to look out for you and chase about. She must be vitally interested in you. Do you follow me? So Larry and I, four days before departing, decided that we must find some sweet young thing and make violent love to her for four days with the result that she would beg to be entrusted with our London affairs. Mac already had things arranged (and is expecting a large box weekly).

So Larry and I looked about hurriedly and immediately we each found an eligible one. Then we showered them with orchids and unloosed the floodgates. Did they fall for it? You bet they did. They'd never heard anything like it before and even came out to see us off (worse luck). But still they've promised to send us everything under the sun and I think the investment will pay interest. If not, the joke is on us. But even at that, it wasn't bad fun. I made a great hit with her mother. I always did have a bigger day with mothers than anybody else.

A heartful of love to you and Father. Your devoted son, Elliott

P.S. I wonder if my letter sounds different. I'm always in a different humor when I write and I suppose they show it. However I flatter myself that they are letters. Yours and Father's might just as well have been written by a machine to a machine.

The following is an excerpt from an Elliott Springs narrative written many years after the war, apparently for a reunion of war veterans.

SPRINGS NARRATIVE: In June of 1918 I was flying SE5As with the 85th Squadron of the RAF over Flanders. The SE had a 180 [horsepower] Hisso motor and would do 125 over the beach for four minutes at 2400 RPM. It would climb at 1800 RPM to 20000 feet in about thirty minutes. We had a way to lean the mixture and close the radiator shutters and it would stall on a turn at 22000 or at least what we judged to be that height, though we had no way to compensate the altimeter or the air speed indicator. The SE had two guns—a Vickers firing through the prop and a Lewis on the top wing. I had a month at the front during which time I smashed three planes on my own field, did a dozen bomber escorts over Zeebrugge and went high hunting with the great Major Bishop VC, who taught me to stalk two-seaters.[9]

FLIGHT LOG: 26 May: Solo flight: 1 hour 20 minutes at 16,500 feet in #1885. Ypres. Maj Bishop and Capt [Horn] patrol.
DIARY ENTRY: May 26: The Major bags a Hun! Got a two-seater. Major Bishop is unquestionably the greatest fighter of the age. Capt Horn takes us up for a patrol.
FLIGHT LOG: 27 May: 55 minutes at American aerodrome [gunnery practice]. Fired 450 rounds.
FLIGHT LOG: 27 May: 1 hour. Sea [gunnery practice]. Fired 550 rounds.

FLIGHT LOG: 27 May: 1 hour 40 minutes. 13000 ft. Ypres. C Flight
 patrol. Fired 300 rounds.

DIARY ENTRY: May 27: The Major gets two Huns and then takes Capt
 Horn and myself up on a patrol. No success. Capt Benbow missing.

85 Squadron, RAF
BEF, Petit Synthe, France
May 28 1917

Dear Mother—

I am not only well but happy. Yes happy—perfectly happy for the first
time in my short but eventful existence. Nothing could possibly be better
and it would have to be a lot worse before I'd feel bad about it. I got some
mail from England today which pleased me considerably. No, don't be
foolish, none of this babbling flapper stuff—just a couple of kindred souls
write to say that I'm missed and that Uncle has been very gloomy since I
departed.

The major got very fed up after tea yesterday [26 May] so went up for
a flip. He saw a Hun two-seater and shot it down—wings fell off. Capt.
Benbow decided he'd go up this morning and stalk one himself. So up he
goes and proceeds to approach a nice fat Hun unseen. But just about that
time six Hun scouts dove on him and chased him all the way back amid a
hail of bullets. He was awfully fed up about it and came back swearing
vengeance. Most comical he was—still had his monocle on—never flies with
goggles—just his monocle—and raging mad.

The major went up alone again this morning and came back in an hour
having shot down two Huns. He met nine of them and attacked them all.
Both of them went down in flames. He's a marvel, is our C.O. He goes up
and shoots down a couple of Huns and then comes down as calm as you
please and spends the rest of the morning playing with the puppies or discussing Jack Harkaway or Diamond Dick.[10] He's the prince of gentlemen
and I think the greatest warrior of them all. He displays the finest type of
courage, is the cleanest fighter, and the most unostentatious man I've ever
known. A stranger might come into our mess and not be able to tell which
was him for several days. He's a wonderful C.O. as well.

I've just been censoring some letters of the men—the mechanics—and
every one of them writes home how lucky he is to be with this outfit. If
there ever was a happy squadron, this is it. And the Three Musketeers are
simply in their glory. We're the "Colored Troops," as they call us. Over here
all colonials are known as "Colored Troops" by their British friends. This being a picked squadron we have quite a number of them. Two of the Colored

The Men of "C" Flight, 85 Squadron. Front row, left to right: Spencer Horn, flight commander; Thompson; Larry Callahan; Mac Grider. Back row, left to right: Malcolm MacGregor; Elliott Springs. This picture was taken early in June 1918. Courtesy of the Springs Close Family Archives, the White Homestead, Fort Mill, South Carolina.

Troops have shot down Huns already, a New Zealander and an Australian. Our squadron's not doing badly and particularly one flight, which is all Colored Troops.

I'm giving a good imitation of a war horse champing at his bit and snorting for the fray. Not a shot have I gotten. I was up yesterday hunting with the C.O. and Capt Horn but we didn't see but one Hun and he was too far away. To get Huns you have to go out by yourself and go far into their territory.

Speaking of the censorship I ran into some awfully funny things censoring the men's mail. The British soldier has an accepted style of writing love letters and he never varies. They are always very formal and distant with here and there an allusion of the most personal nature. He is always subtle and at the same time laconic. For instance—"Dear May—Hope this finds you in the pink as it leaves me. Should I ever come back to Blighty I would like to see you again. I had some nice times with you. Yours truly Bob." And then he puts in fifty or a hundred crosses which he labels "kisses" and maybe becomes bold enough to add a postscript enclosing much love. All of them indignantly disclaim any intention of mixing in French Society, usually in this manner: "No, I will not have any thing to do with these French women. I have not as yet seen any of them which looks as good as English girls. But all of them is good cooks." And so say all of us.

Another one remarks, "The pilot of my machine is slightly windy. I spend most of my time putting on crazy gadgets for him. Every morning all the other officers comes and looks at it to see what new things he can tie to it. I'm afraid he's going to put a Thermometer on it next to take his own temperature. He already has a calendar on it and two mascots." I'm anxiously awaiting a letter from one of my three men to see what they think of me.

I had a long motor trip the other day. Covered about a hundred miles through beautiful country. Never enjoyed a trip more. My French is improving though at best it's a little slow.

A heartful of love to you and Father—I must knock off as I'm going up on patrol as soon as we've had a swim.

Your devoted son, Elliott

DIARY ENTRY: May 28: Capt Horn gets a Hun. The Major gets two more. Capt Benbow reported shot down over Ypres [apparently Benbow eventually returned to the squadron].

DIARY ENTRY: May 29: MacGregor gets a Hun. Capt Baker crashes. Brown crashes. The Major gets a Hun.

85 Sq RAF
BEF, Petit Synthe, France
May 30 1918

Dear Father—

One of the supernumerary pilots is up looking at the war in my machine so for the moment I am unoccupied and will endeavor to tear off a line or two. I hate for anybody else to fly my machine and this is the first time anybody else has touched it. But the flight commander wants this fellow to look at the lines and get his bearings so when something happens to one of us he will be all ready to take the place. Nice fellow he is and a good pilot— a New Zealander, got the DCM for gallantry under fire when he was in the Infantry.[11]

Buying toothpaste in St. Omer. This painting by Norman Mills Price was made well after the war and depicts Springs attempting to speak French in order to obtain a tube of toothpaste. This incident is reported first in his letter dated 30 May 1918 and then in a War Birds *entry dated 29 May. Courtesy of the Springs Close Family Archives, the White Homestead, Fort Mill, South Carolina.*

We've been doing rather well. We have a score board in the mess to keep track of the Huns we shoot down. We don't count any unless they go down in flames or we see them crash. Already our score is eight and there's a big red 8 staring every one in the face. Pretty good, considering that it's all voluntary, as we aren't supposed to be ready for action until day after tomorrow [1 June]. I think it's a record and the wing commander is tickled to death. I'm going to get a Hun this week or bust.

Mac and I went to a French city the other day to get some things and I had considerable amusement working out my parley-vous. We went in one large store and I strolled up to a very pretty little clerk and opened fire, endeavored to inquire for some toothpaste. She didn't follow me at all nor could she interpret my gestures. Mac in the meanwhile was quite captivated and during our conversation kept on making remarks to me about her. She looked at him as if to say she knew he was referring to her and Mac was having a great time. "She's got a pretty face but a square ankle," he would say and she would shoot him a fiery look. "You've got that come hither look, little one, but your figure would go better if bustles were back in style, etc." It was quite comical.

Finally, I got it out of my system. "Avez-vous du savon pour les dents, si vous plait," or words to that effect. She led the way over to the counter and I got my Pebeco[12] and paid for it, completing the transaction in fair French. Then she says to me in perfect English, "Do you want it wrapped or will you take it in your pocket?" We fled without even waiting to stuff it in a pocket.

The squadron amusement is now diavolo.[13] Somebody found a couple of sets in a village nearby and now everyone is concentrated on it. This is some squadron. I'm still doing things to my machine. I've got a new way to fire my guns now. And being very tired of my bromidic cockpit, full of uninteresting gadgets and gauges, I am now decorating so that I shan't be bored when upstairs.

Quite like old times playing with my bus. Though now instead of the spasmodic assistance of Waddy or Charlie,[14] [I] have three expert mechanics at my beck and call who do nothing but look after my bus. They never touch another and thus far they've been pretty busy. However, unless I bring down some Huns in a few days, I'm afraid they'll lose interest in their work.

Enough this time. I must go and shave and wash up for tea. A heartful of love to you and Lena.

Your devoted son, Elliott

P.S. They are changing the score now as the Major just came down and has shot down two more Hun machines—one scout and one two-seater. He's broken the English record now. However, I'll bet he gets another before dinner. You can always tell when he gets one. When he's coming back to land, if he dives on the mess first we know he's got one. If he dives twice we know it's two. Never have I heard of such a man.

FLIGHT LOG: 30 May: 35 minutes. 13000 feet. Ypres. Oil pressure dud [bad engine].

FLIGHT LOG: 31 May: 25 minutes. Coast [gunnery practice]. Fired 300 rounds.

FLIGHT LOG: 31 May: 1 hour 20 minutes. 16000 feet. Armentieres. Chased home by six Albatrosses.

DIARY ENTRY: May 30 [31?]: Fed up I go on a Hun hunt and am successful. Find six and they chases me home. I'll get them tomorrow.

SPRINGS NARRATIVE: One day [31 May] I had overdone the hunting and found myself five Hun scouts. I took a crack at a straggler and thought I hit him before the other four turned and started peppering me. I went home in a hurry and cracked up on my own airdrome.[15]

85 Squadron, Royal Air Force
British Expeditionary Forces, Petit Synthe, France
June 1 1918

Dear Mother—

Well the joke was on me yesterday but there may be a different tale to tell tonight.

Everybody seemed to be shooting down Huns in rather a nonchalant manner so I decided that it was about time for me to get one. So late yesterday afternoon up I go alone and over to the lines. No activity at all, not a Hun in sight. So I climbed up pretty high and went on into Hunland. Between five and ten miles in I was delighted by the sight of a Hun coming towards me and about two hundred feet below. Imagine how thrilled I was. At first I thought he was a French machine as the markings were indistinct so I flew on straight towards him all ready for action—trying to remember everything I had been taught.

Then to my great surprise I found that I was in the center of six Hun machines, silver-bellied Albatrosses.[16] Imagine my consternation! All reason fled from me and I kept straight on into Hunland climbing for all I was worth while the Huns were circling about me. I hadn't the faintest idea what to do. I knew if I turned I would lose height and come down among the six—I could see the face of one just below me—yet I didn't care to go to Berlin. I knew what the Major would do—turn and shoot a couple of them down and chase the rest of them home—but somehow or other I thought I needed a little more experience before trying that—and besides there would probably be some mail waiting on me when I got back. I wasn't nearly as mad at the Huns as some people are—but at the same time they were displaying no affection for me.

So I dissolved myself into a committee of one to devise ways and means of returning to read my mail with the least possible resemblance to a Swiss cheese. I realized that no one could possibly say "Doesn't he look natural"—and I didn't care if the whole world pointed fingers at me and said "There he goes."

Yes I fled, ignominiously, but how I did it, I really cannot remember. It was my greatest "strategic retreat" and for a while I was busy as the humble little bee. Somehow I dived away, though such is usually folly, and I remember wondering mildly how long before my wings would fall off. I was doing well over 250—motor full on, and the last I saw of the Huns, they had given it up and were going back again to the shelter of their own Archie [anti-aircraft fire]. Meanwhile some kind battery opened up on me and I hastened back to the line and ran into the Major just after he had done successfully what I had failed at so miserably.

So, as a Hun hunter I am the joke of the squadron, Mac is still in hysterics, and the Major wants me to tag along with him next time. Somebody else suggests I tag them after I find them. I'm the Bolivar[17] of the squadron and everyone goes out and claims to find mysterious bullet holes in my plane. But still, who knows—I may bag one of them this evening. I'm going to that same spot at the same time, only higher than yesterday, and stay between them and the sun and then—who knows—I may push one of them down.

From all descriptions they are the same ones that chased Capt Benbow home. They played the same trick on him. My Flight Commander, Capt Horn, just got a check this morning for $90,000 so I expect there'll be a big dinner tomorrow night.[18]

Well, I'll be going out now to test out my motor and guns. I've already had the plane rerigged on account of the strain yesterday.

A heartful of love to you and Father. If you show this letter or describe its contents I hope that my ghost may disturb your sleep forever and bring you two double chins. Your devoted son, Elliott

P.S. There was no mail for me from home after all the trouble I took to get back to read it. I think you and Father have treated me outrageously in the matter of writing. T'would serve you both right if this were my last. And a lot you have to do to prevent you taking time to write to me. Other people find time to do. Four letters last night and none from home! Nothing wrong with American mails. Well, don't write, then. Your letters are hardly worth getting due to the care and attention you devote to them.

FLIGHT LOG: 1 June: 1 hour 5 minutes. 15000 feet. Lille. Major Bishop, MacGregor and I bag Huns. MacGregor 2.

DIARY ENTRY: May 31 [1 June?]: The Major gets one. I get one and MacGregor gets two of the six I saw yesterday. Not bad. I chased the remaining two and got a lot of Archie.

85 Squadron, Royal Air Force
British Expeditionary Force, Petit Synthe, France
June 3 1918

Dear Mother—

I will have to write you about this, 'tis too good to keep. I went back the other day after the six Huns who chased me home and Capt Horn and the New Zealander, MacGregor, decided they wanted to hunt too. So we all went together. Just over the lines we saw Major Bishop and went over and joined him and then we saw my six friends of the day before when we were miles in Hunland. They were in different layers again only this time their scheme did not work, as Capt Horn and I took on the top two ones. It developed into a dog fight and for several minutes the sky was full of lead and two Huns started for home. The Major got one, I got one, and MacGregor got two. I being the furthest in, I decided to get one of the two survivors but after chasing them for about five minutes six more joined them and I decided that discretion was the better part of valor.

Then a new chapter in my life began. I am now a changed man. I got sensations I never knew existed before.

About three Hun Archie batteries opened on me and the whole sky turned black. A barrage appeared just in front of me and I swung around just in time to avoid it. Scared—of course I was scared—scared stiff. Heavy clouds below. Where are our lines? I don't know—what does my compass say? Nothing—turning too fast. Archie all around, dive, climb, and dive again. Where are our lines, quick. Ah, the sun, does the sun set in the east or west? Oriens occido—orient occident—sure it sets in the west. Good, then our lines must be there. Pooof—Pooof, right under my wing tips goes Archie and my heart beats 200 higher. Poof, pooof, he's got my range again—dive quick, then turn and climb. This won't do, I'll run for it. So down goes my nose and with motor full on make for the lines, diving [at a speed of] about 200. Archie's bursts are behind me now. He is not giving her enough deflection. Yes he is. Up we go—fine, he's half a mile ahead now, there he comes back and down we go as he comes up.

After an age, he stopped, so I caught my breath and wondered how to get home, as it was getting dark. I still couldn't see the ground but knowing

Billy Bishop and members of 85 Squadron, Royal Air Force. Bishop is standing at the center, hands clasped in front; Spencer Horn is to his right, hands in pockets; Larry Callahan is second to his left; MacGregor is seated on the ground in front of Callahan. Grider and Springs are not in the photo, which was taken in mid-June 1918. Courtesy of the Springs Close Family Archives, the White Homestead, Fort Mill, South Carolina.

I was on our side of the lines I went down through them [the clouds]—trenches—a ruined village—where's home? How can I find my way home? Fairly easy—the others back already all safe and four Huns less to bother us.

The squadron is not doing bad now at all. Our score is sixteen. Long live the Major. Capt Benbow would have gotten a couple only his gun jammed.

This letter is written for your personal amusement only and may the ghosts of those four Huns haunt you if you show it to any one.

A heartful of love to you and father. Devotedly, Elliott

FLIGHT LOG: 2 June: 1 hour 55 minutes. 17000 feet. Nieuport-Ypres. C Flight first patrol.

FLIGHT LOG: 2 June: 1 hour 40 minutes. 15000 feet. Ypres. Crashed landing.

DIARY ENTRY: June 1 [2?]: I go hunting again with Capt Horn but no success. Crash badly landing. Goodby 1885. Big party we made [for] 211 [Squadron] [for] Bobby Loraine.[19]

FLIGHT LOG: 3 June: 30 minutes. 2000 feet. Rely-Dunkirk. Fetched my new bus [6851].

FLIGHT LOG: 3 June: 1 hour 45 minutes. Patrol—Ypres. Benbow missing.
DIARY ENTRY: June 2 [3?]. Go down to Rely for a new bus. 'Tis a dandy.
Go hunting again but no success. The Major gets two more Huns.

85 Squadron, RAF
BEF, Petit Synthe, France
[Undated; early June 1918]

Dear Mother—

I was censoring some of the men's mail the other day and ran across this sentence: "Dear Bill: You remember the big dog back at Hounslow? Well, he ain't got no master now." The dog referred to was a big mastiff belonging to Capt Benbow and we miss his master very much. He was buried near where he fell, with a cross made of a propeller to mark it.

Every one thinks of the English as having a phlegmatic disposition. Nothing could be further from the truth. It is considered extremely bad form to display the slightest emotion. An Englishman will get news of the death of his brother, son, or father, or the elopement of his wife, be awarded the VC or lose a leg and merely raise an eyebrow. And ten minutes later sit down to dinner and show no trace of any emotion. But they feel anything more than any other race. The Frenchman wears his heart on his sleeve and he is easily moved. The American, self analysis is too difficult, but there is more agitation over the death of one American cadet from a flying accident than over the death on the field of five English heroes. The Colonials are somewhat different but have the same general idea.

For instance, we came down from hunting and counted noses and compared notes and found Capt Benbow was not back. After two hours it was evident that he was down somewhere but we all said "engine trouble" and let it go at that. The next morning, still no news. Finally in the afternoon we got word from an Archie battery up close to the front.

Of course, we all felt pretty bad about it and nobody forgot about it for some time but there was no hullabaloo and the subject has not been mentioned since. No rotten sentimentality about it and yet you'd be surprised how deeply these Englishmen feel things and how much sentimentality they have in their nature. I can't do justice to the subject so will cease.

Later—was interrupted by having to go up on a patrol. Nothing exciting happened as the weather is bad. Archie, however, knows no weather except heavy clouds. . . .

I've another patrol to do and then the three musketeers and the Major and Capt Horn are going over to a neighboring squadron to supper. As it's one of the best squadrons at the front it ought to be quite a cheery evening.

I had a letter from [Robert] Kelly from England today and he hopes to be ready to come out in a week or so. The Major is going to try to get him here. I hope we can arrange it.

You've no idea how much there is to learn about the game. When you get to the front you're just beginning and there's something more to learn about machine guns every flight. And then there's the idiosyncrasies of the Hun to be studied as well as geographical conditions. I lost my bearing for a moment the other day and thought I was just above the lines. Imagine my surprise when I got my map out to find that I was twenty miles into Hunland.

A heartful of love to you and Father.

Your devoted son, Elliott

85 Squadron, RAF
BEF, Petit Synthe, France
June 4 1918

Dear Father—

I received your cable yesterday and suppose by this time you have received my address. I cabled it to you before I left London. Many thanks for the two hundred pounds. If I ever do get leave, I shan't have to take it like the prodigal son.

I had another crash yesterday and my bus was smashed all to pieces so I had to go down to an aircraft park by car this morning and fly my new one back. It's a beautiful bus, the finest I've ever flown and after I get my own gadgets put on and have it altered to suit me, it will be much better than my old one. Luck was with me again and I didn't get a scratch.

Made me pretty mad though. I'd just done an hour and a half over the lines and was feeling much relieved to get back when it happened. I had been getting an awful dose of Archie and you have no idea how it makes you feel. A burst of Archie near you sounds like a loud cough and as soon as you hear it you start zigzagging all over the sky. When you hear it, you know that burst won't get you, it's the one you don't hear that does the damage—but it means that the battery has your range and the next one is sure to get you, unless you fool him and sidestep, or zoom or turn. Then he fires where you would have been but weren't.

It's great sport playing with Archie—if you're in humor for it. You can make him waste $5000 worth of ammunition on you without much trouble. And then think how mad the old gunners must get. I'll never be happy until I get a chance to open up on them with a machine gun. Archie simply goes wild then and spouts in all directions while you spin down on him. But it's not considered healthy—it's like trench straffing, you always get a few bullets in you. Mac just came back a moment ago from looking at the war and found a bullet in his rudder. He says he knows the fellow's hang out that did it and so is going back tomorrow and fill his dugout with lead.

You'd be surprised how personal the war in the air gets. Whenever there's anything doing you always know that each little lead pillet or Archie shell was meant for you personally. And when you fire you don't just fire towards Berlin and hope that some Hun stops it. Nope, you wait till you see a special particular Hun, you may wait three or four days for him, and then you let fly. Meanwhile Mr. Hun has been practicing daily and is ready to do an overturn as soon as you start your dive. Or he may fix it up with Archie to range a certain area and then lure you to it.

The Major got two more this morning, which raises our score to eighteen. There has never been a squadron like this before.

A heartful of love to you and Lena.

Your devoted son, Elliott

FLIGHT LOG: 4 June: 1 hour 45 minutes. Patrol—Ypres. I lead a show. Thompson, Trapp and McDonald.

FLIGHT LOG: 4 June: 1 hour 40 minutes. Patrol—Ypres. Broken valve.

DIARY ENTRY: June 3 [4?]: Fed up again I organize a patrol of my own and chase a Hun about twenty miles in. Then get Archied all to hell. The Major gets one.

DIARY ENTRY: June 4 [5?]: No success at all. Don't see a Hun. The Major and Thompson each get one.

85 Squadron, RAF
BEF, Petit Synthe, France
June 5 1918

Dear Mother—

Just a line for your amusement and edification. Have been doing nothing but Hun hunting lately—sometime alone, sometime with one, two, or ten others. We've been fairly successful. It's a fascinating pastime—also a dangerous pastime. You can't beat this squadron—imagine it—we do our regular work and do it well, and then every body gets filled up, grabs some food, some more ammunition and with a whoop up again we all go to chase the elusive Hun.

Poor old MacDonald, from Canada, had a narrow squeak yesterday. We were up chasing a Hun about ten miles over the lines when his engine conked. However, we were up high and covered his retreat and the wind was with him so he just managed to get across the lines and land in a shell hole just this side. Machine ruined, of course, but he's reported safe. How he did it is beyond me, as Archie was firing at him all the way back and he was always in the midst of it and then when he got near the lines they opened on him with machine guns and rifle fire from the ground.

Poor old Mac, he's had hard luck. First he ran into a steam roller back at Hounslow and smashed it and his plane. Then he crashed badly on the way over and had to get a new bus, and a day or so later another machine landed on top of him and crashed that one. He's been constantly fed up.

I've been made assistant Mess President so now am entitled to the use of a tender any time to run around the country. My duties though are very light—the Mess President looks after the food end entirely.

Larry almost got a Hun yesterday. He and the Major and Thompson took on eight Huns and got two of them. Larry hit his all right, but didn't see him crash so doesn't claim it. The Major and Thompson saw theirs go down and crash. Another pilot went out this morning and had a dogfight with two Huns for a half an hour. No results. He chased them into Hunland and then they chased him back.

A dog fight is a fight where several machines on the same level start a free-for-all scrap and everybody shoots at everybody else until enough of one side are shot down to force them to beat it. Then the others can shoot them down. It's not very good policy, but sometimes you can't help it. The best way to fight is to rush in—concentrate your fire on one man and make sure of him—and get out quick. Then if possible and there's a big dog fight going on—dive down again and pick off another one, etc.

You've no idea how much there is to learn about this game. The ability to fly well and shoot straight are but small beginnings.

A heartful of love to you and Father. Devotedly, Elliott

FLIGHT LOG: 6 June: 1 hour 50 minutes. Escort [bombers to] Zeebrugge. 211 [Squadron]. No excitement.

DIARY ENTRY: June 5 [6?]: Big squadron show. See no Huns but find plenty of Archie.

The following excerpt from a letter by Leroy Springs is dated 15 May 1918.

My dear Son:

I have been right much worried about your being transferred to the British service. Of course, it may be all right, but you did not write me anything about it. I think you should write me a full explanation of it. If you would write Lena and me more news about what you are doing, we would appreciate it more than some of the frivolous things you write. Won't you please write me why you were transferred to the British Flying Corps. I think you stood a better chance for promotion in the American Army but you did not discuss it with me or ask my advice. However, I hope you have done for the best but I think you might ask my advice sometimes and I might be of assistance to you. Won't you please write me full particulars and what you expect to do. . . .

Your affectionate father

85 Squadron, RAF
Petit Synthe, France
June 6 1918

Dear Father—

I received your letter of May 15th and was amused by part of it but can't say that I was pleased by any of it. Where and why did you get the idea that I had transferred to the Royal Flying Corps and if so, why not? I wish I could. But the fact remains that I am still wearing an American uniform and still get my pay, if any, from the American Government.

It seems that it is my promotion that worries you. I came over here to fight Huns and not to get my picture in the home papers and give my relatives something to hightone other people about. Of course, I realize that fighting the Huns in person isn't the way to get promoted, but I won't swap my job for General Pershing's. I shall refrain from giving my opinion of Naval Aviation. . . .

So Lena is all tired out from her Red Cross work? Are you sure it isn't from sitting up late at night writing to me? Tell her I appreciate her frequent letters very much. But I suppose it's foolish to expect her to write to me except when the Red Cross has done something grand or you to write to me except when you have something to jump on me about.

Your advice, I believe, at first, was for me to join the infantry or the Pacific Coast Defense or something like that. After you consented to Aviation because you couldn't stop me, you then advised me to stay as far away from the front as possible and become an instructor or something like that. In New York you were infuriated because I was not going along with Brewster, Pyne, etc.[20] Told me I was all kinds of a fool because they were coming back as instructors.

And now you are peeved because I didn't consult you about transferring to the Royal Flying Corps and discuss it with you at 3000 miles range. And now, if I took after you in the matter of correspondence I would close with brief remarks as to the state of my health. But I hardly feel as inconsiderate as that.

I am not only enjoying good health, but the best of health. I could eat ten penny nails and thrive on them. True, my ears are very sore from high altitudes and long dives and my eyes are rather sore from flying without goggles—you don't wear goggles when you're out hunting and your eyelids get blown about—but everybody more or less has those complaints and they only cause a slight discomfiture. My nerves are in excellent condition due to regular doses of Archie and I have long since quit biting my nails. My moral welfare needs no looking after and besides I am at the front. I'm well amused in idle hours as the company is excellent and there are two other squadrons on the same 'drome here and every night is visitor's night. And every once in a while the Hun comes over and drops some pills to break the monotony. So I have nothing to complain of.

I saw a marvelous sight the other day. MacGregor was below me and to the left and was just opening fire on a Hun. The Hun turned and Mac half rolled and while he was upside down and turning, shot down the Hun. Prettiest bit of shooting I ever hope to see, and I could see the whole thing as I was coming down parallel on another Hun.

You needn't shout it around town but I'm going up this evening and shoot down another Hun if I have to chase him all the way back to Berlin.

The squadron is all excited over the affairs of the canine world. They sent me up after MacDonald when he landed just back of the trenches and he returned bringing a mongrel fox terrier with him. He was born in the trenches, so is a real dog of war and he got him from a Tommy. The Major in the meanwhile found another pup in a nearby village and brought it back with him and an Airdale has wandered in and has been adopted. The Major's pup is of unknown origin, at least part rat terrier, so we have quite a collection—four chows—a Belgian police dog—and a part bull terrier in addition to the aforementioned. And they continually fight. The chows are too fat to be ferocious but are excellent wrestlers and very fond of a free for all. If we keep on collecting we ought to have some remarkable brands of dog before long.

You've no idea how sleepy high altitudes make you. As soon as I finish this I'm going to sleep until time to go hunting.

I saw an article of the Major's in the *Saturday Evening Post* of May 11th. Did you read it? However the wording is not his so don't blame him for it.

I saw in the *London Times* where Lt Fleet had been killed.[21] I knew he was going to be. He was too good to live. You remember that I wrote you I dined with him Christmas in London. A scholar and a gentleman he was, always and he stood out over here much more than he did at Culver. The *Times* has published three articles about him. "A prophet is not without honor"—

Thanks very much about doing what you can to send me Page and Shaw's. Would appreciate some more very much.

As regards your paragraph about publicity I again beg of you to say nothing about me. Yes, I know a lot of other boys write and their letters are published. A fellow told me that his father got someone to rewrite one of his letters and then had it published. Naturally he says he will never write again. You promised me that you would never show any of my letters to anyone and that of course, means that you will not read them aloud or any portions of them. I am only writing with that understanding and if my name is ever mentioned in the papers I should feel very badly about it. Of course, I can't hope for you to see my point of view but please have that much consideration for me.

Your devoted son, Elliott

DIARY ENTRY: June 6: Weather dud so Larry, Mac and I go to Boulogne in search of liquor. Bring back a lot—inside us.

FLIGHT LOG: 7 June: 1 hour 40 minutes. Escort [bombers to] Nieuport. 211 [Squadron]. No excitement.

DIARY ENTRY: June 7: I'm having great difficulty getting liquor.

FLIGHT LOG: 8 June: 1 hour. Nieuport. Motor trouble.

FLIGHT LOG: 9 June: 1 hour 30 minutes. Nieuport. Lots of Archie.

FLIGHT LOG: 10 June: 1 hour 40 minutes. Nieuport. Mac Grider gets a Hun.

85 Squadron, RAF
BEF, France
June 9 [10?] 1918

Dear Mother—

Should I ever write a story of the war, I think I should call it "The Dawn Patrol" or "The Twilight Hunt." This morning I rose at three-thirty (two-thirty real time) and at six I was back for breakfast and the Huns had wasted a thousand pounds worth of Archie shells on us. Our hands might have been a touch steadier as we raised a coffee cup but still a little exposure to Archie gives you a wonderful appetite and this Archie gunner was not an amateur—he was a good shot—no beating about the bush with him—his first shot almost made me loop—but after that dodging was fairly easy—and besides the sun was in his eyes.

And then before breakfast I went over to a farmer's house and got some cream—shredded wheat and cream for breakfast—can you beat it—out here where there's supposed to be a war on. I breakfast as at the Vanderbilt. I taught the cook to make eggs Benedict.

But again at eleven I had unmistakable proof that there was a war on and Mac distinguished himself by filling a Hun full of lead bullets. A dog fight developed and Mac was upstairs guarding the others when a Hun dove on him from somewhere he had been waiting. Mac saw him in time and turned quickly which threw the Hun's sights off. The Hun went on by and half rolled down onto his tail. Mac continued turning to keep the Hun's sight off him and then they turned around and around each other maneuvering for position to open fire. After a while the Hun tried to half roll out and Mac let him have it at close range. The Hun went down on his back with Mac still popping at him and was last seen headed towards his future home and breaking all records. Jolly stout effort, as my English friends say.

The dog fight sent another Hun to his doom and all our machines returned safely.

Cunningham-Reid, our pink-cheeked infant, commonly known as Lady Mary, decided that it was high time that he shot down a Hun so went up in search of one the other night. The result has caused much merriment. He found plenty of Huns all right, enough to last him several weeks if taken singly. As near as we can figure out, some of the Huns must have gotten in each other's way getting to him. Either that or their wings fell off when they tried to dive after him. Anyway he's back and is another welcome member of the "sadder-but-wiser" club.

Trapp, a Canadian, met two Huns and chased them home, then they turned around and chased him back. 'Tis great sport.

The only startling thing I've managed to do is shoot my own propeller full of holes. However, it brought me home.

Father asked me in his last letter about my pay. I forget how many francs I'm getting—about a thousand a month I think without flying pay. However, I'd pay twice that for the privilege of doing what I am. And if I didn't like it, there's not enough money in the world to induce me to do it for one day. Pay is a different thing in the Aviation corps to any other. A very good pilot can't be paid enough and a dud pilot is a serious liability—he can prove exceedingly expensive though the good ones are certainly enough expense as it is. . . .

I am getting very very tired of reminding you that I consider and only regret that you should write to me occasionally. I'm fed up with your neglect.

A heartful of love to you and Father.

Your devoted son, Elliott

P.S. The Scotch dentist was a good Christian all right but a rotten dentist. After losing his plugs I decided to locate an army dentist over here. I did yesterday. He was a rotten Christian but a good dentist. He seems to appreciate that with my mouth full of gadgets I could not possibly express my thoughts. So he endeavored to help me out and ease my mind. I certainly forgot my pain. Had I three tongues lubricated with honey, I couldn't equal his outpour. He fairly blistered the walls and I am sure his instruments need no further sterilization. Anyway I am sure that's all they get.

In a weak moment I sent you two photos. We were all feeling very simply, hence the expressions. But we had just decided that the fates could never be so kind to us again and that our physiognomies should be preserved.[22] As soon as Larry gets a Hun now we'll have another taken bearing our spoils.

DIARY ENTRY: June 10: Orders arrive for us to move [to St. Omer, a field about twenty miles south of Petit Synthe]. We pack then wait til tomorrow.

FLIGHT LOG: 11 June: 30 minutes. Dunkirk to St. Omer. Changing station.

DIARY ENTRY: June 11: We fly to St. Omer and dine in town at Officers' Club. Transport arrives and all is well. Good quarters—Nissan huts but rotten drome.

FLIGHT LOG: 12 June: 45 minutes. Looking over country. Thompson leading again.

DIARY ENTRY: June 12: Thompson leads a practice patrol about 20 miles back of the lines.

FLIGHT LOG: 13 June: 1 hour 55 minutes. Ypres to Nieppe. Saw 9 Huns too far over.

FLIGHT LOG: 13 June: 1 hour 50 minutes. Ypres to Nieppe. Hall missing.

DIARY ENTRY: June 13: C Flight muffs one. See 9 Huns below me. Capt Horn's guns jam and we follow him off. All of us get lost. Mac [Mac-Gregor] returns in four hours.

85 Squadron, RAF
BEF, St. Omer, France
June 14 1918

Dear Father—

You can't appreciate the RAF until you see a squadron on the move. The other morning I came back from a dose of Archie without suffering from his hate about six o'clock and, after a good breakfast, strawberries, shredded wheat, and cream, I got tired of baseball and decided to take a nap. About ten, my orderly, bat man or valet, as you choose to call him, shook me and said, "Orders has come, sir, that is to move at twelve o'clock, sir." At four thirty we landed at our new aerodrome. We didn't get supper in the new mess but had breakfast the next morning. We were comfortably fixed by noon. Rather remarkable, isn't it.

Our new quarters are very comfortable. We are up on a wooded hill just above the drome and a pretty glade on the other side of us where we can lie in peace and snooze in the breeze. Not bad at all.

I am learning many things, especially that discretion is the better part of valor, not only the better part of it but about 99% of it. When there are about four Huns above and your immediate vicinity is full of lead and you can see the tracers streaking by you and going behind your wings, well, my boy, it is time to go home. Never mind trying to shoot one of them. Go home and try again tomorrow. How to get home. You are far in Hunland and lonesome. If you put your nose down and head straight for home, you will never tell anyone about it. All the Huns will get a shot at you and you will look like a sieve.

Well, first turn back over 90 degrees and keep turning. They can't keep their sights on you then. Watch the sun for direction and now there's one on your right. Shoot at him. No, don't try to hit him, just spray him for if you try to get your sights on him, you'll have to fly straight and the others will get you. But you put the wind up to him anyway and he turns. Quick, turn in the opposite direction. He's out of it for the moment. Now there's

85 Squadron, Royal Air Force, St. Omer, France, June 1918. From left: Cushing, Dymond, Daniel, Canning, Malcolm MacGregor, Larry Callahan, Elliott Springs, Spencer Horn, Randall, Baker, Cunningham-Reid, Longton, Ross, Carruthers, Dickson, Brown, Brewster, unidentified, Abbott, Donald Inglis. The squadron's SE-5A aircraft are lined up neatly behind them. Grider does not appear in the photo, which indicates that it must have been taken after 18 June (the day Grider failed to return) but before Springs left the squadron. Billy Bishop is also not in the photo; apparently he had left the squadron by this time but his replacement, Mick Mannock, had not yet arrived. Courtesy of the Springs Close Family Archives, the White Homestead, Fort Mill, South Carolina.

another one near you. Try it on him—it works. Turn again, you are between them and the lines. Now go for it, engine full on, nose down.

Two of them still after you—tracers getting near again. Pull up, zoom, and side step and if necessary spray one of them again. Now make for home again. If your wings do not fall off and you are gaining on them, pull up a little. Ah, here's Archie, that means they're far away—woof—that one was close—better turn. You laugh at Archie now—he's a joke compared with the machine guns. You dodge him carefully and roll in derision and hasten home, that is, if you can find it.

That is discretion—many a man has gotten one or even two only to lose to the others.

I have a new motor in my bus which is giving me quite a bit of trouble. My other one chewed up a piston one day but I got back to the drome all right. However, I hope to get it going properly this afternoon. I am rather worried about MacGregor. When I last saw him, we were going down on nine Huns about fifteen or twenty miles the other side of the lines. He got away from there all right I think but it's three hours since I got back and no sign of him yet. I imagine he had engine trouble. If he only gets across the lines! He may have gotten lost. We are all rather anxious.

Oh, I forgot to tell you, we have another dog, even more disreputable than the others. Nationality unknown.

A heartful of love to you and Lena.

Your devoted son, Elliott

P.S. We just got word of MacGregor. His engine was dead but he got across the lines and landed about twenty miles away from here all OK. Quite a relief.

FLIGHT LOG: 15 June: 1 hour 55 minutes. Ypres to Nieppe. Capt Horn gets a Pfaltz. Larry [Callahan] gets a two-seater.

FLIGHT LOG: 16 June: 1 hour 50 minutes. Ypres to Menin. Thompson missing.

FLIGHT LOG: 16 June: 1 hour 45 minutes. Ypres to Nieppe. Nothing doing.

FLIGHT LOG: 16 June: 1 hour 50 minutes. Nieuport to Armentieres. Canning is crazy loves Archie.

FLIGHT LOG: 17 June: 1 hour 50 minutes. Houlshorst to Nieppe. Grider and I [and Callahan?] get a two-seater in flames. (II)

DIARY ENTRY: June 15 [17?]: I lead Mac and Larry to victory. A Flamer!

SPRINGS NARRATIVE: One morning [17 June 1918] I went out early. Mac Grider and Larry Callahan were with me and it was my turn to lead. We crossed the lines above the clouds at 15000 and I saw a flash of light about five miles ahead of me and 2000 feet below. I waggled my wings and pointed and we all went down wide open. It was a Hun two-seater and we converged on him with six guns roaring. The observer was starting swinging his guns but he didn't have a chance. The plane exploded when I wasn't fifty feet above him. Archie opened up on us then and we hurried home but there was a column of smoke all the way to the ground.[23]

REPORT: Combats in the Air, 85 Squadron: 17 June 1918, 6:45 AM. Location: South of Merris, SW of Bailleul; Line Patrol at 2000 feet. Enemy Aircraft brought down: Two-seater. When at 7000 feet I saw EA about ten miles the other side of the lines S of Merris flying northwest. At about 2500 feet I turned and flew towards him and he put his nose down towards our lines. I approached from the east and opened fire at 40 yards range. Tracer seemed to be going into the fuselage and flames burst from EA just back of pilot's seat. He crashed and continued to burn near a crossroad. Kill shared with Grider and Callahan.[24]

85 Squadron, RAF
BEF, St. Omer, France
June 17 1918

Dear Father—

Well, the last few days here have been very eventful. Being confident that you will treat this [as] confidential, I'll tell you about it.

To begin with we went up on a patrol early yesterday morning and just across the line we saw a Hun two-seater. Capt Horn was leading the patrol and signalled to us and then dove after the Hun. He missed and I was the next to get to him. He turned sharply before I got in range and I half rolled to make sure of him. In the meanwhile Callahan just behind me turned higher up and dove squarely on him. The Hun turned over on his back and dove into the ground crashing into some ruins. Then Archie opened fire on us and we scattered for our side of the lines.

We climbed up high and about half an hour later saw about thirty machines in the sky in different layers. Six machines of ours were in the middle layer and we saw them dive on the lower ones. Then I saw one of the Huns above dive vertically for 3000 feet and flatten out and open fire right on the tail of one of our machines. Most wonderful sight I ever saw. I wouldn't have believed it possible. But one of our machines got on the Hun's tail and got him.

About that time we reached the scene of battle and went in. There were machines circling and firing all about us. Worst dog fight I ever saw. Everybody firing at everybody else. Then suddenly everybody pulled out on both sides and Archie opened up. A new bunch of Huns came up and in we went again but there was little action and too much confusion this time. Capt Horn and I went down on one and he got him. The Hun went down in a spin and crashed into a wood. The other bunch shot down two and had one of their men shot up but he got back to our side of the line. MacGregor shot up his own machine but glided back to our side of the lines.

In the meanwhile, the Major went up alone and shot down three Huns; two went down in flames and the other lost a wing.

Then this morning Capt Horn let Callahan, MacGregor and me go out together.[25] I was leading and we flew around for an hour without seeing anything within reach. Then all of a sudden when I had about given it up, I spotted something about two miles in Hunland. I signalled the others and went for him. It turned out to be a Hun two-seater and when I was about 400 yards away and 1000 feet above he turned and the observer stood up and opened fire on me. Remembering my mistake yesterday, I went behind him and turned and dove right on his tail. I could see the observer travers-ing his gun frantically and plastering the sky. Mac in the meanwhile came straight down and Callahan was just behind me. I opened fire at about twenty yards range and after about fifty rounds he burst into flames just back of the pilot's seat where the petrol tank was. So I pulled away but not before I could feel the terrific heat of the flame. Mac had also been plaster-ing him from immediately above and pulled up just before I did.

We were so low then that the machine guns on the ground opened fire and I had the pleasure of seeing a few tracers whiz by. Thank goodness we were too low for Archie.

The Hun crashed from a spiral and flames shot up twenty five or fifty feet high.

So we all met again on this side of the lines and flew gaily home feeling very proud of ourselves.

As near as we could figure out, Mac and I both got the Hun so we shared him and each of us have half a Hun more to our credit. The Major in the meanwhile got two Huns and Lady Mary got one. After Lady Mary got his, his motor cut out and he had to land in Hunland. He made a bad landing and jarred something and broke his landing wires and his motor started again and he got back—thoughtfully assisted by machine gun fire from the ground.

I would appreciate a letter from you regularly.

A heartful of love to you and Lena.

Your devoted son, Elliott

FLIGHT LOG: 18 June: 1 hour 55 minutes. Menin to Estaires. Grider missing but I get the Hun. (III)

FLIGHT LOG: 18 June. 1 hour 55 minutes. Ypres to Nieppe. Saw a two-seater but Capt H[orn] didn't.

DIARY ENTRY: June 18: Mac and I doing high protection spot a Rumpler near Menin. We get it. Mac missing. Oh Christ. Am I to blame.

DIARY ENTRY: June 18: Capt Horn won't believe me when I tell him there's a two-seater over Estaires so I don't get it. Wish I'd gone after it anyway.

SPRINGS NARRATIVE: The next day I went out early again and it was Mac Grider's turn to lead. Callahan had motor trouble so we were alone. Mac did the same thing again and flushed another two-seater. We both hit him at the same time and he went down but didn't burn. There were heavy clouds between us and the lines so we ducked into them. After a few minutes I went out of control because we had no gyroscopes and I spun down about 10000 feet until I came out of them [clouds]. Archie started shooting at me as I headed west for the coast and finally got my bearings over Calais. We never had any word from Mac. We had already lost Benbow and Thompson and I got hell for losing Mac from the flight commander, Captain Horn, though I wasn't leading.[26]

FLIGHT LOG: 19 June: 2 hours. Ypres to Nieppe. Major Bishop gets five Huns.

DIARY ENTRY: June 20: Bishop gets five making 25 in all and we all [travel] to Boulogne to see him off [Bishop was recalled to England]. Everything is going wrong now. Late patrol sees nothing but Archie.

85 Squadron, RAF
BEF, St. Omer, France
June 20 1918

Dear Mother—

. . . I was already in a very bad humor when the paper [from home] came. In the first place I got up at three. Wouldn't Father be pleased to see me spring lightly and exultantly from my couch at that hour! And in the second place the Major has been recalled. Three days ago the order came. They think he's too valuable a man to fight the Huns in person. Perhaps they're right—I'll bet the Huns think so too.

But he certainly showed what kind of stuff he was made of. First he raised unshirted hell about it but it was no good. Then he went up and shot down two Hun machines. The next day he got his orders and ticket. And he went up and shot down three Huns. So today he was to leave at noon and everybody felt pretty bad about it. But he went up at ten o'clock and attacked five Huns. One of them got away by going into the clouds. Then on the way home he saw a two-seater and shot it down in flames. He saw some Hun infantry resting on a road so went down and shot them up regardless of the fact that we lost a good man that way last week and had three planes out of four shot up.

So our Major is gone but if ever a C.O. had the respect, admiration, and love of his unit 'twas him. The mechanics even are disconsolate. He has shot down seventy-two Huns now—twenty five in the past three weeks. And he's made something of this squadron too. So much so that our new Major—who isn't coming for two weeks—is the next best man in the RAF [Mick Mannock]. We all know him and like him. As a matter of fact he tried to get the Three Musketeers to come out with him in his flight when he came out as a Captain in April.

And now in the third place—the worst—the worst possible. Mac Grider is no longer with us. Mac and I were up high protecting an offensive patrol yesterday. We were a couple of thousand feet above and when we were well over the lines I saw a Hun two-seater not so far away. I signalled to Mac and we went for it. I got there first and attacked. I held my fire until I got right on his tail and I could see the observer standing up and firing at me. Then I let him have it—both guns—right into the observer's pit—about 220 rounds—I could see my tracer going into him. Then I had to pull away to fix my guns. I turned around and saw the Hun go straight down and crash into the ground and Mac was just above the scrap turning too.

So I started back for where the lines were, steering by the sun. I looked back and Mac was following. After five or ten minutes I got my bearings and got back to the patrol. But that's the last I've seen of him. I decided he'd gotten lost and [I] went after another two-seater later—no success— and when I returned, still no sign of Mac. I imagine his motor cut out—I don't think Archie could have gotten him—I saw no more Huns about— and I think I killed the observer so I don't believe Mac got hit.

Of course many things might have happened—Mac might have been firing at long range from above and shot up his own prop or gotten a burst in his motor from the observer—or gotten hit by Archie, or lost his way, or attacked another Hun a half an hour later. That's the worst of this game— the uncertainty of it. But I feel sure that Mac is personally safe wherever he has landed. He's a prisoner all right but no one knows how I miss him. No man ever had a truer friend and the fact that we fought together and in unison and harmony shows the confidence we had in one another. And he was as fine a fighter as ever tripped a trigger.

I remember once in Oxford Mac threatened to thrash [an Englishman] if he ever heard him criticizing my method of commanding again. The fellow took it so seriously that he came over and told me what a good commander I was.

Mac is gone but he'll never be forgotten until the Hun's aim improves or my bus goes back on me—or I pass out from irritation at the doings of the Springs family on the home front. I wonder why they don't withdraw the Armies from the field and let the Red Cross fight and win the war for us.

Anyway I hope my ghost haunts you and never gives you a moment's peace. You have all the time in the world to make speeches and run around to hen parties called conventions where they fight the battle of social precedence and waist measurements and yet you have the nerve audacity and bad taste to write me that you have been abed resting from your strenuous labors. I could sleep with great ease right now—three hours' sleep last night. But instead I'm writing to you until time to go up on patrol at seven and try to avenge Mac. May your powdered nose take on the color of an overripe tomato and may you never see your feet again except in a mirror!

I'm completely fed up with you.

And yet somehow I think to myself—there's the folks at home having a lonesome gloom fest around the fire—tired, dusty, bedraggled and footsore from this terrible campaign—and it's the least I can do to drop them a line and try to cheer them up and I'll censor them myself so Father need not worry about the censor's childlike faith in this just-before-the-battle-Mother and you-look-after-the-little-girl-for-me stuff being shaken. And then too Father can say to Mr. Brewster, Mr. Robertson, Mr. Ellis, etc not "my son is slated to be first assistant to the Carbon Paper Purchasing Department" but "my son to my great surprise has proved to be unselfish and in a measure considerate of his family. Integer vitae scelerisque purus."[27] Of course I can't imagine Father saying that but still it's a pleasant thought to contemplate.

A heartful of love to you and Father.

Devotedly, Elliott

FLIGHT LOG: 21 June: 1 hour 20 minutes. MacGregor is also fond of
   Archie.
FLIGHT LOG: 22 June: 2 hours. Great scarcity of Huns.

85 Squadron, RAF
BEF, St. Omer, France
June 22 1918

Dear Aunt Addie—

I'm still alive and this is the proof. Also I'm very well, in the pink of condition as a matter of fact. I look like an overfed Billiken[28] and could eat even you out of house and home. My appetite now is just what you used to think it was when you fixed a dinner for me. Then you used to feel that I didn't do justice to it, and now you would blush because you only had one turkey and three chickens and two cakes cooked. After which I would start chewing the table and chairs just to show you how good my digestion was. After all there's nothing like a little dose of Archie (shrapnel and light explosive) to improve it. He may not come anywhere near you but you won't worry at lunch later whether strawberries will upset you or not. And I've come to believe that people who like their meal hours regular are un-necessarily fussy. If our meal hours vary by less than two hours daily it's because it rains.

A heartful of love.

Your devoted nephew, Elliott

FLIGHT LOG: 23 June: 1 hour 50 minutes. Great scarcity of Huns.
FLIGHT LOG: 23 June: 1 hour 45 minutes. Great scarcity of Huns.
FLIGHT LOG: 24 June: 1 hour 55 minutes. Got a two-seater beyond Kem-mel (IV)

85 Squadron, RAF
BEF, St. Omer, France
June 24 1918

Dear Mother—

Your letter of the 2nd arrived from the Vanderbilt and contained little more than a futile attempt to spread ink over some paper. I'm surprised that you even took the trouble to write at all. And I don't suppose Father has been able to locate a stenographer to tear off a few lines to me. Haven't you been getting any mail from me at all? Apparently not. If you have, you are wonderfully appreciative—I suppose you are heaping coals of fire on my head.

I'm not in a particularly good humor. I got eight letters this morning—not one of which was worth opening except one from the Colonel [Bishop?]

in London. In fact I started to throw most of them away unopened. I'm
fed up.

And besides we spent an hour and a half playing hide and seek with six
Huns a while ago. We were at about ten thousand [feet] and saw them
coming towards the lines considerably above us. We piled into a cloud and
circled around—got between them and the sun and climbed up above
them. Then just as we were about to dive on them and annihilate them,
they saw us and down went their noses homeward bound! A minute more
and we would have had them.

So back to our side of the lines we go amid a hail of Archie—I got a
burst ten feet from my tail—and wait. Sure enough, here they come again,
looking for some cold meat. Again they see us and retire with great haste.
Then we saw them making for another part of the lines and we beat it
down there in time to see them go into the clouds. Down we go only to
drive Archie mad and start him throwing up the earth at us. Finally we
got fed up and came on home in disgust. Saw another of our machines
shoot down a balloon though—wonderful sight. It blew up in flames at
about 1500 feet.

If I were the Kaiser I'd fire the whole Hun Flying Corps. This morning
five of us had to go about seven miles into Hunland pretty low and all
the time there were seventeen Huns sitting up in the sun and they never
attacked us. I wish five of us could get above seventeen of them! One of
them did come down and shoot Trapp up a bit, but he only tried it from
very long range and he did no damage. Long range is no good—hereafter
I don't think I'll bother about opening fire at more than 50 yards range.
The Major says hold your fire until 25 yards if possible. . . .

Just before the Major left we gave a little dinner party to some friends
from far and near and as assistant Mess President and representative of
Bacchus I feel justly proud of the dinner we set before them. Listen:

Soup
Filet of Sole
Potato Chips
Broiled Chicken
Fresh Peas
Cauliflower
Hearts of Lettuce and Tomato Salad
Strawberry Ice Cream (I drove 80 miles to get the freezer) and
An unlimited supply of strawberries
Camembert and Roquefort Cheese
Coffee

How's that, now really? And the vintage was 1906 and I managed to get together an imitation Bronx. Are we proud of our mess? I should say so. And last night we had Broiled Lobster, Filet Mignon, and strawberries as sort of three side dishes. After which we had a little Mozart, Beethoven, and Tchaikovsky on the piano and then toodled off to bed after a game of ball—it's light here until ten thirty. Not a bad life.

That is so long as we have good jobs to do. But if you know you're going ground straffing the next day you don't sleep as well as you might. That's the job we all hate. I'll write you about it sometime but it's not a pleasant subject.

Order up three plates of strawberry ice cream for me and three bottles of Blue Ribbon. Our strawberry ice cream is nearly as good as the Vanderbilt's but there's no Blue Ribbon, Alas! And I can't get any more shredded wheat.

A heartful of love to you and Father.

Your devoted son, Elliott

P.S. Had a letter from Jimmie [Latham] the other day. He's a sergeant in a French Transport Corps. Also one from Bob [Lamont] who is at an Agricultural College somewhere out West. Jim Warren is married and Pabst is still in Italy.

FLIGHT LOG: 25 June: 1 hour 40 minutes. Uneventful.
FLIGHT LOG: 25 June: 1 hour 40 minutes. Top flight [cover] for B Flight.

85 Squadron, RAF
BEF, St. Omer, France
June 25 1918

Dear Mother—

All well and happy and lots of scrapping and I'm getting so fat I think I'll have to diet. Am in a hurry—not much to say—except I want you to send all mail to the Bank—its quickest and surest and when I go to another squadron I won't lose it all. My last crash the propeller was not so badly damaged and I am having you a picture frame made out of one tip of it. It's mahogany and walnut and ought to be very pretty.

A heartful of love to you and Father.

Your devoted son, Elliott

P.S. Frances' [Robertson] birthday is the 3rd of August. Would you please send her a box of candy with my card. Never mind why—just please do it. E. W. S.

FLIGHT LOG: 26 June: 40 minutes. [Flew to] Petit Synthe. Larry and I run up for beer.

85 Squadron, RAF
BEF, St. Omer, France
June 26 1918

Dear Father—

Have not heard from you for a couple of weeks but suppose that pressing business has prevented your writing. By the way, think you'd better write me care of the Bank as my mail comes through quicker that way and it prevents miscarriage of it, as there's no telling where I'll land next.

Things have been much the same. I arose this morning at three so have that week-end-in-the-city feeling as I drank too much coffee before going up and consequently couldn't get back to sleep when I came down. Poor old McDonald returned yesterday after four days' absence. He got lost on the other side of the line and finally found his way back but landed about 150 miles away. His engine went dead next day so we had to send a truck after him, take his plane to pieces, and bring it back in the truck. In the meanwhile he had the time of his life. I'm seriously considering getting lost myself, somewhere near Paris preferably.

I had rather a surprise yesterday. I was some distance back of the patrol and saw a Hun two-seater about three miles across the lines so went for him. I expected [to spend] about 30 seconds close quarters under his tail and then watch him go down in flames. It looked like cold meat. So I started my final drive about 2000 feet above him.

But not so. I had picked the wrong Hun. It resulted in a duel lasting about five minutes and in the end the Hun only dove into the ground from 1000 feet. I hope the pilot is still alive, he was certainly a stout fellow; if his observer had been a good shot I wouldn't be writing this now. However, I don't think there's much chance of his having gotten out of it alive.

But to return to the narrative. Just as I was about to open fire the Hun turned sharply to the left and as I was doing about 200 I couldn't turn. So I pulled up and half rolled and came down on him again. He turned up to the right and forced me on the outside arc giving his observer a good shot at me as I turned back the other way to cut him off from the other side. I tried a burst from the turn but my shots went wide. So I pulled up and half rolled on top of him and opened fire from immediately above and behind. He stalled and side-stepped me but at the same time giving me a non-deflection shot at him. In other words, I didn't have to make allowances for his speed though his observer had a dead-on [shot] at me.

I think I must have hit his engine or tank for he went into a spiral and never came out until 1000 feet. Anyway he had no power and it was simply a question of getting in the final blow. So I kept on firing at him from every conceivable angle and even got so exasperated that I threw an ammunition drum at him (which I don't suppose missed him by more than 500 yards). Then the rest of the patrol arrived and four of us kept a steady stream of lead into him. I left him at 1000 feet as he was apparently done for and I was afraid of machine gun and field gun fire from the ground. So toodled back and joined the patrol carefully escorted by Archie who simply went mad.

The remarkable part of it was that no Hun scouts dove on me. I kept watching the sky all the time expecting a Hun patrol to come down but think a patrol of our machines up high kept them away. Capt Horn and MacGregor witnessed the fight from 18,000 [feet]. Box seats they call their position.

[Part of the letter is missing] . . . descended low over the trenches and had a sham battle among ourselves. Capt Horn and I dove furiously on one another just back of no man's land and Larry and MacGregor rolled and looped desperately trying to get on one another's tails. The boys in the trenches must have enjoyed it. Any way no one fired at us at all and even Archie the Avenger kept quiet until our performance was over. Then we spied some field sport back of our lines four or five miles and we stunted for them for a while. They were very appreciative and stopped the sports and waved frantically.

There were six of us who always flew together and got quite good at stunting in formation. Somehow a movie man heard about it so came over the other day to take movies of it. There are only four of us left but we did our best so if you see any such picture published you'll see me on the left of the leader.

Please remember I am relying on you to consider my letters absolutely confidential. Otherwise I should write you about the weather.

A heartful of love to you and Lena.

Your devoted son, Elliott

FLIGHT LOG: 27 June: 1 hour 30 minutes. Armentieres. Crashed Nieppe forest.

DIARY ENTRY: 27 June: MacGregor, Inglis and I chase a two-seater the other side of Armentieres and both guns jam and my oil goes. Crash in Nieppe forest and land in Duchess of Sutherland hospital.

DIARY ENTRY: June 28: Still in hospital and they won't [let me leave] [entry not completed; no further diary entries until 28 October].

SPRINGS NARRATIVE: Next morning [27 June] I went out again with Mac-Gregor and Inglis. MacGregor was leading. He found a two-seater east of Baupaume and went after him. MacGregor overshot and half-rolled back. I went in close from an angle and got under him. Both my guns stopped. The Hun observer was shooting at me when he could but I couldn't remedy the stoppages. Then I could see the observer's tracer bullets going through my wings and suddenly my oil pressure went dead. There was nothing to do but try to glide back to the lines. I headed for the St Omer salient and the Huns started shooting with Archie, field guns, rifles, pistols, and throwing old tin cans at me. I glided as far as I could and landed down wind in the Forest of Nieppe. Of course, the SE rolled up into a ball and the next thing I knew I was stretched out on the ground with a Tommy pouring something on me. I started crying.

"Why are you crying, Sir?" asked the Tommy. "You're back home."

"But my teeth," I bawled. "My teeth! They're all gone!"

"Oh no, they're not, Sir," said the Tommy. "Here they are."

And he pulled my lips out, which were on the inside of my teeth. I felt better then but I had a hole in my chin. A padre came out and told me to tilt my head back. Then he poured cognac down my throat until I felt better. This continued all day and after dark they sent me back to the squadron in a side car.

When I got back I found my wake in progress which I joined and then a doctor arrived from the wing and took me to the Duchess of Sutherland's hospital. There were only three patients in my ward—an Australian brigadier with his sixth wound, a Chinese coolie without his appendix, and me. A doctor sewed my face up without having to bother with any anesthetic while I chatted merrily. Then he told me to stand up and close my eyes. I did and promptly keeled over.

"Ah ha!" he said. "Concussion!" And he put me to bed.

The next day Callahan and MacGregor brought me a crocus sack full of champagne and we had a binge.

Three days later the doctor said he was going to send me home so that night I put on my flying boots and walked back to the squadron in my red silk pajamas. That was what I was flying in. The doctor came after me but the whole squadron worked him over with champagne and he agreed to leave me. Outside of a mouthful of string, my only trouble was that I was blind from a hemorrhage of both retinas. I lay around a few days until I could see a little and then I got orders to report to the 148th Aero Squadron which was being activated by Major Fowler and Mort Newhall at Dunkirk.[29]

Duchess of Sutherland's Hospital
St. Omer, France
June 29 1918

Dear Mother—

Well, I'm a casualty—that's what comes of playing with these Huns—they have no sense of humor—I had my fingers crossed all the time. And besides that if the Hun had had any sense at all he would have seen at once that both my guns were jammed because I had maneuvered into position and then failed to shoot him down. But that's a mere detail—MacGregor shot one of them down and got back so it's all right only I hate[d] to miss such an opportunity.

But the fact remains that I'm a casualty. But I'm one of the lightest casualties you ever saw. If they hadn't taken my clothes—what's left of them—away from me, I'd leave now. But you can't argue with this doctor. When I arrived I was full of anti-tetanus serum, morphine, and brandy—unusually full. Naturally I acted a bit queer and now the doc is convinced that I am suffering with acute concussion. I hope I can persuade him not to operate. The nurses positively humor me and won't even let me have my bedroom slippers for fear I'll disappear into the woods. I'll bet they even open this letter.

But who wouldn't act crazy with that combination? And who wouldn't rave after they'd gone twenty miles over after a Hun, gotten him and then have both guns jam and then get shot up yourself. Then to come back against the wind at two thousand feet expecting your motor to quit altogether any minute because an oil pipe was gone and have the whole Hun army shooting at you all the way—and good shooting they were doing, too—wouldn't you rave?

Well, if the doc don't change his mind in a day or so I'll not only be a casualty but missing as well. I'll return to the squadron in these yellow pajamas via the window if necessary. The doc can't seem to understand that my relapse yesterday was due to the fact that they showed me my face in a mirror. And you really can't blame me. It's a wreck and the doc's a rotten tailor—he sewed me up all wrong. But you can't expect me to enthuse over an entirely new face that resembles nothing I've ever seen before. I look like a reflection in one of these comic curved mirrors and I don't like my new face at all. It's all wrong. But my hard head still remains uncracked, though my machine gun and the trench parapet that they found it between were both damaged. And they brought my machine back in six lumps.

But my face—oh, mother, it's awful. They'll use me after the war as propaganda—"the horrors of warfare." I haven't gotten my mouth open enough to count my teeth but they don't feel right. At first I thought they were all gone but later it developed that they were just on the wrong side of my lips so my tongue misled me.

And my neck! I'd hate to tell you what it feels like. However Larry went down and flew my new bus up this morning and if I'm not over the lines in four days again, it'll be because I'm in jail for murdering the doc. If you see my name in the papers as wounded don't let it worry you—I'm all right except for my face and it could be a lot worse. It's still all there though a bit confused—I may have to smell through my ears and eat through my nose but still—the worst part of it is that I may have a Jewish nose.

But cheerio—I'll mess up some Huns' faces before you get this and I'll never have to sit for a photograph again.

Devotedly, Elliott

Duchess of Sutherland's Hospital
St. Omer, France
[Undated; late June 1918]

Dear Father—

Just a line to let you know that I am all right and will be out of here as soon as some minor repairs are effected on my face and the Doc is convinced that I haven't got a concussion. He's very much convinced that I have at present.

But that's not the worst of it. I've been promoted and I don't know what to do about it. A telegram came through for me to report to another squadron yesterday as a flight commander [in the 148th Aero Squadron]. I suppose that'll mean a captaincy in time, say three or four months. But I don't want it. I want to stay with 85 where I am reasonably sure of getting some Huns and where all is going well, and where I'll have a flight when Capt

Horn goes on leave. I got a Colonel at once on the phone and refused to accept but he told me that I wasn't doing the appointing this season. Then I got hold of another Colonel and resigned but he only told me there was a war on. So the C.O. is going to get the Colonel to have the brigadier refuse to let me leave 85. That seems to be the only chance. Larry insists I cable you to go to Washington and have it stopped but I'm afraid that would take too long.

It looks like I'll have to go though I can't figure why they would yank me away from 85 like this after all the trouble Major Bishop and Capt Horn took to get me. I don't want to be a flight commander and lead patrols but I would rather lead them myself than follow anyone I didn't have confidence in. I got cured of that some time ago.

This hospital has Johns Hopkins backed off the boards. And the fact that it's portable detracts nothing from it. My face will never be much to look at but I am glad to state that there is no damage done to any of my five senses though they are under slight repairs. So don't worry about me, all is well.

Write me care of the bank and for the love of Pete hasten along some Page and Shaw's and some Egyptian Deities. I'm starved for both.

Devotedly, Elliott

With the 148th Aero Squadron in France— First Combat

July to August 1918

The second operational squadron with which Springs flew was the 148th Aero Squadron, which was in the process of filling out its roster of pilots at the time Springs joined it. Even though Springs wanted very much to return to 85 Squadron after he recovered from his accident of 27 June, he received orders assigning him to the 148th during his recovery. It is unlikely that his accident had any effect on the decision to transfer him to the 148th, as his name must certainly have previously been mentioned as a likely candidate to be a flight commander in that squadron. Unlike some of the better-known squadrons of the U.S. Air Service flying in combat, such as the 94th Aero Squadron, with Eddie Rickenbacker as squadron commander, or the 95th Aero Squadron, to which Quentin Roosevelt was assigned when he died in aerial combat, or the 27th Aero Squadron, to which the Arizona "Balloon Buster," Frank Luke, had been assigned before he was killed, the 148th and 17th Aero Squadrons were not as visible in the news because they were attached to the British army and not to the American army.

The pilots of the 148th and the 17th Aero Squadrons included many who, like Springs, had previously been flying with British units. Another high-scoring American ace from Princeton, George Vaughn, for instance, had been flying with 84 Squadron before he was reassigned to the 17th Aero Squadron. As the Americans hurried to assemble operational aero squadrons, and thus fulfill the promise that had been made the year before (that the American air forces would "darken the skies" over the French front), it was common practice to place American pilots with some combat experience from existing units in command positions in newly formed units. Many new American squadrons were forming in this manner during the summer of 1918, as the American forces eventually succeeded in bringing sufficient men and supplies across the Atlantic to support their air arm.

While the 148th and 17th Aero Squadrons were fully manned by Americans, including maintenance personnel, the British supplied the squadrons with aircraft and assigned them their flying missions. The aircraft assigned to both the 17th and the 148th was the Sopwith Camel, which by the middle of the summer of 1918 was rapidly becoming obsolescent. Its rotary engine could not develop the power necessary to compete with the new and more powerful German aircraft, especially the Fokker D-VII, and the pilots soon realized this fact. However, the Camel had always been one of the most versatile and maneuverable aircraft in the war due to its exceptional turning ability (aided by the torque of its rotary engine); as long as it flew at lower altitudes, it could still be a potent weapon if flown by a skillful and sharp-eyed pilot. The 148th and 17th Aero Squadrons were assigned to the 65th Wing, RAF, and reported the results of their flights up the British chain of command.

Like almost all American aero squadrons, the 148th had been formed in the United States and then sent to France. The 148th was originated in the fall of 1917 and provided with a commanding officer, a few staff officers, and a complement of enlisted men who would become the maintainers of the squadron's aircraft when the aircraft and pilots to fly them arrived. Pilots were not initially assigned to the squadron since they were still in the process of being trained. Additionally, when the men of the squadron were notified that they would be leaving for France, the kind of aircraft they would fly and their mission were not determined until after the squadron had arrived in France; there the American authorities would decide what that mission would be. The enlisted men in the 148th originally trained at Everman and Hicks Fields, near Fort Worth, Texas.

The first squadron commander of the 148th was Maj. Cushman A. Rice,[1] who had political influence in Washington and who claimed to have flying experience, although few people had seen him flying. Few who interacted with him had good things to say about him. Francis "Spike" Irvin, who eventually became the sergeant major of the squadron, noted (with obvious irony) several times in his war diary that Major Rice was fond of giving orders.[2] Under the command of Major Rice, the 148th left Hicks Field on 14 February 1918, traveling by train to the military camp at Garden City, New York. The squadron boarded the transport *Olympic* on 25 February and left New York harbor the next day. The *Olympic* arrived in Liverpool on 5 March, and the men spent approximately two weeks in England before crossing the English Channel to France on 17 March. Early in April the squadron was assigned to duty with 40 Squadron, RAF, near Bruay, France, to learn something of the maintenance tasks involved in keeping a flying squadron airworthy.[3] On the evening of 22 April, a German bomber dropped bombs in the area where the 148th was located, and ten enlisted men were killed. In the middle of May, Major Rice was transferred to the American headquarters in Paris. There was a general sense of relief among the men of the squadron when the major departed.

On 1 June the commander of 40 Squadron (RAF), Maj. R. S. Dallas, was killed in action, a blow that affected the men of the 148th as well as 40 Squadron. As a result of the German advance, on 4 June the 148th relocated to a new field at Serny, near Estree Blanche, where they were attached to 208 Squadron, RAF. After a few days of inaction, the 148th received its new commanding officer, Capt. Morton "Mort" Newhall, transferred from 84 Squadron, RAF, and the unit moved again, this time to a new field at Capelle, three miles south of Dunkirk. The 148th was scheduled to begin work as an operational squadron on 1 July. During the first week of July, the squadron received a full complement of pilots, including Springs, who arrived by 2 July, even though he was still recovering from his accident four days earlier. Springs, assigned as B Flight commander, flew a few flights, mostly bringing Camels into the squadron from the supply field at Marquise. Two other flight commanders also arrived at this time, Lt. Bennett "Bim" Oliver for A Flight and Henry Clay for C Flight. Springs soon suffered a relapse as a result of a reaction to the medicine he was taking and (more probably) the fact that he had not fully recovered from his accident. Springs was essentially absent from the squadron from 8 to 28 July while he recovered his strength.

During his absence the 148th began to fly operational patrols, and Field Kindley of A Flight shot down the first German aircraft on 13 June. Although rainy weather limited their flying activity for the next few days, the men of the unit were designated as operationally ready on 20 July, and Irvin

Elliott Springs
in military uniform
in front of his Sop-
with Camel aircraft,
14 September 1918.
Courtesy of National
Museum of the
United States Air
Force.

noted in his diary that "real war flying started today."[4] That same day
Springs was officially given leave in Paris. However, he was back in the
squadron by 29 July and flew his first patrol two days later. Three days
later, on 3 August, Springs claimed his first German aircraft shot down
while flying with the 148th.

As a flight commander, Springs had responsibility for leading the pilots
of his flight along their patrol or bombing routes and for deciding when
and how to engage enemy aircraft. The other members of Springs's flight
included, at various times, William Clements, Percy Cunnius, Marvin Kent
Curtis (who became a prisoner of war), George Dorsey (wounded), Linn
Forster (killed in combat), Joseph Frobisher (killed in combat), Harry Jen-
kinson (killed in combat), Johnson Kenyon (wounded, prisoner of war),
Oscar Mandel (prisoner of war), Louis Rabe, Orville Ralston, Henry
Starkey, Lawrence Wyly (wounded), and Errol Zistel (wounded). Larry
Callahan eventually transferred from 85 Squadron to the 148th early in
September; there he served as assistant B Flight commander and replaced

Elliott Springs in flying suit in front of his Sopwith Camel aircraft, 14 September 1918. Courtesy of National Museum of the United States Air Force.

Springs as B Flight commander in October. The official squadron history describes Springs as "a fine pilot and flight-leader but more impetuous, more willing to take chances, the last to leave a fight and the first to commence one. He would never desert a pilot in distress. Several times he nearly lost his life vainly trying to save a pilot, who was hopelessly fighting against odds."[5]

The following memorandum was apparently written while Springs was recovering from his injuries. It was composed in response to a request from Maj. Harold Fowler for information pertaining to 85 Squadron's philosophy of conducting combat patrols under Major Bishop's leadership. Major Fowler served as liaison between the British and American forces in the establishment of the 148th and 17th Aero Squadrons, which worked under British control. The information in the latter portion of the correspondence is likely based on Springs's recent experiences in combat.

Duchess of Sutherland's Hospital
St. Omer, France
June 28 1918

Dear Major Fowler—

Time hanging heavy I am taking this opportunity to comply with your request and send you what information I can rake together.

Memorandum for Major Fowler:

85 Squadron worked on the principle that a scout patrol was ordered to perform a definite duty and this duty would be performed best by sticking closely to the job in hand and not by wandering about the skies indiscriminately in search of EA. A line patrol should protect our artillery machines, photography machines, and balloons and harass the enemy artillery and photography machines, and this can best be done by a constant patrol a half mile on our side of the lines at about seven thousand feet and not by chasing ten and fifteen miles into Hunland after EA. The flight organization is too valuable to be jeopardized by taking unnecessary chances. If a Squadron is particularly keen and is anxious to get a lot of Huns, let them go out in twos, threes, or alone between or after patrols, go over high— 17000 feet—and descend as low as necessary five miles over and sweep along the line keeping the sun behind.

It is foolish to fight EA Scouts except when it is possible to start the fight from above. If above and there are no other machines in sight, dive, fire at close range only and then pull up in a climbing turn and go down again. This avoids a dog fight and makes it possible to break off the fight in the advent of the approach of other EA. If below enemy scouts, as soon as they are seen, turn back to our lines and climb into the sun. When above the enemy machines, come down from the sun as before. Great care should be taken in the morning when the sun is very unfavorable. If you cannot attack with the advantage, don't attack.

Engine trouble should be the only reason for a pilot leaving a patrol. Daring without skill is not an asset but a serious menace. If a member of a patrol sees EA which the patrol leader apparently does not see, he should fly in front of the patrol leader and point to EA. If the patrol leader does not lead the patrol down, individual pilots should not attack "on their own." The patrol would thus be weakened and the patrol leader would probably have particular reasons why it is not to the advantage to attack. Often he is maneuvering for better position or sees other EA in the sky.

When on an offensive patrol up high, it is very bad policy to go down low after a single two-seater. The patrol is then rendered ineffective until it can climb up again and the chances of success are too small and the risk from EA above, "Archie," and machine-gun fire [too great] to warrant it.

To guard against going into the air with defective [Vickers machine] guns each pilot after his motor is started should (1) with the CC Gear: unload; pull up the reservoir handle; press and release Bowdoin control; note position of handle and number of bursts; load. (2) with the Kauper Gear: half load; unload; press Bowdoin Control. This ensures that the gear is tripping the trigger, that air has been released from the system, and that guns are ready to be fired. Care should be taken that the first round in the feed block is engaged in front of the pawls; otherwise a double-feed may occur.

With Lewis Gun care should be taken that the magazine is properly placed upon the gun. This can be done by attempting to revolve magazines.

Fussee and return springs should be weighed before each flight.

SPRINGS NARRATIVE: I went up there [to the 148th Squadron] and found they were going to fly Sopwith Camels, a tricky little biplane with a 130 [horsepower] Clerget rotary motor and two Vickers guns firing through the prop. They would do about 90 [miles per hour] level but you couldn't fly level because they would shake your teeth out in forty seconds by the clock. You had to climb or glide. But they could fly upside down and turn inside a stairwell. They would stall at 15000 feet and lose 1000 feet a turn. But they were deadly below 5000 feet if you could suck the Fokkers down to that level.

I was commander of [B] Flight and I had Clements, Mandel, Jenkinson, Frobisher and Curtis as pilots. After I lost Mandel, Jenkinson, Frobisher and Curtis, and Clements went to 17 Squadron across the [C]anal [du Nord], I got Callahan, Ralston, Starkey, Cunnius, and Noel in their places. Bim Oliver had [A] Flight and Henry Clay had C Flight. They had guts with a capital G. Henry Clay died of flu in Coblenz, but before that time he turned in the top performance as a flight leader, and later we staged some great decoy shows when we sucked the whole circus down low and rendered them ineffective henceforth.

We picked up the castoff rebuilt Camels from Aire. No new Camels had been built since January when they became obsolete and were replaced by SEs, Dolphins, Bentleys, and Snipes. But that summer they were still the workhorses below 15000 [feet]. A Camel was at a disadvantage at the beginning of a fight where speed and height were paramount, but in a dogfight down low nothing could get away from it. If the Fokkers didn't get them on their first dive they would often leave them alone and just pick at the stragglers. A Camel could make a monkey out of an SE or a Fokker at treetop level but it couldn't zoom and it couldn't dive. The Dolphin was worthless because the motors were too unreliable and the Bentleys and Snipes didn't get to the front until the Camels and Fokkers had finished each other off. The big scores were run up on SEs and Camels or Nieuports or SPADs. The SPAD was like a truck on an icy road. The Camel's guns were best at 100 yards. Beyond that you wasted bullets because of the terrific vibration.

A rotary [engine] was a completely illogical motor. The propeller was bolted to the cylinders and the crankshaft was bolted to the plane. It had no camshaft and no carburetor. It could be controlled by shorting the sparkplugs—called buzzing, but would catch fire if you did it too long. It always blazed up when started because the gas had to be squirted into the exhaust valve and then pumped out by the pistons before it could fire.

My eyes were still giving me trouble so [the second week of July] I went down to Paris to see a specialist.[6]

FLIGHT LOG: 1 July: 35 minutes. Marquise to Petit Synthe. Getting new busses [Sopwith Camels].

FLIGHT LOG: 2 July: 25 minutes. Marquise to Petit Synthe. Getting new busses.

FLIGHT LOG: 3 July: 28 minutes. Marquise to Petit Synthe. Getting new busses.

FLIGHT LOG: 3 July: 35 minutes. Marquise to Petit Synthe. Getting new busses.

FLIGHT LOG: 5 July: 10 minutes. Dud bus.

FLIGHT LOG: 5 July: 1 hour. Dunkirk to St. Omer [to visit 85 Squadron]. Landed for tea.

FLIGHT LOG: 6 July: 1 hour. [Flight] Test.

148th Aero Squadron
Capelle, France
EWSprings, 1st LT ASSC, AEF France
July 12, 1918

Dear Mother—

Am all right but can't use my eyes. Will write fully in a few days. Doctor says I'll be able to fly again in four or five days but must not read or write.

Write to me care of the Bank.

A heartful of love to you and Father.

Devotedly, Elliott

148th Aero Squadron
Capelle, France
July 18 1918

Dear Mother—

I am overjoyed with the news that I am going to live. Don't get excited—the doctor was never worried about me at all—well, I'll tell you about it.

I can't remember what I've written to you before but risking repetition I'll start at the beginning. I left the hospital and returned to 85 Squadron. In spite of all the C.O. and the Colonel could do I had to accept my promotion [actually a transfer, to the position of flight commander in the 148th Aero Squadron] and depart. In time I arrived here at the 148th American Squadron attached to the B.E.F. [British Expeditionary Forces] and started organizing my flight. First I had to get my machines and then organize the mechanics and train the pilots. I have [Kent] Curtis, [William] Clements, [Linn] Forster, and [John] Fulford of the Italian Detachment in my flight, one Princeton man named [Oscar] Mandel, and another specimen that I've never seen before but who seems O.K. I have B Flight and Bim Oliver, son of ex-Senator Oliver of Penn., who was in command of the first detachment at Oxford, has A Flight. Henry Clay, who came over with Bim, has C Flight, and the C.O. is [Mort Newhall,] an old Curtiss Pilot who came over in December—nice fellow—an old Harvard quarterback and a good organizer.

I got things organized and was almost ready to go and have a look at the war when something slipped up behind me and tagged me and I went out cold when I wasn't looking. You know what a mosquito bite looks like? Well, I look like I had been bitten by a million anapholes [mosquitoes]. From the top of my head to the soles of my feet, inclusive, I am one large bite. My hands, feet, and joints swelled double their size, my eyes closed completely—the remnants of my lips doubled up, my tongue broke out, my face looked like a big lump of red putty, I itched all over, my stomach broke out on the inside and wouldn't receive even water—I ached all over—my head split. And thus the doctor viewed me and listened to my tale of woe. Then says he, sympathetic-like, "you must have been the baby at home." I passed away again. So thus I lay and suffered for several days on one of those portable beds that always collapse. The doctor said it was due to poisoning from a combination of whiskey, brandy, anti-tetanus serum, and morphine and was nothing to worry about. Finally I decided to live and at last got up. But I couldn't walk. The stuff settled in my eyes and knees. So I retired again. Neither could I eat or sleep.

My knees are better now and I get about in a motorcycle sidecar and my eyes are no longer as bloodshot and I can see well enough to write and read a little. A great specialist examined me yesterday and said that I would be able to fly again in four or five days. He said that my case was unique but that I was O.K. and as soon as I got back my strength I would be up and at 'em again. He recommended that I go back to England for a week or ten days' rest but I've been out [of the squadron] long enough and refused to take it. My face isn't quite ready for leave yet awhile.

But you ought to have seen the dinner I knocked over the head last night. 'Twas worse than when I got out of the Johns Hopkins [hospital]. So worry not, I am completely restored but if they ever want to give me any more serum they'll have to hold me and chloroform me first.

Larry flew up to see me and has gotten another Hun. My new machine in 85 has been shot down twice and they got seven Huns in one flight—one patrol, that is. It makes me sick to think what I've missed. 85 has gotten twenty Huns since I left and only lost two men. Even McDonald got one so they must be cold meat. Mac usually forgets to cock his guns or turn his petrol on or something. But I'll have some excitement up here in a few days and then get back my own. Meanwhile I run my flight from my sidecar and my deputy leader leads the flights. A Flight got the first Hun the other day[7] but just wait for B.

Why don't you and Father write? I'm beyond being indignant about the matter and am now just hopeful. Your letter from the Vanderbilt was the last I got. Also got a letter from Page & Shaws but no candy. I enclose ten requests. Use the Bank address. Long before you get this I'll be over the lines again so don't worry about me in the slightest. But for the love of Mike, write to me!

Your devoted son, Elliott

P.S. Please don't pass around the word that I've been sick. The only danger was to my sanity and that's as O.K. as it will ever be. No further possibilities of trouble. The doctor expected me to run around with an empty beer bottle shouting "I'm to be Queen of the May"[8] but I fooled him. Now for the dentist as soon as I can get my mouth open wide enough.

148th Aero Squadron
Capelle, France
July 19 1918

Dear Father—

Your letter of June 9th arrived yesterday. Through some mischance it was forwarded wrong and went to a different squadron some distance away. But a friend of mine saw it there and tied a streamer to it and flew up to 85 and dropped it in front of the hangars. Then Larry got it and brought it up here. The Washington–New York mail service[9] certainly must be a phenomena [*sic*].

I'm getting all right now but they are trying to send me away again. The big mogul of the medical profession recommended that I go back to England for a rest for a couple of weeks. I certainly was tempted but it's no can do. The doc says I can fly day after tomorrow so let them what has nothing to do go on leave. I seem to be all right.

Incidentally, I wonder if you ever made a long trip by night with no lights on the car over a strange road. Try it some time . . . for your nerves. You can't use lights over here at night and I defy anyone to remember roads. A couple of trips more and I'll be singing "For I'm to be Queen of the May" sure enough.

Write me care of the Bank. Also I shall continue to keep my money on deposit there as it is more convenient and should I ever get leave which ought to be in about eight weeks, I'll go back to London.

And I want to go back to London, too. You can't imagine how that doctor tempted me. But I don't want sick leave at all and now I'm all right except for my eyes which the doc says are taking a long time to return to normal. My knees are O.K. and I can walk about with great ease. Have no idea of going on leave—can run my flight all right even though I can't fly.

I drove over to 85 [Squadron] for dinner last night. As fine a bunch they are as was ever gathered together and I got very homesick. The old place is just like home to me, all the batmen, waiters and mechanics seemed glad to see me again and they said my bus is waiting on me whenever I come back for it. I'd go back in a minute if they'd let me.

They've just gotten word that Thompson and Hall are alive and prisoners but no news from Mac Grider and the other two. Hope to hear something soon though.

That doc certainly tempted me with leave but I would much prefer to do my job first and take leave afterward. Tempted isn't the word.

Your devoted son, Elliott

P.S. If anyone complains that I haven't answered their letters, tell them that all my mail has been lost.

Paris, France
July 21 1918

Dear Mother—

So this is Paris! Would you believe it? No, certainly not.

They called me into the office the other day and gave me a ticket to Paris and said they hoped I'd have a nice time. I told them to use it themselves. But no, a lot of trouble had been taken to get it and the General would not like it if I refused to accept it.

So I went in to see the Doc. No, says the Doc, you won't be able to fly for ten days. Run on down to Paris and have a good time. Just remember if you take a drink it'll kill you. I handed him his ticket back. Oh go ahead, he says, you're a nuisance around here anyway. So I could say no more.

It seems that my crash was a little more serious than at first appeared and while I am to all intents and purposes as well as ever, my eyes refuse to return to normal and I can't see much in a strong light.

So I arrived in Paris this morning and came here [hotel not identified] on the recommendation of Bob Lamont who wrote me to try it. It's a small copy of the Vanderbilt only more so and they gave me a suite that makes anything I ever saw look pale. It's decorated like an art exhibit and I get lost in it every time I try to find the bedroom or one of the bath rooms. All for five dollars a day.

I tried to use the telephone a while ago but had to give it up. I can only count up to seventeen in French. And I have ten francs in my pocket. Comprez? And the only person I know in this place is Lorraine Goodrich and I can't get her on the phone.

Tomorrow I see an eye specialist and get the worst told me. And my face has improved so that I will also see a dentist.

A heartful of love to you and Father.

Devotedly, Elliott

P.S. I shall be here seven days.

Paris, France
July 25 1918

Dear Father—

I didn't want to come away from the squadron at all but after four days in Paris I have improved 100 per cent and feel like a new man already. 'Twas certainly the very thing for me.

I had quite a blow though. The [eye] specialist told me at first that my days as a pilot were over. After much argument he finally said that the matter was up to me and if I was that anxious to keep on flying I could probably do so. He said there was no reason why I shouldn't do night flying though as my eyes are all right in the dark. A strong light, though, messes things up.

Rather than have you worry about it I'll explain the trouble. When I crashed the blow on top of my head produced a slight hemorrhage of the retina in the back of my eyes. It is nothing serious and the doc says that time will cure it, maybe a year, maybe five years, but it is sure to cure itself. So don't worry. He is the best eye man over here.

The focus is not affected—I only need dark glasses and am sure I can fly. I'm going to get my five Huns if it costs me both eyes. Rest assured, though, that I shall do nothing foolish. So don't worry. Rather rejoice in the fact that it's nothing worse. I was scared to death for a few days when there was a prospect of being blind for good.

My French is improving but has a long way to go yet. For instance, at 8:30 this morning I called for the valet and sent my uniform out to be pressed. The valet asked how long before I wanted it. A half hour, I told him in my best French. An hour and a half later—no uniform. I called for him and demanded it. He was undisturbed and didn't know what I wanted. After much argument the manager came up. "Ah monsieur," he said, "the valet will have it back at noon." I explained that I didn't care to remain in my suite, pleasant as it might be, until noon. "But did you not tell the valet to return it at noon?" Then I realized that I had used *midi* instead of *demi* and after much mutual apologizing the valet has now gone out in search of my clothes which he sent to some tailor shop. Meanwhile I shall write.

Pabst [Goodrich] is a poilu in the Foreign Legion, training at Fontainbleau[10] but wired me that leave was impossible. Determined to see him, I got a very imposing limousine and took Lorraine [Goodrich, his sister, who was working as a nurse in Paris] and went out to Fontainbleau Monday.

After much difficulty I got to speak with him. Leave impossible, he said. Lead me to your C.O., said I. He took me to a French lieutenant and I at once opened fire. All my wounds I laid bare, weeping constantly. I had not seen my cousin in two years. I might never see him again. I had come from the front to see him. Here, see, is my permission, necessarily signed by two generals and a colonel. Could not my friend cousin come to Paris for twenty-four hours? See, I have for him procured a car.

Well the Lieut fell for my smashed mug and wept with me. He would take me to the Capt and let him hear my request. The Capt was moved to tears but leave for Poilu Goodrich was impossible. However, I could tell my tale to the Major.

The Major showed real sympathy and almost kissed me on both cheeks. But he could not grant me leave. Only the Colonel could grant leave. I had exhausted my store of tears by that time as well as my breath so the Major drew up a formal document telling of my sad plight, my sad past, and my sad future, my failing eyes and worthless lower lip, my comrade's good record, the car outside, etc., and sent it to the Colonel. And lo, in due time Pabst and I started for Paris and spent the next twenty-four hours explaining to the multitude how a poilu could swear in such perfect English.

The next night on the way back we stopped by and got Eli [Springs] and had dinner out at the Fontainbleau and then dropped Eli on the way home again. Eli is doing very well, excellent in fact, and is also looking better than I have ever seen him. He is due to go far in the army.

This town is full of Americans. I've seen everyone I ever knew. Even ran into Captain La Guardia who was up for a few days from Italy. Tried to get some news of Mac Grider through the Red Cross but couldn't. I arranged for parcels to be sent to him and also all the money I have left after I pay my hotel bill here. I think they have designs on my gold teeth though.

But permit me to state that the Paris food is the best in the world. If you ever get a chance run over here and go to the A La Becasse in the Rue Chambertin[11] and call for George, the maitre d'hotel. Disclose your identity to him and he will put before you such food as you never knew existed. True you go out between courses to hock your valuables but it's worth it.

I heard something funny yesterday. An American doughboy drove up in front of where we were sitting in a taxi. He got out and says "Combien que?" The driver held up nine fingers. "Ah, too much, come down." An argument followed and as usual a polite Frenchman stepped up and offered his services as interpreter.

"Thanks," says the doughboy; "I wish you'd tell this hunk of cheese that I don't want to buy his taxi. Even five francs for that ride is a hell of a ride." "Ah," says the Frenchman; then, to the driver, "L'Americain ne vous pas a acheter votre taxi, il vous a acheter de fromage et donnera a vous cinq francs [He doesn't want to buy your taxi; he wants to buy you some cheese and will give you five francs]."

After which the doughboy spluttered like a soda bottle, was pushed into the taxi again, and the driver whirled away merrily and when they disappeared from sight the doughboy's head was still to be seen thrust out of the window and he was still gesticulating wildly with both hands. I wonder where that driver took him.

I sent Lena and Aunt Addie each the finest handkerchiefs that could be obtained in Paris today. I don't know why but I wanted to send them something and that's all I could think of. On this side the presents are different. A man saves your life—you offer him a box of Deities. In then olden days the villain corrupted the beautiful village maiden with promises of jewels and fine silks. Today you whisper in her shell-like ear that you have deux kilos du sucre [sugar] and she will promptly forget home and mother.

I feel though in Paris like a ham sandwich at a banquet. A lower lip which is of no practical value except to enable me to close my mouth and the total inability to consume more than a sherry flip or a prairie oyster combine to make me an ornament, than which there is none such. But the climate and the food are rapidly turning me from a pessimistic invalid into a pink butter ball and I live only from meal to meal.

Your devoted son, Elliott

Paris, France
July 27 1918

Dear Mother—

Well I am an old man. The mirror shows no white hairs but mental reflection shows unmistakable signs of old age.

I have seen the [eye] specialist again and he says that I can fly so I am returning tonight and will be over the lines again Monday. Thank heaven for that much anyway. Day before yesterday I ran into Jimmie Latham. He is a sergeant and was in charge of twenty men, taking them down south to a motor transport school. He turned the tickets over to a corporal and decided to take a later train. Of course he didn't get that train or even the next. He finally got away early this morning. There are some advantages in not holding a commission. An officer is not absent without leave. 'Tis not done.

Also I ran into Colleen Minton and a couple of old Culver [Academy][12] friends so have not been lonely at all. Paris is a wonderful place. It's an education to visit it. And the shops show no sign of war. Wish I was bloated [loaded with money?].

And the food! To a man from the front it is heaven itself. I live on one dish. Filet of Sole a la Maison. It's smothered in truffles and mushrooms and covered with cheese like potatoes au gratin. And the frog legs are fine. I brought some sugar down with me and have plenty of bread so all is well.

Yesterday Jimmie and I were sitting in the Café de la Paix[13] at a table on the sidewalk when I saw something. Then I said "Jimmie, if I thought that Mother would wear mourning [clothing] like that for me, I would take on the whole Hun flying corps with unloaded guns in the original Wright machine." Knowing you would be interested, I marked her costume well. A black tailored suit, moderate length, knee-length coat with a belt, a white pique vest with wing collar protruding, black toque hat with a narrow band of white at the bottom, thus [drawing] and a black veil trailing behind. The face under the hat was the whole show but still the costume was what did the trick. I don't know whom she was mourning for, but he certainly died in a good cause. I was simply open-mouthed and my eyes nearly popped out. Wish you could have seen so you could get it duplicated. I would then withdraw my objections to black and go down cheerfully. The only fly in the ointment was that she was wearing most unobtrusively an American officer's insignia. But what else can you expect? C'est la guerre.

A heartful of love always to you and Father.

Your devoted son, Elliott

FLIGHT LOG: 29 July: 15 minutes. [Flight] Test.
FLIGHT LOG: 29 July: 1 hour 20 minutes. Nieuport—Ypres—Nieppe. Line patrol.
FLIGHT LOG: 30 July: St. Omer—Neippe—Ypres. Chased home by two Fokkers.

148th Aero Squadron
Capelle, France
July 30 1918

Dear Mother—

Back at work and I feel much better. My leave improved me more than anything else that's ever happened to me. I feel like a new man. I was over the lines again yesterday for the first time in three weeks. Very uneventful trip. Couldn't find a thing to even argue with. However I'm going to take a patrol over this evening and hope to stir up some trouble.

I returned [from evening patrol] to find my machine full of holes, thanks to an energetic Hun. But it has been patched up again. Revenge must be mine.

I was talking to Larry [Callahan, who was still in 85 Squadron] on the phone and he was shot down the other day but succeeded in getting the Hun first. That's four to his credit now. His motor was shot away but he landed on our side of the lines.

Major Mannock has been killed—85's new C.O. who took Major Bishop's place. He has 65 Hun planes to his credit and a bullet from the ground got him. He and my old friend Inglis the New Zealander went down to 50 feet after a Hun and got him but on the way back he saw Mannock's machine burst into flames. Too bad. Next to Bishop he was the world's finest and his loss is a blow personally as well as officially.

I am enclosing some pictures taken at 85 before I left. In the group Larry is standing on my right. In the line of machines Capt Horn is in the first machine with "Lobo" the police dog. I am in the second with "Genevieve" the chow and Larry is in the third with "Gwendolyn." No news of Mac Grider yet. Larry says Princess Mary Louise is working through the British Red Cross to try and get information of him.

I returned from Paris with enough money to keep me going until my next pay check so all is well. Think I managed very well. And I must say I got my money's worth. Really can't see why I brought any back. Imagine returning to the Front from leave with any money left! It's ridiculous. But such are the ideas of economy taught me by Father. It'll be four months now before I have another opportunity of violating my Scotch-Irish inheritance of thrift.

A heartful of love always.

Devotedly, Elliott

FLIGHT LOG: 31 July: 2 hours. Ypres—Nieppe. Search of E.A. [enemy aircraft].

FLIGHT LOG: 31 July. 1 hour 55 minutes. Nieuport—Ypres—Nieppe. Line patrol.

148th Aero Squadron
Capelle, France
July 31 1918

Dear Father—

I am very much surprised to find that today I am 22 years of age. Yes surprised. Of course, I knew that on July 31 I would be 22 but I never expected to last until July 31st. I might also say that I am agreeably surprised.

I went out hunting yesterday [30 July] and found a scrap. But getting the worst of it, I was forced to return much against my will. Today has proved the most exciting day in my history. Some day I would like to tell you about it but at present the details are too fresh to be pleasant. If I were a Hun I would hang my head with shame. Only two of my planes got shot up and all returned. Yet for an hour and a half I thought one date would be sufficient for my memorial [the same date for his birth and death]. It's to a hospital didn't you say? Cheer up, I'll fool them yet. But it was some show. There'll never be another like it. Everything from a dogfight to a balloon strafe.

Your letter of July 9th received but as yet no Page & Shaws. Am awaiting it anxiously.

The C.O. is away this afternoon so I'm acting C.O. My only official act thus far however is to send the men for a swim and dispatch someone to look for ice. Larry and Capt Horn flew up and had lunch with me and then went off hunting. I'd like to celebrate my birthday by getting a Hun but a couple of Majors and a Colonel showed up and I had to stick around. Also I have a hunch that you have sent me a check and I don't want to take any chances on missing the evening mail. Did you send four or five figures? I can use either.

You needn't expect much mail from me from now on. In addition to handling the flight, I have two or three patrols a day and run the mess and try to recoup my fortunes all at the same time. And I have to find time to brush my teeth some time. Which reminds me, there'll probably be a great shortage of paper in France shortly. The American army is tearing up all the French money shooting crap with it. You'd be surprised at the appearance of the money now, all torn and folded.

Have heard nothing more of my captaincy. Ought to get it in three or four months with a little luck. Heard that Major Bishop had been decorated again. DFC this time and a bar to his DSO.[14] They ought to knight him. News has been received that Mac Grider was killed in action but we can't figure how. He must have attacked a formation or decided to shoot up the ground. Mannock was shot from the ground. Have got to go up now and test out a new bus.

A heartful of love to you and Lena.

Devotedly, Elliott

FLIGHT LOG: 1 August: 2 hours. Nieuport—Ypres—Nieppe. Line patrol.

FLIGHT LOG: 1 August: 10 minutes. [Flight] Test.

FLIGHT LOG: 2 August: 2 hours 10 minutes. Courtrai—Menin—
   Rouleurs. We do not get a balloon!

FLIGHT LOG: 3 August: 1 hour 45 minutes. Nieuport—Bruges. O. P.
   [operational patrol]. Escort attacked by four Fokkers. Got one. (V)

COMBAT REPORT: 148th Aero Squadron, 9:40 AM, 3 August. Remarks
   on hostile aircraft: Fokker Biplane. Results: Destroyed one E. A. Narrative: Three Fokker Biplanes who had been hovering above us for
   twenty minutes came down after several feints. I turned on one then
   at my level and he turned directly towards me. I opened fire at 100
   yds. range and, after 50 to 75 more rounds, Fokker turned on back. I
   fired 50 to 75 rounds and Fokker went into a dive, and went down
   spinning slowly. Black smoke started issuing from E. A. and it was
   last seen close to ground going down with great vertical speed and
   apparently on fire. Sgnd, E. W. Springs, 1st Lt, Air Service, USA.

FLIGHT LOG: 5 August: 10 minutes. [Flight] Test.

148th Aero Squadron
Capelle, France
August 5 1918

Dear Mother—

Your two letters received but have forgotten dates. We never carry letters around with us as the address would give information to the enemy so
not caring to leave them behind, I always destroy them. Would hate to
have someone else sorting out my mail to determine just what will be
spared for home consumption. I've had to do it for several others already.

I am completely restored now except for my eyes and lower lip. As soon
as I get above 10,000 feet my lip freezes and I can't get it thawed out until
I come down. It's absolutely numb still and not of great value. My eyes are
improving. All together things are looking up.

I managed to push down another Hun yesterday [3 August]. We were
over about 15 miles and there were some Huns above us. One of them dove

on me and began to shoot me up. Naturally I got pretty fed up about it. It's a rotten trick. So I turned around and opened fire on him. Then the poor fool shifted his position too and came head on into me. His guns apparently jammed and I pumped about 250 rounds into him. He turned over on his back and I pumped 100 more into him. He went down in a slow spin and burst into flames. Then I looked up and saw another Hun coming down to avenge his comrade but before he could get me one of my flight up above hopped onto his tail and pushed him down to join his beloved.

I think the Huns must have had a thick night or something. Probably celebrating the capture of Paris.[15] Which reminds me that about two weeks ago early in the morning they captured a Hun two-seater in which they found both pilot and observer in full evening dress and both stewed to the gills.

Reminds me of another story I heard in Paris. They say the American Marines were supposed to make an advance behind the tanks. The advance came off all right. The Marines rode over sitting on top of the tanks. Speaking of Paris I was certainly pleasantly surprised with it. I found comfort there which is almost unknown in Merry England. Am seriously considering moving from London to Paris. As you know the Parisian women are the best dressed in the world but you have no idea by what overwhelming odds they lead their nearest competitors. Except for their shoes which are atrocious. The pictures in [V]ogue [magazine] supposedly taken in the bois are not faked.[16]

And the shops are all that they are supposed to be. I find that I can get leave again if I want it in six weeks and if I do, I think I'll wire Father for an abundance of kale (beaucoup de francs) and send you a lot of stuff which you can't get elsewhere. Wanted very much to send you a little platinum watch I saw to go with your bracelet but they wanted 2000 francs for it. Wonderful linen stuff too.

I had dinner with the Colonel last night and spent a very enjoyable evening. Also got some valuable dope on guns. . . .

Went down to 85 [Squadron] the other day. Their new C.O. has arrived. Poor Trapp is missing. He would persist in going after enemy balloons and they think he got shot from the ground.

A heartful of love to you and Father.

Devotedly, Elliott

With the 148th Aero Squadron in France— Supporting the Allied Advance

August to September 1918

On 8 August, five days after Springs shot down his first German aircraft while flying with the 148th, the Allies launched the Hundred Days Offensive, in which British, French, Canadian, Australian, and American troops attacked German forces all along the western front. The offensive slowly gained momentum, and the Allied forces began to turn the German ground forces back; 8 August was later called a "black day" for the German army by General Erich von Ludendorff, as the turning point in the war when the Germans no longer fought an offensive battle but were forced to fight a defensive war. From that date until the armistice the Germans were in constant retreat.

On 8 August the war in the air intensified significantly, as the German high command relocated a number of German squadrons, or Jastas, to the front lines in France and Belgium to help provide support for the German army. From that date until the end of September, the aerial war was fought continuously with great intensity, as more German aircraft appeared in the skies over the front lines than had appeared earlier in the summer. The effect of this change in the war caused the pilots of the 148th Aero Squadron to face some of the greatest numbers of German aircraft they had seen, and the odds frequently turned against them as German aircraft often outnumbered the American aircraft. If the pilots of the 148th (and their comrades in the 17th Aero Squadron) shot down more German aircraft after 8 August than they had before, they also lost more pilots, and the emotional pressure on the pilots throughout August and September increased significantly as more and more of their fellow pilots failed to return from their combat missions.

In addition to the challenge of escorting British bombers over the lines and attacking German aircraft, the pilots of the 148th were given an additional dangerous mission, dropping small bombs at low altitude and then strafing targets of opportunity on the roads behind the lines. The Camel was not designed as a bombing aircraft and could not carry a heavy load; the maximum load was four twenty-pound bombs. If they were not careful, the pilots could damage their own aircraft by releasing their bombs at a dangerously low altitude. Whenever they strafed the roads, they were susceptible to heavy ground fire from the German forces. According to the squadron records, the first low bombing missions began on 22 August and continued throughout September; these missions ended only when an extended period of bad weather arrived in the middle of October.

During the period from 8 August to 29 September, Elliott Springs participated in some of the most stressful flying of the war, and the stress was increased as the result of his concern about the welfare of the other pilots in his flight. As more of his pilots failed to return safely, he undoubtedly became more and more anxious about his chances for survival. In his letters home, however, Springs seemed to present the same cheerful, confrontational self that he had demonstrated in his earlier letters. If we look only at the letters Springs wrote home during this period of time without taking into consideration his operational activities, we might believe that he was maintaining a positive, aggressive attitude toward the war, that he was seeing the war only as an annoying drain on his time, and that he spent more energy developing an increasingly glib, antagonistic, and even occasionally hostile attitude toward his parents than he did worrying about the war. However, when we examine his other war-time documents—his flight log and especially the records of his aerial victories and ground attack missions while he was in the 148th—we can see more completely the stresses and strains under which he must have been operating in August and September. As we read these squadron records of aerial combat after aerial combat and ground attack mission after ground attack mission, we can begin to appreciate the tremendous mental burden of these repeated daily flights. When we realize that Springs felt responsible for the welfare of the men in his flight with whom he flew, we can begin to feel the emotional weight that

Springs and his fellow pilots had to endure. We should realize also that flying the sensitive but underpowered Sopwith Camel into aerial combat against more capable aircraft such as the Fokker D-VII required physical skill and endurance as well as mental discipline and intestinal fortitude.

In a relatively short period of time, just under two months, this kind of life must have been especially physically and emotionally wearing. What is surprising is not that Springs and many other pilots eventually suffered some kind of physical and emotional relapse during and after the war, but that they did not suffer it sooner and more completely. The other flight commanders in the 148th showed the strain as well. Bim Oliver of A Flight fell ill at the end of July, and his place was taken by Lt. Field Kindley. Henry Clay, C Flight commander, admitted in a letter home written after the armistice that in the "latter part of September, my nerves were pretty near gone," but luckily "the Huns moved their best squadrons [away] from that front [at that time] . . . thereby giving me a rest."[1] The physical and emotional drain on Clay's spirits may have been partly responsible for his death from influenza and pneumonia less than two months later, on 7 February 1919.

The rapidly changing situation along the front lines after the Allied attack began on 8 August caused frequent squadron moves eastward to provide air cover and ground support for the advancing forces. On 11 August the squadron moved from Capelle, where it had been operating since becoming operational in July, to Allonville, about ten miles northeast of Amiens, near the Amiens-Albert Road. A week later, on 18 August, the squadron moved to Remaisnil, about five miles west of Doullens, where the men flew along the Albert-Arras front in support of the advancing British 3rd Army.[2] Flying out of the airfield at Remaisnil for a period of a month, Springs experienced his most difficult and challenging aerial combats. The Allied forces moved farther east as the Germans fell back, and the squadron moved again, on 20 September, to Baizieux, six miles west of Albert, and then moved on 12 October to Beugnatre, just northeast of Bapaume.[3] On 28 October the squadron essentially ceased flying operational patrols, as it prepared to exchange its worn-out Camels for newer aircraft, and the three flight commanders, Springs, Kindley, and Clay, were told to report to Toul for new assignments as squadron commanders. However, the armistice intervened.

FLIGHT LOG: 6 August: 20 minutes. O.P. Returned—one mag[neto] dud.
FLIGHT LOG: 6 August: 20 minutes. [Flight] Test OK.
FLIGHT LOG: 7 August: 45 minutes. Test escort.
FLIGHT LOG: 8 August: 2 hours 5 minutes. Nieuport—Kemmel. O.P.
FLIGHT LOG: 8 August: 55 minutes. St. Omer. Landed at 85 [Squadron]
    [85 Squadron was operating out of Bertangles, just north of Amiens].

148th Aero Squadron
Capelle, France
August 8 1918

Dear Mother—
    The last few days have been fairly exciting ones though I must say that the excitement and strain is trebled for the leader, so possibly the others would call it quiet. But when you are responsible for all that takes place from the time you leave the ground you find the old frazzle on the nerves. I guess I'm taking things too seriously but flight commanders are usually to blame for casualties and even those who have been at it for several years have casualties.
    At tea yesterday a Lt. blew in and announced that he had come to take some movies of us. I at once spoke for the part of the villain, but he explained that this was to be propaganda material and he must have us in action. But he didn't quite know how to get the pictures so he called for suggestions.
    "Why not show the pilots between patrols? Give the public an idea as to what we do."
    "Fine," said the movie man, dreaming of Pearl White,[4] his former subject.
    "All right," said someone. "Get the bones [dice] out."
    But he turned down that suggestion and said he wanted something sort of continuous like "A Day with a General" which he had just done.
    "Well," says I, earnest like, "take a picture of the planes, then insert [the words] 'The Alarm' and have all the pilots rushing down and hopping into flying kit. Then insert 'Our Fearless Airmen Leaping into the Air.' Then the take off."
    "Fine," says he warming up, "that's just the stuff."
    "Then insert 'Two Hours Later' and show the planes returning all shot up. All return but one. Then show a close-up of the C.O. shading his eyes and scanning the skies nervously. But the last plane returns not. Then show the mechanics stroking the lost pilot's hat and shoes tearfully. Show the flight commander tearfully explaining how he was saved by having a Fokker shot off his tail by an act of sacrifice.

Let them summon the Chaplain and hold prayers and then summon the YMCA Secretary and have a song service. Then have the multitude break into triumphant shouts as the long lost plane is sighted, staggering home under its load of lead and just at that moment the General arrives with a sackful of medals.

Get six French women and dress them up as German mothers and have them weep profusely. Then dress them up as American mothers and show them grinning joyously holding up six Iron Crosses. And finish it up with a close-up of the President."

The movie man had been grinning and nodding assent right down to the last and you should have seen his expression change when he got the drift of the joke.

In the end he took the mechanics, pilots, and hangars, some formation flying and then we got a couple of two-seater machines from a neighboring squadron and the two movie men went up. Then I got [William] Clements and [Oscar] Mandel and we got right together with about two-feet interval between our planes and throttled down to about 5000 feet. Then the two-seater flew around us and got pictures from all angles. Then I went over to one of them and flew about ten feet away from his lens while he was grinding away. Then I went over to the other and got about six feet away and the other fellow got some good pictures of us both. You'll probably see them in the States in four or five weeks. The movie man promised to give me some if they turn out well.

I am enclosing the menu of a little dinner party last night which was pulled off within range of the big guns. All honor to France. She may be obliterated but never conquered. This particular café may be shelled and bombed continually but it will take a direct hit in the kitchen to stop a meal.

I've just been censoring some of the men's letters. Very funny some of them. . . . One of them wrote to his mother: "We have a new gun here now. All the Germans it doesn't kill it takes prisoners, and the recoil brings up tomorrow's rations." Another burst forth with this to his girl: "The mosquitoes here are fierce. Last night I put my tin helmet over my face and I'm hanged if they didn't start boring through. So I got my hammer and bent over their beaks so they couldn't get them out. When I woke up this morning I found out they'd flown off with my shrapnel hat."

Have received no packages yet. Send all my mail to the Bank. Can't understand why you have always been prejudiced against using it. If you can get the faintest clue of another address you insist on using it.

A heartful of love, Elliott.

FLIGHT LOG: 9 August: 15 minutes. [Flight] Test.

FLIGHT LOG: 10 August: 1 hour 50 minutes. Nieppe [on the northwest edge of Armentieres]. O.P.

FLIGHT LOG: 11 August : 25 minutes. Dunkirk to Allonville. Flying to new aerodrome [at Allonville, ten miles northeast of Amiens, near the Amiens-Albert Road].

FLIGHT LOG: 12 August: 1 hour 50 minutes. Albert—Roye—Montdidier [east of Amiens]. Line patrol.

FLIGHT LOG: 12 August : 1 hour 45 minutes. Albert—Roye—Montdidier. Line Patrol.

FLIGHT LOG: 13 August: 1 hour 20 minutes. Albert—Roye—Montdider. Line Patrol.

FLIGHT LOG: 13 August: 1 hour 40 minutes. Albert—Roye—Montdidier. Line Patrol. Attacked 9 E[nemy] A[ircraft]. (VI, VII)

148th Aero Squadron
Allonville, France
August 14 1918

Dear Mother—

I'm not feeling too well today. I fought Huns all night in my sleep and after two hours more today I feel all washed out. Yesterday [13 August] produced the worst scrap that I shall ever have the opportunity to indulge in. It lasted about twenty minutes and the participants were nine new type Hun scouts [probably the Fokker D-VII] and myself. I say participants because each Hun fired at me at least once and I fired at each one [once] then several times collectively and individually.

I had just gone down on a two-seater and had become separated from all but one of my patrol when I spotted the nine Huns about eight miles over. The rest of them [the other aircraft in his patrol] were too far below so I decided to take a chance on something being up above to help me. The Huns were about 3000 feet above me so I flew underneath them and waited for them to come down. Two of them did, one on me and one on [Joseph] Kenyon. Kenyon went down and I went up so I was above the Hun on his tail. I sprayed the one coming for me and he turned back so I turned on the one on Kenyon's tail. He went down after I fired 50 to 75 shots in a glide. Think I must have hit his motor. I couldn't follow him down because two more came after me and Kenyon had pulled out as he should have done, as he's a new pilot and had no business there at all.

I turned on the one nearest me and we opened fire at each other head on. I must have fired 200 rounds into him and he went down in a straight dive. Two people saw it so I may get credit for it. The other one and I started a dog fight and after a few moments he pulled away. Then three more came down on me at once. Their machine guns nearly deafened me and all I could do was circle madly to throw off their fire. One of them pulled up and then came down to finish me off. I thought I was gone. However, I turned towards him and forced him to pull up to keep from overshooting. As soon as I saw his nose go up, I put mine straight down with motor on for I knew my time had come as all seven of them were circling up above ready to come down in relays. The Hun dove again and as soon as he opened fire I pulled straight up doing about 250. Of course, he overshot and went by me about fifteen feet away. I could see his goggles and noted all the details of his machine which was black and white checked with a white nose. I turned on him but he was doing about 300 and went up like an elevator. As he went up, I went down and after several repetitions he gave it up and went back to join his yellow comrades and I toodled peacefully back to our lines, moaning Kenyon's loss, for I thought he was done in. But he used his head and got back all right. I tried to shoot up some infantry on the ground but it was too hot for me and I had to come on back.

I've been trying to get some confirmation but as yet have had no success. If all else fails I'm going to get a side car and go up to the trenches and see if I can't get official confirmation. Some one must have seen the scrap and seen the two Huns go down. Unless I can get the confirmation I can't claim the Huns as I didn't see them crash.

Remember this letter is to be shown to no one and no one is to be told about it. If I thought for a moment that you would not consider it secret I wouldn't mention it. Even at that I hesitate. But I feel that if I get away with anything over here you and Father have a right to know about it. And as something may happen to me at any time I feel I ought to write to you about it. But that's all. No one else is to know about it or have an opportunity to use their imagination. I know Father can't see my point of view but please try and explain it to him. If you only knew in what contempt we hold those who play the George game and write home a lot of drule [drivel] for the families to spread around. I know of several who have done well over here and have their pictures in all the papers at home and I feel sorry for them. It's not their fault either. Thank goodness I'm working with the British where such rot isn't countenanced. But my nerves are a bit touchy today and I've got trench mouth[5] as well. And I've got to lead a triple patrol in half an hour.

Larry, Capt Horn and MacGregor wandered in about half an hour ago. They've moved too and are about two miles away. I certainly miss Mac

Grider. And it's good to be near the old bunch again. My machine will probably know the hangars over there as well as over here.

I've never been able to understand these people who go out into the woods with a tent and a frying pan and have a wonderful time. And now that I am possessed of the tent but not the frying pan I understand that form of exercise much less. Bring back, oh bring back my shower and breakfast in bed. True I can't say I'm really roughing it with a valet to bring me hot water and five course dinners every night but if you ever catch me forming a camping party or a country house party, call the doctor. The Castiglione, Savoy, or Vanderbilt are as near as I ever want to get to rustic life.

Devotedly, Elliott

FLIGHT LOG: 14 August: 2 hours 25 minutes. Albert—Roye—Montdidier. Line patrol. Attacked by 20 EA. (VIII)

FLIGHT LOG: 15 August: 1 hour 30 minutes. Albert—Roye—Montdidier. Attacked by four Fokkers.

FLIGHT LOG: 16 August: 2 hours. Albert—Chaulnes—Roye. Attacked by five Fokkers.

The following is an excerpt from a letter by Leroy Springs dated 16 July 1918.

My dear Son:

We have just received your letter to Lena [probably dated 20 June] and are very proud of your continued good record. I judge from your letter that you must have about two and a half or three and a half Huns to your record, so you must soon be an ace. I am glad you realize that discretion is the better part of valor and that you can best serve your country by not taking too many risks, that is, not try to fight too many at once.

I am sorry that your friend MacGregor has been lost.[6] I sincerely trust that he is a prisoner and has not been killed. I know you must miss him very much, as it is hard to part with friends. I hope he has shown up by this time. . . .

Your affectionate father

148th Aero Squadron
Allonville, France
August 16 1918

Dear Father—

Your two letters of July 12 and 24 [and 16 July?] received and brought great joy. I just happened to be over at 85 for lunch and found them waiting on me there. Duplicates also arrived from the London City [Bank] at the same time. No, I am sorry to say, Mac Grider did not come back. Dove in, so the report came in. MacGregor, now a captain, was over with Larry for dinner last night. He was shot down this morning too but managed to glide back to our lines and land all right. He wasn't hurt at all.

We had a good scrap yesterday. I was leading a two flight patrol and when we were about five miles over I saw about 20 Huns above us. I turned so the top flight was in the sun and then took the bottom flight directly under the Huns and waited for them to attack. They did. They came down like a ton of bricks and [it] sounded like a 4th of July celebration. The crackle of machine guns almost deafened you. As soon as they started down we started twisting and turning to spoil their aim and then the top flight came in. For about ten minutes there was the worst dog fight you ever saw. Everybody shooting at everybody else. 20 Huns and 11 of us. The first four came down just above me and [Harry] Jenkinson and we stalled up and opened fire to keep them off. The one I was firing at pulled up again and the one Jenk picked put his nose further down and Jenk went on down after him. Then I saw another one on [Oscar] Mandel's tail so I turned on him and opened fire and he pulled up and zoomed away.

More were coming down then and one went by me after Jenk. I got on his tail and fired about 400 rounds into him. He turned over on his back and I had to pull up to avoid colliding with him. He went down in a slow spin and I tried to follow him down but was interrupted by the crackle of six guns and saw three Huns coming down on me so I was too busy to see where he crashed. But I'm sure he did although I didn't get credit for it unless it was seen from the ground. Several of the others saw him go down though so it counts as "out of control." I managed to get a few shots at one of the three lead ones but he pulled up and the others overshot. My guns jammed then so I had to pull out to cure them. Got them cured and went in again but was promptly leapt upon from above and had a bad time for a few minutes.

Used up all my ammunition so pulled out again and collected my flight as they came out of the scrap. Got organized and led them in again but the Huns beat it home as some [more] of our machines appeared above them.

At least fourteen of them went home. We think we got six of them though we only saw two actually crash. But I'm hoping to get the others confirmed from the ground as we saw six go down. All of us got back except [Lawrence] Wyly and I'm hoping he was able to glide back to the lines.

This morning I had three machines with me and about the same place I saw six Huns hiding in the sun above us. So we flew over to them and tried to get them down. But all they would do was dive on us and fire 50 to 75 rounds and then zoom up again. And they were rotten shots. One of them missed me by 200 yards. Only one of our planes was hit. Kenyon got a bullet in his wing. This lasted for about ten minutes and then the Huns gave it up and went on back into the sun. Then they tried to cut us off by coming down from different directions but they lacked nerve and every time they got well hid in the sun we changed our position and got them out of it. They finally beat it altogether and left us in sole possession of the air and in full view of Archie, who made it pretty hot for us. I'm going to try it again tonight though and maybe I can get a bunch of the yellow Fokkers to fight with us. Fokker machines for scout work altogether.[7] Pretty good machines too only the pilots are dud.

As yet I have been unable to get any confirmation for my scrap with the nine the other day so got no credit for it. I even landed up near the front lines to inquire but no one had seen anything but me trying to shoot up the [German] trenches and getting royally peppered. I'm getting lots of scrapping but no confirmation. I now have three to my credit as destroyed, one shared in flames, and two out of control, all confirmed, and two unconfirmed which don't count. But whatever you do, say nothing about it to any one.

Just this moment I am conducting an examination for promotions among the men. Feel like I am back at college again except that the men can't kick at the questions. Thank goodness. Otherwise I'd be mobbed.

Have heard nothing more of my captaincy. Guess it must have been lost. No promotions have come through for any of the officers yet. The C.O. even is still a Lt.

Picked up some souvenirs for you all while I was at the front. The American army claims to be fighting for democracy, but the British and French say we are fighting for souvenirs. And the doughboys say they are fighting to make the world safe for prohibition.

A heartful of love to you and Lena.

Your devoted son, Elliott

FLIGHT LOG: 17 August: 2 hours. Albert—Chaulnes—Roye. Attacked several times.

148th Aero Squadron
Allonville, France
August 17 1918

Dear Mother—

Your letter of July 24 arrived and I hope you will have the good sense to persuade Father to go somewhere else besides White Sulphur [Springs]. Outside of that your letter was pretty dud. The opinions of you and Father of how to fly and how to fight are doubtless valuable but just the same I wish you would send them to some one else. York [Wilson] could probably use them. They might assist him in cleaning his sword. And you haven't told me a thing about how to use my compass. I shall probably be lost though before you all get the information to me. Think it over.

Yes indeed my birthday was very eventful. The most eventful of 22 years. The little display of fireworks the Huns arranged for me was most complimentary. When I got back I remarked to the sergeant that it was a shame I hadn't taken the children along.

The last couple of days I've gotten real fed up having Huns sitting up above me every time I get five miles over and taking a shot at one every now and then. They seldom come down and fight but sometimes they catch us in an awkward position and they are able to pick off one of us and get him and then run home. They won't fight, they're just head hunters, vultures.

So this morning I called up Larry [Callahan] and Capt Horn, got permission from the Colonel and arranged a little surprise party for the Hun. Capt Horn, Larry, MacGregor and two others flew over head for [the rest of the line is unreadable]. I saw them overhead. I took off with five machines. Then we both started to climb and when we reached the lines they were about four thousand feet above us and four miles away. So I went about six miles over and started patrolling up and down climbing all the time. When I got to 3000 I saw what I was looking for, six Huns up in the sun above me. Pretending I didn't see them I cut off and went right underneath them losing height all the time. It looked like cold meat to the Huns and it was so cold that they wanted to make sure of getting us all and they waited for us to get nearer and turn so they came down to about 1000 feet above us and stayed in the sun. Meanwhile Capt Horn led the others around in back of the Huns and got above them in the sun and then I turned and dived south to bring the Huns on down with their tails towards the others.

It looked for a moment like a slaughtering party was going to be pulled off and everything was ready for the trap to be sprung when the Hun Archie opened up. And Archie fired not at us or Capt Horn, but at the Huns themselves and they varied the color so we could see that it was a signal. Immediately I saw the Huns, who were just beginning to open fire on us, turn and put their noses down for home doing about 300 [miles per hour].

So our game was up and I went down on the carpet after a two seater I saw some distance over. It proved to be one of ours and the same six Huns came down on us and I had [to] duck under the clouds at 1000 feet and dodge machine gun fire all the way back. Then I spotted another machine dodging around in the clouds and he was a Hun. We played Hide & Seek for about fifteen minutes and then some other machines dove on him before I could get a shot at him. Think they got him.

But we'll work our little stunt before long and when we do the slaughter will be terrific. But I don't know which is going to get me first, a bullet or nervous strain. Playing bait is the most desperate game in the world and unless properly played is the most deadly. That's all I have been doing for the past two weeks and it's beginning to tell. I'll never be able to shoot at a bird. I know too well how it feels. I also sympathize with the [man] who dodges the baseballs with his head through a hole.

Word has reached me that my letters are being quoted. There's honor among thieves but darn little among families. I use the profanity with intent hoping that you will be shocked and Father indignant. If I didn't know that 'twould affect you thus there would be no point in using it. I hope nice people will always be displeased with darn etc. It will save learning a new sort of profanity and the army's profanity is not expressive at all, it's only emphatic.

Larry is prostrated. His family passed one of his letters around and it got in the papers. Needless to say he is not going to write any more. I also saw a letter from his father. You could tell it was from his father. You could tell his father had confidence in him. You could also tell his father was a human being. I should like to meet him some day. I imagine he gets on well with Larry's friends. I don't think he will ask me if Larry drinks. If he does, I shall tell him no, he only gargles with it. Think it over.

A heartful of love to you and Father

Devotedly, Elliott

FLIGHT LOG: 18 August: 15 minutes. Allonville to Remaisnil [five miles west of Doullens]. Flying to new aerodrome.

148th Aero Squadron
Remaisnil, France
August 19 1918

Dear Father—

You don't know how pleased I am to be hearing from you regularly at short intervals after a year's absence. Please continue. We have moved again. It's beginning to be a habit. Also a nuisance. So now I go up again alone and get all the landmarks in our new territory, then I take the flight up and lead them up and down the lines until they get the compass bearing of all roads and canals, know all the woods and villages and get the positions of all salients[8] and then we are ready for battle. I now know Mother France pretty well.

There will be a number of professions open to me after the war. I might be a mail carrier, an aerial chauffeur, a map maker, or work in an information bureau at the railway station.

I had dinner last night with our new Colonel. Next to being a Paris bartender I think I'd rather be a Colonel in the Royal Air Force. They live in chateaux, have a couple of cars for short distance work, and any sort of planes when they want to go anywhere in a hurry. The Generals even have a chauffeur for their planes. And they live like Marc Antony did when Cleopatra was keeping house for him. I've dined with three different ones now and I can't remember where I got the best meal. A squadron commander is rather a glorified individual but he has nothing on the Colonel.

The General came over to see us also. He walked up to me unannounced and we started a conversation. I didn't know what he was, his insignia wasn't showing as he had a French coat on and he spoke so familiarly of various matters that I thought he was a Capt so we had quite a little argument. He knew of Larry and Mac and finally it turned out he was the General who let us get with Bishop back in London.[9] These RAF Great Moguls are the greatest in the world. They make Lord Chesterfield appear like truck drivers for polish.

Glad to hear you have the Stutz at home. Think you'd better dispose of it though. I left the keys with the Rea Sprocket Garage in East 31st St.

Glad to hear the mills are doing so well. You must be getting them in fine shape now. My congratulations.

Have run into a lot of old friends around here already. One squadron near here used to be on the same aerodrome with us and I know practically all of the old pilots. The Flying Corps out here is sort of a club anyway. I think I could wander into any squadron's mess out here and see two or three fellows I know pretty well. A pair of wings are better than any fraternity or club.

A heartful of love to you and Lena.

Devotedly, Elliott

FLIGHT LOG: 20 August: 45 minutes. Arras—Bapaume. Weather dud.
FLIGHT LOG: 21 August: 2 hours 5 minutes. Arras south. Escort RE-8.
FLIGHT LOG: 22 August: 1 hour 50 minutes. Arras—Albert. Got two Fokkers. (IX)
COMBAT REPORT: 148th Aero Squadron, 10:10 AM, 22 August. Remarks on hostile aircraft: Fokker biplane—grey and white checked grayish crosses, stripe back of cross on fuselage, white tail, white undercarriage. Results: Destroyed, one; Driven down out of control, one. Narrative: Attacked one of five E. A. and fired a burst of 150 [rounds] at close range. Right hand gun No. 3 stoppage. Pulled up a little, remedied stoppage and attacked E. A. again, who was spiraling. Fired 200 rounds, very close range and E. A. went down in a dive and crashed near the wood south of Velu. Attacked another E. A. on same level and we both went into vertical turn. I was just able to turn inside of him and fired 200 rounds into him with deflection and 100 from off his tail at 25 yds., when E. A. straightened out. E. A. side-slipped and went into a wabbly dive. Was unable to follow him down as [he] got beneath my wing at 2000 ft. Attacked another E. A. who dove east. Had no more ammunition, so pulled out. Sgnd, E. W. Springs, 1st Lt, Air Service, USA.[10]
FLIGHT LOG: 22 August: 2 hours. Arras—Albert. Got one Fokker. (X)
REPORT ON ATTACK ON ENEMY GROUND TARGETS: Lt. Springs, in Camel D-8250, 3:30 PM, 22 August. Dropped 8 bombs from a height of 1500 feet on road just southwest of Ecoust St. Menin. Fired 900 rounds at transport on road southwest of Queant.[11]
COMBAT REPORT: 148th Aero Squadron, 5:40 PM, 22 August. Remarks on hostile aircraft: Fokker biplane, green and white camouflage. Good pilot. Result: Drive down out of control. Narrative: Three E. A. came down on lower flight. One stopped at 6000 ft., another turned east and I attacked the third who was below me at 6000 ft. We exchanged bursts and began maneuvering. After a series of five half-rolls, he turned east and I fired a burst of 100 rounds at close range on tail of E. A. E. A. went over on back and then went into a twisting dive. I followed him down and as I could not dive fast enough watched him [continue]

down in a side-slip. E. A. continued dive into Bapaume. Sgnd, E. W. Springs, 1st Lt, Air Service, USA.[12]

FLIGHT LOG: 23 August: 1 hour 15 minutes. St. Legere [to] Arnheim. Low bombing.

FLIGHT LOG: 23 August: 1 hour 5 minutes. Bapaume. Low bombing.

REPORT ON ATTACK ON ENEMY GROUND TARGETS: Lt. Springs, in Camel D-8250, 7:30 PM, 23 August. Dropped 4 bombs from 1500 feet on road between Ligny and Bapaume. Observed four bursts on edge of road near transport. Fired 700 rounds at transport on road between Ligny and Bapaume. Shot up road from Beugnatre. Saw fire in St. Leger. Heavy ground fire near Bapaume.[13]

148th Aero Squadron, France
Remaisnil, France
August 2[4] 1918[14]

Dear Mother—

Again I've got that feeling, gee, it's great to be alive. The last three days have been particularly strenuous and eventful. Ordinarily I wouldn't be able to sleep at all but I'm getting so hardened to it that I slept like a baby last night. And I'm getting so bored at being shot at that I don't bother to dodge any more. I sat in the midst of Archie bursts yesterday for five minutes and yawned, refused to turn until they knocked me about thirty feet. I used to be scared to death of Archie and fire from the ground. Now it almost fails to excite my curiosity.

To begin with, the day before yesterday [22 August] I had four dog fights. In the morning we attacked five Huns. I paired off with a Fokker on my own level and we maneuvered for a couple of minutes trying to get on each other's tail. I finally got inside him, put 100 rounds into him and he went out of control and crashed into a wood. Another one was after me by that time and we had quite a scrap but he made the fatal blunder of reversing his bank and I shot him down too after pumping 300 rounds into him. Couldn't see whether he crashed or not, as there was another one coming down on me from above. Couldn't get him but then he didn't get me. I was down on the carpet by that time and had to come back low for five miles while the Huns picked at me.

In the afternoon, Henry Clay took his flight down on a two-seater and I stayed up to protect him from some scouts above. Three of the scouts got their nerve up and came down and didn't see me as I was just under some clouds. I hopped one and he beat it home and then I dove on the other. We had a regular old-time duel all over again and we fought down from 8000 feet to about 2000 when he did a bad half-roll and I did a stall turn above him and came right down on his tail. [I fired] 100 rounds and he went spinning down into a little village.

I was very lucky that scrap as he was an exceptionally good pilot and got several good cracks at me. I came back with several holes in my plane to testify to his skill. Two of the Huns I got confirmed as the others saw the fight but the three last week I can't claim unless the Intelligence [section] can confirm it for me later.

Yesterday we did ground straffing. You know about that? Well, I can't tell you because words can't describe it. Orders came through for it the night before and I felt exactly as I did when they used to tell me at the Johns Hopkins [hospital] that I would have the stomach pump at seven the next morning. I didn't mind the pumping much but I slept not a wink thinking about it.

So, I strung bombs all over my little scout and got a piece of steel put under my [seat] cushion and took my flight over the lines about four miles pretty low. I saw what we were after, Hun transport, so I gave the signal and we all went down on the carpet. All the machine guns and field guns were shooting at us but somehow we got through and dropped our messages with pretty good effect and then shot up everything we could see and then raced madly home, zigzagging furiously. As soon as we got back, they told us to get ready to do it again. So over again we went and I saw a road packed with gun linkers. I dropped my bombs on them and then started shooting. My bombs hit on the side of the road and everything scattered. Then we shot up everything we could find, machine gun nests, balloons on the ground, Archie batteries, everything, and though several were badly shot up, we all got back. In all, yesterday I pumped about 2000 rounds in the Huns' back yards and about 1000 into his planes the day before. I feel quite bucked about it.

I'm waiting now for it to clear up enough for me to go up and do some more of it but have gotten quite reconciled to it. It's not worth bothering about. Either you do or you don't and you have very little to say about it. Imagine how I laugh at all the letters from home emphasizing "do be careful." What can we do to be careful? Pass the word about to call it off. Funny about this game. One minute you are inspired to heights otherwise unattainable and think no more of making the supreme sacrifice than of tackling the second egg at breakfast. The next you are so fed up you want to go to a South Seas Isle where they don't know whether war is a vegetable or a new kind of barbed wire.

A duel with a Hun plane—and whether you win or lose is immaterial—you see it through and rejoice then and for a day or so after. The smell of powder up in the air has an effect indescribable. But the waiting around, the hot air, red tape, and pettiness on the ground disgusts you. While you are in the air you are so far above the smallness of [human?] nature and stupidity that the contrast on the ground is disgusting. When you get the spirit of the thing in the air, there's no job too dangerous or difficult to tackle cheerfully and voluntarily with no chance of ever getting credit for it even if you get away with it. And it's fun. But when you're ordered up to go ground straffing or go for balloons you feel that the man who gives the order is nothing more or less than an executioner and if he makes you wait around all day he's nothing more or less than an accomplished torturer.

We're forming two new organizations. One is the "Society for the Extermination of Aerial Amateur Authors." "Sergeant Pilot Wright" is to be our first honorary member and with each fresh paper from home we get a few more names for our list.[15] One "Terror of the Hun" in his article states that "he opened fire 'violently.'" Wonder he didn't break the trigger. He's proud because he got his right over his own aerodrome. Lord, I wish we would catch one within five miles of the lines.

The other is the Committee on Self Defense to Suppress and Prevent from Return Home the Aerial Heroes of the Battle of Paris and Siege of London. There are enough wounded heroes in Paris to win the war if you ever get them near enough to the front or move the front back to them. They are all members of the "I wanted to go to the Front but important executive work . . ." Club.

How's the Battle on the Texas Front? Isn't it a shame the dear boys can't get over, no matter how hard they try? How are the Naval Aviators getting along? It must be awful guarding New York Harbor. Ask Father if he isn't glad I didn't become an air instructor. Possibly I am in a good humor but then you haven't seen real men going west every day like I have. Real men, that love fighting.

Devotedly, Elliott

FLIGHT LOG: 24 August: 1 hour 15 minutes. Bapaume. [Kent] Curtis gone west. Shot down during low bombing. [Curtis was not killed but became a prisoner of war.] Attacked by five Fokkers.

REPORT ON ATTACK ON GROUND TARGETS: Lt. E. W. Springs, in Camel D-8250, 5:15 PM, 24 August. Dropped 4 bombs on road between Beugnatre and Vaulk-Vrancourt. Fired 700 rounds on gun limbers going into Vaulk-Vrancourt. Heavy machine gun fire from Beugnatre. Engaged 5 Fokkers unsuccessfully 1600–12000 ft.[16]

148th Aero Squadron
Remaisnil, France
August 25 1918

Dear Mother—

The first shipment of Page & Shaw's arrived today and brought great cheer. I now have enough sugar to corrupt half the population of Paris between the ages of 18 and 21 of the gentler sex and the wives of four generals and eight colonels. Please tell them hereafter to send me only Egyptian Deities and mixed chocolates and marshmallow Genesis. I am sending some of the sugar to Pabst and Lorraine Goodrich. Pabst can then use her share and use his as best he sees fit. The Paris charmers will laugh at jewelry, scorn frat pins, bread tickets and Hun souvenirs, but just mention the fact that you have some sugar, well it's like getting careless with a limousine at the Frolics.

I wonder what your idea of a battle is? Well, I'll give you mine and you can change yours as much as is necessary and then hightone the new preacher when he tries to put something across.

I went out about five last night loaded with specially selected lead pellets [twenty-pound bombs] and took [Linn] Forster along with me. [Joseph] Kenyon went a half hour before and [Kent] Curtis was to come a half hour later. We flew very low, the clouds were at 3000 feet and very heavy. When we got up to the lines, I saw about 40 white puffs of smoke in a line about 20 feet off the ground. That was a barrage. As the puffs would die away, more would take their place. Nothing could be seen on the ground at all. Further along was a village and high explosive shells were rapidly obliterating it. I would see several buildings rise about 20 feet, disintegrate, muck fly about, and then as it settled I would hear a dull report and my machine would wobble from the concussion. A mile more and nothing but the rattle of machine guns below and an occasional burst of Archie or field guns about us. Two miles more and I saw some Hun artillery on a road. I signaled to Forster and we went down on the carpet. I dropped my bombs on them and then started to chase one limber up the road.

Then I saw some troops just off the road and I put 500 rounds into them. Machine gun fire from the ground was pretty hot and then I heard a crack, crack, crack, pitched in a higher key. I looked around and just below the clouds coming down on me were five Fokker biplanes. Two of them were firing and I could see the tracer coming towards me from their guns. I twisted and turned and looked for Forster. He was underneath a low cloud and the Huns didn't see him. They drove me back still twisting. I was right on the carpet in the midst of the little village. Then I started back low zigzagging and eventually reached a point that I knew was occupied by our troops and drew a deep breath. Shells were bursting everywhere, shrapnel in the open spaces with its white puff and high explosive with its cloud of dust and debris on the trench parapets. Here and there were tanks, some belching lead and others a mass of flame or a misshapen mass, hit by field guns. I was down very low but saw very few dead bodies but a number of dead horses. The ground was all pockmarked and what little vegetation remained was a light straw in color from the gas. Further down I saw the Huns using gas, a thin layer of brownish green stuff was drifting slowly along the ground from a trench about 300 yards long. But no men were to be seen anywhere. Only horses and tanks, mostly abandoned.

The Fokkers had left me and were hovering about in the clouds waiting for someone else. Forster was nowhere to be seen. I looked my plane over carefully and found no holes so started back. I was there in sight of our reserve lines where the advanced artillery was banging away. I got an idea. The Huns were in the clouds. Why not beat them at their own game? So I climbed into the clouds and headed towards where I thought they ought to be. The clouds were intermittent so I had to climb up to 9000 before I got above them so I could see any distance. I saw my Huns, seven of them now, and worked down on them from the sun. Then they went into or under a cloud and I lost them. Then I got lost myself. Then I found out where I was and saw my Huns again, four this time. Then a cloud got between us and I lost them.

So I came down through a gap and deposited the rest of my ammunition in the Hun trenches and along the roads and went on a personally conducted sight seeing tour of the Battle. I saw everything, advance trenches, reserve trenches, tanks, reserve tanks, armoured cars, artillery in action, support [columns] going up, demolished towns, cuts that were once railway cuts, thousands of yards of barbed wire, in fact the whole battle was there.

I got back, circled just above the hangar and when the sergeant signaled me with a [flare] pistol that my bomb racks were clear and nothing was stuck on my undercarriage, I landed. Forster had already gotten back safely but Kent Curtis was shot down by one of the Huns. A fine fellow he was, possessed of an excellent sense of humor, once a teacher of French and German at a Missouri college, once a guide in the northern woods, and a gentleman above reproach. His witty remarks will long ring in my ears, and he was a musician with few equals. [Erwin] Shaw, from Sumter, South Carolina, had also been reported missing and [William] Deetjen, my right hand man at Oxford. We've lost [men] very heavily lately. I'm waiting around now for another ground straffing show. As soon as I get my information as to the position of our troops and up we go to clear the way in front of it.

But Lord, how this business is getting to me. Last night the old restlessness overtook me and no sleep could I get. It's not your nerve that's affected but nerves. It's your stamina, your power of endurance, that's hit by this game. A man comes out here with no nerve or nerves, and as he develops one, the other comes along. Don't think for a moment that nerve is just born in a man, it ain't. Recklessness, foolhardiness, fearlessness, yes, but nerve, no. Nerve is cultivated and may or may not include recklessness. It is the ability to carry through anything anywhere without faltering. A man who rushes into a fight and then lets his hand shake on the trigger hasn't got it. And the fool who doesn't know when to be afraid hasn't got it. He'll get scared some day and spill the beans. But a man with nerve is a hardened, tempered individual who may be scared to death, but fear to him is like water on a duck's back.

Well I just got the location of the points I wanted and orders to take the air in twenty minutes.

A heartful of love to you and Father.

Devotedly, Elliott

FLIGHT LOG: 25 August: 1 hour 20 minutes. Bapaume. Low straff.
    [George] Siebold missing on low straff.
REPORT ON ATTACK ON ENEMY INFANTRY: Lt. E. W. Springs, Camel
    D-8250, 6:00 PM, 25 August. At 2000 ft., fired 750 rounds at transport
    just east of Beugny and just north of Fremicourt.[17]

148th Aero Squadron
Remaisnil, France
August 27 1918

Dear Father—

I'm certainly getting a run for my money these days. Eight holes in my plane when I got back last night from the scrap. But it was a good scrap. You see the Huns knew that we were shooting up and bombing a certain road about five miles over. And it was annoying them. And we of course knew that he would make an effort to stop it. So we planned accordingly. I took my flight over low, 3000 feet. A Flight was just above me and Henry Clay took his [C Flight] over at 5000. Above was Tipton and Hamilton with a whole squadron [the 17th Aero Squadron] and up on the ceiling were some more Allied machines. I crossed over and shot up the road. An Archie battery was annoying us. So I shot that up also.

Then things began to happen. Coming towards us out of Hunland were five Hun two seaters in wing tip formation at 2000 feet. Now that's the coldest meat in the world and I began to gloat in anticipation. They saw me and came straight on. Aha, says I, a trap; we'll go easy. But all looked well. I took my flight down on them and broke up their formation. Then each of us hopped a Hun and A Flight came down to complete the slaughter.

But was I surprised? You bet I was. I had the hardest scrap of my career. The buses proved to be the latest type of Hun two seater fighters [possibly the Hannover CL II] and one of them almost got me. I got rid of him and slipped under another's tail. Put two or three hundred rounds into him and he went down in a dive. I thought I had gotten him but I followed him down and he leveled off. Awfully inconsiderate of him. The fight continued and five more Huns arrived unannounced. I looked up and saw [Henry] Clay having a big scrap at 5000. Still higher was another scrap in progress. So we fought on but every way I would attack a Hun, a stream of phosphorus would greet me in the wake of lead. Finally my ammunition gave out just as a lone Hun and I were having it out by ourselves over in a far corner. But I did have the satisfaction of chasing him home. He didn't know I had given out of ammunition.

It appears that the whole thing was a carefully arranged trap. The two Huns down low were bait. They figured all of us would hop them and then thirty or forty Huns up high would come down after we were split up and finish us off. Meanwhile the two seaters could defend themselves by sticking together for a few moments. But the only Huns up high who got down were shot down. The ceiling men shot down two, [the William] Tipton and [Lloyd] Hamilton crowd [from the 17th Aero Squadron] got one, Henry Clay got one, and we got two of the two seaters. One Hun got away up high and was passed on down by consecutive layers and was finally shot down by [Oscar] Mandel at 500 feet. Altogether it was a successful afternoon. I hope the Hun continues to arrange such nice parties for us. He's getting pretty clever these days though. Every time you cross the lines you run into some of his little tricks and you have to be pretty cute to dodge them.

I heard that Alex Matthews was killed yesterday. Too bad. Also E. D. Shaw of Sumter has been missing some time.[18] If you know his people you might write them a letter of sympathy. There's a good chance that he may be alive and a prisoner. Fine fellow. We came over together.

Ernest [Mount] cabled me that he was married. Yesterday I cabled him to draw on the Bank of Lancaster for $500 and also cabled you asking you to honor it. Also I'm fairly low [on money] myself and I may get a week's leave before long if I don't get to the "Queen of the May" stage before then. And just to remind you, I'm still expecting you to say nothing about what I'm doing over here. My letters are strictly confidential and secret, written for yours and Lena's consumption only.

A heartful of love for you both.

Your devoted son, Elliott

FLIGHT LOG: 27 August: 2 hours 15 minutes. Arras-Cambrai Road. 15 to 20 Fokkers. Got one. (XI)

COMBAT REPORT: 148th Aero Squadron, 1:10–1:30 PM, 27 August. Remarks on Hostile Aircraft: Fokker biplanes—grey and white— orange strip on fuselage. Pilots very good—very stout. Results: Crashed. Narrative: We attacked six E. A. southwest of Souchy. I fired a burst into one, and he half-rolled and went down in a dive. About five minutes later we attacked six more E. A. near Prionville. I fired about 300 rounds into one, who turned over on back. I contin- ued firing and followed him down. E. A. went down through thick clouds in a slow spinning dive. Sgnd, E. W. Springs, 1st Lt, Air Ser- vice, USA.[19]

148th Aero Squadron
Remaisnil, France
August 28 1918

Dear Aunt Addie—

Your letter arrived the other day and was very welcome. I've forgotten the date and as we are not supposed to have letters or anything to give away our identity on our person, I can't look it up.

No, Aunt Addie, I am not in a YMCA. It just happens that this is the only writing paper I can locate at this moment. Can't imagine where this came from. By the heading up in the corner you might think I was down at Marseilles or over in England. Don't be hightoned by it, it doesn't mean anything. Instead I have a grand stand seat at the big scrap and it's worth coming a long way for. I've had the opportunity of seeing tanks in action, gas attacks, and barrages in large numbers. I got too curious one day and saw [something] on the ground that interested me so I went down to have a good look at it. It slipped my mind that said object was on the Hun side of the lines and it never occurred to me that the machine gun fire I heard below me was aimed in my direction. All of a sudden I realized that it was a personal matter as something whistled by me leaving a yellow streak—tracer bullets—and I certainly made that particular spot as vacant as possible.

Got shot up a little but not much. A plane traveling at 100 to 130 miles an hour is a pretty hard target and you don't accomplish anything unless you hit the pilot, motor, or the control cables. I've seen machines come back with thirty or forty bullet holes in them. One of our men last week was wounded in five places, had his motor and one control shot away and still was able to get back just inside our lines.

A heartful of love,

Your devoted nephew, Elliott

148th Aero Squadron
Remaisnil, France
August 28 1918

Dear Mother—

I did a most futile and absurd thing yesterday—I went to the dentist! Think of it! But he told me that they would last a month longer without any work so I let it go at that.

Had a good scrap yesterday [27 August]. Henry Clay got a two seater—shot its wing off—and I got a Fokker Biplane. Got it confirmed, too, luckily. One of the fellows below saw it spin down and crash and then burst into flames on the ground. Just before we had a scrap with seven of them but we were too far over and the wind was against us so we had to pull out of the fight before anything happened.

Saw still another bunch of Huns but some other machines of ours got to them first. These Huns are getting entirely too ambitious. They're almost getting offensive! Before long one of them will actually come up to the lines! All because they got by with one good show. It was the same bunch that got Tipton, Hamilton, Campbell, Williams [all from the 17th Aero Squadron], and lastly [George] Siebold in A Flight. It's von Richtoven's Old Circus and have entirely the wrong idea about this war. It's up to us now to show them who owns this front. You can always tell them by their orange and red fuselages.

Tipton and Hamilton were the two best American pilots. The French-trained American "Aces" can't touch them. And Campbell and Frost [all four pilots were from the 17th Aero Squadron] were the next best with the exception of Callahan. All five of them had each shot down more than three Huns but it's not the number that counts—it's the way they did it. Siebold had two to his credit. And now in three days, Tipton, Campbell, Hamilton, Frost, Siebold, Curtis, Matthews, Todd, and Ritter [are gone].[20] I'm feeling really depressed. Tipton and Hamilton and Frost were Flight Commanders in the 17th American Aero Squadron which is the only other [American] squadron besides us operating with the British.

I'm trying to get Larry Callahan in my flight and I think I can. If so it ought to help a lot as my nerves are worn to a frazzle leading all these patrols and I can trust Larry to take a lot of work off my shoulders. Leading patrols is one of the most difficult jobs I want to tackle—particularly when the matter is complicated by multiple flights that you have to watch out for. And you get all the responsibility. [If] a man is lost—it's the Flight Commander's fault often.

When Bishop first got his flight, he took them on patrol, five of them, and came back alone. After that he only lost one man in five months. Mannock was different. He got more Huns than Bishop but he lost men regularly doing it by taking too many chances. And finally he went west himself. And then there's the famous Capt Trollope [J. F. Trollope of 43 Squadron, RFC]. He lost three entire flights in succession, going west himself with the third. But he accounted for thirty Huns himself besides those that must have gone down with those who never came back. I'm trying to steer the middle course. I want to get Huns, and I try to do my work, but at the same time I'm trying to go easy on the lives of the men who are depending on me to pull them through.

Well I'm due for another show so will go on down and get ready.

A heartful of love to you and Father.

Devotedly, Elliott

FLIGHT LOG: 29 August: 2 hours 20 minutes. O.P. [Operational Patrol]
    Lots of Fokkers.
FLIGHT LOG: 29 August: 2 hours 15 minutes. O.P. Working with 60
    [Squadron]. Dud.

148th Aero Squadron
Remaisnil, France
August 30 1918

Dear Father—

No mail in the last few days but hope there's some on the way. Lots of action lately. I've been shot at so much lately that I feel like a duck. I seem to spend most of my time dodging and I'm getting to the point where I feel lonesome and neglected unless some kind Hun is cracking away at me.

The Hun is doing nothing now but setting traps for us. Yesterday I had three men with me and I saw seven Huns about ten miles over. We maneuvered about for five or ten minutes and finally I got there in closer to the lines and got above them. Everything looked propitious and I led [the flight] down on them. But as I went in I had a good look around and caught sight of eleven more Huns coming down on us so I pulled out and beat it away. Fortunately the other three [in the flight] had enough confidence in me and passed them up too and followed me back.

So I waited my chance and when the eleven retired to wait for more easy meat I got around the other side of the seven and went in again. We were too quick for the eleven to come down on us so the seven beat it home without waiting for them. I almost got one. I got on his tail and put a hundred or so rounds into him. [Henry] Clay and his flight were down below and saw us go in. He said he was quite tickled to see me hop one and then to see him start down in a spin. But the Hun got control again at 2000 feet, leveled off, and went on home. I thought sure I'd gotten him and would have followed him down and finished him off but we were too far over and there were too many Huns about so we had to call it off. You have to be awfully careful how you wander about because the Hun has concentrated a lot of machines here and is always setting traps. And if he catches anything in his traps he knows how to make a killing of it.

You meet some Hun squadrons who are rotten and you can mop them up with no trouble and the next day you run into a crowd that will reverse the process if you give them half a chance. Just lately we have been scrapping with Richthofen's old circus and I can certainly testify that they are good. They've spoiled several afternoons for me. However, we are not asleep by a long shot and if they aren't careful they'll get a dose of their own medicine.

Larry Callahan is coming to my flight next week and then I may be able to lay off for a week. I need a little rest. My nerves are in rotten shape and my eyes are going back on me again. Don't laugh when I say "nerves." It's no joke. Long patrols and ground straffing will get any man in time.

I'm waiting now to go up and shoot up a road about three miles over. It'll have to be done from 1000 to 2000 feet and it's a nasty joke. I don't mind the actual show; it's rather fun, chasing Huns down a road, bombing their lorries and cars but it's rotten to have to sit around and wait for your turn to go up. And then if you get by with one show you have to go up a while later on another and so forth.

I wish you and Lena would write more.

A heartful of love to you both.

Your devoted son, Elliott

FLIGHT LOG: 31 August: 1 hour 25 minutes. O.P. and ground straff. One bomb on undercarriage [One bomb remained attached to aircraft, unknown to Springs].

FLIGHT LOG: 31 August: 1 hour 25 minutes. Ground straff Prionville.

REPORT ON ATTACK ON ENEMY GROUND TARGETS: Lt. E. W. Springs, Camel D-8250, 7:15 PM, 31 August. Dropped 3 bombs on road east of Pronville. No transport seen. Approximately 15 E. A. seen.[21]

FLIGHT LOG: 1 September: 1 hour. Ground straff Prionville.

REPORT ON ATTACK ON ENEMY GROUND TARGETS: Lt E. W. Springs, Camel D-8250, 12:30 PM, 1 September. Dropped four bombs on transport on road between Manacourt and Etricourt. Fired 350 rounds into transport.[22]

148th Aero Squadron
Remaisnil, France
September 1 1918

Dear Mother—

The rumor is correct—there is a war on over here. After the last patrol I counted seven bullet holes in my plane and [George] Dorsey got back with twenty or thirty in his, one spar, one rib, two longerons, and one control [cable] shot away and the axis pin shot out of his flying wires. I don't see how he made it.

[Errol] Zistell was missing for three hours but finally turned up with a Hun Major General's slippers as a souvenir. His motor had conked and he glided back just this side of the lines and managed somehow or other to land between the shell holes. He found the trouble—broken wiring on the magneto—and fixed it. Then some officers took him into their dugout. They had just captured the Hun general and they gave him the slippers. And being a flying man they, of course, killed the fatted calf for him. The very best corks were popped and he even partook of issue rum which is not to be sneezed at. So he felt very brave and after getting his bus started up he managed to get off the ground and then, full of Dutch courage, he went about seven miles over and dropped his eggs on some Hun transport and shot up some infantry. Quite a good show.

I don't know how much damage I did to the Hun last night but I certainly put the wind up myself. We went over low and saw some transport and I released my bombs and shot them up. Then I saw a fight going on above me so I climbed up to join it but was too late to get in. Fooled around until dark and then came back low. I always come down over the trenches now. It seems to buck up the infantry a lot to see their planes about them. So I come down to about ten or fifteen feet and they stick their heads out and wave furiously. I wave back which seems to please them a lot and if I find a particularly enthusiastic bunch I circle around and stunt for them some. The Scotch troops are always very friendly and appreciate stunting.

Well I came back that way and some distance back of the lines I did a quick turn to avoid a tree. Then something flashed and I was blown about fifty feet up. My [fuel] tank! I thought, but the machine was all right. A bomb then, yes it must have been, so I circle around and sure enough I had dropped a bomb but fortunately no one had been nearby. It must have gotten caught on the undercarriage. Were there any more stuck and about to go off when I landed? So I twisted and squirmed to shake off imaginary bombs but nothing happened so I came on back to the aerodrome. It was dark by that time but my sergeant kept firing a flare pistol and I found my way back by it. And I made the most careful landing of my career. I might have been landing on eggs.

Everybody came rushing out because Forster had seen the bombs still hanging on in the air and had tried to tell me about it but had lost me in the clouds when I went [up] after the scrap. I remember then his signaling to me but thought at the time that he was calling my attention to Huns above.

The worst of this low straffing game is that you don't get a chance to get into any scraps. You get shot at all the time from the ground but Hun planes seldom attack and you're too low to get to any of them.

The C. O. and I are dining with the General himself tonight. I don't know why we are thus honored but think there's a trick in it somewhere. Probably he's got some particularly dirty job for us and wants to kid us along that he's doing us a favor. But we're sure to get a knock-out dinner and all the raspazass will be there. I'll be sure to make a few breaks and tell a few Colonels and Majors things they shouldn't know.

A heartful of love to you and Father.

Your devoted son, Elliott

148th Aero Squadron
Remaisnil, France
September 1 1918[23]

Dear Mother—

The Springs family seems to be about as honorable as the German Red Cross. Or possibly you and Father don't understand my wishes in regard to publicity. Why was the *Lancaster News* permitted to bootlick Father by mentioning my connecting with Bishop? How did the editor even find out about it? Well, it's got to stop! What I write home is for you and Father only. Aunt Addie, Aunt Bleeker, Uncle Alva, or anyone else whatsoever regardless of whether they-knew-me-when-I-was-too-young-to-resent-it or not are not to be told [anything except] that I am in good health and, when last reported, sober.

And if anybody writes me again that "doubtless you hope to be an ace" I'll send them an infernal machine. I am not an "ace" don't want to be an "ace" and never will be an "ace." We don't have "aces" here. This "ace" stuff makes me tired. Call it off, wash it out! Also this individual effort stuff is all wrong. If I get any more Huns than [the other] men in my flight it's because I'm a better shot. If they don't get Huns it's because I'm a bad leader as much as anything else. My job is not to get Huns myself, but to lead my flight to the detriment of the Hun. It's as bad a faux pas as asking General Foch how many Huns he shot in the Marne show. "Say, Bill. How many Huns did General Pershing kill? None? Well, he's no good."

With the French and Franco-Americans it's different—decidedly different. I don't pretend to know their system but just wait and see which system wins out. I'll admit they have good press agents but I'm glad we are [not] burdened with them. Those press agents wipe out the Hun flying corps every week. And watch out for a man named Cushman A. Rice. He's a major and saw the Hun lines one day from a distance, from the ground. I hear he's back in the States now telling the folks how he killed some odd number of Huns.

The C. O. and I dined with the General the other night.[24] He's one of the most influential men in the Royal Air Force and certainly the most interesting. There were also a couple of Majors about and a very important Colonel so I felt properly hightoned. I was glad to find out that the invitation was not issued because we were Americans but because we had really done good work and our work was appreciated.

I felt much as I felt when dining with Father's influential friends except that I didn't have to pass up anything and drink ginger ale. As both of us are 1st Lts still they didn't quite know where to put us but finally they put

Mort [Newhall] on the right and me on the left of the General. We could help each other out.

But when the talk drifted to flying and fighting I was certainly not handicapped by rank as I was the only man present who had done battle with the Hun in recent days and I certainly slid them some hot dope right off the fire that afternoon. The General will feel bad for a week about what I told him in regard to ground straffing. That is, of course, if he listened to me. He seemed to. But I have to hand it to the R.A.F. great Moguls. They all know their job from A to Singapore. This particular Brigadier General was a Major General in London when I was training there and took a lower rank to come out here to be in on the show. The Headquarters was in a chateau of course and it goes without saying that I got the best meal I've had for a long time.

I had a letter from Larry [Callahan] from London. When he comes back from leave he will be in my flight. Hun papers please copy. Poor old [Field] Kindley had the breeze put up him properly yesterday. He got a bullet right through his goggles and two others in his office [cockpit].

A heartful of love to you and Father.

Devotedly, Elliott

FLIGHT LOG: 2 September: 1 hour 35 minutes. Canal du Nord. Disaster
   itself. 15 Fokkers. [Linn] Forster, [Joseph] Kenyon, [Joseph] Frobisher,
   [Oscar] Mandel missing.[25]

148th Aero Squadron
Remaisnil, France
September 3 1918

Dear Father—
   Yesterday I got mixed up in the hottest battle of my experience. It was a dog fight par excellence. The clouds were at 5000 feet with intermittent thundershowers and I was working just underneath them with three men. "A" flight was working over the same [section of the] front with me and we had a lot of artillery observation and contact patrol machines up which I was protecting. I saw a dozen or more Hun scouts some distance over on the edge of the cloud and kept my eye on them. Finally I met them about four miles over and took a crack at them but there were too many so withdrew and waited for them to split up. They didn't and so I went back and got "A" flight and went in again. The wind and numbers were against us but the Huns were after our low machines so I had to take them on. I

hopped the higher of the two formations and was in turn attacked by some others.

Plainly the Huns meant business and so did we, so there you are. As soon as I would get on the tail of one Hun, another would get me and as soon as I would shake him off there would be another. Forster shot down one off my tail and got in a bad position himself. Two got him with one above waiting for me. He dove under me and I took the one on his tail. But before I could get him there was one on my tail shooting at 25 yards range. I could see the tracers going two feet over my head. I had to circle twice under him before he stopped firing and pulled up. I looked at my wings and [saw that] my left lower wing [had] buckled. I went into a spin. I thought the machine was falling to pieces and reflected with pleasure that I had forgotten my pocketbook. I thought of Mac [Grider] and how glad he would be to see me.

But my plane held together, just four ribs had broken just back of the main [wing] spar and I got out of the spin all right in time to hop a Hun who was after one of our machines down low. I was on the carpet by that time and had to come back. I climbed up and found Kindley and we went back to clean up. All the Huns had gone home though and we counted three machines on the ground, two of them Huns, so we came back.

I don't know how many Huns we got out of it. I'm the only one of my flight who returned [four pilots from B Flight failed to return]. "A" flight lost one man and claims three Huns. One of our Archie batteries confirms three for us and reported one of our machines landed under control. I think that was probably Forster as that Hun must have hit his engine.[26]

But anyway we saved our two seaters and got quite a few of the Huns even though we were outnumbered. And it was a fair scrap. No trickery or dirty work as is usually the case. We had no option but to fight and we weren't far over. Of course I feel pretty bad over it but I'll get my own back shortly.

I got four new machines this morning and we'll get some new pilots to-morrow. It means a lot of work now. I've got to train my flight and get the machines in proper tune and it takes time to train a bunch of pilots even after they are proficient in handling the machine and guns. My old flight was so good too. Good fellows, good pilots, all tried and true.

I hate to part with my old machine too but she's pretty far gone and I'm having it rebuilt and taking one of the new ones. I've done over 100 hours over the lines on it. That's more than the life of an ordinary plane. Very few last that long. But it's been shot up so much and had so much strain that she was hardly seaworthy any more. I'll be too busy now to take any leave. But they may only have been shot in the engine or petrol tank and have landed safely in Hunland. There's always that chance. Well, I must go up to the sheds now and see how my new machines are coming along.

Your devoted son, Elliott

FLIGHT LOG: 3 September: 1 hour 20 minutes. Bapaume north. Practice O.P.

FLIGHT LOG: 4 September: 10 minutes. Test OK.

FLIGHT LOG: 4 September: 50 minutes. Bapaume. Practice patrol.

FLIGHT LOG: 5 September: 1 hour 50 minutes. Canal du Nord. 18 to 20 Fokkers. Got 1. (XII)

COMBAT REPORT: 148th Aero Squadron, 5:15 PM, 5 September. Remarks on Hostile Aircraft: Fokker biplane, regular camouflage, white rudder, black tail. Not aggressive. One monoplane very fast. Result: Destroyed, one; Driven down out of control, one. Narrative: Five Bristols returning from Cambrai were attacked by a number of Fokkers who did not press the attack after we flew toward them. After some preliminary diving and zooming, four E. A. attacked. I engaged one who was shooting at Lt. Cunnius. After a burst of 50 to 100 rounds E. A. half-rolled and went down in a spin. Was unable to follow him down as another Camel dove towards me with E. A. on [his] tail firing. Lt. Jenkinson, in Camel, went beneath me and I half-rolled on E. A.'s tail. After a burst of 100 rounds, E. A. half-rolled and dove east. I followed him down and fired another burst at 1000 ft. E. A.'s dive became steeper and E. A. disappeared east of canal. I saw smoke coming from this point which continued for some time. Sgnd, E. W. Springs, 1st Lt, Air Service, USA.[27]

FLIGHT LOG: 6 September: 10 minutes. Test OK.

FLIGHT LOG: 7 September: 2 hours 15 minutes. Canal du Nord. Forced one two-seater down. (XIII)

148th Aero Squadron
Remaisnil, France
September 8 1918

Dear Mother—

Your letter of August 5th arrived. You say among other things "I write at least once a week, and yet every letter from you complains of not having heard from home." So you pride yourself on writing once a week do you? Well, maybe so. So you think you are doing well if you can spare the time from your arduous duties (rats) to scribble me one letter a week? You think that one letter every seven days should overpower me with joy? Well, you've got another think coming. And I am very tired of dwelling on the subject in my letters. And what poor, rotten, weakly, weekly letters they are.

So you are expecting me to come back covered with bars, stripes, and decorations? Wouldn't you rather have them send you the bric a brac under a separate cover? I suppose that with my splendid "Culver training" and unequaled advantages—oh well what's the use?

We had quite a good scrap yesterday. I was up with my new flight[28] with "A" flight above me and we ran into about fifteen Huns. They were above us and about five of them came down on my flight. Things were pretty hot for the moment and I saw a Hun get on the tail of one of my new men. I got on his tail and he went down in a spin after a few shots. I started down after him but looked around and saw another of my flight with a Hun right on his tail pumping away. I pulled up and my [man's] machine dove underneath me with the Hun hot after him. I half rolled and came down on the Hun's tail and started contributing a few nails for his coffin. The Hun half rolled and went down but I had a hunch it was a trick so followed him on down. That was at 9000 feet and at 1000 feet the Hun leveled off and I was right on his tail and finished him off. He landed in a clump of trees. All of us got back and only two machines were shot up.

Kindley followed down the one I left in a spin and got him. [Henry] Clay got two the other morning and [Clayton] Bissel got one also. We're gradually getting our own back again. Clay got one down the other day on our side of the lines and went up that night to get some souvenirs off of it. But he wandered into the evening barrage of hate and was lucky to get back at all. However he's gone up there again this afternoon to see what's left of it.

We did succeed in getting a piano and a lot of other stuff for the mess from an abandoned town. Perfectly good German piano. Also we got a big van—much bigger than the moving vans at home—more like the big lunch wagons—and we hauled it back here and fixed it up and are now using it for a kitchen. When we move next time we won't miss a meal.

The movie man was back here yesterday and says the pictures he took of me up in the air came out fine and are the closest pictures ever taken in the air. They're probably being shown in the States now. He wants to get some more but we have no two seaters handy.

Just at present I occupy a unique position in the squadron. I am the only man who has three different and distinct kinds of itch in addition to the hoof and mouth disease. I seem to have fallen heir to all the trench curses except fleas. I have enough different kinds of ointment to stock a chemist's shop. Everyone has some sort of itch and some even have two varieties but I'm the only one who has all three. The Doc is quite proud of me.

I've got my old bus all fixed up with new wings, new tail, new engine, and new guns and am so fond of it I'm going to keep it instead of taking one of the new ones. My mechanics here are exceptionally good and as I've just gotten some promotions through, they work like demons.

A heartful of love to you and Father.

Devotedly, Elliott

FLIGHT LOG: 9 September: 20 minutes. Test OK.
FLIGHT LOG: 9 September: 20 minutes. Test.

The following excerpt is from a letter by Leroy Springs dated 7 August 1918.

My dear Son:

I have just received a letter from you written from the Duchess of Sutherland Hospital, France, without date but I notice it is postmarked July 11th. Lena has received one from you dated June 28th and one dated July 10th. We, of course, are very much disturbed to hear that you have had an accident. We do not know whether it was an accident or whether you were shot in the face or what and are very much surprised that we have not heard from you before regarding same. We had a cable from you about the 28th of July stating all well.

Now, my dear son, I do not think it fair to treat us this way. You should have had us cabled when you were hurt and your letter is so unsatisfactory to us. You do not state how you were hurt, what the accident consisted of, whether you were shot down in your machine, or how it happened. I am very much worried but thankful that you are out again. Please sit down and write us full particulars and do not deal in frivolities. These are serious times and I wish you would write us seriously and write us facts and do not leave us to guess at things. I am awfully sorry you have been wounded and hope it will not leave the scars you intimate in your letter. You claim you are very much disfigured. I hope you will be careful and not go out too soon.

As regards your promotion, of course, I am glad to hear of it but you did not tell us what it is, except that you will be flight commander, but you do not state what your commission will be, whether it will still be First Lieutenant or Captain. . . .

I am also distressed to hear in your last letter to Lena written about July 19th that you had serum poison. You did not state how this occurred. Did you take treatment after you left the hospital? I wish you would always write particulars and, as above stated, leave off frivolities.

You frequently call your friends by their given name or a nickname but never write us where they are from or who they are. We do not know who Larry is or who MacGregor is or your other friends. It would be of interest to us if you could tell us who they are and where they are from and please arrange some way to have us cabled in case you get hurt again. . . .

Your affectionate father

148th Aero Squadron
Remaisnil, France
September 10 1918

Dear Father—

I received your letter of August 7 and note that you are anything but pleased with my letters. I might return the compliment with emphasis. To take up your letter in detail: How could I cable you [when he was wounded] from a hospital close to the lines? It isn't being done this season. I wrote you that I was not seriously hurt, only my face mashed up and that I expected to return to flying shortly. I think I then wrote you that I was flying again and that I was all right except for a few minor scars which have all disappeared now except one on my chin.

Whenever you are injured they give you an injection of anti-tetanus serum at once. I mentioned that and later I told you that I had poisoning from it. I wrote you that I had been promoted to flight commander, which ordinarily means a captaincy but that it would probably be some time before I got it. Such is the case and I am still a lieutenant. Just as Mort Newhall, the C.O., is still a lieutenant as his majority has not come through yet. You say my letters are full of frivolities. Yours aren't even pleasant. I can arrange my affairs much better through London than through Paris as I am operating with the British.

I have at last succeeded in getting Larry Callahan in my flight. He arrived yesterday. Also got a man named Ralston who was attached to 85 [Squadron] and got a couple of Huns while with them. He was in MacGregor's flight. I wrote you I think that MacGregor had been promoted. So now Captain Horn is the only one in the original C Flight left down there.

So I've had to become an instructor in addition to my other jobs, as Larry and Ralston have never flown the type of machine we have here.

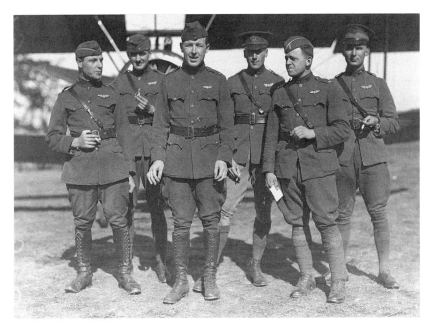

Elliott Springs and some members of B Flight, 148th Aero Squadron, 14 September 1918. From left to right: Lt. Percy Cunnius, Lt. Sydney Noel, Lt. Elliott Springs, Lt. Larry Callahan, Lt. Orville Ralston, Lt. Harry Jenkinson Jr. Courtesy of National Archives.

But they are such good pilots that they will have no trouble with them. All single-seater scouts, though, fly a good deal the same. After they get used to the motor they'll be all right. I expect to take them over the lines with me the day after tomorrow. I certainly ought to be able to raise unshirted Cain with the Huns with them behind me. Both of them good shots and know the game. We have the mess anteroom decorated with souvenirs from a Hun two-seater that [Henry] Clay shot down. And Larry livens us up with music extracted from our Hun piano.

There was a Captain Henry Fleetman here for dinner the other night. He said he used to be mixed up with the Parker Mills through his Commercial House in New York and spent quite a bit of time in Columbia and Spartanburg in 1910. Have you disposed of the Stutz yet? Better do so.

We have had quite a bit of social life lately. Every night we are invited to another squadron for dinner and celebration or have some of them over here. I'm going to make my batman social secretary as I have engagements already for the next four evenings. The [squadron] adjutant is away on leave so as usual I'm the goat. For the next two weeks now I'll be adjutant and pretty busy. If they don't make me a general before long I'm going to strike. I've about reached my limit anyway. I long for the life of the care-free. This responsibility is getting on my nerves. However, I'll probably tell some colonel where to head in before long and get what I want shortly—the life of the carefree.

A heartful of love always, your devoted son, Elliott

P.S. Have a heart. Your letters must be copied from "Life in a Monastery." Your linen can't be as bad as mine if I smile every week.[29]

148th Aero Squadron
Remaisnil, France
September 12 1918

Dear Mother—
    We've had some bad weather the last three days so have had rest which has been quite beneficial. I certainly needed it as I was getting quite low and now feel much revived. It's all in the game, of course, but every now and then we do get reminders that there is such a thing as the future and—oh, well, I can't explain it.
    I'm getting aged and decrepit. My age is wearing me down. Day before yesterday, Major [C. M. "Billy"] Crowe and Capt Horn flew over from 85 [Squadron] to warn me that a bunch of them were coming to dine with us and cause trouble.[30] 'Twas quite a compliment so we made elaborate preparation. But somehow I've become about ten years older than they are and I couldn't quite enter into the party with my old zest. Ordinarily the Major was entitled, ex officio, to make the most noise and I claimed second place, ex officio, but I was out of place this time and was quiet and dignified to the point where it was impolite. Poor old McDonald wept profusely over my transition.
    Last night we were guests of [Henry] Clay's old squadron [43 Squadron] and we heard that an exceptional dinner could be had at a little village some 10 kilos away. Ten of us altogether arrived and found that the report was correct—soup, lobster, peas, breast of chicken or pheasant or something similar, salad and cheese did very well. It was a little place, formerly a private house, and there were two British colonels, a couple of stray Australian and Canadian majors and a sprinkling of Scotch and French dining there also. And a charming French M'mselle was directing the affair. Of course the international competition for her favor was very keen and as usual with true British politeness all the officers ignored each other.

Finally we put Larry [Callahan] in front of the piano and almost immediately everyone became bosom friends. And M'mselle graciously and im-
partially danced with each one in turn. Picture it to yourself, one charming
lady entertaining fifteen officers from all parts of the globe for several hours!
A couple of the English officers were so affected by Larry's rag[time play-
ing] that they gave an excellent imitation of the Gaity chorus and put on a
very good ballet.[31] We all parted friends and we're going over some night
to dine with a couple of the English officers at their mess.

Tonight we are going over to a neighboring squadron [the 17th Aero
Squadron] for dinner. Bob Vaughn is over there and has been decorated
with the DFC (Distinguished Flying Cross) and they are celebrating it. I
heard that MacGregor is going to get it too. Bishop got it when he was out
here with us. Quite a few Americans have been recommended for it but
something has been holding them up.

Larry tells wonderful tales of London. He spent part of the time with
Bishop who is now a Colonel and head of the Canadian Flying Corps and
all covered with red tabs. He saw our old friends and was informed that I
had been killed in July. I don't know how that got started. They killed me
down in Paris in May.

Capt Horn wants me to take leave at the same time he does and go over
to London with him. However it can't be done. I've moved to Paris and am
afraid his company is too rich for my blood. He'll probably produce another
$1,000,000 check about that time and buy something expensive which I
would have to share. Yes it's me for Paris at the earliest opportunity.

Larry also reports that every blonde and every brunette in [London] is
weeping for Grider. He says Billie Carleton was more dramatic over Mac
than she was in "Fair and Warmer"[32] but has recovered sufficiently to become engaged to another American officer. Quite a few of our very best
and most promising young warriors are taking something unto themselves
over here. Thank goodness Pabst is far away from his wop Princess or
Dago Duchess or whatever she was. I wonder who Ernest married? No
word from him yet except the cablegram.

I have a VMI[33] man in my flight now. Quite a nice fellow, and a good
pilot—[Henry] Starkey from Roanoke. I am now up to strength again but
can use eight pilots if I can get them. Am trying to get Bob Kelly [an old
Oxford acquaintance] for the eighth. He's still in the hospital in London
from his crash but ought to be out shortly.

A heartful of love to you and Father.

Devotedly, Elliott

P.S. Again I insist my letters are private and secret! See to it!

FLIGHT LOG: 13 September: 2 hours 35 minutes. Cambrai-St. Quentin.
FLIGHT LOG: 14 September: 2 hours 10 minutes. Canal du Nord.

The following excerpt is from a letter by Leroy Springs dated 14 August 1918.

My dear son:

I am very proud of your promotion and trust you will get a captaincy after you are ready to go on duty with your division. From your letter [dated 19 July 1918], I understand you have been promoted to commander of Squadron B. I was in Charlotte Monday and Columbia Tuesday and everybody was asking about you and seemed to be very much interested.

Now my son you should not be so particular about people not knowing what you are doing. It is hardly fair to your friends and my friends. It is a compliment and no disgrace that you are fighting for your country and there is no reason why they should not know what you are doing. I will not attempt any band wagon play nor give you any undue credit but there is certainly no reason why I should not tell my friends when they ask what you are doing and also that I should not tell them when you have had an accident and are in the hospital. You certainly do not want to come out of the war and have nobody know what you did but have them thinking you acted as a dummy. I will certainly have discretion enough not to tell anything that I should not tell but it would appear very strange to my friends if I should decline to tell them anything about you.

Even Bishop and other aviators have been writing to the newspapers full accounts of their fights. Of course, I do not propose to do anything like that but you should not wish me not to say anything about anything you are doing in the war, as I am very proud of your record. I hope you will soon be well and yourself again and that you will have further promotion. At the same time, take good care of yourself and be very careful. We have reason to be very thankful that your accident was not more serious. . . .

Your affectionate father

148th Aero Squadron
Remaisnil, France
September 14, 1918

Dear Father—

I am just in receipt of your letter of August 14 and was glad to hear from you even though your letter was very uninteresting, containing less than a paragraph of news. Your views on publicity are too well known to me to need any explanation. But remember that I have your promise over your signature as well as your spoken word in New York and a cable to respect my wishes and show my letters to no one, read them to no one, nor reveal their contents. If I did not trust you to keep that promise I would not have written.

Is not that clear? If you betray my confidence I shall cease to communicate with you at all. I have tried to be considerate of you and write often and be a dutiful son. If you care for my continued confidence don't forget your promise. I feel flattered that you are proud of my record but have patience. If I'm not shot down in the next six weeks I'll pull off something that you can really talk about.

And why do you persist in getting everything wrong. I distinctly wrote you that I was in command of B Flight, 148th Squadron, and I am still a Lieutenant but had heard rumors that my captaincy is somewhere on the way. I hope you gave Frances the wrong address to send the box to. Her motives are unquestionably good but her execution is rotten. If anybody wants to send me any sox tell them that I have over 3 dozen pairs mostly hand made but that the original pair I left New York with is still going strong and that I have at odd times given away two or three dozen pairs in addition to innumerable sweaters, mufflers, gloves, etc., which are remarkably inferior to the kind you can buy anywhere.

I had the busiest hour of my existence yesterday. We were on patrol and during that time I had a scrap with four two-seaters at different times and four Fokkers all at once to say nothing of the maneuvering. I forced one of the two-seaters to land just back of their lines and was lucky [to] get back after the scrap with the others.

At the first I saw a Hun two-seater just over the lines about ten miles away. Instead of going towards him I went into Hunland and cut him off so attacked him from the east and let one of my men get on his tail. But the Hun was good and squirmed away. So I dove east and cut him off again but we were too far over and too low down to do any good.

I saw another one [in] a few minutes under a cloud, so climbed up on top of the cloud and came out east of him. We had quite a fight and his observer certainly made things hot for me. Every time I'd get in close the observer would have two guns on me and I would simply get sprayed with explosive bullets. Finally I got underneath him and forced him to dive. Then I went straight in and nailed him. He continued his dive with the observer still firing at me and I had to get east of him again and take him from the front. We were about four miles over then and at about 500 feet. I got another crack at him and he went down and landed. Rather inconsiderate of him.

Then my troubles began. Machine guns from the ground, pom poms, and field guns made my trip back to [the] lines about as interesting as I could stand it. Then to top it off two Fokkers came down on me. I don't know why they didn't get me. Probably because some of my flight who had lost me before were up above. I couldn't find any of our machines about, so hung around the lines to see what the Fokkers above were going to do. And lo, at 7000 feet were four Fokkers in good formation and above them at 10000 to 12000 were about twenty more.

I climbed for all I was worth and the four Fokkers passed right above me. It was a trap. They wanted some of our machines to tackle the four and then the others hiding in the sun would come down and mop up. I figured that they would not break up for one lone machine so kept climbing. I thought that one Fokker would attend to me and then I could shoot down a Hun on our side of the lines, go down and land near him, and collect souvenirs.

But the whole outfit ignored me. So I decided that they were after our balloons so kept climbing under them. Finally I got underneath the rear one of the four and opened fire. He turned, and before I could get him, the leader did a climbing turn and quarter rolled onto my tail. I hadn't expected that. It wasn't according to Hoyle at all.[34] It wasn't fair. I turned, myself, and [then] all four of them opened fire [on] me. The matter began to appear serious.

I looked about. Not another one of our machines in the sky. Time to call it a day and quit. But how? There were clouds at 2000 feet so I violated the laws of aerial tactics and dove. That was what one Hun was waiting for and right on my tail he was. I banged my rudders about to spoil his aim and put her over the vertical. I was doing about 250 and I looked back to see him gaining on me and firing with both guns. The clouds looked 20000 feet below me. There was only one thing to do. I didn't like to do it but I had to. I put on full rudder and aileron and twisted around then pulled up my nose. Somehow my wings stayed on and by the time the Hun got anywhere near me I was in the clouds. Instead of going thru I pulled right out again just in time to see the Hun charging down after me. He saw me though and went on through and back to his lines before I could find him.

My plane was flying sideways due to a drooping wing, so I came on back. Had to have it completely rerigged and new struts put in as the strain was too much for it. It's my same old bus that I've had since the 4th of July and I'd hate for anything to happen to it.

A heartful of love to you and Mother. Your devoted son, Elliott

FLIGHT LOG: 15 September: 2 hours 10 minutes. Canal du Nord. Larry
Ralston and I got a two-seater. Numerous Fokkers. (XIV)

COMBAT REPORT: 148th Aero Squadron, 10:40 AM, 15 September.
Remarks on Hostile Aircraft: Halberstadt, gray. Very good pilot.
Hannoveranner, grey and white. Fokker biplane. Result: Destroyed,
one-fourth; driven down, one-half. Narrative: Leading lower flight,
we cut off a Halberstadt and attacked from East and below. After a
good burst E. A. turned west. Lt. Cunnius attacked from rear above as
I attacked from below and I observed his tracer going into observer's
cockpit. E. A. dove east with smoke issuing from fuselage. Observer
ceased to fire at me and followed him down to 500 ft. and was forced
to pull up due to ground fire. Later Lt. Ralston and I attacked a Hannoveranner over Bourlon Wood at 300 ft. E. A. disappeared after long
bursts. Ground fire fairly active. Flew underneath two Fokkers and
two Hannoveranners who refused to attack. Sgnd, E. W. Springs, 1st
Lt, Air Service, USA.[35]

FLIGHT LOG: 15 September: 2 hours 25 minutes. Canal du Nord. Very
little activity.

148th Aero Squadron
Remaisnil, France
September 16 1918

Dear Mother—

. . . It appears that if anything is going to happen, I'm the Jonah. I had
another ragtime patrol yesterday. I was leading a patrol of five machines
and there were thick clouds at 4000 feet. I expected a lot of two seaters to
be out so made my plans before I left the ground. Just across the lines I
spotted a Hun two seater north of me and got up into the edge of the
clouds. According to the plan I went east full out and caught the Hun nap-
ping. One man came with me and the other three went north. The Hun
put his nose down for home but I beat him to it and opened fire from in
front of him. To give the observer a shot at me he had to turn north and I
went under him. The observer was cracking away in good shape at me but
his aim was poor and as the pilot turned into me I got a good burst in and
evidently killed the observer. Then according to plan, as the pilot turned
to get away from my fire, [Henry C.] Starkey [Jr.] came straight down on
him and it was all over. He went down smoking badly.

A two seater is a hard thing to tackle. The observer has nothing to do
but empty his guns into you while you are maneuvering up close. One two
seater can usually lick one scout, but I've found that by taking them from

the east and letting the observer concentrate his fire on me, one of the others slips onto his tail and nails him without interference.

Later it cleared up and we got mixed up with four Fokkers who for some reason wouldn't fight with us. I went down after another two seater but he got too low and too far over and I couldn't get him. Came back at 300 feet and the boys in the trenches had great sport [with] me all the way. Tried again with the same results.

Now comes the funny part. One of the patrol left and went home for all he was worth. Then [Harry] Jenkinson started circling around me wildly. He evidently wanted to tell me something. I looked about—no Huns. He came up alongside and started making motions. He pointed down, rotated his arm, and held up one finger. What the blazes? Something about a wheel. I made a motion like a wheel and he nodded and held up one finger. Aha, one of my wheels is gone. I held out my left arm and he nodded. Then I have no left wheel. Damn that observer. I knew that I couldn't possibly land without crashing—probably badly—with a whole wheel missing so debated the matter. I went through imaginary drills. Cut off petrol and switch so as not to catch fire, undo safety belt, take off goggles, and pancake in the canal [Canal du Nord]. No, never get out alive. Pancake in the woods—no, nobody would be able to get to me for some time. Will have to land on the 'drome. I raked forth my knowledge of geometry and psychology and began to figure.

A stiff breeze blowing, good. If I land with the wind on my left, it will hold up my left wing a little, but it will probably tear off my right wheel and flop me over. Still, we'll have a try.

When I got near the 'drome I saw why [Orville] Ralston had left the patrol so suddenly. Here he was in another machine with a spare wheel with him. He flew along side me and I nodded. It seems he'd rushed back, told everyone, and had come up to show me a wheel. But in his excitement he had crashed his own bus which was piled on the aerodrome.

Everybody was on the 'drome firing Very pistols at me to attract my attention and the mechanics were running about with wheels in their left hand. The ambulance was all cranked up and everything was ready. I took a look at the wind and got back a way.

I threw away my goggles, cut off the switch and petrol and made sure my belt was tight and braced my left hand in front of my face on the guns. Then I put her in a right hand side slip and came down. Just before my wing touched the ground I leveled off vertically [horizontally?] and got my [right] wheel and tail on the ground with my right wing low—headed into the wind. Still doing about 55 miles an hour, so [I] could hold her level for

Elliott Springs in front of upended Sopwith Camel aircraft. Springs, who had just crashed this aircraft in landing, appears pleased with the results. Courtesy of the Springs Close Family Archives, the White Homestead, Fort Mill, South Carolina.

a second. Then I banged on full right rudder and got the wind on my left. It worked! She was losing her speed and it looked as if I was going to get away with it. No, before I could lose enough speed, I lost control, my wheel-less axle stuck in the ground, and over I went, but very gently. All I broke was my propeller and my top wing.

Now the funny part is that there was a movie man on the 'drome to take some pictures and he had his camera all set and had taken a movie of the whole thing—even the ambulance, the mechanics with wheels, and all. You may see it some day. It was taken for the Signal Corps and will be shown everywhere.

I'm seriously considering having a glass floor put in my cockpit so I can see my undercarriage. I'll feel uneasy every time I land now. I saw a fellow land some time ago with one wheel gone and he messed up his machine and himself pretty badly. Run the Stutz into a stone wall at 50 miles an hour and get a similar sensation.

The General was over here the other day and patted me on the back. Said he didn't consider it my fault that I lost my flight but that it was a good show from start to finish. That doesn't make me feel any better though nor bring me back good men. The matter is too involved to go further. A heartful of love.

Devotedly, Elliott

FLIGHT LOG: 16 September: 2 hours 25 minutes. Canal du Nord.

FLIGHT LOG: 17 September: 2 hours 25 minutes. Canal du Nord.

FLIGHT LOG: 18 September: 2 hours 15 minutes. Havrincourt. Shot up ground by Bahle.

REPORT ON ATTACK ON ENEMY GROUND TARGETS: Lt. E. W. Springs, Camel F-6192, 8:00–8:15 AM, 18 September. Fired 700 rounds from altitudes of 500–1000 ft. into troops and transport on roads from Ribecourt to Marcoing and Sonnet Farm to Bohavis with marked effect.[36]

FLIGHT LOG: 19 September: 2 hours 20 minutes. Cambrai balloons.

FLIGHT LOG: 20 September: 2 hours 10 minutes. Canal du Nord. Jenk [Harry Jenkinson Jr.] down in flames. (XV)

COMBAT REPORT: 148th Aero Squadron, 2:55 PM, 20 September. Remarks on Hostile Aircraft: Fokker biplanes. Regular camouflage, white undercarriage, white noses and white stripes on fuselage. Pilots very good. Result: Crashed, one. Narrative: Leading lower flight to balloon east of Marcoing which was pulled down to ground, I saw E. A. north of Cambrai at 4000 ft. I returned to lines and went north along the Canal. Four E. A. proceeded west and coming through clouds we met them at 6000 ft., both at the same level. E. A. climbed east and we climbed north. E. A. climbed above us and were joined by another E. A. I attacked one which was firing at Lt. Jenkinson and fired a good burst at close range. Center section of Fokker began smoking and it went into a stall and then a slow spin. Went to assistance of Lt. Jenkinson again who was fighting one Fokker with two other above. Attacked one Fokker, [which was] firing at Lt. Jenkinson, and one Fokker attacked each of us from above. Lt. Jenkinson's machine burst into flames and I returned. Later saw three camouflaged objects on Marcoing-Ribecourt Rd., apparently gun limbers. Fired remaining ammunition into them from 1500 ft. to 1000 ft. Sgnd, E. S. Springs, 1st Lt, Air Service, USA.[37]

148th Aero Squadron
Baizieux, France
September 20 1918 [21 September]

Dear Father—

Your letter of August 26th arrived and I was very glad to hear from you.[38] You seem to have been worrying a lot over nothing. To ease your mind I'll repeat. When I went to the hospital, I had my oil pipe shot away when about ten miles [over the lines] and crashed just this side of the lines when my motor burned out and landed in some reserve trenches. My face was smashed up but outside of that I was all right. They gave me anti serum of course and later it took effect. Also my eyes refused to return to normal. They still bother me a little but not much and they are improving steadily.

Just as the commander of a company is a Captain, so I am supposed to [be], as a commander of a Flight, but as yet my promotion has not come through. I expect it pretty soon though. As to Huns, I think I am officially credited with nine. That is I have nine confirmed. I think I've gotten about six others for which I could get no confirmation.[39]

You object to my frivolity. Let's compromise. You write me and throw in something cheerful and bright every now and then and I'll write you and tell you what I'm doing to win the war and how I sit up nights trying to keep from ever smiling. . . .

Don't you think yourself that I get enough of the war as it is without having you rub it [in] all the time in every letter and insist that I keep my thoughts active and correspondence confined strictly to it? Even at night my three varieties of itch keep my mind from wandering too far from the war.

I went out after balloons yesterday [20 September] but didn't get any. Went after two but the Huns pulled them down before I could get to them. Then I saw some Hun planes and we began maneuvering for position. I went into the clouds at 7000 [feet] and dodged in and out to watch them. There were some more of our machines above and I was counting on them to come down and clean up. But like the Huns they couldn't follow us on account of the clouds. We won at maneuvering and came out of the clouds just beside four Fokkers and a Halberstadt. We were two or three miles over and the Huns turned east to draw us over. There was a strong wind so I could [not?] afford to go, but turned northwest and started back trying to get the Huns to attack us close to the lines. They did and the battle was on.

Starkey went after the two seater, [Sidney] Noel got a spar shot away right at the first dive and Jenkinson and I started fighting with the other three. One got on my tail and kept me busy until I got one off Starkey's tail who in turn hopped on me. I had two after me and Jenk had two after him. I got rid of mine and went over to help Jenk. Shot one down off his tail and then he started east after another one. He was putting up a wonderful fight but there were too many of them and I had to go in again as there were three after him. I took the one on his tail and the other two hopped us from above. A lucky shot winged Jenk and he burst into flames not thirty yards from me. All the Huns then came after me and things looked bad. I turned towards the lines with three after me. The wind had blown us about three miles over. I turned under one Hun and dove. They were after me like a shot of course. So I pushed my stick forward and went over the vertical with engine full on doing about 300. The Huns gave up as some of our machines came up just at that time and chased them back.

Now comes the funny part. I pulled my stick back and nothing happened. I couldn't get out of the dive. Controls shot away. So I cut off the motor, pushed her further over the vertical and yanked her out. She came out and my wings didn't come off though both my top wings buckled on the leading edges and when I got back I had to have a new set.

Losing Jenk has hit me pretty hard. He was the best man I've had except Larry and he was the only one left of the flight I started with in July. He hasn't missed a scrap since he started except when he was on leave the last [of] August.

When I reported the [results of the] flight to the Colonel, I couldn't say whether my Hun had crashed or not so they wouldn't give me credit for it. I didn't see it crash and said so. I'm glad I did now because some one in the top flight saw the fight from a distance and saw my Hun go down, crash, and burst into flames on the ground.

We have moved again [to Baizieux, six miles west of Albert, about fifteen miles southeast of their previous field at Remaisnil]. In another two months I will have been on every drome in France I think.

A heartful of love to you and Lena.

Your devoted son, Elliott

148th Aero Squadron
Baizieux, France
September 20, 1918

Dear Mother—

Enclosed you will find some clippings which interested me very much. You must have learned a lot of interesting things at Winthrop. The fact that all our women folk at home are patriotic and are learning all about bird life and public speaking just makes our chests burst with pride. It makes us glad we are in the army. It makes us glad we are in France. I hope I go to Siberia next.

The Women's Committee of the Council of National Defense is certainly taking a step in the right direction. A man is killed in action—certainly somebody ought to swank about and get his glory. But I have a better suggestion to make. Why not benefit the living as well as swank for the dead? Why not help out those who live through it. Let the bona fide wives of dead heroes wear mourning and the gold star. Let the war brides of lucky cannon fodder wear mourning and two gold stars and let the would-be wives of wise and eager to fight belligerents wear black stockings with gold stars. Let the anxious but unsuccessful ones wear the gold stars on any color stockings. Thus could every woman swank, mourn, and advertise all at the same time, and the itinerant doughboy would be saved much curiosity and vain labor.

Yes the Women's Committee of the Council of National Defense is certainly on the job when it comes to helping win the war. The American attitude towards soldiers is without parallel or equal and beyond the imaginative concepts of Jules Verne or H. G. Wells. Every day I hear something new which makes me glad I am in France. Schopenhauer was right.[40] Tell me, are there nothing but fools left in America?

If it were the lower classes who indulged in the poor rotten cheap sentimentality, that even the French peasants scorn, I could understand it. But no, in America our best people have proved the contention of democracy that all are equal by showing how poor low democracy's best are, and stooping to a level that aristocracy's servants would scorn. Of course, American people are proud that their men are fighting for what they think right (even though a lot had to be forced to) but at the same time they go about proclaiming it to the world, taking credit for it, boasting of it, advertising it, and endeavoring to transfer the pride in the soldier to the pride in one's self. Will American families wear the decorations, wound stripes, and service chevrons of their beloved also? Why not?

Why do people get their sons letters published? Do the gentlefolks in England or France permit of such a thing? You bet they don't. They value and treasure them and consider [them] secret if not sacred. The common people sometimes do but even they look down upon such things.

One thing I will say. America's attitude has turned out a fine army of fighters. When they get into battle they fight to the finish because the people at home have shown them just how valuable life is.

I also saw in the paper where some sterling youth was in the Naval Flying Corps—a fine youth of old fighting stock and the hope of young

America who upholds her honor etc etc. Then what is he doing in the Naval Flying Corps? I think more of a man who is a ground officer in the Army Air Service than of all the stunt pilots in the NFC. I just make that remark apropos of comparing service stars as such. Just because your son is in the QMC [quartermaster corps] don't let anybody hightone you about it. Everybody wants to fight for their country but not many want to get hurt doing it.

If you have a star up anywhere about the house or anywhere else for me TAKE IT DOWN! Is it necessary to advertise in order to prevent any one from thinking that a slacker lives there? I say all this in dead earnestness. Every officer about the mess agrees with me. I've been thinking about this and much more and want to communicate it to you before it's too late. I'm going on a balloon strafe in an hour. Well who knows? But I want to leave behind with you a protest against certain things which are beneath contempt.

And another thing. You and Father seem to be so tickled about my being over here and yet you will not do but one thing for me. You send me money or its equivalent in small doses. But waste time or thought on me? Never. Cash in small amounts? Sure. Articles I write for. Yes possibly if it's not too much trouble. But sit down and think out something you can do for me, figure out something I would like to have, take time and write me decent letters regularly? Never.

A lot of credit is due to you for sending me the Lancaster *News* and Charlotte *Observer.* Yes a lot. You can get anyone to do that just as well as you can if not better since my address has not changed since January.

Being with the BEF [British Expeditionary Forces] as I have been, I suppose you think I get Puck, Life, Theatre Magazine, Vanity Fair, Metropolitan, Saturday Evening Post etc regularly. I usually see Life, which I detest, and sometimes the Saturday Evening Post because some of the officers get them from home. The Charlotte Observer gives me only news which should be contained in your letters. There are two people in London who write me oftener and better letters than you do.

Listen here, on September 15th I received a letter from you. What's in it? Advice about not flying if my eyes are bad. I've been doing two to four hours over the lines a day since July 30 and now I get your highly valued advice. Many thanks. How do you think I get along without your advice on certain subjects. Do you honestly think that the advice of you or Father about flying or military matters means a thing to me. If I knew what the paragraph was I wouldn't bother to read it. Can you imagine it otherwise? Six weeks after I make a decision I get a lot of worthless advice about it. Think it over! Father says my letters are frivolous. Yours and his are worse than that. They are foolish annoying worthless uninteresting and not amusing. If you can't do better just quit writing and spare my temper. First thing you know I'll be writing you how to run your house and what to serve the Red Cross Committee for luncheon six weeks after the luncheon takes place. Have a heart. . . .

The closing salutation of the above letter is missing.

FLIGHT LOG: 24 September: 2 hours 20 minutes. Canal du Nord.
FLIGHT LOG: 24 September: 1 hour 50 minutes. 53 Fokkers. Plane shot all to Hell. (XVI)
COMBAT REPORT: 148th Aero Squadron, 7:40 AM, 24 September. Remarks on Hostile Aircraft: Fokker biplanes. Regular camouflage. Broad blue stripe just back of cross on fuselage. Pilots exceptionally good. Preferred to shoot from a stall. Results: Crashed, one. Narrative: Leading top flight, attacked from above, fight between seven Fokkers and lower flight. One Fokker was firing from a stall and I attacked him. We both fired head-on. Fokker refused to turn away. I pulled up and turned. E. A. did one turn of a spin and tried to stall up underneath me. I got in rear and above and got in a good burst. E. A. went down in a dive and crashed near Bourlon. Engaged a number of other E. A. but was decidedly unsuccessful. Three E. A.s got hits on my plane. Later was being attacked by three Fokkers and Lt. [Henry] Clay came back into fight and relieved me. A number of Fokkers came up above us. Sgnd, E. W. Springs, 1st Lt, Air Service, USA.[41]

148th Aero Squadron
Baizieux, France
September 24 1918

Dear Mother—
    Father would certainly rather make mischief than eat but why on earth is he so determined to blackguard me when I am 2000 miles away? And you seem to be a great help. In other words I got a letter from Olive [Kahlo]. She said nothing directly but reading between the lines I gather that she doesn't like either you or Father. She mentions several things that were said which I consider not only tactless but unkind, unforgivable and disloyal to me. I hate to think that you stood by while all this was going on and said nothing. Then you write to me and carefully avoid the subject. I thought something was wrong.

Another and a minor matter but it rather pains me. Why did both you and Father tell Olive that I had written to you all that I should go to England if I got a long leave? I'm not at all troubled with the Christian Virtue [of] Forgiveness; don't forget that. And there's a very small chance that someday I may come back to you all, after I'm kicked out of every other place, and I'll take good care to impress my sentiments regarding parental treachery. In other words—leave me and my affairs alone!

And aren't you patriotic too. Yes. If it gets your name in the papers—sure. And yet you want me to give up fighting and take one of these damn safety first jobs. Somebody has got to fight and yet you in full possession of all your faculties are hoping that I am physically unfit and will be sent back to instruct. Yes, I know that it's how most families feel, it's quite the usual thing—but it's certainly a disgusting attitude. Now sit down and write me that you are glad I'm at the front, glad I'm fighting and will continue fighting until they get me and when I am shot down you will rejoice with me that I have achieved a glorious end and regret only that I could not have postponed that end. And don't write me that you want my life spared at the cost of someone else's. If I do return let it be through my own skill.

But I'm in a bad humor today. Mostly because I've been worried about Larry [Callahan]. We had a fight at 7 o'clock this morning and we got no word from him until noon. A spar broke and his right wing buckled in the fight. He went down in a spin but got out and side slipped back to our lines and landed in no man's land upside down. He's not back yet and I don't know what's happened to him except that he was uninjured enough to give his name and organization and reported no injuries.

But permit me to remark it was the warmest fight I've ever been mixed up in. There are nineteen holes in my machine, two spars shot through, a bolt shot out of my propeller, and the machine generally scorched by inflammatory bullets. I didn't get hit myself but I could smell the phosphorous as the stuff went by. Yes, I could—no joking. The fight started [when] Clay, who was leading the bottom flight, hopped seven Fokkers at 12,000 feet. Kindley took his flight in too, and I dove in from above just as four more Fokkers came in from the east. There were fifteen of us and about fifteen Fokkers but more Fokkers kept coming up. They had set a trap but we sprung it for them.

When I first went in I took a Fokker head on and we got off by ourselves and had a pukka aerodrome fight. I finally got on his tail and put in about 150 rounds; he went over and down and I watched him crash near a railway about three miles over. I went back in and hopped another but another hopped me and I had to turn to fight him. About ten more Fokkers came up and things got pretty hot. One stalled up underneath me and got a burst in my right wing before I could turn into him. I decided it was about time to get out of it as I saw about twenty more Fokkers coming up from the east. But the Fokkers didn't want to quit a bit. Three of them got on to me and I had to keep turning to throw their aim off. One of them opened fire from the side and got a shot in my prop and a few more in my wings while I was turning towards him. Good shooting it was. Another one took me from the other side and shot up the other wings. Things looked bad. I could smell phosphorous and burning petrol and thought I was on fire. I didn't dare spin because they'd pepper me while I was going into it.

Just then Clay saw me having a rotten time and came to my assistance and a couple of other machines came down so the Fokkers quit and waited for help from above which came promptly and we cleared out. Clay got one, [Field] Kindley got one, also [Lawrence] Wyly and [Walter] Knox crashed one apiece. And all of us got back except Callahan, who's all right, [Louis] Rabe, who landed unhurt [on] our side of the lines, and [Errol] Zistel, who ran into a wireless aerial on the way home. He's in hospital, badly shaken up but not seriously injured. Altogether there were 53 Huns there, as an Archie battery told us over the phone, and the fight lasted over ten minutes. Later in the day the other American Squadron [17th Aero Squadron] up here shot down five so we had a very good day. My machine is so badly shot up that I'm going to get a new one much as I hate to part with it. But I'm afraid it's done its time—I've had to have seven new wings on it in the last three weeks.

A heartful of love to you and Father.

Devotedly, Elliott

FLIGHT LOG: 25 September: 2 hours 5 minutes. Canal du Nord. Big scrap but I'm out of luck.

FLIGHT LOG: 26 September: 2 hours 20 minutes.

FLIGHT LOG: 27 September: 2 hours 20 minutes. Cambrai-Havrincourt Wood. Clay and I get one Hanoveranner. (XVII)

REPORT ON ATTACK ON ENEMY GROUND TARGETS: Lt E. W. Springs, Camel E-1586, 9:10 AM, 27 September. Dropped 4 bombs on railroad siding near Marcoing with good results. Fired rounds at two balloons west of Cambrai.[42]

COMBAT REPORT: 148th Aero Squadron, 9:55 AM, 27 September. Remarks on Hostile Aircraft: Halberstadt two-seater, regular gray camouflage. Results: Crashed, one-half. Narrative: Saw five Halberstadts coming from Cambrai and got into sun and cut off one. Attacked

directly from behind and fired 150 rounds at close range, while Lt. Clay was firing from underneath his tail. We were then attacked by another E. A. from above. Last saw [first] E. A. in dive. Later I attacked another two-seater Halberstadt between Bourlon Wood and Cambrai. Fired about 200 rounds into it and was dived on by an SE-5 before I could see what happened to E. A., which was last seen turning northeast. Sgnd, E. W. Springs, 1st Lt, Air Service, USA.
FLIGHT LOG: 27 September: 25 minutes. Test. Very good bus.[43]

Springs's flight on 27 September was the last flight recorded in his flight log. It was also the last combat flight he flew with the 148th Aero Squadron.

148th Aero Squadron
Baizieux, France
September 27 1918

Dear Father—

The war has been conducted entirely to my satisfaction these past four or five days. I've done my four hours over the lines with an abundance of fights and then spent the rest of the time wandering about the place in the back seat of a comfortable touring car with an extra windshield to keep the wind off my face. Pretty hot stuff. I sort of hate to draw my pay. By the way, I'm getting about $235.33 a month now. Observe I didn't say earning that. I said getting that, quite a difference. You'll have to boost the ante and give me more than that 70 cents a day you've promised all these years. You know I won't be able to live on less than a dollar a day after this.

Larry turned up all right after the big scrap. A main spar went and his wing folded at 12,000 feet about four miles over. By the grace of God and the slightly used but still reliable long-handled tooth brush he managed to turn and side-slip back on his good wing and crash in no man's land. Rather remarkable.

Next day I saw eight Huns below me. Two of them were straggling. They looked like cold meat so down I went. Got on the tail of one and was so intent upon making sure of him that I disregarded the others. My mistake. All of a sudden I realized that all the noise was not coming from my machine guns. I looked about and three or four Huns were firing at me. I couldn't see any of our other machines so was quite annoyed. Clouds below, can I make it? Here's Larry with two on his tail. We dove, banging our rudders around and watching the tracers go by. I never saw clouds so far below me. Finally the clouds enveloped me and the crack crack ceased. Pulled up and Larry and I went back in. The other flights had come down and a general scrap was on. Got in the scrap but couldn't get anything. Two of the others got a Hun apiece though.

Next morning we had quite a war. There were heavy clouds at 3000 and we caught a two seater in there about four miles over. He went down on the carpet and I was right on his tail when my motor cut out. Nice thing to have happen. I was just about to pick a place to land when a couple of cylinders picked up and I got over the lines and finally I got it running again. But there was a machine like mine on the ground crashed so my flight came back and reported me as down.

When my motor came back I was feeling very belligerent so climbed up and went back. Saw five two seaters and Clay's flight some distance away after a balloon. I went over and signaled to him and dove on the nearest two seater right out of the sun. Clay got underneath him and we each put about 250 rounds into him. Then he dove into the ground. Felt so good then that I went after another but was not so successful. I fired quite a bit at him but he was armored. Couldn't see what happened to him as I got attacked myself. Not a hole in my machine though when I got back. Put a new motor in and it was as good as ever.[44]

A heartful of love to you and Lena.

Your devoted son, Elliott

148th Aero Squadron
Baizieux, France
September 28 1918

Dear Mother—

No mail for the past three days. Hope you've got a lot on the way. Clay and I have located the two seater we shot down yesterday and it is now about 1000 yards [in on] our side of the lines. We are going up tomorrow and get what's left of it. If they don't shell us too badly I'll send you the iron crosses as souvenirs.[45] I've also got a Fokker somewhere near there but don't know whether I can get to it or not.

My main difficulty lately has been running the mess. We've moved again and where we are situated it's fairly hard to get anything but regular rations. Have to go a good ways to get tomatoes, chickens, lettuce, and such stuff. Which just reminds me. If I ever should get home and find you in the act of "keeping house" I should speak hard words. I recall with horror your domestic duties which you would have me understand were bearing down heavily upon you. Please remember that an establishment should appear to run itself to everyone but the person running it.

In addition to being flight commander, adjutant, and O.C.B. [officer in charge of booze?], I've been running the mess here for the past three weeks. That is, I feed a couple of dozen officers at a place where food as such is food only. And I've found it no difficulty at all. I have a mess sergeant and two cooks and we have the reputation throughout the R.A.F. of having better food than any other squadron in France. We always have four course breakfasts and dinners and our fame has spread. I'm really quite conceited about it.

Never let me hear about the troubles of housekeeping again. Why, I ran a house in London for about eight weeks. A big four-storied house and I had only two servants. True, there were just the three of us but we had a continual stream of company. The whole squadron used to come in. All the Americans who came to London that we knew and a lot that we didn't, would come around. I would never know how many to expect for anything. And I never had any coupons of any description. I would never know how many we were going to have for breakfast until midnight because often some friend would take one of the extra beds rather than try to find a taxi at that hour. Larry at the piano was too much of an attraction. Until you know wartime London you can't appreciate it.

Can you imagine keeping house under such circumstances? Yet the place was always clean and my only real trouble was replacing things as we broke them and getting fuses for the electric stoves. And it wasn't as expensive as it sounds. It did cost quite a bit which Larry, Mac, and I shared, but nevertheless it was cheap at ten times the price. Our kitchen was famous. We even entertained a General there and there's more than one lady [who] cooked on that stove whose pictures appear in all the papers regularly.

Yes, housekeeping is so simple that only a woman would complain of its difficulties. I wonder if I spent more on my house than you do in eight weeks on yours. Of course our rent and breakages were pretty high but even at that.

I'm getting so stagnant here that I'm seriously considering getting lost some day and landing accidentally in Paris. Could very easily break a wheel that would take several days to repair. Think I could enjoy a few hours of Paris and a couple of meals or rather banquets at the Alabecasse.

But to really appreciate Paris you have to be about ten miles in Hunland with Archie all about you, three Huns on your tail, and a dud engine. Then you think of Paris with joy, I may even say you enthuse over Paris, "thrilled to a peanut," so to say n'est pas.

Well, some day, when dreams come true I'll check my limousine outside and stroll into the Alabecasse and be greeted by George like an old friend

and get the best of everything. It will be just like returning to the Vanderbilt, except for minor details.

A heartful of love to you and Father.

Your devoted son, Elliott

SPRINGS NARRATIVE: [While I was with the 148th] I had a wheel shot off
in the air. I shot my own prop off a dozen times, I had a little bomb stick
to my undercarriage and I have been a nervous wreck ever since. I still
wake up at night with the sound of screaming wires and the smell of brim-
stone. I have seen twenty pilots at dinner when the phone rang with orders
for the dawn patrol. After they got the orders not a pilot could lift a glass
to his mouth with one hand. Ring a phone at dinner and they still can't.[46]

"In Hospital," the
Armistice, and After

October 1918 to January 1919

After flying an intense and nerve-wearying number of missions in the 148th Aero Squadron in August and September, Springs suffered another physical setback at the end of September and once again traveled to Paris to recover, leaving Larry Callahan in charge of B Flight. Spike Irwin, sergeant major of the 148th Aero Squadron, reports that he and some other men were able to travel to Paris on a ten-day leave and on 8 October met Springs, who entertained them in the evening.[1] Although Springs was not present in the squadron for most of the month of October, he did not miss much of the action as, after the middle of the month, bad weather and then plans to relocate the squadron kept the planes on the ground most of the time. When Springs did return to the squadron, at the end of the month, it was only to travel to Toul and then to Tours as he and the other two flight commanders, Kindley and Clay, awaited orders to take command of new aero squadrons. However, the armistice of 11 November caused all further plans for the development of new squadrons to be cancelled, and the men now waited to return to the United States after the war ended.

Springs evidently suffered two relapses of some kind, the first, less debilitating, in Paris during the first half of October and the second episode, much more serious, after the armistice, from 13 November until the first of December. During the second episode, he admits in a 13 November entry in his diary (in which he resumed writing on 28 October after a four-month lapse), he had to go to the hospital, where he remained essentially immobilized for two weeks. One of the comments in his diary written on 15

November suggests that he was so distraught that he was considering suicide (by jumping out of a window), but his enervated condition prevented that action. It is possible that he was exaggerating his condition, but the tone of the entry suggests otherwise. The severity of his debilitating condition is indicated by the fact that he wrote only one letter home in a one-month period between 13 November and 14 December, and in that one letter, dated 30 November, he admits that he had tried to write several letters home but had "torn them up" because they did not express his "sentiments" correctly. The letters that he wrote after the armistice lack the usual Springs energy, caustic wit, and confrontational commentary. As he says elsewhere, he had really never expected to survive the war, and now that he had, he had difficulty making the emotional adjustment.

Springs's psychological fragility was certainly shared by a number of other aviators, and what we know today as post-traumatic stress disorder syndrome existed then; the term commonly used was "shell-shock," associated with the condition of the men in the trenches returning home. More properly for the aviators, the term would better be called "air combat shock," indicating the nature of the affliction causing them some difficulty. When we realize how troubled psychologically Springs and his fellow aviators were when the war ended, we should not be surprised to learn that there was invariably an adjustment period required for these individuals to return to something like normal behavior in a peacetime world.

Springs's correspondence ends abruptly with his last letter home, dated 1 January 1919 to his stepmother, Lena. We know that he returned to the United States early in February, so the intervening four weeks were probably occupied with movements from one holding camp to another, likely starting at Toul and ending at a French port. Because Springs had been among the first American aviators to arrive in Europe, he would have been among the first to return home, especially as he had indicated no desire to remain associated with military service. It is clear that his flying experiences remained indelibly impressed on his mind as he continued to process those memories in fictional form throughout the 1920s, especially in his most successful version, his very popular *War Birds: Diary of an Unknown Aviator.*

In Hospital
Paris, France
October 9 1918

Dear Father—

Just for the moment I'm in bed with a beautiful case of grippe but ought to be out in a few days. I'm a complete and total nervous wreck though why I should be at this stage I can't figure. I'm a chattering idiot they tell me and I'm expecting my hair to turn gray daily. However a little flying ought to soothe my nerves. Major MacDill is still trying to get me but I have no intention of going there.[2] I want a squadron, I want to be a major and I'm going to stay at the Front at all costs.

But you needn't announce to the world that I am a Major. I'm still a 1st Lt.[3] Henry [Clay] and I wander about and let all the American aces hightone us. They think that [what] we are wearing [British Distinguished Flying Cross (DFC)] is a service ribbon, probably for ambulance work. Everybody that drives an ambulance gets a lot of funny colored ribbons. When I was in Paris I wore my coat all the time so I wouldn't have to answer questions about what it was. Typical conversation:

"Say, Lieutenant, pardon me but would you mind telling me what that decoration is you have? It's a new one on me."

Look of extreme contempt. "It's British."

"Is it for service in a certain campaign?"

More contempt. "No."

"Then it's for valor?"

"It's the D.F.C."

"Did you get it for getting a Hun?"

"No."

"What's it for, then, please?"

"They sometimes give it to people who get more than five."

"Oh, then you're an Ace. Congratulations."

"NO! I'm not an Ace! That's a French vegetable. We don't have 'em with the British."

"Oh, thank you, sorry to bother you."

Clay is going to kill someone before long. I heard him conduct that dialogue five times in one café! We used to laugh at Major Fowler and his M.C. [Military Cross] but it's no joke. It's like everybody stopping you and asking the name of your tailor. You could hang around the British for ten years with a cocktail shaker pinned on your chest and no one would question you about it.

I suppose you are still very wrought up about my financial condition. Don't worry. I wouldn't have wired you unless I needed the money. And you must admit that when I cable you for money it tells you where I am. That's a discount. However I'll cable you in a few days to let you know I haven't died with double pneumonia or anything. And I won't ask for money. Several of my very worst debtors paid me an aggregate of 1140 francs this morning. That'll feed me for a week. Have some more to come. It's bad to have much money in your pocket though. The bunch is too clever at rolling elevens. Did I ever tell you about teaching the British Colonel to shoot crap? It's a good story, remind me some day. He didn't get either the gold cigarette case or my gas mask.

Think it's about time you sent to Boston for a Textile engineer to come down and locate the exact bottom of the mill. If I started in again at my old job of trucking cotton to keep the negro labor amused and contented, people might say that I was being pushed up by parental influence. Tell Mary Williamson she'd save a lot of work by just mailing me the short-hand dictation of your letters.[4] I can measure the length and know exactly what I've done wrong.

A heartful of love to you and Lena.

Your devoted son, Elliott

In Hospital
Paris, France
October 11 1918

Dear Mother—

Well, here I am in Paris again. Thanks to Father's excellent financial arrangements though I have no cash so must wait here until the reply to my cable for money and then I shall proceed to Nice.[5]

Doesn't it seem reasonable to you that I should know more about how to manage my bank account on this side of the water than anyone else? I cabled the London City Midland and they replied that my balance was five pounds. I then went to the Comptoir National and they had not only never heard of me, but didn't want to hear of me and didn't care to do business with me or the Hanover National. So I strolled over to Morgan Harjes and Co., Boulevard Housman, and opened an account there where you can address me if you prefer though the London City is better. Now I wouldn't say it is better without a reason. You might slip that bit of information to Father. So daily I trail over to Morgan Harjes and inquire if my cable has come. Luckily I hadn't drawn my last month's pay and I charge everything to the hotel bill.

Pabst came in and spent Saturday and Sunday with me. Asked me to send his love to you. Lorraine Goodrich is nursing here and I've had dinner with her twice. Lunched yesterday with Major Fowler's two sisters who are in town for a few days from the Front where they are nursing. Very charming they are. Tonight I am dining with Coleen Minton who's stationed here. I called up Eli but he's away taking his examination for a commission.

My stomach is improving steadily but I have to be pretty careful about what I eat. I'm in the hands of a specialist who's OK.[6] As soon as it's well enough I'm going on back to the front whether my leave is up or not. I prefer the front to all the places I've ever been.

As I was going out yesterday I heard my name shouted and who should it be but Lois Meredith[7] who greeted me with a resounding but not otherwise unpleasant smack. She was just back from entertaining "the boys in the trenches" and was on her way elsewhere with Margaret Mayo's Entertainment Unit.[8] She was leaving in an hour or so consequently I didn't see much of her. Funny what a uniform will do. She was never affectionate in the slightest in ye olden days.

For Christmas I am having some handkerchiefs sent to you. I'm having a dozen initialed and then sending along some more unmarked. You can either have them marked yourself with your own initials or have someone else's initials put on them and send to them as a present. I just thought you might want to send some to your mother. I mention this so you won't be hurting my feelings at all if you do. I am also sending some to Father and Aunt Addie. They ought to reach you about three weeks after this does. I hope my taste is not too atrocious but I had no one to advise me about the selection.

My French is improving but is still nothing startling.

I ran into Major La Guardia who was on his way back to the States from Italy. He was well-covered with wop ribbons. He told me he had just seen Major MacDill and that MacDill had applied for me as an instructor in his Aerial Gunnery School. Of course I shan't accept. Ordinarily I'd like to do it but just at present there's a war on and I have business at the Front. I'm particularly anxious to return as soon as possible because I have several new ideas about how to shoot down the elusive Hun with the least possible inconvenience and the delay is rather irksome. You have to get away from the front to get real bloodthirsty.

A heartful of love to you and Father.

Devotedly, Elliott

Hotel Continental, 3 rue de Castiglione
Paris, France
October 12, 1918

Dear Father—

I presume you got my cable and are wondering what it's all about. As you probably have surmised, I am on leave and as you may guess also with[out] funds. From what you said I had judged that you had arranged for the Comptoir Nationale to finance me. Particularly so when the London City [Bank] proved to be dry. But when I went to the Comptoir [they] refused to do anything about it and had evidently never heard of me. So I went over to Morgan Harjes and Company[9] [on the] Boulevard Hausman and opened an account and establish[ed] a forwarding point for mail there and cabled you for cash. I asked for $1500 because it [is] embarrassing to get caught short over here. Then I drew my last month's pay and am now waiting for a cable from you. My stomach or my imagination is improving rapidly and all is well except I caught a cold yesterday and am feeling rotten today as a consequence.

Major MacDill applied [for] me as an instructor at his School of Aerial Gunnery which is rather flattering but at the same time impossible. I've already taken steps to make sure that the application is refused. I got some good news today. Three of the men I lost have been reported as prisoners. Curtis, Mandel, and Kenyon. There's no hope for Forster or Jenkinson. Also my old friends Tipton and Frost are prisoners also. It's almost like a resurrection. If only Mac [Grider] would show up but that's beyond the realm of possibility now! Larry and Ralston each shot down a Hun just after I left. I'm rather anxious to get back to say the least.

You can write to me either at Morgan Harjes and Company, the London City Midland Bank, or direct to the squadron. Just 148 Army Aero Squadron will get [to] me.

A heartful of love to you and Lena. Devotedly, Elliott

In Hospital
Paris, France
Posted 19 October 1918[10]

Dear Mother—

Well, here I am in hospital again. Don't be worried, the ground hasn't come up and hit me again. Do you remember the sad condition I was in when you and Father escorted me to the Johns Hopkins [hospital] in 1914? Well, I arrived here in exactly that condition day before yesterday, the raw

egg expression on my face and feeling like I'd swallowed the 7th pit of hell.
The Doctor examined me and put me through my tricks. He produced a
bellows apparatus with a gadget on it. Blow says he. I blew with all my
might for 30 seconds. Why don't you start? says the Doc and I slowly
passed away. The Doc seemed to think I was due for six months instructing or hightoning or something but I soon convinced him that I must be
back at the squadron in two weeks from that day even if I had to go without my stomach.

Finally we compromised. I'm to take two weeks of leave and go to Nice
or Cannes and bask in the sunlight. In the meanwhile I stay here in
hospital—that is, I sleep in the hospital and look at breakfast there. The
Doc has prescribed all sorts of medicine for me but I got some belladonna[11]
and milk of magnesia at a drugstore and take it instead. With the result
that I am improving rapidly and actually knocked a steak in the head
today without having to resort to the Roman relief.

The days I spend here at the Hotel[12] in pleasant and philosophic con-
templation of life in general and the R.A.F. and W.A.A.C.[13] in particular. I
have known the maitre d'hotel, the headwaiters, and the bartenders since
I left England and I am well attended to. Henry makes a most excellent
eggnog, also a very good coffee flip so I am not lonely or idle. And every
ten or fifteen minutes some old friends wander in. Last night Grid [Keith]
Caldwell blew in with his three flight commanders. Grid used to break up
most of our furniture for us on guest night at 85 Squadron. Last week he
had a collision in the air and was reported killed. His squadron resorted,
literally, to tears. About eleven that night Grid strolled in. His left wing
had given away in the collision and he had started down in a spin. So he
got out of the seat and crawled out on the spar and balanced the machine
and came down from 15,000 feet that way. Just before it hit the ground he
jumped and landed in some bushes, unhurt. The squadron sat up all night
celebrating and he led the dawn patrol. He was with Bishop eighteen
months ago.[14]

The world is much smaller than the old saying would have you believe.
My roommate in hospital I knew at Oxford. Seven other R.A.F. officers on
the same floor with me I knew at various training squadrons. A couple of
Infantry officers I knew at the Savoy. Capt Horn was here for lunch yes-
terday. I saw Pansy George Whiting this morning.[15] A half a dozen others,
I have assisted, or been assisted by, in fights over the lines. And so on.

Pansy Whiting is probably the most unique character in the U.S. Army.
Always broke, he manages to put up the best front of any man in France.
His wardrobe is so carefully selected and so well groomed is he that he is

known to the R.A.F. and U.S.A.S. as the immaculate conception. He speaks carelessly of his yachts, his racing cars, his horses. The Vanderbilts he doesn't like and he always snubs the Astors. He drove up this morning in a limousine and stepped forth clad in everything but the kitchen stove— shining boots, stick, spurs, and all, even a fine fur collar on his coat. I was most impressed. Had I not known him I would certainly have taken him for Pershing's A.D.C. [aide-de-camp].

George ranged up to me and offered me one of his priceless cigarettes and spoke of me becoming his guest for the rest of the day. I pled a bad stomach and finally took another eggnog. George was magnificent. He called for the maitre d'hotel and gave him minute instructions as to how to prepare lunch. I stretched a point and shared the magnificent feast. George confessed that he was just returning from the pestilence hospital where he had been treated for scabies, commonly known as trench itch. However George was none the less magnificent.

George insisted on paying for the lunch and then ere we parted he told me that he was going to do me the honor to permit me to lend him 200 francs. I knew it was coming so I had it ready. It's worth the price of admission to see George in action. He returns to the front tomorrow. I've known him for over a year now, intimately, and he never ceases to endeavor to hightone me despite what I know about him. Ye ancient swashbuckler probably turns over in his grave.

In walking about the town I espied in a shop window a handkerchief. Now it is the habit of Tommy, Doughboy, Aussie, and Jock to send their womenfolk a certain kind of French embroidery, usually a handkerchief with flags or Vive la France, or To My Darling embroidered on them. I don't know whether it was the eggnog or the sea air but I strolled into said shop and purchased for you one of the very best as a souvenir de France. Then I returned here with my trophy of war and exhibited it. Everyone admired it—something dainty for swell occasions! Did you ever read O. Henry's story of the tramp and the doll?[16] Well the story was repeated somewhat today. Everyone drank the health of the handkerchief, the motto, you, me and Henry's. It developed into quite an occasion and the last I saw of the clan they were off to buy likewise.

In censoring letters for the [unit name censored] I've run into 100 or so of them [handkerchiefs] on the way home. You might carry it next time you are in Charlotte but don't exhibit it too publicly or the W.C.T.U. [Women's Christian Temperance Union] will be sending over another delegation. By the way did you read a book called "Out to Win"?[17] If not, do so and read what is said about delegations. I agree with him.

I also note with great pleasure, pride and relief that America goes dry on the 1st.[18] You know the history of the Jews I suppose. You find them everywhere but Palestine.

Devotedly, Elliott

In Hospital
Paris, France
Posted October 19 1918

Dear Mother—

I wonder what you think of the WAACS and WOES, that is if you think at all now and I have no reason to believe that you do. I very often find time to think of shoes and ships and sealing wax and I wonder how valid my conclusions are. I know nothing at all of the WOES or for that matter of any American Women's Organization (Thank God) but I do know quite a bit about the English VADs [Voluntary Aid Detachment], WAACs [Women's Army Auxiliary Corps], Chauffeuresses, and Nursing Sisters and I have a tremendous admiration for them. They are cheery hard workers who are happy to be just left alone, though never with a chip on their shoulders. Always pleasant when spoken to and altogether very efficient.

Official investigations have proved that putting a woman into a uniform does not affect her virtue one way or the other except she has free will about the matter. That I suppose is the average officer's attitude but that's taking them collectively and of course there are no two alike. The thought that challenges me is, what of the individual? And what will be the attitude of the individual man?

The clinging vine type is not always in demand, but at the same time isn't nearly every man afraid of a woman who has tasted of independence and flourished? Does a man dare take unto himself a wife whom he respects for her accomplishments more than she respects him for his? And won't the woman after all be hard to please?

These WAACs aren't social butterflies attracted by the uniform. They aren't the brainless little fools you find swarming around a Red Cross sign at home because it's the popular thing to do. These girls have brothers in the service, they know what they are up against, and they join up in spite of it. Do you think they'll ever be willing to return to their former position? Will they consent to the sub rosa methods of their former days after having breathed the same air as the other sex?

I have never denied the single standard. But I have always denied the right of any one to arbitrarily decide what that standard shall be. I confess

I don't see the light yet but I am certain that neither of the two standards in existence today is fit to encompass the other. The women of the war will stand for neither of the two. One standard will be their right but I'm not at all sure to which side they will incline.

Of course no one at home will have sense enough to try to interpret the handwriting on the wall but you might sit down sometime and write me about the signs of the times. Of course, wit isn't allowed to flourish in the Springs household but you might with each letter include a couple of jokes clipped from Puck or Judge[19] to make up for the deficiency of the text.

Oh, I'm forgetting the war for the moment. How careless of me. I should be shot at dawn. I'm afraid I'm only martial and not military. The war, in my opinion, should only be conducted between two and four. As it is, it interferes with everything.

And just to add a little spice. The WAAC costume is excellently designed. With one failure however. Each individual attempts to get a skirt as short as possible. The average length is about two inches below the knee. And yet modesty is supposed to be the woman's cardinal instinct. Bah!

Devotedly, Elliott

P.S. Better not show this to Father. He might bite through all your best China at lunch.

Paris, France
Dated 19 September [but probably 19–22 October] 1918[20]

Dear Mother—

Well I suppose I should write you some of the details of my visit to Paris though I don't suppose you will be greatly interested. However—

Well first there's the affair of the Belgian taxi.

Taxis are very scarce here and when you want one you're never able to get one. Several days ago I cornered one and told him to take me to the American quartermaster. "Monsieur," he says, "give me a few American cigarettes and any time you want me I am yours." So I gave him some cigarettes and ever since I have owned his taxi. I merely tell him what time to come for me and he is always there. The only difficulty is that he knows no more about Paris than I do and consequently we have great difficulty in finding any place. He's a Belgian and new to Paris. I can reckon myself one of the wealthiest men in Paris though with a taxi always at my disposal.

Then comes the affair of the Brigadier.

I was calling up Lorraine Goodrich from the Continental [Hotel] when I noticed an American doctor, a Captain, standing beside me wearing the

British Military Cross. I congratulated him and we were both glad to see someone who had been with the British. We waxed enthusiastic over our friends the British. Just about that time a British Brigadier came in. He shone from top to tip. Boots, spurs, pink breeches with spotless strappings, tunic covered with decorations, brass hat, and a batman carrying his luggage. We both looked at him with pride. Any one could tell at a glance what sort of a soldier and gentleman he was.

"There," remarked the doc, "is hot stuff."

"You said it. I've got my money on him. That's the sort of man I like to buy a drink for."

The Brigadier registered and strolled over our way. The Doc walked up to him and saluted.

"Sir," he said, "pardon us this intrusion, but this other American and I would like to buy you a drink."

I wanted the floor to open and swallow me but it didn't and I could only stammer.

The Brigadier saw the M.C. on the Doc's chest and smiled.

"I see you've served with us. Certainly I'll be delighted after I've seen my room. Thank you. I'll join you in about five minutes."

I fled in disgrace. I haven't seen either the Doc or the Brigadier. I expect they enjoyed the evening.

Next is the affair of the Camion.

Picture to yourself, Paris, 9 P.M. A two-ton Camion is going from garage to garage trying to get a burner for the gas [head]lights. On the Camion sits your humble servant. The Camion is driven by a beautiful American girl. No burners can be found.

We return to the hotel and hold a council of war. There are six American girls in French nurses' uniforms and myself. I express myself very decidedly but am not even heard. The decision is that they will proceed to the front at once in spite of the absence of lights. I enquire the sector [to which they are traveling] and am informed that they have a five to six hour drive ahead. I give my opinion again but am overruled. Finally in desperation we manage to swipe one burner from a car in a nearby garage. The nurses pile in, scorn my offer to accompany them and start for the front. I collapse and seek my belladonna.

Scene II, several days later.

The same Camion is discovered. Hitched behind is a trailer the size of a moving van. I am told that it is to be a portable kitchen. Again my offer of assistance is declined without thanks. I am not even allowed to crank it for them. Again they depart and I am seized by mingled emotions.

My stomach is much improved and I expect to return to the front in several days. I'm getting more and more impatient all the time.

A heartful of love to you and Father.

Devotedly, Elliott

Paris, France

Dated 28 September 1918 [but probably written toward the end of October][21]

Dear Mother—

Not long ago I was in a city not far from the lines. A city undamaged save where an odd bomb had fallen. A city where the street cars ran and where there were cafes and hotels and civilians. I strolled into a place where the attendant wears a white jacket and where there is a rail made of brass and tables and chairs. And where the greeting is "What'll you have?" and where the uniform is incomplete with a smile and a Dry Throat.

Few were partaking of the sacrament and their faces suggested no other such performance. I looked about. I had never been in the place except I saw half a dozen comrades of other battles. Seated at a table alone was an R.F.C. Captain with a vacant expression on his face. Before him were many glasses—empty. His right arm hung limp at his side—apparently overworked. He looked like the sort of fellow who would call a bartender by his first name.

He saw me.

"Sit down, America."

I did.

"What'll it be?"

"Thanks, but I'm on the wagon."

He seemed grieved. "But you've got wings on. And today is Wednesday."

"Yes, but that's why I ride the wagon."

"How so?"

"Carbuncles on my liver," I explained, "internal prickly heat from anti-tetanus aggravated by machine gun fire from a two seater."

"I know nothing about motor boats," he said. "George, scramble two martinis for us."

"The Flying Corps," he continued, "is not what it used to be."

"No," I agreed with him. "The Huns certainly are practicing shooting too much."

"It's not that," says he, "but it's no longer a gentleman's game."

"Our Mess is out of port, too," I admitted.

The drinks arrived. A cheer-oh and we operated our elbows and adam's apples in unison.

"Well," he continued, "when I started up for my last patrol, the C.O. comes up to me on the tarmac, and says he to me,

'You will take your flight to the lines and split up. You will then all of you fly up and down in front of the enemy's front line at the height of fifty feet for two hours. You will then be relieved by "B" Flight.'

"Says I, 'by the sacred extensions of the Harry Tate, what the almighty constantinereo type C is the idea?'

"'How the empennage should I know? Brigade order. Have you any documents on you which might aid and abet the enemy?'"[22]

"So I go up and follow directions. For half an hour I saw nothing but shrapnel and nothing saw me. Then all of a sudden holes began appearing all around the cockpit and the next thing I knew I came to in a shell hole with my bus on top of me. The Hun started shelling me and things were getting uncomfortable when our infantry came over the top and went on by me. Some stragglers picked up the bus and sorted me out. I nearly got run over by a couple of tanks and got inside one and they let me work a machine gun for 'em. They were a good bunch, those tankers, so I stayed up there a week as the machine gun officer got plugged. Then I met a General testing out his limousine so here I am."

"But why," I asked, "did you have to do it?" asks I. "Oh George, another pair of your martinis."

"Two pair, George," said he, and pulled a paper from his pocket and pointed to a paragraph. I read: "on the [22nd] the Air Force and the Infantry cooperated successfully. Our low-flying machines drowned the noise of our approaching tanks and permitted us to take the enemy by surprise. Several of our machines have not returned."

I could not restrain a smile.

"But," says I, resting my elbow, "you have nothing on me. Haven't I shot up transport and chased Hun artillery about like a trooper? Haven't I bombed Hun generals' limousines and shot up Archie batteries? Haven't I shot up balloons on the ground and taken Pom Poms head on? Haven't I escorted two seaters to every objective from Zeebrugge mole to the Munich brewery?[23] Haven't I been chased into Holland twice on the same day? What kick have you got?"

"Listen, America," says he, "You haven't been an aerial chauffeur like "I have. One week they had me dropping ammunition to the front line in parachutes. Another week I was a cavalryman. They had me leading a troop around. I'd go ahead and locate the enemy by kidding them into shooting at me. Then the cavalry would know where they were and wouldn't [go] there, naturally. Then some yanks got too ambitious and decided to go to Berlin. They kept going till they ran out of everything. So they had us floating around at fifty feet, ten miles over, trying to locate the ten lost tribes by their collar ornaments. We found them in a wood, at least that was the only place we didn't get shot at from. They turned loose the Australians on them and sent us back to drop food to them. The Handleys knocked out about half of them dropping ammunition on 'em."

"Well, didn't I hop a two seater last week. Nice fat old D.F.W. caught with his fingers in the jam.[24] I filled him full and he went in flames and what do you think—what do you think—what do you think? Both of them hopped out in parachutes, in parachutes!"

"Yep, we'll be matching to see who wins the war yet. And using our props as scythes!"

"It's true," says I, warming up my elbow, "but what are you going to do about it?"

"Do?" says he. "Well, I'm reported in paces somnet, or pro patria, or in loco parentis or something.[25] I'm going to your country and become a postman."

"No," says I, "better not; your insides will get rusty [a reference to prohibition]. That country is inhabited by nice people."

"That's so," says he. "I did hear something like that. Didn't the W.C.T.U. or the I.W.W. or the A.C.L. or somebody start the war to get all of the men out of the country so they couldn't vote against prohibition?"[26]

"No, that's not quite it. When Rheims was threatened everybody knew what the cellars there contained, so we had to go to war and then Congress made the country dry to stimulate recruiting. All the men with a thirst went abroad and then they made it permanent."

"Well," says he, "you haven't got an extra seat in your car have you?"

"Sure," says I, "unless George here will sell me enough to fill it. In which case we'll both walk."

"George," says he, "is it true you can mix four martinis as quick as you can [mix] two?"

[The closing comments, if any, are missing.]

DIARY ENTRY: October 28: Depart with Sam Eckert [squadron commander of the 17th Aero Squadron]. Back to 17th Squadron. Lunch at Amiens. Maj Fowler and I dine at Amiens.

DIARY ENTRY: October 29: Back to Squadron. Ordered to go to Toul. Machines [Sopwith Camels] all returned. Clay and I to get squadrons.

148th Aero Squadron
Beugnatre [Bapaume], France
October 29 1918

Dear Mother—

Well, I have returned to the squadron and must say that I am glad to be back at it again. Managed to return in a Cadillac so had a very pleasant trip.

I'm very proud of my American citizenship and all that but permit me to remark that if ever I go to Paris again I shall conceal the fact. It costs you about 200% [more] because you are an American. Prices have doubled since I was there in July. A meal cost you $8 a plate and uniforms and boots are out of the question. I had to pay $60 for a decent pair of shoes and puttees. Of course, francs mean nothing to me, so I probably got rid of a lot more cash than I should have. However, why worry. I'm back in the land where there is no tomorrow and yesterday's memories fast recede.

This is confidential, but I've got it straight from Major Fowler that I am going to have a squadron of my own. I was recommended for it shortly before I went on leave. That'll mean beaucoup de Huns because I shall be able to fly anything I feel inclined [to] and have a roving commission. That is, I can wander out alone, with one or two [others], or take my whole squadron with me. I want Larry and Bim Oliver for Flight Commanders if possible and think I can get them.

Thanks to you my supply of Dieties still holds out though the Page and Shaw's disappeared the first day.

A heartful of love to you and Father.

Your devoted son, Elliott

P.S. Address: Morgan Harjes & Co, Boulevard Hausman, Paris

DIARY ENTRY: October 30: Fool around all day doing nothing.
DIARY ENTRY: October 31: Visit 85 Squadron at Foucacourt near Cateau in Crossley.[27]
DIARY ENTRY: November 1: Squadrons go by cattle train. Mort [Newhall], Kindley, Clay and I go by Cadillac. Spend night in Amiens.
DIARY ENTRY: November 2: Arrive Tours and go to Grand [Hotel].
DIARY ENTRY: November 3: Stick around and do nothing.
DIARY ENTRY: November 4: Start for Toul, spend night at Lignes [probably Ligny-en-Barrois]. Hell of a trip.
DIARY ENTRY: November 5: Arrive Toul and find everyone arrived and very fed up. Clay and I report to Colombey-les-Belles and find no squadrons available.[28]

DIARY ENTRY: November 6: So go back to Toul and lay around.

DIARY ENTRY: November 7: Jesus Christ what a place! What an Army! Chills and fever [and] am sick as a dog.

Toul, France
November 7 1918

Dear Mother—

Well, I turned down the job of chief instructor at the School of Aerial Fighting again and am still waiting around to take command of a squadron. Expect to get a machine and go out and look for a Hun in a day or so. I'll be using a strange machine[29] and strange guns so don't expect much success at first.

I want you to do something for me. Next time you are in New York get a nice leather registry book, have it marked "Italian Detachment" and make the following explanation to the manager of the Vanderbilt. When the Detachment broke up just a year ago [when the men left Oxford University in two groups], I announced that I would provide a registry at the Vanderbilt where they could all put their home address, date of return, and any news of missing members. Also their New York address and length of stay. Thus some of us might some day get direct accounts of those missing. A few are going home as instructors and it might be well to start the registry.

Another thing I want done. I want the old White place at Fort Mill fixed up for me.[30] There's a good chance now that I may get to live there. I feel you will know better what to do to it than anyone else. You needn't say why you are doing it but draw on Father for the limit—mortgage the mills if necessary—and fix it up right. Also buy me a good pair of overalls. Also make Father get rid of the Stutz.

A heartful of love to you and Father.

Your devoted son, Elliott

DIARY ENTRY: November 8: Sick in bed same. Am going to Vendre [?? town not identified] and try to get back in shape again.

The following excerpt is from a letter by Leroy Springs dated 9 September 1918.

My dear Son:

. . . We were glad to hear from you and to know that your eyes are all right. I have been very much distressed about same and I am glad that they are all right and that you are able to take charge of your squadron but hope you will take good care of yourself and be careful and not take any more risks than you can help. It is certainly a big compliment to you to have been transferred as squadron commander of squadron B of the American forces but you do not give your address in France. . . .

Now, my dear boy, I want to say to you again to be very careful and not take undue risks. I do not like to be writing you letters of this kind, as I want to write you nothing but encouraging letters, but I cannot see why you should be wanting additional funds outside of what the government is paying you. All your expenses are paid and I am told there is little or nothing to spend money for in Europe. Nearly all the men are sending at least half of their money back. . . . I know the boys here are sending most of their money home.

I am anxious to gratify you and to have you have everything you want but there is such a thing as getting in the habit of being a spendthrift and I cannot see for the life of me why you should need additional funds, except at some occasional rest room where you may dine. It will not help your standing for you to spend money recklessly and your friends will discredit you, also your commanding officer. You should not be thinking so much about pleasure and eating now as about taking care of yourself and making yourself efficient and serving your country faithfully and making a good record. Your commanding officer will not be inclined to promote you if you are frivolous or reckless in the expenditure of money. They will not be willing to put you in charge of other men unless you maintain your dignity and show your ability to handle other men.

When your cable came [. . .], I did not understand that you wanted me to honor a draft for Ernest Mount. The cable read "amount" and I thought you had drawn a draft for this. I am surprised at same. Now my dear son, I am not unreasonable about this, but it is very hard, after your grandfather and I have worked so hard for our money, to have you throw it away on strangers. You are under no obligations whatever to Mount except that you were at college with him for a year. I have never done anything like that in my life. You have never made any money in your life and it is unreasonable of you to expect me to dish it out like this to strangers when I have so many poor relatives. . . . I want to gratify your every wish but it is unreasonable for you to be expecting me to be paying out money to strangers this way to be squandered when I have worked so hard to save your grandfather's estate and save something for all of us in order that we may be independent. . . .

I am afraid you think I am a much wealthier man than I am and also that your part of your mother's and grandfather's estates is more than it is.

You must disabuse your mind of that fact. All we have is invested in cotton mills and the income from them from now on will be very small, as the government will take about 75% of our profits, only allowing us a fair interest on our investment. As everything I have is invested in cotton mills, with the exception of a little land, and it will be an easy matter for the mills to go to pieces after the war and we lose everything, it stands us in hand to be conservative and we certainly have no money to waste on other people.

I am afraid you do not realize the importance of knowing the value of the dollar and how to save it. It would simply mean disaster to you if you get into this habit and become a reckless spender of money and allow other people to impose on you. . . . You cannot serve your country with the credit you should nor will you make the business man you should, if you develop into a reckless spendthrift and do not know how to get the value for your money. You must know that my ambition in life is to do everything I can for you and Lena and your future happiness and it is not my pleasure to take issue with you about things that your good sense should tell you are wrong. As above stated, I regret very much to write you in this way. It is not the amount of money involved but it is the principle of the thing. . . .

Your affectionate father

The following excerpt is from a letter by Leroy Springs dated 14 September 1918.

My dear Son:

We have just come back from Columbia. Lena and I spent yesterday down there on war work business. She is one of the vice chairmen of the state on the next Liberty Loan drive. She is kept busy all the time on her Red Cross work and other things. . . .

I am very sorry I wrote you as I did about Ernest Mount but you must understand that I did it for your own good. I could not understand why you were allowing him to draw on me for $500 but in one of your last letters to Lena you stated he had gotten married. I suppose you were sending him this as a bridal present. I must say I never give bridal presents that cost more than $150 and, if you had cabled me to send him a present, it would have been more appropriate.[31]

However, I am very sorry I wrote you as I did, as you are fighting for your country and I would hate to write you anything that would make you think I was not willing to do anything in the world for your pleasure that was reasonable but I want you to understand that there is nothing in getting in the habit of wasting money and spending it on people who do not appreciate it and besides it is unreasonable and extravagant. . . .

The following excerpt is from a letter by Leroy Springs dated 28 September 1918.

My dear Son:

. . . It will not do for you to keep up perpetual flying too long, as you might get restless and can't sleep. I only suggest this, but leave it to your good judgment what is best to do. It would be an easy matter for you to get a furlough or for me to get one for you. You have been in active service now for fifteen months, three months training and twelve months on the other side and there is such a thing as overdoing a thing. I am distressed to learn that you have lost so many of your friends. I hope they were not shot down but that they are prisoners. They are certainly a gallant lot of fellows. . . .

. . . Lena has been very busy at home with the Red Cross work and also in connection with the Fourth Liberty Loan. She and I both are active in this work and have to keep busy all the time. . . . We had a campaign meeting here today to start the new drive for Liberty Bonds. We will have to sell about $375000 worth of bonds in this county and are depending on the farmers to take a large number of them. I have been appointed County Chairman to raise about $20000 for the YMCA, YWCA, Catholic order, and Jewish order, which have all been combined in connection with the work overseas. Our county has contributed eagerly and liberally to all demands made upon them and I am proud of their record. . . .

Your affectionate father

Toul, France
E.W. Springs, 1st Lt A.S.
Squadron Commander
Unattached [Not assigned to a squadron]
November 9 1918

Dear Mother—

I think you might discontinue sending me the Charlotte Observer. I'm fed up with it. It only aggravates me. I'm infernally sick of reading in each issue where "Mrs Walter Lambeth and little daughter Mary Wisdom" are, that "Miss Calvine Scott is the attractive younger sister of Miss Julia Baxter Scott, daughter of Mr and Mrs J. M. Scott," and the location of Mrs Gordon Finger's relatives. No offense to those mentioned. In addition to that I read where the many friends of Mr and Mrs —— will be delighted to read that their son has safely arrived at the training camp at Plattsburg. I also learn that the following people may puff out their chests: his aunt,

Mrs ———, his cousin, Mr ———, and his uncle, Mr ———. In addition, Mrs ——— was a sister of Miss ——— and Mr ——— and that she is President of ——— and keenly interested in Red Cross work.

I can't remember when there's been anything in it of interest. If you see anything that you think might interest me please pass it along. Otherwise it's a waste of postage. I'd like to have the Lancaster News though.

I've had numerous experiences with the American Army. The first thing that happened was I was placed under arrest by an A.P.M.[32] because I have no American passes or orders. The fact that I had a pocket full [of] British ones made no difference. I am still awaiting the verdict. If Father writes a long line of admonishment, advice, and regret I shall cease to be his son.

I've run into quite a few differences from the British. The censor can't object to my mentioning these two. You doubtless read in the papers where American pilots shoot down enemy planes on the American side of the lines and then land beside them. None of the British squadrons I have been with ever got a Hun on our side of the lines. I did most of my fighting five to seven miles over and two I fought twenty miles beyond the lines. That makes every difference in the world.

Also if two or more pilots get the same Hun they don't share [the credit for] him. Every pilot who fired gets full credit. That runs up Henry Clay's and my score considerably. The British Pilots are universally modest and reticent. I don't think anyone embarrassed me by asking me the number of planes I had [shot down] until I got to Paris. I couldn't tell them because I didn't know exactly. I don't know exactly yet. I think the British give me 12 and $1/4$ but by American figuring it will be 14.

By the way I have quite a bit of bric a brac from the Hun plane Henry [Clay] and I got which I will send you when I get a chance. We shot it down about five miles over the lines during a push and our infantry took that territory immediately after. Rather funny—but we could each trace our own shots and both of us had hit the cockpit, tanks, and pilot. Henry was below and I was above so it was no trouble at all. It also turned out that there were two others firing at us and more up high but the trap was not sprung as some of our machines above protected us.

God. I'm itching to get into it again.

A heartful of love to you and Father.

Your devoted son, Elliott

P.S. Father's last letters positively make me homesick. How I shall rush home where my gentle sense of humor is so worthily appreciated! Throw away the rubber plant and the plush sofa and the brown derby and pearly grey fedora and install a picture of Ben Franklin and an embroidered motto,

"A penny saved is a penny earned," and another, "Filial is Financial," and feed the calf. And next time Father is trying to hightone someone, just remark "Too bad he's such a fool about spending money. Why when on leave he [Elliott Springs] thinks nothing of spending $25 on dinner when he could get a perfectly good one for $22. And do you know he lent $300 to a man who had shot a Hun off his tail one day and when the man was killed, he was such a fool that he wouldn't try to collect it by writing to his people. While in Europe he cashed over $1500 worth of checks for friends and that cost him $105 because [one] fellow was killed. Oh, he's a worthless spendthrift, and will only throw away what very little he's got." Just say that once. And then you might add that he's beyond money, now. A man doesn't go through the fire and come out counting his money.

That doesn't mean I have holes in my pockets. Even now I am planning to get to England and hope to do so before the French get the gold out of my teeth. The English people show a marked consideration for Americans.

No sign of my squadron yet so I'm wrestling with a bad case of grippe. I find myself otherwise in good health though a complete nervous wreck. E.W.S.

P.P.S. Please send me a Christmas Box containing Fruit Cake and Page and Shaws.

EW Springs, Morgan Harjes Co, Paris.

DIARY ENTRY: November 11: The Armistice. Spend night on platform in Toul with Jean [Gene?] Delmont as guard.[33]

Toul, France
November 11 1918

Dear Mother—
    Peace! The bells in town began ringing at eleven and the Band struck up the Marseillaise and the Star Spangled Banner at twelve. The French are still dancing in the streets.
    But I can find no enthusiasm. I went to bed a free man and I awoke with a millstone around my neck called tomorrow which pulls and pulls and will hang there 'til the grave. No more can I laugh at conventions, colonels, and cocktails, no more can I speak of shoes and ships and sealing wax with equal objectivity.

There is no longer the "Front." There is no longer that place where every man is known by his merit, where a grim though sure justice prevails, and where there is always a haven of rest for those whom the world treats ill. Expiation is now withdrawn—everyone puts on their kid gloves. Pandora's box flies open again and Repentance and Remorse rush upon us.

The Music for the Dance of Death has ceased, the Dancers are making ready to depart, draining the last drop of punch as they go. Tomorrow— thick heads, brown tongues, The King is dead, whom shall we crown in his place?

A new country is before us—"The Land of Might Have Been." A huge army of occupation must enter it at once.

Peace! I find myself alive. Strange—I hadn't considered that possibility —I must alter my plans—quick, my kid gloves—doctor, how about my lungs? Has the high altitude knocked them for good? And how about my liver—how long does it take Sorisis[34] to get you?

Yes, Bill, I know you are thinking of your wife. I doubt if you can re- member what she looks like. But you do remember that she has large feet, doesn't know how to dress, and all she's good for is to see you off to war and form a picturesque background for your heroic sacrifice which didn't come off. And your family don't like her.

And a lot of enthusiasm is aroused over finding a marble top behind each brass rail and stalls drawn up in front of it. Goodbye to the great American digestion.

Peace! We've shoved it down the Germans' throats; now let's go find it ourselves.

Love, Elliott

The following cable from Leroy Springs is dated 11 November 1918.

Congratulations peace. If unwell think should arrange come home promptly. Love. Answer.

Toul, France
[Undated, but probably soon after 11 November 1918]

Dear Father—

I am writing this in anticipation of the abolition of censorship but don't know when I'll mail it. You are undoubtedly curious about where I was located in France, so get a big map out now and I'll elucidate. We started from Hounslow just west of London and landed at Folkestone to get weather reports. Our next stop was at Marquise (between Calais and Boulogne) for orders. Then our next stop was at our aerodrome about a mile from Dunquerque (Dunkirk).

While there we patrolled from Nieuport to Ypres but as there was more activity between Ypres and Armentieres, we used to go south of our beat looking for Huns. We used to escort the bombers over Bruges and Zeebrugge, which were about twenty to twenty-five miles over the lines. Usually we went out to sea and came in over Holland and then back over there. Archie was worse there than anywhere else on the line.

After two or three weeks we moved to St Omer and our aerodrome was about two miles east of the city. Our sector of the front was from the Forest of Nieppe to Houthulst Forest just north of Ypres.

My first fight took place near Armentieres, my second near Estaires, third over Courtrai, fourth over Neuse Englise and I was finally shot up over Armentieres and landed just north of the Forest of Nieppe.

Then I left the 85th Squadron and went to the 148th Squadron, which we organized at Dunquerque, working more or less between Dixmude and Nieppe. The next Hun I got was between Bruges and Ostend after a raid on Bruges. Then we moved to Amiens for the push down there and had our aerodrome at Allonville. The 85th Squadron moved to Bertangles just north of us. We stayed there as long as the battle raged and worked from Albert to Chaulnes, to Roye, doing most of the fighting between Chaulnes and Roye.

Then we moved to Doullens and had two days rest to prepare for the big push. The push started from Adinfer Wood and we kicked off with four days ground straffing around Croisilles, St Leger, Queant, Bapaume, Beugny, and Havrincourt, Goureaucourt and Bourlon later on. That's when we had our hardest fighting. The Hun concentrated all his best machines there and we had to fight as well as ground straff. You could always find a fight along the Arras-Cambrai and Cambrai-Bapaume roads. I had a dozen or more fights near the Canal du Nord and its junction with the Scarpe. The two-seater Clay and I got possession of was at Fontaine Notre Dame between Bourlon Wood and Cambrai. I suppose by this time you have received the cross I sent to you which I cut off the side of it. It was a Hannoveranner of the latest type, the kind that gave us so much trouble.

Then we moved to Albert and finally to Bapaume. We were going to move to Le Cateau when we were withdrawn from the British [army] on the 1st of November and sent to Toul where we were when the Armistice was signed. Mac Grider was buried near Armentieres where he fell. Mannock was killed at Estaires, Jenkinson at Aubigny (near Cambrai), Siebald at Bapaume. Capt Benbow's cross stands before Ypres where he fell.

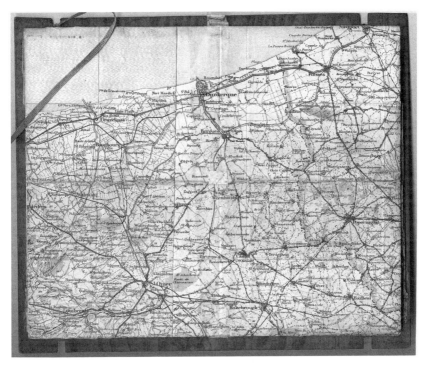

Two photos of maps used by Elliott Springs. These maps, compressed accordion-style and attached to both sides of a small board, helped him identify his position flying along the front lines. Courtesy of the Springs Close Family Archives, the White Homestead, Fort Mill, South Carolina.

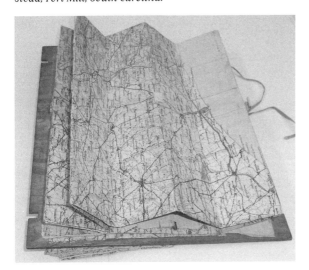

When the weather was bad, you'd find us at Calais, Boulogne, Freport, Dieppe, or sometimes up prowling around the front. I went from Bapaume to Paris to Toul by Cadillac and it was a very pleasant trip. Enjoyed it very much.

No matter where I go or what I do, the best part of me will always remain between Zeebrugge and Armentieres, and in front of Cambrai. There I lived a life, a long lifetime, there lie my companions, and many adversaries and there also lies the biggest part of myself.

I know every tree, every village, every road, every canal, every little wood, every little change of color between Nieuport and Roye for twenty miles on either side of the lines, from Boulogne to St Omer to Arras, to Roulers, to Amiens to Montdidier on our side, Zeebrugge to Roulers, Menen, Courtrai, Lille, Valenciennes, Le Cateau, St Quentin. I've spent a couple of hundred hours up above it, looking first down, then up, searching below as well as above. I can close my eyes and my mind becomes a huge map whose accuracy has been tested hundreds of times.

I've flown between the piles of ruins of Nieuport, Dixmude, Ypres, Bailleul, Arras, Bapaume, Albert, Villers-Bretonneux, Montdidier, and their memory will always be a sear. The first four are the worst, you almost need a map to tell where they were. Bailleul, Estaires, Meteren are simply pushed to one side and flattened. Arras is a huge shell, the buildings are practically all standing, but they are hollow and full of holes. Bapaume, Albert, and Bruay are piles of red brick. Villers-Bretonneux is just a collection of dusty walls and a city pulverized to dirt. Montdidier like Ypres seems to protest mutely with its masonry which will not crumble though but few walls remain.

In Ypres there are no walls standing north and south. There are some east and west. It gives you the appearance of furrows. Then for miles around there is a flat brown expanse of mud and dust which from above seems to be boiling. You can't place a pin point on a spot that hasn't been hit by a shell. The same is true of the Somme [battleground]. The Menen Road, once lined with poplars, has a few stumps to mark it. Houthulst Forest is just a red patch with maybe fifty stumps left—a ghostly sight. Nieuport, when you come down low over it, looks as if some child had been drawing in the sand.

A heartful of love always.

Your devoted son, Elliott

DIARY ENTRY: November 12: Arrive Paris. Dine with Major Fowler and sister.

Men of the 17th and 148th Aero Squadrons, Toul, France, November 1918. The men of the 17th Aero Squadron are on the left side of the propeller; the men of the 148th Aero Squadron are on the right side. Standing, left to right: members of the 17th Aero Squadron including George Vaughn Jr., A. F. Everett, W. W. Goodnow, John Donoho, Howard Burdick, Frank Dixon, J. A. Myers, I. P. Corse, Ralph Snoke, William Armstrong, and commanding officer Capt. Sam Eckert. Continuing on, left to right: members of the 148th Squadron including commanding officer Capt. Mort Newhall (in front of the propeller hub), Charles McLean, Sydney Noel, J. R. Hogan, Larry Callahan, Clayton Bissell, unknown (face blocked by the next man in line), Field Kindley, W. B. Knox, Foster Marshall, William Taylor, Thomas Moore, George Dorsey, Elliott Springs, and W. E. Cravens. Kneeling, left to right: members of the 17th Aero Squadron including Edward Lubbers, Ernest Mason, William Schadt, William House, Martin Giesecke, William Clements, and Leonard Desson. Continuing, left to right: members of the 148th Aero Squadron including Jesse Creech (holding dog), Henry Starkey, Louis Rabe, Henry Clay, William Colgan, John Welsh, Bennett "Bim" Oliver, Percy Cunnius, Orville Ralston, and Lawrence Wyly. Courtesy of National Archives.

Paris, France
November 13 1918

Dear Father—

As there's no squadron available for me at the present moment and the war is over, I was ordered south to be chief instructor at some place, don't know exactly where. So I am passing through Paris on my way there.

Everybody is rejoicing and Paris is decorated with flags worse than 5th Ave was when Joffre was there. I'll rejoice too as soon as I get rid of my indigestion. In the meanwhile I only scowl at everyone and demand another war.

I am greatly surprised to find that I have actually lived through the war. But as I have lived through it and will see you all again there's little use in my writing about anything as I'll get to tell you about it in detail.

The Fort Mill Mfg Co will be the next thing I take to pieces to look at the works but I won't tell anybody in the meanwhile so it won't hurt your credit. Start sounding for the bottom!

What do you think of my bringing home a plane with me. I can get a good one in England fairly cheap. If you approve send me some money. Send me some money anyway. I'll be sure to need it. Address Morgan Harjes, Paris, from now on.

A heartful of love to you and Lena.

Your devoted son, Elliott

DIARY ENTRY: November 13: Very sick. Got to go to hospital. Oh Christ.
DIARY ENTRY: November 15: Gradually go insane. Shall I try the window. No. Cowardly.
DIARY ENTRY: November 24: Get up and walk about. Too weak. Back to bed again.

Paris, France
November 30 1918

Dear Mother—

I've written a half dozen letters to you in the last couple of weeks but have torn them up as none of them expressed my sentiments correctly. Have forgotten when I mailed the last one. I'm back here in Paris for a few days getting my teeth fixed as there was nothing to do down at Tours. I'm trying to arrange to get to England but for the moment it doesn't seem possible. May be able to get over later though.

I ran into [Fred] Shoemaker on the street yesterday and I must tell you about him. He was one of my staunchest supporters in the Italian Detachments and when last I heard of him he was missing in action. He told me a long tale and he looks as if he'd been through it all right. He was shot down three months ago but landed safely. A bullet entered his face just in front of his left ear and came out of his right lower jaw, shattering both jaws. His teeth were all wired up to hold his jaws together. He eats by pushing soft stuff through a gap.

In such condition he escaped from a German hospital in Belgium, wandered about for fourteen days and finally worked through the Hun lines and got to Lille just as the Armistice was signed and is now in hospital here. He said [Grady] Touchstone was in the same hospital with him with a broken jaw also but couldn't get away as he did. He's a remarkable fellow anyway. Once was a mail carrier in Alaska and ran a dog sled all winter. About 6' 3" and weighed about 210. Now he's a mere shadow. I'm going to see him again tomorrow.

This visit to Paris is very quiet as I'm broke. Pabst will be in tonight but I expect he's broke too. Now the war is over and there is a tomorrow in store for me again. I'm becoming farsighted when it's too late. I've got several hundred francs but they've got to go a long way. Not like in the old days when you spoke of tomorrow with the same definiteness and conviction as the resurrection. And now that I have actually survived the war I don't feel like cabling for more. In other words, I am no longer careless and carefree but a man weighed down by one horrible thought—tomorrow!

Have you gotten the Black Cross from the Hun plane yet? Or the two packages of handkerchiefs? Your letter of November 9 I got yesterday at Morgan Harjes telling me you'd gotten the sketches.

Prices over here now are unbelievable. Everything has soared till you have to be a multimillionaire to keep yourself even looking respectable. And then on top of that is the 10% tax on everything—even food. However, you can eat here at the [military] club for a couple of dollars a crack. Well the big job's done anyway. I was going to say—why worry—but I'll never be able to use that expression again which I used to apply to everything.

Well, get Fort Mill ready for me.

A heartful of love to you and Father.

Devotedly, Elliott

Paris, France
December 14 1918

Dear Father—

As I cabled you yesterday I am going to get two weeks leave and I need some money. My stomach was not in good shape so I went to hospital here and they are fixing me up. And in a few days they are going to give me two weeks leave and I shall probably go to Nice.[35] Then with a little luck I shall start home. Hurrah!

It will probably take some time to get on a boat as I shall have to go to a concentration camp and get a detachment of troops, get them into shape and await orders and passage. I figure I ought to get home some time in February.

Don't worry about me. Nothing wrong, just a touch of flu and the same old hyperacidity. Am feeling all right now but the Doc says I ought to lay around here a little while longer.

The School of Aerial Gunnery is closing down so they won't need me down there [at St Jean de Monts]. So unless they send me back to the front to take command of a squadron, which I don't think they will, I see nothing to hold me up though I haven't actually got orders yet to do anything but report down to S.O.S. Headquarters after my leave.[36]

I would like to go home through England but don't think I can arrange that. I'll cable you from time to time about what's going on.

A heartful of love to you and Lena. Your devoted son, Elliott

Paris, France
December 14 1918

Dear Mother—

I am becoming more and more overjoyed at the thought of getting home. In fact I am so anxious to see you all again that I'm passing up everything [all military assignments] on this side in an effort to get back. It will take some wangling but I figure on being with you some time in February. It seems a long time away but that looks like the best I can do.

My stomach has been misbehaving so I'm getting it fixed up here. But it's nothing to worry you. And the two weeks' leave will fix me up fine. But why bother about writing now when I'll see you soon and spend the first week just telling you about what happened over here. I'm going to either Nice or Biarritz on leave—probably Nice. I've certainly been lucky about getting leave over here.

A heartful of love—a very large heartful of love to you and Father. Your devoted son, Elliott

Paris, France
December 18 1918

Dear Aunt Addie—

My thanks for the bond. I appreciate it very much. I am sending your [Christmas] present today. When in Paris, I got Lena some of the finest hand woven handkerchiefs in the world. And she was so delighted with them that I have gotten some for you for Christmas. I hope you will like them. Though I know you have a lot of nice ones already.

I am still hoping to get to Chicago for Christmas but don't know yet whether I can or not. Many many thanks again. And Merry Christmas.

Devotedly, Elliott

DIARY ENTRY: December 24: [Hugh] Fontaine departs.
DIARY ENTRY: December 25: Fontaine and I lunch at Becasse [?]. Dine
    with the Goodrichs at Becasse.
DIARY ENTRY: December 26: Get out of hospital and stay at Edward VII.
DIARY ENTRY: December 27: Depart for Tours. Find Fontaine there.

The following excerpt is from a letter by Leroy Springs dated 11 November 1918.

My dear Son:
... I feel that I have so much to be thankful for that you have been safely spared to us. We have been so constantly uneasy about you for fear that you would not be returned, as you have been in such a hazardous part of the service.

I am very much afraid, owing to the high altitudes at which you have been flying and the nervous strain you have been under that your physical system is not what it should be and that you are suffering from indigestion such as you had when you were eight years old and also again when you were at Princeton. I realize what it is and I honestly think, in justice to yourself and me, that you return as early as possible. If you want to go back to Europe at some future day you may but I think you should return now. Remember you have been away almost fifteen months and have not been at home for almost eighteen months. You have been through a great deal of excitement and a great strain and it is certainly due you that you should come home and rest up. As the war is ended, you will not be needed in Europe any longer.

I am afraid you have been eating too many sweets and high seasoned food, which have gotten your digestion all out of order and it will be no pleasure to stay over there in such a condition. Now look at it sensible and act sensibly and remember I am thinking about you constantly and shall be very uneasy until your physical condition is what it should be. . . .

With love and best wishes and hoping that you will decide to come home at an early date, I am always

Your affectionate father

Tours, France
December 27 1918

Dear Father—

You write as if nothing were easier than getting home. I thought I had enough trouble getting over here but it's nothing to getting back. And where do you get the idea that I'm not breaking my neck to get back? Why keep giving me reasons why I should return? I know a lot more than you do and I'm just as anxious to get back as you are to have me there if not more so. When I get there you can bet I won't find fault with the place but dollars to doughnuts you're going to start cussing me out as I enter the door. But I warn you—you'll fight the war alone—I've got enough of it.

As the matter stands now I ought to get my orders through in about a week and go to a port where I shall probably have to wait around for two to five weeks. Then voila I shall sail. That is if all goes well. But it is slow—very slow. I don't think that any Air Service men have sailed yet though everyone seems to be doing just as I am—waiting around—while the French take the gold out of our teeth.

I'm well fed up. I'm tired of waiting around—I'm tired of leave—I'm tired of bridge—tired of gambling, and tired of spending money.

Many thanks for the $1000—it ought to get me home unless the Frogs double up on the prices again. The Vanderbilt charges like child's [play] compared with a modest French back room estaminet. The meal I had in Paris cost 135 francs exclusive of the liquid. But we should worry—I've still got the gold cigarette case.

For the moment I'm very comfortable. Fontaine and I have a big comfortable room and bath at the hotel here and are living like lords. Callahan writes from Issoudun that he, [Bim] Oliver, [George] Vaughn and [Orville] Ralston are having a rotten time at the camp there awaiting orders too. Unless something happens soon I may go back to Paris for a couple of days. This waiting around is not my idea of a pleasant occupation.

A heartful of love to you and Lena. Your devoted son, Elliott

The following cable from Elliott Springs is dated 29 December from Tours.

Awaiting embarkation orders. Some delay. Home six weeks. Love Springs.

DIARY ENTRY: December 31: We buy up all cordials and throw a party.
   Buz Law . . . [possibly Bradley Lawton?] wins all our cash at Poker.
DIARY ENTRY: January 1, 1919: New Year's dance at the town hall in
   Tours.

Tours, France
January 1 1919

Dear Mother—
   New Year's Greetings!
   HA! HA!
   And I hereby resolve during 1919 to be as lazy, worthless, selfish, arro-
gant, and as crooked as I please and see if it doesn't get me more than trying the opposite in 1918. Pardon my patting myself on the back but my
present position seems to indicate that in other words I am officially out of
luck. I can't get to England, I've got to hang around concentration camps
and drill for four or five weeks, and maybe I'll get back provided they trace
all my papers and I get rid of the scabies. Meanwhile 2nd Lts just over
from the States bawl hell out of me on all occasions and I have to say
"please" if I want to ask for any information. I suppose I ought to feel lucky
if these brave soldiers don't court-martial me.
   Outside of that I'm doing very nicely thank you. I have my health and
some money and those two items mean a lot more than the army now the
Hun is finis.
   At the New Year's Ball (attended by General Harbord[37] and 86 military
policemen) I saw Eli [Springs], Lee Skipper, Stuart Gilchrist, and Howard
Conway.[38] All were looking well. [William] Plyler from Kershaw I saw
here at the hotel.
   I was informed yesterday that I had been posthumously awarded the
D.S.C.[39] Don't know where the rumor started but if you hear it don't
believe it. I am neither posthumous nor D.S.C. The Barflies Union in Paris
shoots me down in flames once a week. One fellow actually described my
funeral to me. It took place September 12th about three miles the other
side of the lines and the news came through the prison camps. I was shot

down in flames. Unfortunately it was [Linn] Forster who had the opportunity of finishing it right and pulling the grand finale.[40]

I suppose you all know from the papers that all promotions were stopped November 11. I had a letter from General Patrick informing me that the order was the reason I am returning as a 1st Lt.[41] Of course, I was just tickled to death. Made me feel so good. I'd swap my D.F.C. for another one. Thank Heaven I'm above all that stuff now. I don't care whether I'm a general or corporal.

They gave me a blank to fill in. Did I desire to remain in the Regular Army, Reserve Corps, or get immediate and complete separation. I'll bet you can't guess what I put. Anyway, I'm coming home. I may be grey and tattered but I'm on my way.

And listen—if I get home and find that a lot of drivel has been spread around about me, I'll remain between ten and fifteen minutes. If it wasn't for Father I'd take a wonderful job I've been offered on this side. But if I find that I return a ridiculous object I shall be tempted to disregard my filial piety and follow my natural inclinations.

And if there is any criticism about the financial arrangements of the Springs household from Aunt Bleeker just tell her for me that Father has been exceptionally generous, beneficent, and prompt in relieving my financial difficulties and the fact that I have to cable and ask for it doesn't make any difference so long as I get it since Father doesn't see my pass book and doesn't know when I run out. That the only times I've been broke were when I forgot to cable. Also you tell Father he's reflecting on both of us when he broadcasts the statement that I've been cabling to him for me. It's come back to me through various channels.

If you were at the mercy of these French people you'd need money too. And yet I read where some Senators proposed canceling France's debt to the U.S. Wait a year and we can ask the French to cancel our debt to them. Yes I know the drivel the papers and magazines feed you. I used to marvel that the British didn't love the French as I felt they should. Vive la Franco-American. Vive la beaucoup d'argent. At one of the theatres in Paris they have changeable price cards: Francais 2.50, Anglais 10.00, Americaine 20.00. It always gets a laugh.

I don't know what's the matter with me today. You naturally expect to feel bad in the morning but it's nearing tea time. Yes I still have to have tea at 4:30. I invited both Eli and Lee to dinner. They didn't know whether they could make it or not. After which (the dinner) I shall NOT go to the dance at the Y.W.C.A. Hostess House. So saying, he put his honor in his pocket and strode forth in search of excitement.

As soon as it clears up Fontaine and I are going to get a plane and fly over to Issoudun to see Larry, Bim, and the crew who have been sitting around in the mud for six weeks.

A heartful of love to you and Father.

Devotedly, Elliott

Conclusion

Elliott Springs's Postwar Career as a Writer

When Elliott Springs returned to the United States early in 1919, he did not settle down in Fort Mill. Instead he investigated alternative forms of employment, working for a brief period for the LWF Aircraft Company of Long Island, where he and Field Kindley, another 148th Aero Squadron pilot, participated in an abortive cross-country race featuring LWF aircraft.[1] Accompanied by Larry Callahan, he embarked on a voyage to Europe in 1921 to revisit some of the places he had seen during the war, but he was immediately distracted by the presence on board the ship of Frances Ley, daughter of a wealthy New York businessman. He married her a year later. During this time his father, Leroy, continually requested that Elliott start to learn about the textile business, but Elliott was reluctant to become a South Carolina businessman, believing that lifestyle did not suit him. The period from 1922 through 1925 was marked by a series of disagreements, often heated, between Elliott and his father about Elliott's role in the family business.[2]

Partly in response to a challenge from his father to demonstrate that he could make money instead of spending it, but mostly due to his own inherent interest in writing stories, Elliott began to write narrative accounts of his World War I flying experiences. One of the first was a series about training for and flying in the war. These narratives were collectively called "Back in '17" and were published in *Air Service* magazine in 1925 and 1926. About the same time he began a longer work, which he called "Diary of an Unknown Aviator"; it was eventually published in *Liberty* magazine in 1926 as "War Birds: Diary of an Unknown Aviator" because the publisher of *Liberty*, Joseph Medill Patterson, believed that such a title would have greater appeal for readers.

War Birds: Its Success, Composition, and Controversy

The story of *War Birds* is told in diary form, following the adventures of an eager "anonymous" American airman from the time he begins his training in October 1917 until his death in aerial combat, which occurs, according to events in the book, late in August 1918; the last dated diary entry in *War Birds* is 27 August. The book describes the career of the airman as he crosses the Atlantic with 150 other American flying cadets, completes training in England and Scotland, and travels to France as a member of the British 85 Squadron, led initially by its famous commander, the Canadian flier and high-scoring ace Maj. William "Billy" Bishop. The anonymous aviator flies with 85 Squadron until his death. It is evident from these facts that the career of the anonymous airman is strikingly similar to that of Elliott Springs and his two closest friends in the war, Larry Callahan and John McGavock "Mac" Grider.

In addition to the 1926 trade edition of *War Birds,* Springs prepared a limited autographed edition of 210 copies, that number representing the number of American fliers in the cadet detachments with which he trained in England.[3] These special copies included additional materials not present in the trade publication: three large group photographs; a roster of the men indicating those who had been wounded or killed; and a special dedication page autographed by Springs and four of the men who had been responsible for the training of the men or the preparation of the book.[4] These men were Leslie MacDill, the major who led them across the Atlantic; Geoff Dwyer, who served as liaison for the men after they arrived in England; Bennett "Bim" Oliver, who was the commander of one of the cadet detachments in England (Springs was the leader of the other detachment); and Clayton Knight, who drew the superb illustrations in the book. Oliver was later a flight commander in the 148th Aero Squadron with Springs. Henry Clay, the third flight commander in the 148th, had died on 7 February 1919; had Clay lived, it is likely that Springs would have included his name on the autograph page. Apparently family members of the men assigned to the original Oxford training detachments were offered the opportunity to purchase copies. This effort suggests that Springs saw the book as a testament to the achievements of all the men in the original American training detachments, however great or small their individual contributions to the war might have been. Springs had prepared the special edition of this book before it was bought for publication in *Liberty* magazine. His name, however, did not appear as editor or author in either the limited edition or the first trade edition.

War Birds achieved classic status practically from the day it first appeared, initially as a series of episodes in *Liberty* magazine, from August through November 1926, and then as a book published by Doran that year.[5] It has been republished several times in subsequent years and remains a favorite of readers because it vividly describes the perils of flying and the pleasures of off-duty socializing in a colorful, colloquial style. The book was a popular success when it was printed and has remained popular in the years since its original publication.[6] It earned the approval of flying veterans such as Sholto Douglas, commander of 84 Squadron of the Royal Flying Corps during the summer of 1918, who called the book a "splendid and heart-warming story," one that would appeal especially to those who flew in the war.[7] R. R. Money, another English pilot in World War I, called the work "one of the finest books of the war in the Air."[8] Even Lawrence of Arabia, T. E. Lawrence, wrote to tell Springs that *War Birds* was one of "the sharpest, reddest, and liveliest" war books he had read.[9] Both the initial *Liberty* issues and the later book included excellent illustrations by Clayton Knight, an exceptionally talented artist and a pilot in 211 Squadron during the war.

Although Springs's name was associated with the story from its first appearance in *Liberty* magazine, the issue of the book's true authorship soon arose: who really should be given credit for *War Birds*: Elliott Springs or his deceased squadron-mate John McGavock Grider, whose life the entries appear to describe? An anonymous 1934 columnist in *Time* magazine stated that with the publication of *War Birds*, Springs had "started a great cycle of War-time aviation literature." The same writer, acknowledging that the book was the diary of an unknown aviator, slyly suggested, however, that "few literary wiseacres believed that Mr. Springs did nothing more than edit the manuscript."[10] T. E. Lawrence, writing to Springs in 1931, seemed to sense that the book grew from a mixture of sources and requested that Springs annotate a copy, for "record purposes," of how the book grew in Springs's mind and under his hand: "Nobody but yourself knows how it was built," he wrote, "and it would be famous and fascinating to put on record its parts and origin."[11] Springs refused to be persuaded to do this, however, and his written response to Lawrence indicates his strong reluctance to do so: "You suggest that I annotate a copy of it for history's sake to show how it grew. That is just what I don't want to do. If it lives, I want it to live as Mac's diary, not my novel. The controversy will be forgotten in a few years and then perhaps the book may be revived and read by a new generation on its own merits. My hope is that it will be a monument to Mac's [John McGavock Grider's] memory. He has no other."[12]

The "controversy" to which Springs refers in his letter to Lawrence was a disagreement with some members of the Grider family, who had questioned the issue of authorship. Grider's older sister, Josephine, was well aware that Grider had associated with Springs and Larry Callahan during the war because Grider had written about the men in his letters home, letters that provided a fair sample of his writing style, which she recognized in the early pages of *War Birds*. Because the diary entries appeared to be by someone other than Springs but described training and combat experiences similar to those of Springs's best friends, Callahan and Grider, and Grider was the only one of the three who had not survived the war, how was it possible for a diary that Springs insisted contained the words of someone else (Grider) not to be in fact written by that person?[13] If the words were Grider's, then surely appropriate recognition was due. The Grider family believed that these must be the words of their deceased relative, and they suggested that the family should receive appropriate credit and compensation. Springs initially resisted the efforts of the Grider family, saying that their attempt to establish Grider as the author of *War Birds* would not have beneficial results, in that whatever the outcome of any legal proceedings, the ultimate effect would be to destroy the achievement and reputation that the book had earned as a result of publication.[14] Springs's statement appears to confirm the role of the Grider diary in the composition of *War Birds* while suggesting that attempting to determine the extent of its role in the book would be harmful to the best interests of all concerned.

That Springs admitted the central role of Grider's diary in the composition is suggested by the fact that he eventually came to an agreement with the Grider family for the use of the diary and by writing an introduction (the "foreword," printed in the later, "popular" editions, which appeared after July 1927) in which he acknowledged his role as editor and confirmed the primary authorship of the "unknown aviator" (whom he never specifically identified, however). As he says in the foreword, "Would you dig up the Unknown Soldier and identify him to satisfy curiosity?"[15] According to the 1927 foreword, Springs insisted that the diary belonged to a friend and that all he did was edit it for publication: "He was very definite in his ideas and I agreed to respect them."[16] Of course, with Grider dead, there would be no way of verifying the intentions of the "unknown aviator."

When he was threatened with a lawsuit by members of the Grider family, who wanted to share in the profits from the sale of the book, Springs was able to persuade them not to proceed with it, agreeing, however, to give them a substantial payment ($12,500) in exchange for their compliance.[17] In a letter to Preston Boyden, a Chicago attorney who was involved in the issue, Springs stated that *War Birds* was "based largely on my letters, my diary, and my combat reports. I also used [Eugene] Barksdale's diary and supplementary matter given to me by [Robert] Kelly and [Larry] Callahan."[18] Springs states that this diary "became the actual history" of the 210 U.S. Air Service flying cadets who traveled to England to train for the war, and that it was for the "survivors" of these men that the publication of *War*

Birds was intended.[19] Springs thus suggests that the diary of the "unknown aviator" had a greater significance than presenting the unique experiences of one individual; it represented the experiences of all. Possibly it was for the reasons Springs gave in his foreword, especially his statement that he was merely following instructions, that the Grider family acceded to Springs's request.

Yet while maintaining that he was only following the instructions of the anonymous aviator about the disposition of the information in the diary, Springs clearly wanted to receive credit for writing the book. Springs's biographer, Burke Davis, says that in writing *War Birds,* Springs "thought of the nameless diarist as Mac Grider, [but] the narrative was in fact Elliott's own, focusing on the adventures of the Three Musketeers. . . . [Springs] used Mac's shipboard diary only in his early pages, [while] the action of the book took place over the eleven months following Grider's final entry. Elliott's account, in fact, continued for more than two months after Grider's death and described events of which he [Grider] could have known nothing."[20] Grider died on 18 June 1918, and yet the last dated entry in *War Birds* is 27 August. Grider could never have written about events that occurred after his death. A letter written many years later, in 1971, by one of the Grider sons appears to support this statement: with the original shipboard diary of his father in his possession, George Grider wrote that "every syllable of *War Birds,* dated after October 1, 1917, was written by Colonel Springs."[21] In addition, according to Davis, Springs privately "conceded that only one paragraph as written by Grider remained in the published version."[22] However, this statement, as we will see, is not exactly accurate.

If Springs agreed that the diary described Grider's life, he went to great lengths to make it clear that while the *War Birds* diary might be a testament to the memory of Mac Grider, it was, in fact, uniquely the product of Springs's creative energies. To determine just how much of the book can be attributed to either Springs or Grider requires a careful examination of the source materials used for its composition. Determining how Springs used his sources in *War Birds* is not a simple task; the most important include two Grider diaries (not one, as is commonly thought) and the letters that Springs wrote to his family during World War I.

The assumption, made by Davis, members of the Grider family and other readers, is that Grider wrote only one diary, which detailed the troop ship *Carmania*'s crossing of the Atlantic from 17 September until 1 October 1917, events described in the first twenty-four pages of the book, and that the remaining pages of *War Birds* must have come from Springs's own experiences. However, this is not the only Grider diary. Tucked away in the Springs papers is another diary, covering the period 3 October 1917 to

7 February 1918.[23] This diary is not in Springs's handwriting and contains accounts of activities that Springs could not have known about directly. It refers to Springs in the third person and describes activities in which Springs was not involved, especially during the period of time he parted company with Grider and Callahan during their training in England, from early November until the middle of January, when they reunited. Although the owner's/writer's name is not shown in the diary, this has to be the continuation of Grider's diary: the style and handwriting closely resemble those of Grider's first diary. Additional internal evidence is provided by the fact that the writer refers directly to members of the Grider family or friends, including "Jopie" (Josephine), Grider's older sister, as he did in the first diary. In examining the pages of *War Birds* we can see that in fact Springs drew heavily from this second diary as well.

Comparison of the pages of this diary to the text of *War Birds* shows that Springs borrowed frequently from Grider's first and second diaries in the first one-third of the book, up to page 69 of the 1926 edition (*War Birds* entry dated 28 January 1918). Springs borrowed heavily from all entries in Grider's first diary and from all but 10 of the 68 pages in the second diary. Springs seldom quotes wholesale from the Grider diary. Instead he typically borrows a sentence or two, modifying the phrasing, and then enhances the event with recollections and descriptions of his own. In modifying the Grider entries Springs was able to clarify or enhance Grider's visual descriptions of their surroundings, to provide situations for humorous anecdotes, and to amplify Springs's role in the narrative by including some of his own actions and thought processes.[24] Davis may have assumed that only one Grider diary existed (the shipboard diary). In all, Springs made use of the words or details of about one half of the 68 handwritten pages in Grider's second diary. Springs seldom copied verbatim; typically he simplified the style and added supplementary details. Of the 69 pages in *War Birds* where Springs borrowed from Grider, the Grider material constitutes a little over one third of the text, and most of that was significantly modified by Springs in the fashion described above.

Why did Springs need to use the Grider diaries? For one reason, he did not keep a diary himself until 1 January 1918 (or, more accurately, this is the only diary included in the Springs World War I papers). However, the contents of this diary show that Springs was not a particularly good diarist. He certainly was not as interested in recording details as Grider was. Springs's entries are uniformly short, generally uninteresting, and uninformative—almost exactly the opposite of his letters home. Here are some sample entries, taken from four days in January (these are the entire entries for each day; clarifying editorial comments are shown in brackets):

Jan 18, 1918: Much tattered and torn [Thomas] Herbert and I get back at 3 to find we're in for a big strafe [for being out late]. So we make a last night of it and go up to Stamford. Cal [Larry Callahan] and Mac [Mac Grider] arrive from London.

Jan 19, 1918: The C.O. gave us hell but no C.B. [confined to barracks]. Hoorah. I get in 1 hour in a machine which had been condemned. Christ I'm lucky. And I certainly was doing some splitassing.

Jan 21, 1918: I get in two hours solo. I can loop, spin and Immelman with great gusto but I find V[ertical] banks very difficult.

Jan 22, 1918: Capt Horn takes me up for a little stunt instruction and then turns me loose on a [Sopwith] Pup. Great stuff—I get away with it but bend an axle.

It is easy to see why Springs made such extensive use of Grider's diaries. For the days in which he wrote entries in his diaries, Grider gave much more detailed and complete accounts than Springs did, and his style reflects the excitement and enthusiasm typical of the men in the detachment who were part of the great adventure of flying in England and France. Grider had begun his diary entries on board ship and continued them through the early months of training, thus providing essential details and descriptions that effectively captured the actions and ebullience of the eager young apprentice aviators. It is easy also to see why Springs came to think of the diary entries as a kind of unofficial log in terms of the record of events and personnel of the entire detachment.

There is some evidence that a third Grider diary, in which Grider continued to record events after 1 February 1918, existed. The evidence for this is indirect since no third diary has been discovered. One factor in support of a third diary is that the second diary ends with no indication that it is intended to be the final book. At the end of the second diary, Grider's training was still under way, and the London social life of the "Three Musketeers" was just building momentum. There is a second reason to believe that a third diary existed; in one of Grider's letters to his good friend Emma Cox, dated 2 February 1918, he thanks her for the items she sent him, including a "log": "Just received your picture and the little service book. I will keep the log book up to date and try and keep as near the truth as an imaginative nature will let me. Of course when I get to the front you won't blame me for putting in a few extra thrills just to vary the monotony."[25]

The timing of this letter is significant; it is dated 2 February. Grider's final diary entry (in his second diary) is dated 5 February. Interestingly, Josephine Grider Jacobs, Grider's sister (whom he referred to as "Jopie"), who was the author of *Marse John Goes to War,* in which this letter appears, interrupts the letter to make this comment: "It is to Emma Cox that the credit is due for suggesting the diary that later was used as 'War Birds,' edited by Elliott Springs."[26] But this diary could not have been the diary that was included in *War Birds* because the dates are wrong; the diary that all acknowledge was used in *War Birds* covers the dates September to October 1917, and yet Grider says that the diary that Emma Cox sent arrived in February 1918, four months later. In a later letter to his friend Emma, dated 27 February, he reports that he is "keeping the service record [log] up to date, fill[ing] it in every night and try[ing] to stay as near the truth as possible."[27] In a later letter he reports to Emma that he is continuing to be "faithful to our little service record."[28] It appears likely, therefore, that Grider began a third diary.

However, it is also possible that the third diary was never completed—or included in *War Birds.* In the first place, as the training schedule intensified, Grider's diary entries were fewer and covered less detail. In October, for instance, Grider made five entries in his second diary. In November he made eight. However, he wrote only one in December (6 December), one in January (1 January), and only two in February (5 and 7 February). Grider admits in the second diary that he was having difficulty maintaining his diary entries on a regular basis: in his next to last entry, 5 February, he states that he "can't keep it [the diary] up it seems."

Other internal evidence that Springs did not rely on a third Grider diary is suggested by the changing style of *War Birds;* stylistically the *"War Birds"* diary entries written after those in February sound less like the awed innocence of the Grider boy from the Deep South and more like the knowing, worldly wise Springs, a southern boy transplanted to the East Coast. In the pages that follow the last material definitely attributable to Grider, the style becomes generally more opinionated, ironic, and cynical—the kind of style of which Springs was master. However, it is also true that there are relatively few passages of style or content in *War Birds* similar to those provided elsewhere in the Springs letters written between the middle of February and the end of May (between pages 70 and 155). It is possible that Springs may have used additional Grider material in those pages. There is no solid evidence for a third diary, no copy existing in the Springs papers. If it existed, Springs may have disposed of it, possibly because it contained detailed references to Grider's social activities in London, and those descriptions might have been too vivid for family members to read.[29] If Springs kept the first two Grider diaries as a record of his, Callahan's, and Grider's training experiences in England, however, it is likely that he would have kept any additional diaries for the same reason.

Springs did, in fact, make a number of alterations to protect the identity of the central figure in *War Birds*. The reader of *War Birds* would not know, for instance, that its "anonymous author" (Grider) was married with two children. John McGavock Grider had married Marguerite Samuels of Memphis, Tennessee, in 1909 and was the father of two sons, John Junior, born in 1911, and George William, born in 1913.[30] Apparently the youthful Grider's marriage to Marguerite (Grider was seventeen when he married) did not last, and she returned to live in Memphis and kept custody of the two boys. The unhappy marital relationship may have given Grider a reason for volunteering so readily for the war; he would have been twenty-five in 1917. Grider refers to his boys in a poignant passage in his diary entry for 9 November, three days after the Oxford detachment was divided:

> Lord I have the blues. The worried worried blues. It's raining and cold as blue blazes. Anderson [probably Robert Anderson, who eventually flew with 50 Squadron, RAF, and became a prisoner of war] was in our shanty playing his guitar. How that boy can play. He got out a piece of stick and played "Sweet Lei Lei Lua" just exactly like the Victrola at home used to play it. I could close my eyes and see the old living room at Grider with a big fire burning and Goodlookin [Grider's nickname for Marguerite Samuels] undressing John and George in front of it while I laid on the settee or the chaise lounge and read or smoked. I didn't know how good it all was or could have been. I guess every thing will be all right now because I don't really expect to go back. I do want to see the kids bad. John is seven [six?] on the 23rd. My how old that kid is getting to be. I bet he is six feet high. I will write him a long letter on his birthday.

The disturbing juxtaposition of his concern for his children with his fatalistic outlook (he does not "expect to go back") suggests the ambiguity of Grider's feelings about leaving his home and family. Springs did not include this passage in *War Birds*.

In his final diary entry of his second diary, dated 7 February, Grider briefly relates a meeting with one of the women he and the others had met in London: "Had an adventure tonight with a charming unsophisticated damsel in St. Alban's. Name Madge. Pretty with eager big blue eyes and the reddest lips I ever saw. My conscience haunts me. Oh well. Take the fruit the Gods provide." These comments are also not included in *War Birds*. There are many similar passages in the second diary, in which Grider describes his socializing activities (which Springs tactfully omitted from *War Birds*). It is possible that these are the reason that Springs kept the diary with his own papers and did not send it to the Grider family. Of course, had he returned the second diary to the members of the Grider family, they would have had even more evidence of how much Springs had depended on the Grider materials to fill in the details of his story. It is doubtful that Grider ever "gave" his diary to Springs; many soldiers and aviators kept diaries during the war, but these were usually private comments with specific details relating to training or combat activities that could not be reported in letters home due to the review of censors. Diaries could also record social activities that were not necessarily intended to be shared with others, especially close family members. Springs undoubtedly obtained the diary when he (and possibly Larry Callahan) packed Grider's possessions after Grider failed to return from his last flight on 18 June 1918; it was standard procedure for friends of a missing aviator to examine the aviator's personal belongings and to withhold any militarily sensitive materials and any items that might be personally embarrassing to the family (such as love letters from female friends in England, in this case). It is probable that Springs spotted Grider's diaries and withheld them.

Although we can show that Springs used portions of the Grider diaries throughout the first 69 pages of *War Birds,* the fact is that the book is 276 pages long, and Springs had to rely on his own creative energies and experiences to provide the material for the remaining 200-plus pages; those include all of the combat flying activities, episodes that all readers agree provide some of the most interesting episodes in the book. One of the primary sources was the file of letters that Springs wrote to his parents. As mentioned above, later sections of *War Birds,* especially after the final dated entry that can be linked to Grider's diary (7 February), display the characteristics of Springs's sharp and occasionally caustic wit, as displayed in the letters he wrote home to his stepmother, Lena, and his father, Leroy.

Davis says that Springs used much of the material from his letters home, copying passages verbatim into *War Birds.*[31] He states that Springs "documented his adventures in France thoroughly—not to say exhaustively—in a diary, in almost daily letters to his parents (chiefly to Lena Springs), and in his flight log. . . . They were almost certainly written with future publication in mind."[32] However, neither Springs's diary nor his flight log is filled with descriptive details. Springs did use portions of his letters home in *War Birds,* especially in the last third of the narrative, using them increasingly after 18 June, the date of Grider's death.[33] However, given the hazardous conditions under which Springs was living at the time, as well as his own fully developed fatalistic outlook, it would be unlikely that he was seriously thinking about the possibility of using them for "future publication." Like Grider and other aviators, he repeatedly expressed doubts about his safe return from the war.

The Grider character in *War Birds* is presented as if he were continuing to fly in 85 Squadron. For example, the anonymous aviator's diary notes that on 21 June, two days after Grider's death, Billy Bishop was recalled to England; this was the actual date of his recall. On 23 June the anonymous aviator's diary records a discussion in which the men of 85 Squadron are asked whom they prefer as their new commanding officer, and the preference is for Mick Mannock, who had been a flight commander in 74 Squadron. Again, something like this discussion actually occurred. The anonymous aviator's diary also records Springs's accident on 27 June, the actual date on which Springs was shot down and injured. On 2 July the anonymous aviator's diary records that Springs has been transferred to a "new American squadron up at Dunkirk," the 148th Aero Squadron. The aviator's diary records the fact that Mannock arrived about the middle of July and was shot down on 20 July, dates and events that correspond almost exactly with the historical facts. After these dates, however, links to real actions and events in the aviator's diary become much more generalized, and the narrative drifts away from any realistic historical time-based framework. The appeal of *War Birds* resulted from Springs's own synthesis of events in the actual combat environment in which he and his fellow pilots worked, in addition to his effective manipulation of the material in his own letters as well as the Grider diaries—all of these elements being united by the creative glue of his reconstruction process.

It is a fascinating and rewarding exercise to read *War Birds: Diary of an Unknown Aviator* alongside the World War I letters of Elliott Springs, to see how Springs's individual experiences in training and in combat correspond to the accounts given in *War Birds.* In *War Birds,* Springs has added a wealth of contextual details by blending his own experiences, as described in his letters, with those provided by the Grider diaries and topped off, as it were, with historical and factual details gained from looking back at the events of World War I with seven years of hindsight.

One additional aspect certainly influenced his attitude about his authorship of *War Birds*: his determination to acknowledge the participation of the other 200 men who shared many of the training and combat experiences of Grider, Springs, and Callahan. This emphasis is evident in the initial autographed edition, in which Springs listed in an appendix the names of 206 men who were members of their training detachments with an indication of whether they had been killed or wounded during training and combat. In the later popular editions this list was omitted, but the names of 113 men appear in the "anonymous" aviator's diary entries, 30 of them several times. Springs may well have gotten his idea for recognizing the participation of these men from Grider's diaries, which mention the names of many individuals. Including these names was clearly Springs's way of making the adventures of one aviator applicable to all. We can see the germ of the idea in a 7 November letter he wrote to his stepmother just prior to the armistice, when he was beginning to realize that in spite of his long-held expectations, he might actually survive the war; in the letter he makes the following request:

> Next time you are in New York get a nice leather registry book, have it marked "Italian Detachment" and make the following explanation to the manager of the Vanderbilt. When the Detachment broke up just a year ago, I announced that I would provide a registry at the Vanderbilt where they could all put their Home Address, date of return, and any news of missing members. Also their New York address and length of stay. Thus some of us might some day get direct accounts of those missing. A few are going home as instructors and it might be well to start the registry.

It seems clear that Springs was beginning to think, even before the war ended, of developing a document that would record the activities of those who had traveled to England with him the year before. The idea of creating a record of the achievements and sacrifices of the men with whom he flew—epitomized in the experiences of John McGavock Grider—was important to him.

However, if it was so important to Springs to commemorate the life of Grider in *War Birds,* why is Grider's name never mentioned in the book? This is especially puzzling since Springs added a picture titled "The Three Musketeers of 'War Birds'" in the trade edition, although he did not give the names of the three individuals in the picture (Springs, Callahan, and Grider), grouped familiarly in military uniforms with pilot's wings prominently displayed. Why would he not state the name of the one individual whom all readers knowledgeable about the history of American aviators in World War I would probably know? Perhaps he believed that if he had acknowledged the name, it might be too obvious that he had borrowed Grider's writings for his own benefit, although he did not seem to be especially concerned about the issue of giving credit. Part of the answer may lie in the fact that he saw *War Birds* as *his* book, which describes his route to and through the war as he experienced events and emotions that impacted him psychologically as well as physically.

If he had wanted to, he could have written his own postwar memoir, as many other aviators and soldiers were to do, but he chose not to do so.

Instead in *War Birds* he described his experiences in the context of the company of good men who traveled with him, including many who failed to return. The names of others are mentioned frequently. It is clear, in his letters and in *War Birds,* that he was saddened by the loss of so many eager young men like himself, and no one more so than Grider, to whom, for reasons we can never fully know, he was especially attached. It is also clear that he felt some sense of personal responsibility for the fact that Grider failed to return from the flight that Springs was leading when they were flying with 85 Squadron. Springs felt a deep sense of loss when he returned from flights in the 148th Aero Squadron with fewer men than were with him when he departed; in one instance he was the only one to return. If he had identified Grider as the central character in *War Birds,* the book would have been about Grider. By leaving the flyer unidentified, the narrator represented all American airmen who had suffered a similar fate. As he said in the foreword to the 1927 trade edition, Springs saw *War Birds* as the "actual history" of the 210 men who trained at Oxford, and it really was intended to tell the story of the "unknown aviator" of World War I. Springs undoubtedly was thinking of the ceremony that had occurred on 11 November 1921, when the American "Unknown Soldier" had been brought from France to Arlington National Cemetery. His determination not to reveal Grider's name must have resulted from his cultural as well as personal sense of symbolic association with the meaning of Grider's death.

Although the focus of attention in this section has been on the ways in which Springs incorporated material from the Grider diaries and his own letters into *War Birds,* this discussion does not mean to suggest that *War Birds* is a derivative effort, that it is *merely* a compilation of various aspects of its source materials. It must be observed that the greater part of *War Birds* consists of Springs's creative representation of his various training and combat experiences, and the work includes descriptions that enhance and clarify comments that Springs makes in his letters. The events and attitudes represented in the Grider diaries and his own letters home enabled Springs to generate a narrative of the air war during World War I that truly captured the authentic flavor of the times.

Springs's Other Books about World War I

The phenomenal success of *War Birds: Diary of an Unknown Aviator,* both in magazine form and then in book form, enabled Springs to embark, at least briefly, on a literary career. In the seven books that followed *War Birds,* Springs drew heavily on his flying experiences, often recycling them in slightly different forms. His use of these experiences is most extensive, of course, in *War Birds*. With two exceptions the subsequent books were collections of short stories, nearly all of which had been previously published in popular magazines. By far the two most important of these are *Nocturne Militaire* and *Above the Bright Blue Sky*. *Nocturne Militaire*, published in 1927, includes eight stories describing Springs's training experiences in England and his combat flying in France. Each of the eight stories is dedicated to an aviator whom Springs knew in the war; the names include Larry Callahan, Jake Stanley, Robert Kelly, Bim Oliver, and Billy Bishop. The two stories that bear most directly on Springs's career are "Caveat Emptor," which describes in detail aspects of his social life in London in the spring of 1918, and "Iliad 1918," which summarizes his flying career in 85 Squadron and the 148th Aero Squadron. "Iliad 1918" reads almost like an autobiographical account, as Springs provides the actual names of many of the men with whom he flew.

Most of the nine stories in *Above the Bright Blue Sky* (1928) continue in the same fashion; "Aeneas Americanus," for instance, describes in fictional form the difficulties of adjusting to life in the United States after the war ended. Some of Springs's best stories are included in this volume: "Sore Subjects"; "Cornwallis, We Have Come"; "Fed Up"; and two stories titled after the identification numbers of aircraft in Springs's 148th Aero Squadron, "5618" and "9214." "Sore Subjects" describes the successful efforts of an American aviator to escape from enemy territory after being shot down; it is dedicated to Capt. T. E. Tillinghast, from the 17th Aero Squadron, who managed, in fact, to accomplish the events described in the story. "Cornwallis, We Have Come," dedicated to Maj. Leslie MacDill, describes many of the incidents that Springs and his fellow cadets experienced during their stay at Oxford University in the fall of 1917.

The first of the two aircraft stories, "5618," describes how the main character in the story, a flight commander named Henry, whom we can easily imagine as Springs himself, is able to repair one of the squadron aircraft that has crash-landed near the lines and, after it is officially "written off" the list of available aircraft, to return it to operational flying use in the squadron, thus giving his flight an additional aircraft. More important than the administrative trick Henry is able to play on the higher-ranking administrative officers in the wing, however, are the vivid details describing the nearly insurmountable odds against which he, and the pilots of the 148th Aero Squadron, had to fly. The second aircraft story, "9214," describes the futile effort of Henry, the flight commander, to arrange for the "accidental" destruction of one of the flight's older, chronically underpowered aircraft so that it could be replaced with a faster, more reliable aircraft.

Told to assign to one of the pilots in his flight what he believes is a nearly suicidal mission to shoot down an observation balloon, Henry decides to fly the mission himself in the suspect aircraft, believing that neither he nor the aircraft can possibly return safely. In spite of overwhelming odds, however, Henry and the aircraft return. Although the focus of both "aircraft" stories appears to be on administrative or maintenance issues, the stories provide vivid accounts of the difficulties of flying Sopwith Camels in combat against overwhelming odds, the kind of situations that the men of the 148th Aero Squadron (and its companion 17th Aero Squadron) faced from the middle of August through the end of September 1918.

The best story in the book, however, is "Fed Up," told without the usual Springs biting humor. Told in the standard third-person narrative form, the story describes how the flight commander, Henry, must fly once again against difficult odds.[34] The impact of the story is one of emotional heaviness, as Henry forces himself to fly again and again in spite of his sense of inevitable failure and death. The seriousness of the tone is indicated in the story's dedication, the longest of any that Springs wrote: "To those gallant comrades who I saw fight their last fight—Lieutenants Trapp, Thompson, Hall, Grider, Forster, Mandel, Kenyon, Hamilton, Siebald, Curtis, Frobisher, Jenkinson, and Avery. Their vacant files were never filled." Of the thirteen men listed by Springs, over half were killed, and the remainder became prisoners of war.

The first of his novels, *Leave Me with a Smile* (1928), describes the problems faced by Henry Winton, a returned war flier, as he attempts to adjust to a peacetime world after the end of the war. Clearly patterned after Springs's own situation, Henry Winton despairs of the life that faces him as he prepares to take over his father's textile mills. Although it lacks the interest of the stories of aerial warfare, the novel offers a respectable example of the narratives describing the experiences of returning war veterans, the "Lost Generation" of the 1920s. Springs's 1930 novel, *Contact,* is similar to *Leave Me with a Smile* in its emphasis on postwar adjustments, but it differs in that it includes a description of the war as well as the peace that follows. It is as if Springs realized that reader empathy for combatants facing a postwar peacetime adjustment could not be developed if the reader did not fully understand what the hazards of war (especially the war in the air) were like. Springs's final novel (if it can be called that), *The Rise and Fall of Carol Banks* (1931), is really a collection of stories, some of them published several years earlier, all having to do with the central figure, Carol Banks, whose character traits and career closely parallel those of Springs. Springs's later collections of short stories, *In the Cool of the*

Evening (1929) and *Pent Up on a Penthouse* (1931), contain few stories of the war in the air. The tales in these books are about life in a postwar world and are, generally speaking, less interesting than his earlier stories, at least to readers eager to learn about flying episodes.

After World War II, Springs published one final volume, *Clothes Make the Man,* which includes materials and photos related to his creative advertising campaign for Springs Mills as well as several of his earlier stories, mostly from *In the Cool of the Evening* and *Pent Up on a Penthouse;* he must have believed that these were too good to lie dormant in his earlier, less popular publications. Springs first published the book in hardback format in 1948, and it was reissued again in 1949 in hardback form. The book was subsequently published in softcover format throughout the 1950s, usually with some new material added and old material deleted. The final issue was published in 1958, the year before Springs died.

After Leroy Springs died in 1931, Elliott Springs finally came to the job he had resisted for so many years, running the Springs Mills. Although the history of his life to that point might not have suggested success in that line of work, he did with his father's textile business what he had done with anything else he had set his mind toward, whether flying or writing: he put his unique stamp on it and made it work. According to one history of the Springs Mills, "When his father had died, the business was shaky. The rundown plants were valued at $7.25 million and had sales of $8 million. Twenty-eight years later, when Elliott died, the plants and property were valued at $104.5 million and sales were $163 million. The number of employees had climbed from 5,000 to 12,000; looms had increased from 7,500 to 17,000; spindles had increased from 300,000 to 836,000. In those 28 years, $95 million was spent on expansion and modernization."[35]

One of the last books in which the writing of Elliott Springs appears is entitled *Pilot's Luck* (1929). It features the excellent artwork of Clayton Knight, who illustrated *War Birds.* In addition to contributing a number of selections from his stories and *War Birds,* Springs wrote a foreword to the book that concludes with the following summary of the air war's impact on pilots generally and himself personally:

> It was the most dangerous of all sports and the most fascinating.
> It got into the blood like wine. It aged men forty years in forty days.
> . . . What human experience can compare with it? No man could last
> six months at it and remain normal. Few could do it two months. The
> average life of a pilot at the front was forty-eight hours in the air, and
> to many that seemed an age.

Is it any wonder that pilots became fatalists? Is it any wonder that those who survived fear a drab and boring existence more than they ever feared Hun machine-guns? No man who has ever pressed triggers above the bright blue sky will ever be happy keeping books.[36]

Elliott Springs died in 1959 from the effects of pancreatic cancer.

Appendix A

American Military Personnel Mentioned in the Letters

Elliott Springs mentions the names of more than ninety military personnel in his World War I letters, diary, and flight log: fellow students, higher-ranking authorities, personal acquaintances, members of his combat squadrons. These names are listed below in alphabetical order according to the first letter of the individual's last name; information about these individuals is provided, including units to which they were assigned and when Springs knew them. The names of many of these individuals are mentioned only once; other names are mentioned more often; while some, especially those of Springs's two most important friends, Larry Callahan and John McGavock Grider, are mentioned frequently. Where relevant, page references are provided to the following sources: V. Lansing Collins, *Princeton in the World War* (1932); Mauer Mauer, *The U.S. Air Service in World War I* (1978); James J. Sloan Jr., *Wings of Honor: American Airmen in World War I* (1994); and Lucien H. Thayer, *America's First Eagles: The Official History of the U.S. Air Service, AEF (1917–1918)* (1983).

AINSWORTH, HAROLD. One of the "Oxford Group" of cadets, he was killed in an aircraft accident on 9 December 1917 (Sloan, *Wings of Honor*, 222).

ARMSTRONG, WILLIAM J. He attended ground school at Oxford and received flight training in England. He was first assigned to 209 Squadron, RFC, and then was transferred to the 17th Aero Squadron, which he joined on 23 June 1918. He was wounded in combat on 12 August 1918 (Sloan, *Wings of Honor*, 220, 230).

BARRY, RUTLEDGE B. He trained with the Oxford cadets and received flight training in England. He was assigned to the 93rd Aero Squadron from 14 August 1918 until the armistice and according to the roster in the autographed edition of *War Birds,* was wounded either in training or in combat (Sloan, *Wings of Honor*, 220, 292).

BISSELL, CLAYTON L. He trained initially in Toronto, Canada, and then received flight training in England. After being assigned to the 148th Aero Squadron on 1 July 1918, he flew with that squadron until the armistice (Sloan, *Wings of Honor*, 14, 223, 231).

BOSTICK, BONHAM HAGOOD. After graduating from Princeton in 1919, he trained in the Princeton aviation program, traveled to England on board the *Carmania*, attended ground school at Oxford, and continued his training in England. He was assigned to 43 Squadron, RAF, on 11 April 1918 and was wounded one week later, on 18 April 1918. He recovered from his wounds and flew with the RAF until the armistice (Collins, *Princeton in the World War,* 459; Sloan, *Wings of Honor,* 219).

BREWSTER, SIDNEY A. A classmate of Springs at Princeton (class of 1918) and a fellow southerner whose family was known to Leroy Springs, he trained in the aviation program at Princeton and sailed for France at the end of August 1917, approximately three weeks before Springs sailed for England. Brewster stayed briefly in France, then traveled to Italy, where he completed his aviation training at Foggia. He then served briefly with the Royal Naval Air Service before flying as an instructor in France. He flew with the 11th Aero Squadron, a bombardment squadron, from the middle of September 1918 until the armistice (Collins, *Princeton in the World War,* 420–21; Sloan, *Wings of Honor,* 248, 306).

BULKLEY, HAROLD KIDDER. A classmate of Springs at Princeton (class of 1919), he trained at Princeton, sailed to England, and trained at Oxford. He was killed in a midair collision with another student on 18 February 1918 (Collins, *Princeton in the World War,* 460).

CALLAHAN, LAWRENCE (1894–1977). From Chicago, Illinois, he was one of the "Three [American] Musketeers" who impressed their British friends with their flying and socializing skills. Callahan met John McGavock Grider when they attended ground school at the University of Illinois before they sailed to France and joined the "Oxford Group" of aviation cadets. He served first in 85 Squadron, with Springs and Grider, and stayed in 85 Squadron for two months before joining Springs in the 148th Aero Squadron on 24 August 1918 (Sloan, *Wings of Honor,* 195, 198, 204, 220, 231).

CAMPBELL, MERTON L. After attending training at Oxford and completing flight training in England, he was assigned first to 54 Squadron, RFC, and then to the 17th Aero Squadron, which he joined on 21 June 1918. He was killed in action on 23 August 1918 (Sloan, *Wings of Honor,* 220, 230).

CARLTON, DONALD E. He trained at Oxford and was receiving flight training in England when he was killed in an aircraft accident at Spiddlegate on 19 February 1918 (Sloan, *Wings of Honor,* 222).

CASTLE, VERNON. Originally named William Vernon Blyth, he was a successful dancer and entertainer and married his longtime dancing partner, Irene Foote, in 1911. He joined the Royal Flying Corps in 1916 and flew as an instructor pilot and an operational pilot. On 15 February 1918 he was killed in an aircraft accident at Benbow Field near Fort Worth, Texas, where he had been assigned as an instructor pilot. He had abruptly turned the aircraft in which he was flying with a student to avoid an aircraft flown by another student; both students survived the crash.

CLAY, HENRY R., Jr. He attended ground school at Oxford University and completed his flight training in England. He was first assigned to 43 Squadron, RFC, and on 2 July 1918 was transferred to the 148th Aero Squadron, where he was assigned as C Flight commander. He was transferred to the 41st Aero Squadron on 8 November 1918 and was assigned as squadron commander. He died of influenza in Coblenz, Germany, on 17 February 1919 (Sloan, *Wings of Honor,* 202, 220, 231, 380, 388).

CLEMENTS, WILLIAM T. He trained with the Oxford cadets and after completing flight training in England was assigned to the 148th Aero Squadron from 23 July to 28 August 1918, at which time he was transferred to the 17th Aero Squadron, where he replaced Lloyd Hamilton as C Flight commander (Hamilton had been killed in combat on 24 August). He remained with the 17th Aero Squadron until the armistice (Sloan, *Wings of Honor,* 203, 220, 229, 230).

CUNNIUS, PERCY E. He trained in Toronto and completed flight training in England. He was assigned to Springs's flight in the 148th Aero Squadron on 18 August 1918 and flew with the squadron until the end of the war (Sloan, *Wings of Honor,* 224, 232).

CURTIS, MARVIN KENT. He attended ground school at Oxford and received his flight training in England. After being assigned to the 148th Aero Squadron on 4 July 1918, he was shot down on 24 August while flying in Springs's flight and became a prisoner of war. After the war he became a writer of stories for boys (Sloan, *Wings of Honor,* 220, 232).

DAVIDSON, WILBUR L. He trained with the Oxford cadets and received his flight training in England. He was assigned to 210 Squadron, RFC, on 3 April 1918 and was wounded in action a month later, on 11 May 1918 (Sloan, *Wings of Honor,* 219).

DEALY. This individual is identified in Sloan, *Wings of Honor* (194), as Eugene Wheatley, killed in training on 10 March 1918. He was not one of the "Oxford Group" of cadets.

DEETJEN, WILLIAM L. One of the original "Oxford Group" of cadets, he completed his flight training in England and was then assigned to 104 Squadron, RFC, on 28 May 1918. He was killed in combat on 30 June 1918 (Sloan, *Wings of Honor,* 219).

DEGARMO, LINDLEY. From Florida, he trained at Oxford and was receiving flight training in England when he was killed in an aircraft accident at Stamford on 16 February 1918 (Sloan, *Wings of Honor,* 222).

DORSEY, GEORGE C. He attended ground school at Oxford and received flight training in England. Assigned to the 148th Aero Squadron on 4 July 1918, he was wounded during aerial combat on 16 September 1918. He returned to duty with the squadron on 21 October 1918 (Sloan, *Wings of Honor,* 220, 232).

DWYER, GEOFFREY J. Originally trained to fly at Governor's Island, New York, he was sent overseas in command of a group of fifty-three aviation cadets, who landed at Liverpool on 2 September 1917, approximately one month before Springs and his group arrived. Both his and Springs's detachments trained at Oxford University (Thayer, *America's First Eagles,* 26, 247).

ECKERT, SAMUEL B. He came to England in October 1917 but moved immediately into the flight training program as he had previous flying experience in the United States. He was assigned first to 84 Squadron, RFC, on 5 April 1918 and then to 80 Squadron, RFC, on 9 June. On 23 June he was assigned as commander of the 17th Aero Squadron, in which capacity he served until the armistice (Sloan, *Wings of Honor,* 202, 229–30, 315).

ELLIS, WALKER MALLAM. A graduate of Princeton (class of 1915), he sailed for France on 17 July 1917 and went through flying training in England and France. After serving in France from June to July 1918, he returned to the United States in August 1918 (Collins, *Princeton in the World War,* 297).

EVANS, CHARLES T., Jr. After training at Oxford and receiving his flight training in England, he was assigned to 209 Squadron, RFC, on 11 May 1918. He was killed in action eleven days later, on 22 May (Sloan, *Wings of Honor,* 219).

FONTAINE, HUGH L. He joined the 91st Aero Squadron, an observation squadron, on 22 February 1918 and served with that squadron until 17 August, when he transferred to the 49th Aero Squadron, a pursuit squadron. He was wounded in action on 24 October and sent to the hospital to recover (Sloan, *Wings of Honor,* 183, 259).

FORSTER, LINN H. He attended ground school at Oxford and completed flight training in England before being assigned to Springs's flight in the 148th Aero Squadron on 4 July 1918. He was killed in combat on 2 September 1918 (Sloan, *Wings of Honor,* 204, 224, 232).

FOWLER, HAROLD. A major and later a lieutenant colonel, he was the U.S. Air Service liaison officer to the British Expeditionary Forces from mid-May 1918 until the armistice. He originally enlisted in the Royal Flying Corps in 1915 and then transferred to the U.S. Air Service in October 1917. He served as the focal point for coordinating the assignment of all U.S. Air Service personnel into British squadrons and for American squadrons (the 17th and 148th Aero Squadrons) that flew under British operational control. He was primarily responsible for bringing Springs (and other pilots) into the 148th Aero Squadron (Sloan, *Wings of Honor,* 192, 200–202, 205, 218, 291).

FROBISHER, JOSEPH C. He received flight training in England and was assigned to the 148th Aero Squadron on 4 August 1918. He was shot down and wounded on 2 September while flying with Springs's flight and died of his wounds on 10 September 1918 (Sloan, *Wings of Honor,* 204, 229, 232).

FROST, HENRY B. After attending ground school at Oxford and flight training at various fields in England, he was assigned to 209 Squadron, RFC, and then to the 17th Aero Squadron, which he joined on 21 June 1918. He was shot down on 26 August, wounded, and became a prisoner of war (Sloan, *Wings of Honor,* 202, 221, 230).

FRY, CLARENCE. From Columbia, Tennessee, he trained with the Oxford cadets. He was killed in training on 28 March 1918 (Sloan, *Wings of Honor,* 222).

FULFORD, JOHN H. He trained at Oxford and received flight training instruction in England. He was assigned to the 148th Aero Squadron and flew with that squadron until 5 September 1918, when he was reassigned to the American training school at Issoudun, France (Sloan, *Wings of Honor,* 221, 232).

GARVER, ROY O. He trained with the Oxford cadets and was killed in a flying training accident on 26 January 1918 (Sloan, *Wings of Honor,* 222).

GILE, HAROLD HATCH ("HASH"). He was a fellow Princetonian (class of 1915), sailed for England on the *Carmania,* and trained at Oxford and other locations in England. He was assigned to 49 Squadron, RFC, on 25 May 1918. He was shot down on 13 June 1918 and became a prisoner of war until the armistice (Collins, *Princeton in the World War,* 299–300; Sloan, *Wings of Honor,* 219).

GOODRICH, FREDERICK PABST. A fellow Princetonian (class of 1917), he served in the American Ambulance Field Service in Italy early in 1918 and then entered training as a French artillery officer during the summer of 1918. His sister, Lorraine Goodrich, was working in Paris as a nurse in the summer of 1918 (Collins, *Princeton in the World War,* 384).

GRIDER, JOHN MCGAVOCK ("MAC") (1892–1918). From Grider, Tennessee, he was one of the "Three [American] Musketeers" who impressed their British friends with their flying and socializing skills. He first met Larry Callahan when they went through ground school at the University of Illinois during the summer of 1918. He and Callahan then met Springs at Mineola before they sailed together on the *Carmania.* He failed to return on 23 June 1918 from a mission that Springs had been leading (Sloan, *Wings of Honor,* 195, 198–99, 219).

GRIFFITHS, EDWARD A. After completing his training in England, he flew with the 8th Observation Squadron from 16 August 1918 until the armistice (Sloan, *Wings of Honor,* 221, 323).

HAMILTON, LLOYD A. He trained at Oxford and received his flight training in England. He was assigned to 3 Squadron, RFC, in the spring of 1918 and was transferred to the 17th Aero Squadron on 21 June. He was killed in action on 24 August 1918 (Sloan, *Wings of Honor,* 202–3, 221, 230).

HAMMER, EARL M. He trained at Oxford and received his flight training in England. He was assigned to 84 Squadron, RFC, on 17 April 1918 and was killed in action on 19 May 1918 (Sloan, *Wings of Honor,* 219).

HARBORD, JAMES G. Earlier Gen. John Pershing's chief of staff, at the end of the war he was a general and was placed in charge of movements of troops and supplies.

HERBERT, THOMAS J. He trained at Oxford and received flight training in England. He was assigned to 56 Squadron, RFC, from May through August 1918. He was wounded in action on 10 August 1918 (Sloan, *Wings of Honor,* 219).

HODGES. He is identified only as a flying student in training in England.

JENKINSON, HARRY, JR. He began his training in Toronto, Canada, and completed training in England. He was assigned to the 148th Aero Squadron on 1 July 1918 and was killed in action flying in Springs's flight on 20 September 1918 (Sloan, *Wings of Honor,* 224, 232).

KELLY, ROBERT A. He trained with Springs at Oxford and was eventually assigned first to No. 3 Squadron, RFC, and then to the 25th Aero Squadron, attached to the British army, just as the war ended (Sloan, *Wings of Honor,* 206, 221).

KENYON, JOSEPH D. He received his initial training in Toronto, Canada, and then completed flight training in England. He was assigned to the 148th Aero Squadron on 22 July 1918. On 2 September he was shot down and became a prisoner of war (Sloan, *Wings of Honor,* 204, 224, 232).

KINDLEY, FIELD. An Oxford cadet, he received his flight training in England and was assigned initially to 65 Squadron, RFC, for four months in the spring of 1918 before being assigned to the 148th Aero Squadron on 1 July 1918. He became A Flight commander on 30 July. In October he was designated as a flight commander in the 25th Aero Squadron, but the armistice ended further operational flying (Sloan, *Wings of Honor,* 202, 204, 221, 232, 352, 388).

KNOX, WALTER B. One of the "Oxford Group" of cadets, he received his flight training in England. He was assigned to the 148th Aero Squadron on 4 July 1918 and flew with that squadron until the armistice (Sloan, *Wings of Honor,* 221, 232).

LAGUARDIA, FIORELLO. During World War I he was assigned as a representative of the Army and Navy Aircraft Board in Italy and traveled across the Atlantic on the *Carmania* along with the group of 150 aviation cadets of which Springs was a member. After making his way to Italy, he was eventually joined by Albert Spalding, who was assigned as his adjutant. LaGuardia was eventually assigned as commander of Squadron 5a of Group IV from August to October 1918. He later became mayor of New York City for three terms from 1934 to 1945 (Sloan, *Wings of Honor,* 304).

LAMONT, ROBERT PATTERSON. A fellow classmate of Springs at Princeton University (class of 1919), he joined the ambulance corps of the American Field Service in France in June 1917. While engaged in ambulance work, he was badly wounded by an explosion and lost his left hand on 7 October 1917; he was discharged in December (Collins, *Princeton in the World War,* 473).

LANDIS, REED G. He trained at Oxford and received flight training in England. He was then assigned to 40 Squadron, RFC, where he remained until he was assigned to the 25th Aero Squadron as commanding officer on 23 September 1918. He was not able to obtain sufficient aircraft for the squadron to become operational until a few days before the armistice (Sloan, *Wings of Honor,* 206, 221, 377, 379, 388).

LATHAM, JAMES HOBLIT. A fellow classmate of Springs at Princeton (class of 1918) he served in the American Field Service Ambulance Corps in France from May to September 1917. He joined the U.S. Army and became an instructor in the U.S. Army's Motor Transport School from July to October 1918 (Collins, *Princeton in the World War,* 437).

LEYSON, BURR W., JR. He attended ground school at Oxford and received flight training in England. Although Springs suggests that Leyson had been injured during flight training, that injury does not appear to have affected his flying program, as he flew with 73 Squadron, RFC, from 11 May to 10 June 1918, when he was shot down and became a prisoner of war. He subsequently became an author and wrote several aviation books (Sloan, *Wings of Honor,* 219, 380).

MACDILL, LESLIE. He learned to fly at North Island, near San Diego, California, in 1916. Assigned to take a contingent of aviation cadets to Italy on the *Carmania* in September 1918, he traveled on to Italy with a small group of mechanics and staff officers after the cadets were ordered to stay in England for further training. In the summer of 1918 he reported to the U.S. gunnery training school at St Jean de Monts on the coast of France. He was killed in an aircraft accident near Bolling Field, Washington, D.C.. on 9 November 1938. MacDill Air Force Base, near Tampa, Florida, is named in his honor.

MANDEL, OSCAR. He was a fellow Princetonian (class of 1916). After completing his flight training, he was assigned to the 148th Aero Squadron on 3 July 1918. He flew with the squadron until 2 September, when he was shot down and became a prisoner of war (Collins, *Princeton in the World War,* 352; Sloan, *Wings of Honor,* 204, 229, 232).

MARSHALL, FOSTER G. He trained in Canada before arriving in England in the fall of 1917. After completing his flight training, he was assigned to the 148th Aero Squadron from 4 July 1918 until 30 October 918, when he transferred to the 41st Aero Squadron (Sloan, *Wings of Honor,* 225, 232, 380, 388).

MATTHEWS, ALEX. Springs knew him at the Culver Military Academy before they went through training with the "Oxford Group." He flew with 84 Squadron, RAF, and was killed on 17 August 1918 (Sloan, *Wings of Honor,* 227).

MOONEY, THOMAS F. After attending ground school at Oxford, he received flight training in England. He was killed in an aircraft accident on 22 April 1918 (Sloan, *Wings of Honor,* 222).

MORROW, JOSEPH C. In the spring of 1918, as a lieutenant colonel, he was assigned as U.S. Air Service aviation officer in London, England. He was succeeded on 15 June by Col. C. R. Day. He was then assigned as commander of the 3rd Corps of the U.S. Air Service in France (Mauer, *U.S. Air Service in World War I,* 2:237; Thayer, *America's First Eagles,* 251–52).

NATHAN, THOMAS C. ("CUSH"). A close friend of Springs, he attended ground school at Oxford and was killed in the flight training program at Ayr, Scotland, on 20 March 1918 (Sloan, *Wings of Honor,* 222).

NEWHALL, MORTON L ("MORT"). He enlisted in the U.S. Air Service in April 1917 and was assigned briefly at Kelly Field, Texas, and Selfridge Field, Michigan, before arriving in England, where he was posted to 84 Squadron, RFC. He was then selected to become a flight commander in the 17th Aero Squadron but was soon transferred to the 148th Aero Squadron, where he was assigned as squadron commander on 26 June. He served in that capacity until the armistice (Sloan, *Wings of Honor,* 193, 202, 229, 230, 232, 315).

NICHOL, CLARK B. He attended ground school at Oxford and was receiving flight training in England when he was killed in an aircraft accident in February 1918.

NOEL, SIDNEY Q. He trained in Toronto and completed his flight training in England. He was then assigned to Springs's flight in the 148th Aero Squadron on 1 September 1918. He flew with that squadron for the remainder of the war (Sloan, *Wings of Honor,* 225, 232).

OLIVER, BENNETT I. ("BIM"). He attended ground school at Oxford and received flight training in England. He was initially assigned to 84 Squadron, RFC, and was transferred to the 148th Aero Squadron on 30 June 1918. He was initially assigned as A Flight commander, but his place was taken by Field Kindley when he became ill on 30 July 1918. He returned to duty on 26 October (Sloan, *Wings of Honor,* 200, 202, 221, 232).

ORTMEYER, ANDREW ("ANDY"). He trained at Oxford and was receiving flight training in England when he died in an aircraft accident at Ayr, Scotland, on 8 March 1918 (Sloan, *Wings of Honor,* 229).

PATRICK, MASON. A general in 1918 and head of the U.S. Air Service in France, he replaced Gen. William "Billy" Mitchell.

PLYLER, WILLIAM H. After training in Toronto, Canada, and completing flight training in England, he was assigned to the 27th Aero Squadron, a pursuit squadron, on 25 March 1918. He was shot down on 13 June and became a prisoner of war (Sloan, *Wings of Honor,* 134, 225).

PUDRITH, CHESTER A. ("CHICK"). He attended ground school at Oxford and received flight instruction in England. He was killed in an aircraft accident on 30 April 1918 (Sloan, *Wings of Honor,* 222).

PYNE, PERCY RIVINGTON, JR. Like Springs, he was a Princeton student (class of 1918) who attended the military aviation training program conducted at Princeton during the summer of 1917. He sailed for France on 25 September 1917 and went through the French-American training program at Issoudun and Tours from October 1917 through March 1918. After a brief visit to Italy, he returned to France and eventually flew with the 103rd Aero Squadron from June 1918 until the armistice (Collins, *Princeton in the World War,* 445–46; Sloan, *Wings of Honor,* 92).

RABE, LOUIS W. He trained in Toronto, Canada, and completed his flight training in England. He was assigned to the 148th Aero Squadron on 2 September 1918 and flew with that squadron until the armistice (Sloan, *Wings of Honor,* 225, 232).

RAFTERY, JOHN HOWARD. A classmate of Springs at Princeton (class of 1919), he completed aviation training at Princeton with Springs, sailed to England with Springs on the *Carmania* in September, trained at Oxford University, and served with the 8th U.S. Aero Squadron in France from August 1918 until the armistice (Collins, *Princeton in the World War,* 481; Sloan, *Wings of Honor,* 221, 324).

RALSTON, ORVILLE A. He trained in Toronto and completed flight training in England. Initially assigned to 85 Squadron, he was transferred to Springs's flight in the 148th Aero Squadron on 6 September and flew with that squadron until the armistice (Sloan, *Wings of Honor,* 225, 232).

RICE, CUSHMAN A. Raised in the Minnesota farm country, he was commissioned as a major in the U.S. Air Service and was initially assigned as squadron commander of the 148th Aero Squadron, which he brought from the United States to France in the spring of 1918. He was awarded aviator's wings, though few who knew him ever saw him actually fly an airplane. He was not especially popular, and there was a general sense of relief when he was relieved as squadron commander on 13 May 1918 and reassigned as a staff officer.

RITTER, ROLAND H. He attended ground school at Oxford and received flight training in England. He was assigned to 56 Squadron, RFC, on 11 May 1918 and was killed in combat on 24 August 1918 (Sloan, *Wings of Honor,* 219).

ROTH, JAMES E. One of the Oxford cadets, he was assigned to fly Handley-Page bombers late in the war (Sloan, *Wings of Honor,* 210).

SHAW, ERWIN D. From Sumter, South Carolina, he trained with the Oxford cadets and after completing flight training in England was assigned to 48 Squadron, RFC, in May 1918. He was killed in action on 9 July 1918 (Sloan, *Wings of Honor,* 219).

SHOEMAKER, FRED T. He was one of the "Oxford Group" of cadets and received flight training in England. He was assigned to the 11th Aero Squadron, a bombing squadron, on 9 September 1918. He was wounded and shot down five days later, on 14 September. He became a prisoner of war and returned to the United States after the war (Sloan, *Wings of Honor,* 221, 245, 249).

SIEBOLD, GEORGE V. He trained in Toronto, Canada, and received his flight training in England. He was assigned to the 148th Aero Squadron on 3 July 1918 and was killed in action on 24 September 1918 (Sloan, *Wings of Honor,* 203–4, 225, 232).

SPALDING, ALBERT. A famous concert violinist, he enlisted for army service when the United States entered the war. After being recognized as a violinist, he was assigned as a member of the group that traveled to England on the *Carmania* and was elevated to the position of instructor of Italian; however, he continued on to Italy with the rest of the Italian contingent after the flying cadets stayed behind in England. In Paris he received a commission and was assigned as adjutant for Maj. Fiorello LaGuardia in Italy and eventually trained as an observer. He resumed his career as a concert violinist after the war ended. His career in the U.S. Air Service is described in his autobiography, *Rise to Follow* (1943), 210–57.

STAHL, WALTER A. He attended ground school at Oxford and received flight training instruction in England. According to Springs, he was injured in a flying training accident, which apparently delayed his assignment to an operational unit. He was assigned to the 11th Aero Squadron on 9 September 1918 and flew with that unit until the armistice (Sloan, *Wings of Honor,* 221, 249).

STANBERRY, ELWOOD D. He attended ground school at Oxford. He was killed on 12 April 1918 in an aircraft accident during flight training in England (Sloan, *Wings of Honor,* 222).

STARKEY, HENRY C. He trained in Toronto and completed flight training in England. He was assigned to Springs's flight in the 148th Aero Squadron on 23 August and flew with that squadron until the armistice (Sloan, *Wings of Honor,* 225, 232).

STOKES, JAMES ("JIM"). Originally from Nashville, Tennessee, he attended ground school at the University of Illinois with John McGavock Grider and traveled to England on board the *Carmania.* He attended ground school at Oxford and further flight training in England. His post-training assignment is not known.

TABER, ARTHUR RICHMOND. A classmate of Springs at Princeton (class of 1917), he completed aviation training at Princeton, sailed to England on the *Carmania,* and studied at Oxford. He was assigned to the American aviation schools at

Tours and Issoudun, France, in February through April 1918 and then flew as a ferry pilot at Orly Field, Paris. He died in an aircraft accident in France on 11 February 1919 (Collins, *Princeton in the World War,* 410–11; Sloan, *Wings of Honor,* 107).

TIPTON, WILLIAM D. He trained with the Oxford cadets and was assigned to No. 3 Squadron, RFC, before joining the 17th Aero Squadron. He was shot down and became a prisoner of war on 26 August 1918 (Sloan, *Wings of Honor,* 202, 221, 231).

TODD, ROBERT M. He was trained in Toronto, Canada, and received flight training in England. He was assigned to the 17th Aero Squadron on 23 June 1918 and was shot down and became a prisoner of war on 26 August 1918 (Sloan, *Wings of Honor,* 202, 229, 231; see also Robert Todd, *Sopwith Camel Fighter Ace* [1978]).

TOUCHSTONE, GRADY R. He was one of the "Oxford Group" of cadets and received flight training in England. He was assigned first to 98 Squadron, RFC, and then to 40 Squadron, RFC. On 8 August 1918, while flying with 40 Squadron, he was shot down, wounded, and became a prisoner of war (Sloan, *Wings of Honor,* 206, 220).

VAUGHN, GEORGE AUGUSTUS, JR. A Princeton classmate of Springs (class of 1919), he trained at Princeton and Oxford University. He attended gunnery school at Ayr, Scotland, at the same time as Springs and reported that "Springs and I were invited to all local parties; he taught the Scots to make American cocktails, and I played the piano" (George A. Vaughn, Jr., *War Flying in France* [1980], 71). From May to August he was assigned to 84 Squadron, RAF; from the end of August until November he was assigned to the 17th Aero Squadron, which, like Springs's 148th Aero Squadron, was attached to the British army. At the end of the war he was credited with twelve aircraft and one balloon destroyed (Collins, *Princeton in the World War,* 490; Sloan, *Wings of Honor,* 203–4, 222, 231).

VELIE. He is identified only as a flying cadet killed in a flying accident in England.

WALKER, SAMUEL J. He trained with the Oxford cadets and was later assigned to No. 1 Squadron, RFC (Sloan, *Wings of Honor,* 220).

WARREN, JAMES STRATTON. A member of the Princeton class of 1917, he served in the American Ambulance Service in France from July to October 1917. He returned to the United States and enlisted in the U.S. Army on 5 January 1918 and served in the 40th Engineers in the United States (Collins, *Princeton in the World War,* 414).

WHITING, GEORGE C. He trained with the Oxford cadets and received flight training in England. He was first assigned to 43 Squadron, RFC, and then was assigned to the 148th Aero Squadron on 1 July 1918. He was admitted to the hospital, ill, on 23 September 1918 (Sloan, *Wings of Honor,* 222, 232; see also W. P. Taylor and F. L. Irvin, *History of the 148th Aero Squadron* [1957], 62).

WILSON, DONALD A. He attended ground school at Oxford and received flight instruction in England. He flew with 64 Squadron, RFC, and was assigned to the 25th Aero Squadron when the war ended. If he did receive an injury during flight training, as Springs indicates, it was not serious enough to remove him from flying status (Sloan, *Wings of Honor,* 222).

WILSON, YORK LOWRY. A Princetonian (class of 1915), he entered military service in August 1917. He served with the 5th Division of the U.S. Army in France from July through October 1918. On 31 October he was severely wounded in the battle of the Argonne. He returned to the United States in April 1919 (Collins, *Princeton in the World War,* 327).

WINSTON. He is identified only as a flying cadet training in England.

WYLY, LAWRENCE T. He received flight training in England and was assigned to the 148th Aero Squadron on 1 July 1918. He was wounded in combat on 15 August and admitted to the hospital. He returned to duty on 25 August and continued to fly with the 148th until the armistice (Sloan, *Wings of Honor,* 204, 229, 232).

ZISTELL, ERROL H. He trained with the Oxford cadets, receiving his flight training in England. First assigned to 43 Squadron, RFC, he was then assigned to the 148th Aero Squadron on 2 July 1918. He was hospitalized from a wound he received in aerial combat on 3 October 1918. After the war he became the commanding general of the Ohio Air National Guard (Sloan, *Wings of Honor,* 14, 222, 232).

Appendix B

Springs's Use of the Grider Diaries in *War Birds*

The following examples illustrate how Springs modified the descriptions in the Grider diaries for use in *War Birds: Diary of an Unknown Aviator.* In the early pages of *War Birds,* Springs used the Grider entries to provide visual details of the English countryside. Here is a portion of Grider's 3 October 1917 diary account:

> So this is England. We landed at Liverpool yesterday morning and took a train right at the dock for Oxford. We came right through the most beautiful country I ever saw. It reminded me of Grimm's fairy tales. The greenest fields imaginable and no fences just hedges and occasionally a stone wall. We did see some fences too but very few and they were boards, no wire. I think the biggest field I saw was about 60 acres and they ranged down to 1 and $\frac{1}{2}$ acres. Most of the fields were pasture land or seemed so. They were covered with this intensely green grass. I saw a good many hay stacks so I guess they must cut this grass and cure it. You should see the hay stacks like houses and covered over with a thatch—woven and pegged down, thick. And never a frame house. All the houses were the softest red brick. I mean the softest colors. And all pretty or I should say picturesque and never an inch of ground wasted even on the railroad right-of-way which was all in grass except some lines for a mile or two we would pass vegetables.

This is the passage as it appears in *War Birds*:

> So this is England. We landed yesterday morning and took a train right at the dock for Oxford. . . . [Then follows a paragraph describing the change in orders assigning them to England instead of Italy; this paragraph would have been added by Springs.]
>
> We came thru the most beautiful country I ever saw. It reminded me of Grimm's Fairy Tales. The greenest fields imaginable and no fences, just hedges and occasionally a stone wall. We did see some fences too, but very few and they were board, no wire. I think the biggest field I saw was about sixty acres and they ranged down to about one and a half acres. Most of the fields were pasture lands or seemed so. They were covered with this intensely green grass. I saw a good many hay stacks, so I guess they must cut this grass and cure it. There was never a frame house, all the houses were the softest red brick, I mean the color, and all pretty too, or I should say, picturesque, and never an inch of ground wasted even on the railroad right-of-way, which was all in grass except where it was planted in vegetables. (*War Birds,* 1927, 24–26)

As a comparison of these two passages shows, Springs has copied Grider's description almost exactly, making only minor punctuation changes. This may be the paragraph of the diary that Springs admitted using (Davis, *War Bird,* 110).

When the men arrived at Oxford, this is how Grider described his living quarters in his diary:

Jim Stokes, Springs, Larry Callahan and I have a room together in Christ's [Church] College, Oxford University. Our barracks is about 100,000,000,000 years old. The stone is crumbling away and the whole place is old old and has the charm, dignity and beauty that only centuries can give. Our mess hall is like a chapel, with stained glass windows and the most wonderful paintings all around the walls. The ceiling is a mile high and is beamed or whatever you call it, it's an inverted V and has the old black wood inside showing with cross fancy business on it. [entry of 3 October 1917]

This is Springs's version in *War Birds*:

I am living in Christ Church College in a room with Callahan, Jim Stokes, and Springs. Stokes and Springs had a stateroom together on board ship. Our barracks are a million years old, I know, because it took that long to cool off to this temperature. The stone is crumbling away and the whole place is very ancient and has all that charm and dignity that only antiquity can give. Cardinal Wolsey and Henry VIII built it or had something to do with it. I haven't found out whether they got fired from it or gave money to it. Either one makes a man famous. Our mess hall is like a chapel, with stained glass windows and the most wonderful paintings all around the walls. The ceiling is very high and is beamed. It's an inverted V and has the old black wood inside with the cross fancy work showing on it. (*War Birds,* 1927, 26)

Here Springs expands Grider's entry to add details about his life on the ship (he roomed with Stokes), to add a joke about Wolsey and Henry VIII, and to simplify Grider's description.

On 6 November, Grider wrote the following entry in his diary describing his visit to Nottingham:

Callahan, Schlotzhauer, Leach, and I went to Nottingham Sunday and had supper.

Believe me it was some town. I never saw such a place since I was home. There were about a million women there and every one of them smile at you when they pass and most of them speak to you. I never knew there was such a place. I couldn't imagine it. No men except just a very few officers and no civilians at all except old men and boys.

This is Springs's version as it appears in *War Birds*:

Cal, Schlotzhauer, Leach and I went over to Nottingham Sunday and had supper. Believe me, it is some town. There have never been any troops quartered in Nottingham and there are no camps near it and all the men have been gone for three years. I never knew there was such a place. The women clustered around us all the time and talked to us as if we were a new species. (*War Birds*, 1927, 46)

We can see that Springs economizes on Grider's diary style, simplifying some details but expanding others, especially in his explanation of why the women of Nottingham were pleased to see the American cadets in their uniforms. The first sentence, for instance, is almost verbatim from Grider, while the last is Springs's clarification and amplification of Grider's ideas.

Another entry from the same date shows how Springs added details about himself not present in Grider's account. Here is a portion of Grider's entry for 6 November 1917:

> Springs together with nineteen others is posted to a flying school. Stillman is in charge and I am now a platoon leader and eat at the head table with the other NCOs and the English officers.

Springs expanded this brief section significantly:

> Stillman is in charge now and I am a platoon commander still. When Springs was trying to decide whom to appoint in his place, everyone wanted Bird as top sergeant. Springs likes Bird but isn't so particularly keen about Stillman but he said he was afraid of Bird so he put Stillman in as top and made Bird second in command. Somebody has got to hold this crowd down and Bird has been in too much devilment already to be effective on his own responsibility. Stillman is a fine fellow and certainly looks the part. He's six feet seven and a half and weighs over 200. He used to play end on Yale. (*War Birds*, 1927, 47)

Here, Springs has added details about his reasons for selecting the man to succeed him as top sergeant of the detachment. None of these details is in Grider's diary, but Springs wanted this information included in the book, primarily to illustrate how he made an important decision that affected the men in the detachment. While many of these "adjustments" to Grider's diary are intended to amplify and clarify the actions of other men in training, most importantly they provide details about Springs himself. Even from these few examples, we can see that Davis's comment that "Springs used only a few paragraphs from Grider's diary" is not accurate (Davis, *War Bird*, 103). This also indicates that Springs wanted the book to describe his experiences as well as those of Grider.

Appendix C

Springs's Use of His Letters Home in *War Birds*

Even in the details of the events that occur early in *War Birds*, such as on the ship across the Atlantic, there is evidence of Springs's use of material from his letters. The basis for the description of discovering the famed violinist Alfred Spalding in their midst is laid out in Springs's letter to his stepmother written on board the ship (*War Birds*, 1927, 19–20). Another early example involves Springs's description of a young British lieutenant at Oxford. In a letter dated 17 October 1917 he writes:

> There was a little [British] lieutenant here last week—looked about 17 and I was kidding him about trying to hide his new commission by making his Sam Brown belt look old. "Oh that," says he, "not a bit. The belt was my brother's. He went West last month. An Albatross got him." And he showed me a stain on the belt. Just a kid and he's off to France now—smiling. And they are all sportsmen, through and through.

This is what appears in the 19 October diary entry in *War Birds*:

> I was talking to a little English cadet who had an old battered Sam Browne [belt] and I asked him was he trying to look like a veteran. He smiled and said, "My brother wore it two years. He was killed by Richthofen." There seem to be a lot of them after that bird [Richthofen]. (*War Birds*, 1927, 37)

Springs changed the original details to emphasize the youth of the cadet (originally a lieutenant) and to glamorize the nature of the German adversary (Richthofen specifically, not some unknown pilot flying an Albatross).

An instance in the 22 October diary entry in *War Birds* (40–41) describes the unfortunate efforts of an English colonel who tried to find out which drunken soldier pushed him in the dark while he was coming home from a party (he believed it was one of the American cadets, but according to Springs, it was one of his own officers). This episode is described in some detail in Springs's letter to his stepmother dated 1 November.

In the same diary entry in *War Birds*, there is a brief account of Springs's success as a boxer:

> We had a boxing tournament last week. Springs and I went in and won our first bouts, but got knocked out in the second round. Pudrith and Jake Stanley each won in their classes and got a trip to London over the week-end as prizes. (44)

This is how Springs had described it in his 1 November letter:

> We had a big boxing contest last week. All the RFC men and the Americans. I went in and to my surprise, was put in the heavyweight class, drew a 190-

pounder the first crack. I got by for several nights and then lost out in the semi-finals. However I won a trip to London out of it—three days leave—but I couldn't take it—had to stay here to look after things.

Normally, Springs referred to his letters for details, which he modified in his retelling in *War Birds*. On a few occasions, however, he did use larger portions almost word for word, as in the following description of the cockpit of his SE-5 aircraft. Here is his account from a letter to his father dated 12 May 1918:

> This afternoon I've got to synchronize my gun gears, set my sight, and adjust my compass—then I'm ready. You ought to see the gadgets on it. The cockpit looks more like an engine cab than anything else. Compass, air speed indicator, radiator thermometer, oil pressure gauge, two gas pressure gauges, tachometer, compensator, two gun trigger controls, synchronized gear reservoir handle, hand pump, two switches, pressure control, wheel altimeter, gas pipe shut-off cocks, shutter control, thermometer, two cocking handles for the guns, booster magneto, spare ammunition drums, map case, throttle, joystick, and rudder bar. How's that for something to keep your eye on? Possibly you can understand why flying requires concentration.
>
> Of course, I can't resist the temptation to add a few devices of my own and have also put in a cupboard and shelf for spare goggles, machine gun tools, map, cigarettes, chewing gum, etc. You know when you're in the air for two or three hours at a time you get awfully bored.

This is what appeared in the 14 May entry for *War Birds*:

> To-morrow, I've got to synchronize my gun gear, set my sights, swing my compass and then I'm ready. Death, bring on your sting, oh, grave hoist your gold star!
>
> The bus certainly is plentifully supplied with ga[d]gets. The cockpit looks like the inside of a locomotive cab. In it is a compass, airspeed indicator, radiator thermometer, oil gauge, compensator, two gun trigger controls, synchronized gear reservoir handle, hand pump, gas tank gauge, two switches, pressure control, altimeter, gas pipe shut-off cocks, shutter control, thermometer, two cocking handles for the guns, booster magneto, spare ammunition drums, map case, throttle, joystick, and rudder bar. That's enough for any one man to say grace over.
>
> Of course, I can't resist the temptation to add a few devises of my own and have also put a cupboard and shelf in for spare goggles, machine gun tools, cigarettes, etc. I am also decorating my cockpit. When you're in the air for two or three hours at a time, you get awfully bored. (*War Birds*, 1927, 139, 140)

These passages in *War Birds* are almost identical except for a few small changes. Of course, it is easy to understand why Springs copied this list verbatim: it was the most efficient way to do it.

In other cases he copied what he had said because he was pleased (we can assume) with the style in which he expressed himself in his letters, as in this example from a letter to his stepmother dated 20 September 1918:

The Women's Committee of the Council of National Defense is certainly taking a step in the right direction. A man is killed in action—certainly somebody ought to swank about and get his glory. But I have a better suggestion to make. Why not benefit the living as well as swank for the dead? Why not help out those who live through it. Let the bona fide wives of dead heroes wear mourning and the gold star. Let the war brides of lucky cannon fodder wear mourning and two gold stars and let the would-be wives of wise and eager to fight belligerents wear black stockings with gold stars. Let the anxious but unsuccessful ones wear the gold stars on any color stockings. Thus could every woman swank, mourn, and advertise all at the same time, and the itinerant doughboy would be saved much curiosity and vain labor.

The angry, cynical humor of this passage could hardly be bettered, which is undoubtedly why Springs kept it nearly intact when he repeated it in *War Birds,* his only changes being to clarify the style of the passage and the hierarchy of women's mourning decorations:

The Women's Committee of the Council of National Defense is certainly taking a step in the right direction. They have issued special rules about Service Stars regulating how people may proclaim to the world at large that a member of their family is a hero. A man is killed in action—certainly somebody ought to be able to swank about and get his glory! But I don't think they go far enough. Why not benefit the living as well as swank for the dead? Why not help out those that live through it? Let the bona fide wives of dead heroes wear a gold star with an edging of mourning. Let the war brides of lucky cannon fodder wear two gold stars and mourning. Let the would-be wives of eager and successful belligerents wear a single plain gold star and black stockings. Let the anxious and unsuccessful ones wear gold stars and colored stockings. Thus every woman could swank, mourn, and advertise all at the same time, and the itinerant doughboy would be saved much curiosity and vain labor. (*War Birds,* 1927, 254–55)

More important, however, is the use he makes of many combat episodes that appear in his letters. Normally, Springs did not copy his combat episodes directly into *War Birds.* There is a good reason for that: he is supposed to be telling the story of the anonymous aviator, not his own story. Because he established the ground rule that the narrator remains a member of the British 85 Squadron, Springs had to write a narrative that is consistent with that scenario. However, he knew with greatest clarity the combat actions that happened to him personally. Springs's most intense aerial combat occurred after he transferred from Bishop's 85 Squadron to the American 148th Aero Squadron on 1 July 1918. Because the 148th was attached to the 65 Wing of the Royal Flying Corps, which included 85 Squadron, and his missions, like those of 85 Squadron, were directed by the British authorities, he was familiar with the flying missions and activities of the men in 85 Squadron even after he left the unit. It was therefore a moderately simple task for Springs to transpose his own aerial actions to those of another man. One particular situation can give us a good example of how he did this.

On 2 August he wrote to his stepmother about a ground-straffing action in which he had recently participated (but as a member of the 148th Aero Squadron):

> Yesterday we did ground straffing. You know about that? Well, I can't tell you because words can't describe it. Orders came through for it the night before and I felt exactly as I did when they used to tell me at the Johns Hopkins [hospital] that I would have the stomach pump at seven the next morning. I didn't mind the pumping much but I slept not a wink thinking about it.
>
> So, I strung bombs all over my little scout and got a piece of steel put under my [seat] cushion and took my flight over the lines about four miles pretty low. I saw what we were after, Hun transport, so I gave the signal and we all went down on the carpet. All the machine guns and field guns were shooting at us but somehow we got through and dropped our messages with pretty good effect and then shot up everything we could see and then raced madly home, zigzagging furiously. As soon as we got back, they told us to get ready to do it again. So over again we went and I saw a road packed with gun linkers. I dropped my bombs on them and then started shooting. My bombs hit on the side of the road and everything scattered. Then we shot up everything we could find, machine gun nests, balloons on the ground, Archie batteries, everything, and though several were badly shot up, we all got back.

In retelling this episode through the eyes of his anonymous aviator in *War Birds,* he had to change the perspective slightly (though, as we will see, he still manages to keep the Springs experience). This is the *War Birds* version:

> Yesterday we did ground straffing down south. That's my idea of a rotten way to pass the time. Orders came thru after dinner and all night I felt just like I did before the operation. I shivered and sweated all night. I took off with four little twenty-pound bombs strung under my fusilage; then we flew over about four miles across the lines at three thousand feet. [Captain Horn] gave the signal when he saw what we were after which was Hun transport and we split up and went down on the carpet. All the machine guns on the ground opened up and sprayed us with tracer and a few field guns took a crack at us but we got thru somehow and dropped our messages with pretty good effect and shot up everything we could see on the ground. I saw what looked like a battery and emptied my guns into it and then chased home zigzagging furiously. As soon as we got back, they told us to get ready and go out and do it again. So over we went and this time I saw a road packed with gun limbers. I dropped my bombs on them and then started raking the road with my guns. My bombs hit right on the side of the road and everything scattered. Two planes were shot up pretty badly and A flight lost a man. Don't know what happened to him. (*War Birds,* 1927, 244, 247)

In comparing the two passages, we can see that Springs retained the reference to his physical ailment but made it general enough that it could apply to almost anyone. He also substituted Capt. Spencer Horn, his flight leader in 85 Squadron, as flight leader instead of himself, which was his standard substitution throughout

War Birds. The specific details of the raid are almost identical, but the event Springs is describing is not about 85 Squadron. By this time Springs was a flight leader in the American 148th Aero Squadron. Although the 148th was attached to the British army and flying in support of British forces (as 85 Squadron would have done), the pilots were now flying in an American unit, not a British one.

Throughout the latter pages of *War Birds,* the flying activities of the character he calls "Captain Horn" are in fact those of Springs. In a letter he wrote to his father dated 16 August 1918, Springs mentions the actual Captain Horn, who continued to fly in 85 Squadron after Springs departed, and Larry Callahan, who had remained in 85 Squadron after Springs had been transferred; by this time Springs had been in the 148th Aero Squadron for two and a half months:

> So this morning I called up Larry [Callahan] and Capt Horn [in 85 Squadron], got permission from the Colonel and arranged a little surprise party for the Hun. Capt Horn, Larry, MacGregor and two others flew over head. . . . I took off with five machines. Then we both started to climb and when we reached the lines they were about four thousand feet above us and four miles away. So I went about six miles over and started patrolling up and down climbing all the time. When I got to 3000 I saw what I was looking for, six Huns up in the sun above me. Pretending I didn't see them I cut off and went right underneath them losing height all the time. It looked like cold meat to the Huns and it was so cold that they wanted to make sure of getting us all and they waited for us to get nearer and turn so they came down to about 1000 feet above us and stayed in the sun. Meanwhile Capt Horn led the others around in back of the Huns and got above them in the sun and then I turned and dived south to bring the Huns on down with their tails towards the others.
>
> It looked for a moment like a slaughtering party was going to be pulled off and everything was ready for the trap to be sprung when the Hun Archie opened up. And Archie fired not at us or Capt Horn, but at the Huns themselves and they varied the color so we could see that it was a signal. Immediately I saw the Huns, who were just beginning to open fire on us, turn and put their noses down for home doing about 300.

This is the version of this episode as it appeared in *War Birds*:

> We got permission from the colonel to put on a joint decoy stunt with Springs. Cal and Springs worked out the details. The point of the story was that the Hun was supposed to be surprised. [Captain Horn] led and the five of us flew over to 148's drome and rendezvoused at five thousand feet at five yesterday afternoon. We both climbed on the way to the lines and they crossed at about thirteen thousand. We stayed back and climbed up to seventeen thousand and had four planes from A flight up above us. We stayed between Springs and the sun and kept about five miles from him so that Huns wouldn't see us. He worked on over about twelve miles getting some Archie. Then six Fokkers came up to see what was going on and the Archie ceased. It looked like cold meat to the Huns but they wanted to make sure of it and took their time.

They came down to about a thousand feet above Springs and he dove back towards us to get them in proper position for a thorough slaughtering. Everything was working beautifully and we were waiting for the Huns to start their dive. The trap was all ready to be sprung when the Hun Archie opened up. They didn't fire at us or at Springs but at the Huns. The Huns got the signal and must have seen us as we started down for they put their noses down and beat it back for all they were worth. We didn't get within two miles of them. (*War Birds*, 1927, 251–52)

Grider had died on 18 June and so could not have participated in either of the missions described above.

A detailed list of comparisons between Springs's letters and the use he made of them is shown in the following table. As can be seen, Springs's reliance on information in his letters home increases significantly after the final entry in Grider's second diary (7 February 1918).

Comparison of Springs Letters to War Birds *Material*

Topic Discussed	Springs Letter	Date	Pages in *War Birds* in Which Material Appears
Albert Spalding, violinist	to stepmother	on board ship	19–20
Young English cadet	"	17 Oct.	37
Angry English colonel	"	1 Nov.	40–41
Boxing match	"	"	44
Decision to divide men	to father	6 Nov.	44–45
River Styx	to stepmother	19 Nov.	54
Aircraft crash (on fire)	"	6 Feb.	75
Callahan piano playing	"	9 Feb.	71
Springs diving at machine gun pit	"	26 Feb.	81
Deaths of DeGarmo, Bulkley, Carlton	"	"	82
Death of Montgomery	"	11 Mar.	83
Callahan accident	"	"	83
London air raid	"	"	72–73
Bostick accident	"	7 May	118
Death of Pudrith	"	"	106
Callahan: trouble with motor*	to father	12 May	139
Aircraft cockpit**	"	"	139–40
London theater*	"	"	140
Americans in England*	"	"	141

Topic Discussed	Springs Letter	Date	Pages in *War Birds* in Which Material Appears
Springs's flying accident	to stepmother	14 May	147
Visitors at departure for France	"	"	147–48
Departure for France	"	23 May	150–52
Lack of women in France	to father	25 May	157
Major Bishop's toothpaste	"	"	159
Grider shooting at wind vane	to stepmother	26 May	164–65
Supernumerary pilot*	to father***	30 May	159–60
Squadron record, planes shot down*	"	"	161
Springs buys toothpaste*	"	"	158–59
Squadron plays diavolo*	"	"	159
Aircraft mechanics	"	"	163–64
Major Bishop downs two planes*	"	"	164
Springs's ill-fated effort	to stepmother	1 June	166–67
Springs's first victory	"	"	171
Archie (anti-aircraft fire)*	to father***	4 June	168
Archie*	"	"	169
Personal war in the air*	"	"	167–68
Cream from farmhouse	to stepmother	9 June	179
Aerial combat	"	"	180
"Lady Mary"*	"	"	183
Trapp dogfight	"	"	183
Springs shoots own propeller	"	"	183–84
Moving the squadron*	to father***	14 June	195
New quarters*	"	"	196
Discretion the better part of valor**	"	"	235–36
New motor*	"	"	197
MacGregor*	"	"	197–98
Death of Captain Benbow*	to stepmother***	15? June	161–62
English disposition*	"	"	162
"Loyalty Menu"*	"	"	198
Squadron party*	"	"	198
Letter from Kelly	"	"	198
Learning the game*	"	"	198–99

Comparison of Springs Letters to War Birds *Material (continued)*

Topic Discussed	Springs Letter	Date	Pages in *War Birds* in Which Material Appears
Callahan's victory*	to father***	17 June	209
Aerial combat*	"	"	209
Worst dogfight*	"	"	210
German pilot down in flames*	"	"	200–202
New major	to stepmother	20 June	210
MacDonald gets lost	to father***	26 June	203–4
Springs is surprised**	"	"	206–7
Archie the avenger*	"	"	208
Movie photographer	"	"	208–9
Springs's accident	to stepmother	29 June	219
Major Fowler visits	(to Maj. Fowler)	(not mailed)	216
Death of Mannock	to stepmother	30 July	233
Springs's birthday	to father	31 July	241
Great to be alive**	to stepmother***	2 Aug.	243
Ground straffing**	"	"	244
Sergeant Pilot Wright**	"	"	253
"I'm not feeling well"**	to stepmother***	14 Aug.	248–50
Living quarters*	"	"	250–51
Decoy stunt*	to stepmother***	17 Aug.	251–52
Decoy stunt (con.)**	"	"	252–53
Callahan's letters	"	"	253
Visiting general	to father	19 Aug.	251
Aerial combat*	to stepmother	25 Aug.	257–59
Springs has a wheel shot off	to stepmother	16 Sept.	264
Springs's accident (29 June)	to father	20 Sept.	218
Women's Committee**	to stepmother***	20 Sept.	254–56
Callahan missing	to stepmother	24 Sept.	262
Callahan missing	to father	27 Sept.	262

Notes

* Partially verbatim
** Extensively verbatim
*** Letters quoted extensively

Notes

Introduction

1. Elliott Springs is credited in various sources with either eleven or twelve aircraft destroyed. In his flight log he indicates seventeen aircraft destroyed, but an aviator could not officially be credited with a "kill" unless visual confirmation of the aircraft's destruction was provided, either by other pilots or by observers on the ground. A common maneuver, used by pilots on both sides when they encountered serious difficulties in combat, was to enter a spin (which could suggest incapacity by the pilot and also create a target that would be almost impossible for an opposing pilot to hit), spin down to a low altitude, and then recover at the last moment and fly to safety at low altitude. Unless the aircraft was actually observed to strike the ground, the claim that an aircraft had been shot down out of control could not be counted as a victory.

2. Davis, *War Bird,* 9. Davis's book provides a useful overview of the life and accomplishments of Elliott Springs, although it does have some incomplete information, at least in that portion that discusses Springs's World War I activities and subsequent books.

3. Ibid., 13.

4. Fitzgerald left Princeton to join the army in 1917 (his junior year) and did not return to Princeton; John Peale Bishop graduated with honors.

5. See Vaughan, *An American Pilot in the Skies of France,* 105-25, for a description of the standard American gunnery school experience, at least as it was conducted in France in the summer of 1918. The introduction also contains an account of the American flight training experience in World War I.

6. That is, Springs crash-landed as a direct result of combat activity twice; he also had at least two mishaps on landing while flying with 85 Squadron and the 148th Aero Squadron. In addition he had at least five forced landings or accidents during landings in his flight training.

7. In the American system, men in training to become pilots were called cadets and were given enlisted military ratings. Only after they successfully completed their pilot training programs could they become officers, starting with the rank of lieutenant.

8. In his letters home and in his 1918 diary, Springs recorded the deaths of at least ten of his fellow aviators during training.

9. This letter, quoted in its entirety later, is also quoted in Davis, *War Bird,* 5.

10. Grider, *War Birds,* 173-74.

11. Ibid., 175-76.

12. Quoted in Davis, *War Bird,* 112.

13. In his biography of his father's war-time experiences, *The Courage of Early Morning,* William Arthur Bishop relates that his father valued Springs's social

contributions to the squadron but worried about Springs because he "suffered from moods so black that it was all Bishop and the rest of the squadron could do to keep Springs from committing some restless act" (153). Bishop does not indicate a source for this statement, and it may be possible that this is his interpretation of the comments in *War Birds,* as Bishop appears to believe that *War Birds* is the actual diary of John McGavock Grider. (The extent to which *War Birds* includes material in Grider's diary is discussed in more detail in a later section.) However, these particular comments—about black moods and reckless acts—are not found in *War Birds.*

14. Taylor and Irvin, *History of the 148th Aero Squadron.*
15. I retain Springs's World War I spelling, "straffing"; today the word is spelled "strafing."

Chapter 1: Princeton and Mineola

1. The development of the Yale Aero Club and its transition to a U.S. Navy aeronautical training unit in World War I is described well in Wortman, *The Millionaire's Unit.*
2. A review of the evolution of the military training program at Princeton from 1916 through 1918 is included in Collins, *Princeton in the World War,* xi–xxxvii; the development of the aviation facilities at Princeton is discussed on xx–xxi.
3. Group photographs showing these individuals, plus others in the aviation training group, can be found in Vaughn, *War Flying in France,* 4–5. Vaughn shared many of Elliott Springs's training experiences and eventually flew in the 17th Aero Squadron, which was employed by the British in the same manner as Springs's 148th Aero Squadron.
4. Taber discusses his Princeton training program in letters to his father published in *Arthur Richmond Taber,* 62–78. Taber died in an aircraft accident after the war ended, on 11 February 1919.
5. Ibid., 69–74.
6. The 1917 *Nassau Herald,* the Princeton yearbook, lists Springs's nickname as "Cave Man," which might indicate something about his attitudes toward women.
7. Lena Springs was Elliott Springs's stepmother; Aunt Addie was his maternal grandmother's sister.
8. Elliott Springs was a member of the Princeton water polo team.
9. Mr. Cohn is not further identified.
10. Classes at Princeton were not suspended.
11. Robert Patterson Lamont, Princeton class of 1919, was Springs's roommate during the 1916–17 academic year. During World War I, Lamont drove ambulances in the American Field Service. He was released from the American Field Service after he lost his hand when a shell exploded near his position on 7 October 1917. See Collins, *Princeton in the World War,* 473.
12. On 26 March 1917 a special meeting of the Princeton faculty voted that a senior who left college and was accepted for active military service by the government should be recommended for his degree in June if his college work for the previous terms was complete. Springs remained at Princeton until he graduated.

13. After his freshman year at Princeton, Elliott went to the hospital at Johns Hopkins University to be treated for stomach problems, apparently ulcers, an affliction that bothered him throughout his life (Davis, *War Bird,* 24).
14. Springs was definitely not an "officer," though he may have seen the special authority that he was allowed to wield as an indication of supervisory status. Another possibility is that he was a cadet officer. As he was not yet officially in the U.S. Army, any cadet rank he may have had was assigned by authority of Princeton University, not the army.
15. Elliott's unannounced trip to White Sulphur Springs, West Virginia, during Easter vacation was probably prompted by an urge to visit a female acquaintance, Freda Kahlo; he sent his father the hotel bill.
16. Leroy Springs had purchased the Lancaster and Chester Railway in 1896 and continued to operate it. Elliott took a personal interest in the L&C when he became president of the Springs Mills many years later.
17. Springs attended Culver Military Academy in Culver, Indiana, from 1911 to 1913 (Davis, *War Bird,* 19–23).
18. No change was made in the Princeton graduation date.
19. This was H. R. Rice, one of Leroy Springs's assistants and eventually executive vice president of the Springs Mills (Pettus and Bishop, *The Springs Story,* 117).
20. That he had a rank of lieutenant, even a cadet rank, seems highly unlikely; he probably was trying to impress his father.
21. Again this seems unlikely. He could not officially become a member of the U.S. Army until after he graduated from Princeton.
22. Princeton University did not close. Springs may have been trying to create a false sense of urgency, again possibly to encourage his father's attention or sympathy.
23. Springs's war record documents, located in the alumni files of the Seeley G. Mudd Manuscript Library, Princeton, New Jersey, indicate that Springs entered U.S. Army military service in May 1917. No particular date is given, but the official acceptance must have occurred between 1 and 15 May. He was not yet an active member of the military forces, as he was still a student at Princeton University, and presumably was listed as a member of the reserve forces. He was sworn in to active duty after graduation, probably on 29 June, the date on which Arthur Taber was sworn in.
24. The club is probably the Quadrangle Club, Princeton's prestigious literary club, which had previously rejected Springs's application to join.
25. "Papa Fixe," not further identified, was apparently a Princeton faculty member.
26. There is no evidence that Springs received any special honors recognition upon graduation from Princeton University. Leroy Springs may have meant that he felt honored that his son completed the Princeton academic program successfully.
27. *Little Lord Fauntleroy* is a novel by Frances Hodgson Burnett that was published originally in *St. Nicholas Magazine* in 1885–86. In the story a young American boy is invited by his English grandfather to live in England and become an aristocrat. Instead of adopting aristocratic behavior, however, he causes his grandfather to become more caring and compassionate toward others.

28. Sidney Erskine Brewster was a Princeton classmate (class of 1918) of Elliott Springs. He was also a fellow southerner whose family was known to Leroy Springs; his name reappears frequently in subsequent letters. More information about him is included in appendix A, this book. See Collins, *Princeton in the World War,* 420.

29. Aunt Carrie was a housemaid.

30. This information was obtained from the Elliott Springs alumni files in the collections of the Seeley G. Mudd Manuscript Library, Princeton, New Jersey.

31. About 1 July responsibility for instruction in the Princeton aviation program passed from Princeton University to the U.S. Army, which provided an instructor, Capt. Adlia H. Gilkerson, who had graduated from West Point. Although other students complained about the stringent military requirements now being enforced, Springs did not complain.

32. The date on the letter, a typed copy, is 2 June 1917, but given the events described, it must have been written early in July.

33. The photograph to which Springs refers, though not included in this book, is in the Springs files at the White Homestead in Fort Mill, South Carolina.

34. Internal evidence suggests that this letter was written prior to Springs's graduation from Princeton. Therefore he could not have completed his program and would not have received any military rank. Springs seems to be enhancing his actual situation, perhaps to impress his aunt.

35. The Vanderbilt Hotel, located at 4 Park Avenue, was completed in 1913. It was one of the newest and most impressive hotels in New York City when Springs was attending Princeton University, and it served as Springs's favorite center of operations when he visited New York City. It was converted to apartments in 1966.

36. The Nassau Inn, one of the oldest inns in Princeton, is a historic landmark building, dating to 1756, and it continues to offer food and lodging to Princeton visitors.

37. *Arthur Richmond Taber: A Memorial Record . . . ,* p. 75.

38. Handwritten record, Springs files at the White Homestead in Fort Mill, South Carolina.

Chapter 2: Across the Atlantic to Oxford University, England

1. The RMS *Carmania* was a large passenger ship launched in 1905 as part of the Cunard Line. After World War I began, the ship was converted to an armed merchant cruiser and troop ship, involved in carrying Americans and Canadians across the Atlantic Ocean. After the war ended, the ship continued to operate until 1932.

2. George Vaughn Jr., a fellow Princetonian, also flew during the short stay at Mineola.

3. Springs was probably flying one of the Curtiss JN-4 "Jennies" whose wings had a steeper dihedral angle (which caused them to tilt noticeably up from the fuselage, unlike the normal Curtiss Jenny, on which the wings extended more or less at a right angle from the fuselage) and, being unused to its handling characteristics on landing, cracked it up. See Bowers, *The Curtiss JN-4,* 5.

4. Camp Mills was a military camp near Garden City on Long Island.

5. Alfred Spalding, an American concert violinist, enlisted in the American army as a private in 1917 and, according to Springs's version, was spotted by Elliott Springs and brought to the attention of the military authorities, who soon elevated Spalding to a position of higher rank. Spalding, in his autobiography, *Rise to Follow,* 213–16, gives a different account: he says he was first noticed by a Captain Swann, who brought him to the attention of Maj. Leslie MacDill and Capt. Fiorello LaGuardia, who then gave instructions to Springs (whom Spalding describes as a "temporary sergeant") to oversee his welfare on the trip across the Atlantic. As usual Springs is enhancing events to impress his parents. Spalding sailed on the *Carmania* and eventually served as an executive officer for future New York mayor Fiorello LaGuardia in 1917–18 in the U.S. Air Service in Italy, where Spalding completed training as an observer. After the war ended, Spalding continued his career as a concert violinist until the 1940s. His experiences in World War I are described in *Rise to Follow,* 213–57.

6. In September 1862 German chancellor Otto von Bismarck gave what became known as his "Blood and Iron" speech, in support of German unification, in which he stated that German national power would come not from discussion and making speeches but from "iron and blood" (*eisen und blut*).

7. This statement is not exactly true; a number of Princeton men sailed on the *Carmania,* including George Vaughn Jr. and Arthur Richmond Taber.

8. Frederick Pabst Goodrich (Princeton, 1917) served initially in the American Ambulance Field Service in Italy and then entered training in French artillery (Collins, *Princeton in the World War,* 384). His name (as well as that of his sister Lorraine Goodrich) appears frequently in Springs's letters.

9. Springs was not at the head of a detachment of "officers" at this point; they were *potential* officers maybe, after they completed their training. As usual Springs enhances the facts slightly.

10. *Baby Mine* was a farce by Margaret Mayo that starred Iris Hoey. It was first produced on Broadway in 1910 and then became a Vaudeville hit. It opened in London in 1911.

11. Beau Brummell (George Bryan Brummell, 1778–1840) was an Englishman with a flair for elaborate dress and a fondness for gambling. He died penniless.

12. All are famous English portrait painters. Thomas Gainsborough (1727–88) painted portraits and landscapes; Sir Joshua Reynolds (1723–92) specialized in portraits and was one of the founders of the Royal Academy; and George Romney (1734–1802) specialized in portraits.

13. *Per ardua ad astra,* a Latin phrase commonly translated as "through struggle to the stars," is the official motto of the Royal Flying Corps.

14. Watt Tyler led the Peasants' Revolt in England in 1381 during the reign of Richard II. He was killed by members of the king's party when negotiations between the peasants and the king went awry.

15. Capt. Albert Ball was a famous English aviator. Born in 1896, he died on 17 May 1917 prior to his twenty-first birthday. A legendary air fighter, he was one of only eighteen pilots to be awarded the Victoria Cross (approximately equivalent to the American Medal of Honor).

16. Happy Hooligan was the central character (a cheerful but penniless hobo) in a popular American cartoon strip created by Frederick Burr Opper that ran from

1900 through 1930. He was a cheerful clown whose clothing was ragged and unkempt.

17. John Masefield, author of many volumes of poetry and Poet Laureate of England from 1930 to 1967, participated early in World War I as a medical orderly and then visited the United States to read his poems but also to measure American interest in the war. In 1917, when Springs and his fellow cadets were at Oxford, Masefield was living in the area. In 1918 Masefield visited the United States for a second time and devoted much of his time to speaking to soldiers about to depart for the war in Europe. He was therefore well known in the United States as well as in England.

18. "Laurence Hope" was the pseudonym of Adela Florence Nicolson (1865–1904), who wrote poetry that employed the language and images of India and the northwest frontier (the border with Afghanistan), where she and her husband, Col. Malcolm Nicolson, a British officer, lived. After his death she committed suicide at the age of thirty-nine. It is not clear whether Springs is complaining about the subject of the poetry or its style.

19. George Berkeley was an influential English philosopher (1685–1753). His 1709 publication, *An Essay towards a New Theory of Vision,* attempted to explain how humans estimated the distance, size, and situation of distant objects. Berkeley attempted to account for ways in which humans could know the truth of the external world following the principles of Descartes, who said that the senses could not be trusted (and thus began philosophy's detailed discourse on *epistemology,* the study of how we can know what we know). Berkeley's theory of vision would be relevant to a pilot's ability to estimate distances to targets in order to shoot at them successfully and to lead (fire ahead of) moving targets (such as other aircraft) accurately.

20. An invitation was extended to Springs and the men in his unit by Clara Anderson (Mrs. Robert Anderson) of Cincinnati, Ohio, to visit on Saturday, 27 October, between 4:00 and 7:00 P.M. Apparently Springs misread the invitation.

21. Lamont was wounded by an explosion that caused the loss of his left hand on 7 October, and he was eventually discharged from the ambulance service in December (Collins, *Princeton in the World War,* 473).

22. Walker Ellis was a fellow Princetonian (class of 1915) who went into the Air Service (Collins, *Princeton in the World War,* 297).

23. The Winton Motor Carriage Company made deluxe automobiles in Cleveland, Ohio, from 1904 until 1924. A Winton was one of the first to be driven across the United States in 1903. One of the best-known models during the World War I years was the 1915 Winton Six Limousine.

24. Sir Gilbert Murray (1866–1957), originally an Australian, was a scholar who specialized in ancient Greek classic literature and translated many of the works of Sophocles, Aristophanes, and Euripides. He was the Regius Professor of Greek at Oxford University.

Chapter 3: Flight Training in England

1. *Arthur Richmond Taber,* 89.

2. Springs may be exaggerating his situation slightly here. If he had to choose 20 men to attend a school where active flight training was to begin, he would naturally

(it seems) choose the men who had had some previous flying experience. While it is not possible to determine which of the 150 men had accumulated some previous flying experience, it is unlikely that all 150 had. He probably chose 20 men who had the most flying experience (which would have included himself).

3. The early Curtiss JN series of aircraft featured the Deperdussin flight control system, in which a control wheel that was mounted in front of the pilot controlled the ailerons mounted on the wing and a rudder bar controlled the rudder. Later JN-4 models replaced the Deperdussin control with a control stick in the floor of the cockpit, which became the standard control system for subsequent aircraft. Evidently a few Deperdussin-type aircraft remained in the training program in England at the time Springs was in training. See Munson, *Aircraft of World War I*, 45.

4. Frank Stanton was an instructor in the Aviation School at Princeton (Vaughn, *War Flying in France*, 4b).

5. Knitted or crocheted helmet liners helped to cushion the rigid flying helmets the students wore; they also added warmth on cold days.

6. The Carolina and North Western Railroad.

7. Hadrian (Publius Aelius Hadrianus, emperor of Rome from A.D. 117 to 138), known as one of the "good emperors," ordered the building of Hadrian's Wall across northern England in A.D. 122.

8. Alfred Noyes (1880–1958) was an English poet and writer who taught at Princeton University from 1914 until 1923. Springs apparently was a student in at least one of the courses Noyes taught at Princeton.

9. Regius Professor of Greek at Oxford University.

10. Made in Massachusetts, Page and Shaw's candy was popular during the period. The company was known for the quality of its chocolates.

11. The Moirea, the three sisters of the fates, according to Greek mythology, are Clotho, who spins the thread of life of each individual; Lachesis, who measures the thread of life; and Atropos, who cuts the thread of life.

12. Calliope is the classical muse of epic poetry.

13. The Latin poet known as Horace (Quintus Horatius Flaccus, 65–8 B.C.) is best known for his four books of odes. Springs says he is thinking of Horace's twelfth ode; possibly he has ode 11 of book 1 in mind:

Tu Ne Quaesieris

Ask not ('tis forbidden knowledge), what our destined term of years,
Mine and yours; nor scan the tables of your Babylonish seers.
Better far to bear the future, my Leuconoe, like the past,
Whether Jove has many winters yet to give, or this our last;
THIS, that makes the Tyrrhene billows spend their strength against the shore.
Strain your wine and prove your wisdom; life is short; should hope be more?
In the moment of our talking, envious time has ebb'd away.
Seize the present; trust to-morrow e'en as little as you may.

This translation is from *The Odes and Carmen Saeculare of Horace, 3rd ed., Translated into English Verse*, by John Conington (1825–69), M.A. Corpus Professor of Latin at the University of Oxford.

14. There is no date on the letter, but the envelope is postmarked 25 November.

15. Thomas Cook of England (1808–92) developed the first modern touring agency and, later, a bank designed to serve financial needs of travelers. After the death of Thomas Cook, the family kept the business running for several years before it was sold. It continues to be well known today as a travel agency. The phrase "Cook's Tour" was used to refer to someone moving continuously from one location to another with a short stay in each.

16. Frances Robertson and Olive Kahlo were female acquaintances of Elliott Springs.

17. This is probably A. H. Robbins, then superintendent of the Springs Mill at Lancaster, South Carolina.

18. The Goring is a luxury hotel in London, built in 1910; located close to Buckingham Palace, it is still in operation today.

19. There is no date on the letter, but the envelope is postmarked 5 December.

20. *Particeps criminis* is Latin for "partner in crime."

21. This is a reference to Shakespeare's *Macbeth,* in which the Scottish King Macbeth sees the ghost of Banquo, whose death he has just arranged, sitting among guests at a royal entertainment.

22. Florenz Ziegfeld (1907–31) produced a series of elaborate theatrical productions on Broadway from 1907 through 1931 called the Ziegfeld Follies. These featured talented Vaudeville artists, singers, and pretty girls; the 1917 Follies featured Eddie Cantor, Fanny Brice, and Will Rogers.

23. The reference to Emma Loe is unclear.

24. William Tecumseh Sherman (1820–91), an important Union general during the U.S. Civil War, was reported to have said that "war is Hell" in comments he made first to the graduating class of the Michigan Military Academy (19 June 1879) ("William Tecumseh Sherman" at *Wikipedia.Org.*).

25. The *Christian Observer* is a publication issued by the Presbyterian Church since 1813.

26. Simpson's-in-the-Strand Restaurant, located near Covent Garden, has served customers since 1828.

27. Sherry's was a stylish New York restaurant located, at the time that Springs would have patronized it, in Manhattan on Fifth Avenue.

28. Another stylish New York restaurant, Delmonico's was also located, at the time Springs would have visited it, on Fifth Avenue. It closed in 1923. A modern version is located at 56 Beaver Street in Manhattan.

29. Murray's Club was a popular nightclub located in the Soho section of London.

30. Alex Matthews had attended Culver with Elliott Springs and was one of the American aviation cadets going through training in England.

31. This is probably a reference to another of Florenz Ziegfeld's Broadway reviews, *Midnight Frolic,* which was staged in the early 1900s.

32. Frascatti's was a popular restaurant located on Oxford Street in London.

33. Egyptian Deities, a brand of cigarettes made with Turkish tobacco, was popular at the time. Barking Dog is a brand of pipe tobacco still made by House of Windsor.

34. Meyerowitz flying goggles were used by pilots and race car drivers to protect their eyes from the effects of wind at high speed.

35. Possibly Monteagle, Tennessee, a resort area.
36. *The 13th Chair* was a play written by the French playwright Bayard Veiller and produced on Broadway in 1917.
37. *Here and There* was a comedy that ran in New York City in 1916 and featured the actor Walter Stull. It ran in London at the Empire Theatre in November 1917.
38. *Bystander* was a British weekly tabloid magazine that ran reviews and topical articles. During World War I it ran copies of the "Old Bill" cartoons by Bruce Bairnsfather. It was started in 1903 and continued until 1940, when it merged with the *Tatler*. The *Sphere,* an illustrated tabloid publication published during the war, featured articles on the war and other topical issues. The *Illustrated London News* was a weekly publication that featured current topics often illustrated with drawings and then with photographs. It began publication in 1842 and continued on a weekly basis until 1976. It too included the writings of Bruce Bairnsfather, creator of "Old Bill." *Graphic* was an illustrated weekly publication that began in 1869 and featured articles addressing social issues as well as current news events.
39. The Winton, one of the earliest American automobiles, remained in production until 1924.
40. Stern Brothers is a department store that still operates in New York City. Tiffany's is a well-known jewelry store that continues to make fine products.
41. There is a conflict in dates here. In this letter to his stepmother Springs refers to events that, according to his diary dates, had not happened yet. But the date of the letter is correct, and the internal logic and time line of the events described in his letter suggest that he might have gotten the dates in his diary wrong, which could easily have happened as it was unlikely that he took the diary with him on his unsuccessful trip to Thetford to bring an aircraft back to Stamford. He probably got his dates wrong when he backfilled his diary after his return to Stamford.
42. *Peter Pan,* by James Barrie, appeared first as a story and then as a play that was staged in 1904. *Alice in Wonderland,* by Lewis Carroll (Charles Dodgson), is an illustrated fantasy that was first published in 1865. *Spoon River Anthology,* by Edgar Lee Master, published in 1915, is a collection of personal observations spoken in poetic form by several (deceased) former residents of Spoon River; their poetic statements describe commonplace events in their lives in a matter-of-fact, often emotionless manner. In his reference to *Peter Pan, Alice in Wonderland,* and the *Spoon River Anthology,* Springs is effectively representing a life of strangeness, fantasy, and death, probably comparable to the feelings he might have been having at this point in his training program. Even if he was making this comparison to unsettle his parents, it also may possibly be an accurate characterization of his frame of mind at that time.
43. The Battle of Mons, 22–23 August 1914, was the earliest battle fought by the British forces in World War I.
44. Military Cross.
45. Springs must be referring to Robert Louis Stevenson, but the story he tells appears to be his own version of a tale Stevenson might tell, not one he did tell; Stevenson's poem "Ticonderoga" is similar in spirit, if not in detail. But the

moral of Springs's Stevensonesque tale is clear: death will come inevitably, so it is pointless to hoard one's wealth. This is yet another of Springs's messages to his parents, one that combines his special blend of fatalism with a not-too-subtle hint not to worry about how much money he spends.

46. It is a little difficult to determine Springs's meaning here. From the context of the message, we might suspect that he is referring to a lack of alcohol. But if Springs's knowledge of the formulaic versions of chemical compounds is reasonably complete, as his use of the chemical symbols seems to indicate, then he should have remembered that the correct chemical formula for alcohol found in beer and liquor is ethyl alcohol, CH_3CH_2OH. C_2H_5OH is grain alcohol, and $C_3H_5(OH)_3$ is glycerin, neither of which is recommended for human consumption. It is likely that he intended to write the formula for ethyl alcohol but could not recall the exact formula at the time he was writing.

47. Typically "ferry pilots" were pilots who had completed flying training and were waiting for assignment to an operational squadron. While waiting for their assignments, they ferried new aircraft from the fields near aircraft factories to the units that needed the new aircraft.

48. Capt. Spencer Horn, RFC. This is the same Captain Horn who apparently recommended to William "Billy" Bishop that Springs, Grider, and Callahan be brought into 85 Squadron.

49. The Savoy, located on the Strand in London, was built in 1889 and became known as London's "most famous hotel." It is one of London's most opulent hotels.

50. This is apparently a reference to the short story "The Last of the Troubadours," by O. Henry (William Sydney Porter).

51. *Intolerance* was a 1916 silent film directed by D. W. Griffith, director of *Birth of a Nation. Intolerance* depicted four different stories of intolerant behavior set in four different time periods.

52. "Gunga Din" is one of the best-known poems by Rudyard Kipling. Published in 1892, it describes a British soldier's account of the service provided by his native Indian water bearer, who dies saving the soldier's life.

Chapter 4: Preparing for Operational Flying in England

1. Turnberry, near Ayr, Scotland, is best known in modern times as the home of the British Open golf tournament. A nearby flying field provided a range for aerial gunnery practice during World War I.

2. *Fair and Warmer* was a comedy written by Avery Hopwood (1882–1928) in 1915. It opened in London in the Prince of Wales Theatre in 1918 and featured Billie Carleton and Hallye Whatley in the two leading women's roles. The relationship between Mac Grider and Billie Carleton was apparently more serious than casual, and Carleton apparently became depressed after Grider left for France. Billie Carleton developed a serious drug habit, whether over an unhappy love life or for other reasons; she died on 27 November 1918, apparently from the effects of an overdose. See Hohn, *Dope Girls,* 67–84.

3. Of the five men Springs mentions in his diary, three eventually were killed in combat, one was injured in combat, and one was shot down and became a prisoner of war.

4. Johnnie Walker was a famous brand of scotch whisky, which featured in its advertisements the figure of a tall Scot.

5. "Annie Laurie" is an old Scots poem attributed to William Douglas (d. 1748), who supposedly had been in love with a young woman by that name. The poem has apparently been modified by others since it first appeared and in the twentieth century became a popular song.

6. It is not clear how Springs came up with the term "raspazass," which meant something like socializing at a level of intensity, sophistication, and affluence well above the average flying cadet's social standing and economic resources.

7. *Puck* magazine, published weekly from 1871 until 1918, featured political cartoons and political commentary. It was founded by Joseph Keppler in St. Louis, Missouri, and was eventually bought by William Randolph Hearst shortly before it ceased publication. *Life* magazine continues to be published today.

8. Wellington House is a distinguished old structure located on Wellington Square in Ayr, Scotland.

9. The Scottish poet Robert Burns (1759–96), author of "Auld Lang Syne" and "Scots Who Hae Wi' Wallace Bled," championed the Scots dialect in much of his poetry. Burns was from Ayrshire, where Springs was practicing his aerial gunnery techniques.

10. The troop ship *Tuscania* was torpedoed and sunk on 5 February 1918 as it approached the coast of England. Over two thousand American troops were on board, of which approximately two hundred were lost. The survivors were carried by various vessels to England, where they wore a variety of makeshift clothing until they could be suitably dressed in military uniforms. Three American aero squadrons were on board the ship: the 100th, 158th, and 263rd; these consisted primarily of enlisted men.

11. Vernon Castle was born in England and moved to the United States, where he met his future wife, Irene. They became stylish dancers and demonstrated new dance steps that became popular. They worked as a team until Vernon joined the Royal Flying Corps during World War I. After service in France, he was assigned as an instructor in Texas, where he was badly injured in an aircraft accident and died on 15 February 1918.

12. Mary Pickford (1892–1979) was born in Canada, moved to the United States as a young girl, and began acting in plays, portraying Little Eva in *Uncle Tom's Cabin*. She eventually became a popular movie star, acting in silent films such as *Hearts Adrift* (1914), *Rebecca of Sunnybrook Farm* (1917), *Pollyanna* (1920), and *My Best Girl* (1927). She married three times; her second husband was Douglas Fairbanks, and her third was Buddy Rogers, both popular movie stars. She did not transition successfully to talking films but remained active in the movie-making industry for many years.

13. The student named Dealy is identified in *Wings of Honor* (194) as Eugene Wheatley, who was killed in training on 10 March 1918. The student named Velie in the next diary entry cannot be further identified.

14. Neither Ipers nor Montgomery can be accurately identified.

15. Built in 1888 in Westminster (the West End of London), the Shaftesbury Theatre was noted for its large stage and popular stage hits. It was severely damaged by German aerial attacks during World War II.

16. This is probably a reference to *The Bing Boys Are Here: A Picture of London Life, with a Prologue and Six Panels,* a musical with music by Nat D. Ayer, lyrics by Clifford Grey, and book by George Grossmith Jr. and Fred Thompson. It opened at the Alhambra Theatre in London in April 1916 and continued until it was replaced with an updated version, *The Bing Boys Are There,* which ran from February 1917 until February 1918, at which time it was replaced with a second update, entitled *The Bing Boys on Broadway,* which continued until well after the armistice. The actor-singer George Robey starred in the first and third reviews. The musical review ran during the last three and a half years of the war, and its music was synonymous with the war.

17. "DH" is a reference to either the DeHavilland DH-4 or DH-9 aircraft, both of which were used as bombing or reconnaissance aircraft. The other aircraft mentioned in the verse are described in later notes.

18. "Quirk—nickname for a certain machine [the BE2, an observation aircraft]" (note provided by Springs in the letter; information in brackets supplied by the editor).

19. "R.A.F.—Royal Aircraft Factories; RAF wire is a special kind of wire" (note provided by Springs).

20. *To-night's the Night,* a musical set in London, by Paul Rubens with lyrics by Paul Rubens and Percy Greenbank, opened in New York in December 1914 and in London in April 1915.

21. "Rigger—carpenter in the Aviation Corps" (note provided by Springs).

22. "Joy-stick—the [flight] control lever" (note provided by Springs).

23. "Henri—nickname for a training machine [the Henri Farman]" (note provided by Springs).

24. "Heavy-handed—et tu Brute (aussi Moi)" (note provided by Springs). This reference is not clear; perhaps Springs is referring to his own flying technique.

25. "F.E.—a type of machine commonly called a 'Fee' [F.E. 2B]" (note provided by Springs).

26. "Propeller—observers often drop magazines into them [in aircraft in which the propeller is in the rear of the fuselage]" (note provided by Springs).

27. "C.B.—confined to barracks" (note provided by Springs).

28. "A Broken Doll" was a popular song from the 1916 musical *Samples,* written by James W. Tate; the musical also featured songs by Herman Darewski and Irving Berlin.

29. "Downwind landing—only fools and experts land down wind or cross wind" (note provided by Springs).

30. "When You're All Dressed Up" was a 1914 song written by Benjamin Hapgood Burt and made popular by the singer Billy Murray.

31. "Dud—rotten, poor, washout" (note provided by Springs).

32. "Ev'ry Little While" was a popular song from the 1916 musical *Some,* written by James W. Tate, sung by Lee White.

33. "Conking—going dud, bitched, getting out of order" (note provided by Springs).

34. Air mechanics, also referred to as Ack Emmas.

35. "What Do You Want to Make Those Eyes at Me For" was a song in the musical *A Better 'Ole: The Romance of Old Bill,* which opened in August 1917 and continued until after the armistice. The musical featured the comic World War

I veteran Old Bill, a creation of the cartoonist-soldier Bruce Bairnsfather (1887–1959). Bairnsfather became an artist prior to his role as a machine-gunner in World War I; he took part in the unofficial truce during Christmas of 1914, when he and some other British soldiers briefly socialized with some German soldiers. After participating in the second battle of Ypres in April 1915, he was brought back to England suffering from wounds and the effects of shell shock. He began to draw cartoons depicting life in the trenches, featuring "Old Bill," a phlegmatic character with a large walrus moustache. *A Better 'Ole* was a musical based on situations depicted or suggested by his cartoons. His "Old Bill" cartoons were initially published in the *Bystander* and became symbolic of the British soldier's trench experiences, similar to those of Bill Mauldin's American cartoon characters "Willie" and "Joe" in World War II.

36. "Rumpty" was the Maurice-Farman training aircraft widely used to train pilots in the RFC; "SPAD" is a reference to either the SPAD VII or, more likely, the SPAD XIII. The letters "SPAD" came from the initials of the manufacturer of the aircraft, Societe Pour Aviation et ses Derives.

37. Waddy Thomson was an employee of Springs Mills.

38. Lord Chesterfield (Philip Dormer Stanhope, fourth Earl of Chesterfield, 1694–1773) was a British politician and public figure whose distinctive oratorical skills did not bring him the political and social success he hoped for. He was described by one biographer as a "selfish, calculating, and contemptuous" man who "practiced dissimulation till it became part of his nature." He is best remembered as the author of a series of letters to his son offering advice on how to succeed in the world. Chesterfield County in South Carolina was named after him, as was the Chesterfield brand of cigarettes.

39. Springs's stepmother, Lena Springs, taught at Queen's College in Charlotte, North Carolina, before marrying Leroy Springs. Now Queen's University, the school began as the Charlotte Female Institute in 1857.

40. Florenz Ziegfeld (1907–31) produced a series of elaborate theatrical productions on Broadway from 1907 through 1931 called the Ziegfeld Follies. These featured talented Vaudeville artists, singers, and pretty girls; the 1917 Follies featured Eddie Cantor, Fanny Brice, and Will Rogers.

41. Daisy DeWitt was one of the Ziegfeld girls.

42. Leroy Springs had suggested, in a letter dated 27 February, that Elliott visit a Commander Arthur, a family relation, in Admiral Sims's office in London.

43. This is probably Foster G. Marshall, who trained in Canada and eventually became a pilot in the 148th Aero Squadron.

44. *The Prince of Pilsen,* by Gustav Luders and Frank Pixley, was a musical comedy first staged in 1902 on Broadway and later performed at the Shaftesbury Theatre in London for 160 performances. It continued to be revived through the 1920s. The plot involves an American beer manufacturer traveling in Europe who is confused with the Prince of Pilsen (a city in Czechoslovakia known for its pilsner beer) by a hotel concierge in Nice, France. Eventually the real prince arrives at the same hotel and, for his own amusement and his interest in the American beer manufacturer's daughter, pretends to be a commoner. The reference is wittily appropriate: Springs is likening himself to the American (beer drinker) who is mistaken for royalty, except in Springs's case he is mistaken for

a member of the elite fraternity of skilled war pilots to which his limited flying experience should not allow him to be admitted.

45. In accepting a commission as an officer, Springs had to be formally discharged as an enlisted man.

46. The Elysee Hotel, located near Lancaster Gate in London, is within walking distance of Kensington Gardens.

47. Gen. John Pershing was the top-ranking American general in Europe.

48. James Herbert Gustavus Meredyth Somerville, second Baron Athlumney (1865–1929), was the great-great-grandson of James Somerville, who had served as Lord Mayor of Dublin. The title was created in the Peerage of Ireland and became extinct with the death of Lord Athlumney in 1929.

49. "Willie the Weeper" was best known as a popular song played by jazz bands in the 1920s. The lyrics tell the story of a man who was a chimney sweep and a drug user by night. Under the influence of the drug, Willie dreams of places he has never seen and experiences he will never know; different versions take him in his dreams to Siam, Turkey, the North Pole, Monte Carlo, and Egypt. The poem on which the lyrics are based is an old ballad of unknown origin. Most versions of the poem conclude with this stanza:

> Now this is the story of Willie the Weeper;
> Willie the Weeper was a chimney sweeper.
> Someday a pill too many he'll take,
> And dreaming he's dead, he'll forget to awake.

Springs's dream of a luxurious dinner in the Vanderbilt Hotel nicely matches the hallucinatory nature of some of the episodes of the poem.

50. Nathaniel David Ayer (1887–1952) was an American-born songwriter who moved to England and composed several musical revues, the most notable of which during World War I were his *Bing Boys* series of musicals from 1916 to 1918.

51. "The Spring Maid" was an American adaptation of *Die Sprudelfee,* an operetta by Heinrich Reinhardt (1865–1922), an Austrian composer. First performed in Vienna in 1909, it opened on Broadway in 1910. No song with the title "The Three Trees" is listed among its musical numbers, however.

52. Thomas Mooney was one of the original flying cadets who came to England on the *Carmania.*

53. Manfred von Richtofen, also known as the "Red Baron," was the most famous of all German pilots; he was killed on 21 April 1918. George Guynemer was a top-scoring French ace with fifty victories; he failed to return from a mission on 11 September 1917. Oswald Boelcke, the mentor of von Richtofen, had forty victories when he died on 28 October 1916. Alfred Ball was an English ace with forty-four victories; he died on 7 May 1917. Max Immelman, another high-scoring German ace, died on 18 June 1916. Christopher Draper, a British pilot who flew with the Royal Naval Air Service during World War I, is commonly called "the Mad Major." However, Springs may have had another flier in mind, as Draper survived the war and wrote an autobiography entitled *The Mad Major.* Adolphe Celestin Pegoud was the first French pilot to score five aerial victories; he became the first French ace and was killed in August 1915. James

McCudden, an English ace, had fifty-seven victories when he died on 9 July 1918, about two months after Springs wrote this letter.

54. The phrase "shoes and ships and sealing wax" is from Lewis Carroll's poem "The Walrus and the Carpenter," which appeared in *Through the Looking Glass* (1871), the sequel to Carroll's *Alice in Wonderland* (1865).

55. The Military Cross is a British military award.

56. Bonham Bostick, a Princetonian, was wounded in combat on 11 April 1918 and eventually returned to active service with the Royal Flying Corps prior to the end of the war (Collins, *Princeton in the World War*, 459).

57. Of the six names mentioned here, only two were killed; the others were injured, and most of those were able to return to productive flying status. Springs seems to be overly dramatizing the situation, probably for optimal personal effect on the part of his parents.

58. Princess Mary Louise was one of three children (and the only daughter) of King George V of England and Queen Mary. Her older brother became King Edward VIII after the death of their father, George V (who reigned from 1910 until 1936). Edward VIII abdicated his throne after ruling for less than a year to marry the American divorcée Wallis Simpson. During World War I, Princess Mary Louise was active in a number of activities supporting the war effort. In May 1918, when Springs met her, she would have been twenty years old.

Chapter 5: With 85 Squadron RFC in France

1. The change from Royal Flying Corps (RFC) to Royal Air Force (RAF) came about as a result of the decision to join the flying units of the British army and navy into a single command. British flying squadrons held the designation RFC prior to 1 April 1918.

2. Bishop chose the following three men to be his flight commanders in 85 Squadron: Capt. Spencer Horn, Capt. Arthur "Lobo" Benbow, and Capt. C. B. A. Baker. The other men with whom Springs, Callahan, and Grider flew most often included Malcom MacGregor, from New Zealand; Beverley MacDonald, from Canada; Donald Inglis; and Alec Cunningham-Reid, whom Springs referred to as "Lady Mary." Other pilots whom Springs mentions are Carruthers, Brown, Thompson, Trapp, Hall, and Canning (first names not known). Undoubtedly there were additional pilots in the squadron not named by Springs.

3. Murray's was a popular nightclub located in the Soho section of London.

4. The Criterion Theatre, built in 1873, is located on Piccadilly Circus in Westminster, London. The Criterion Restaurant adjoined the theater.

5. Although Burke Davis states that Col. Dwight Morrow and Col. William "Billy" Mitchell were present at Hounslow for the departure of 85 Squadron (Davis, *War Bird*, 53), the "Morrow" that Springs mentions in his diary was probably Lt. Col. Joseph C. Morrow, at that time the U.S. Air Service aviation officer in London. The officer named "Mitchell" cannot be identified with any certainty. It seems unlikely that it was Gen. William "Billy" Mitchell as at this time he was fully occupied by events in France: on 19 May he was at Toul, France, when he received word of the death of Raoul Lufbery, who fell from his airplane during aerial combat, apparently because he had failed to secure his seat belt; on 20 May he attended Lufbery's funeral; and on 27 May at Toul he

received word of the death of his younger brother in an aircraft accident at Colombey-les-Belles (William Mitchell, *Memoirs of World War I* [New York: Random House, 1960], 199–204). It seems highly unlikely that Mitchell would have traveled to England, attended the departure of the men of 85 Squadron, and returned to France in less than one week's time.

6. The Victrola was a wind-up record player made by the Victor Talking Machine Company and housed inside a wooden cabinet. The records played at 78 rpm, and sound was projected through a large horn located inside the cabinet.

7. *Winged Warfare,* by William "Billy" Bishop, was published by Doran in the United States in 1918 and was immediately popular.

8. Springs is apparently referring to Billy Carleton.

9. Undated manuscript in Elliott Springs World War I materials, South Caroliniana Library, University of South Carolina, Columbia.

10. Jack Harkaway was a hero of the British "penny dreadful" stories, which were inexpensive and cheaply published, written by Bracebridge Hemyng in the late 1800s and early 1900s. They were published by Frank Leslie in America, where they were known as "dime novels." Diamond Dick was a similar hero, whose exploits took place primarily in the American West.

11. The pilot was Malcolm MacGregor.

12. Pebeco, a tooth-cleaning paste sold in a tin tube, was made by the German firm of Beiersdorf (which is still in existence and is best known today for its Nivea brand of skin cream). Pebeco sold well from 1900 until 1920 and was made under license in a number of other countries besides Germany.

13. Diavolo is a solitaire card game played with two decks.

14. Waddy Thompson worked for the Springs Mills Company; "Charlie" (last name not known; perhaps Charles B. Skipper) apparently did so as well. See Pettus and Bishop, *The Springs Story,* 53.

15. Undated manuscript in Elliott Springs World War I files, South Caroliniana Library.

16. Springs is probably referring to the Albatross DV, one of the premier German fighter planes, which was introduced in 1917 and continued in service until the end of the war.

17. This is possibly a reference to Simón Bolívar (1783–1830), an important South American leader, whose political effectiveness was compromised by his strong sense of idealism in forming effective political states. Exiled to Europe, Bolivar died from tuberculosis before he could leave South America.

18. There is no information about why Captain Horn should have received such an unusually large amount of money.

19. Robert Loraine (1876–1935) was a well-known actor on the London stage before he became involved with early aviation, and he was the first to fly across the Irish Sea in 1910. When World War I began, he flew as an observer in 3 Squadron and was wounded by shrapnel. He then flew as a pilot in 2 Squadron and 5 Squadron. He was commander of 40 Squadron for a time. In the summer of 1918 he was squadron commander of 211 Squadron, which flew Bristol Fighters; 211 Squadron was stationed at the same field as 85 Squadron.

20. Sidney Brewster and Percy Rivington Pyne, fellow Princeton aviators (both class of 1918), did not accompany Springs and some other Princeton men to

England. They sailed later and, after receiving additional training in France and Italy, flew with American aero squadrons until the armistice.

21. W. A. Fleet had been one of Springs's instructors at Culver Military Academy.

22. This may be a reference to the famous "Three Musketeers" photos, one of which is included here.

23. Undated manuscript in Elliott Springs World War I files, South Caroliniana Library.

24. This is the only aerial combat report from 85 Squadron in the Springs papers.

25. In this letter to his parents, Springs writes "MacGregor," but the 85 Squadron combat report and Springs's later narrative clearly indicate that the third pilot was Grider. This mistake in names (writing MacGregor when he should have written Mac Grider) may have helped to contribute to his father's later confusion when Elliott referred to both MacGregor and Mac Grider as "Mac."

26. Undated manuscript in Elliott Springs World War I files, South Caroliniana Library.

27. *Integer vitale scelerisque purus* translated means "Upright in living and blameless of crime," from the Latin poet known as Horace (Quintus Horatius Flaccus, 65–8 B.C.).

28. A Billiken was a charm doll created by an American art teacher, Florence Pretz, in 1908. The Billiken looked like a chubby elf with pointed ears and was usually seated with arms at his side and legs stretched out in front of him.

29. Undated manuscript in Elliott Springs World War I files, South Caroliniana Library.

Chapter 6: With the 148th Aero Squadron in France—An Accident and First Combat

1. Maj. Cushman A. Rice was an unusual individual. The only son of a Minnesota politician, Rice served as an officer in the American army in the Spanish-American and Philippine wars. He was a world traveler, a big-game hunter, and a socialite in Manhattan, and he had a fondness for expensive cars. It is not clear how he managed to be assigned as a major in the U.S. Air Service; after leading the 148th Aero Squadron to France, he was replaced as squadron commander in June 1918 as the squadron was transferred to British control and was prepared for air combat. One researcher suggests that he was the model for Gatsby in F. Scott Fitzgerald's *The Great Gatsby* (Dan Hardy, "Cushman Rice: The Man Who Was Gatsby?," *Writing in the Margins* [Spring 2008]).

2. See Irvin, *Francis L. "Spike" Irvin's War Diary*, 1–2.

3. Ibid., 1–6.

4. Spike Irwin, *War Diary*, 12.

5. Taylor and Irvin, *History of the 148th Aero Squadron*, 22.

6. Undated manuscript from Elliott Springs World War I files, South Caroliniana Library.

7. The first German aircraft was shot down by Field Kindley on 13 July 1918 (Taylor and Irvin, *History of the 148th Aero Squadron*, 82).

8. The line is from a poem by Alfred, Lord Tennyson, entitled "The May Queen" (1833), in which the main figure, a young girl, keeps repeating this line even though (or because) she has been profoundly disturbed by unnatural activities that are occurring around her.

9. On 15 May 1918 the U.S. Post Office initiated the first air mail service with the help of U.S. Air Service pilots.

10. The community of Fontainebleau is located about thirty miles south-southeast of Paris and is centered on the Chateau de Fontainebleau, formerly a palace used by many French kings. During World War I it was used as a military training facility.

11. This is a short street north of the Seine River and about two miles east of the center of Paris. The restaurant/bar A La Becasse was located at 11 rue de Caumartin during World War I, but it is no longer there. The best-known restaurant/bar named A La Becasse today is located in Brussels, Belgium.

12. The Culver Academy, a military preparatory school founded in 1894, is located in Culver, Indiana. Springs attended Culver from 1911 to 1913.

13. Located at the Place de l'Opera, the Café de la Paix is one of the oldest and best-known cafés in Paris.

14. These were significant military medals, including the Distinguished Flying Cross (DFC) and the Distinguished Service Order (DSO).

15. Springs is being humorously ironic here; the German offensive in June was intended to enable the German army to capture Paris, but the attack failed to achieve that objective.

16. *Vogue* magazine began publication in France in 1914. The "bois" probably refers to the Bois de Boulogne, a large park in central Paris.

Chapter 7: With the 148th Aero Squadron in France—Supporting the Allied Advance

1. Written in a letter dated 12 December 1918; see Skelton and Williams, *Lt. Henry Clay,* 153.

2. See the account of the support provided by the 148th and 17th Aero Squadrons to the British army during the difficult days of late August and September, in Mauer, *U.S. Air Service,* 1:331–34.

3. Ibid., 152–53.

4. Pearl White (1889–1938) was an American actress who appeared in over two hundred films. She is best known as the heroine of *The Perils of Pauline* and *The Exploits of Elaine,* silent films made in 1914. Physically fit, she performed her own stunts in films for many years.

5. Trench mouth is a severe form of gingivitis.

6. Leroy Springs is mistaken; it was Mac Grider who was missing, not MacGregor, but his confusion was helped by Springs's error in names in a previous letter home.

7. Something appears to be missing from this sentence. Perhaps Springs's meaning is that Fokker aircraft are well suited for combat patrol flying.

8. A "salient" is a military position that projects into enemy lines.

9. The British general Springs refers to here could be Gen. Sir John Salmond, who was commander over all British squadrons in the area as well as the two American squadrons assigned to support the British army, the 17th and 148th Aero Squadrons.

10. Taylor and Irvin, *History of the 148th Aero Squadron,* 93.

11. Ibid., 129.

12. Ibid., 94.

13. Ibid., 131.
14. Although this letter is dated 2 August 1918, internal evidence suggests that the date should be 24 August.
15. "Sergeant Pilot Wright" is not identified; presumably the name was listed as author of an article about flying in World War I with which Springs was not pleased, probably because of what Springs perceived as inaccuracies or even fabrications in the story.
16. Taylor and Irvin, *History of the 148th Aero Squadron,* 140.
17. Ibid., 148.
18. Erwin D. Shaw was with 48 Squadron RFC and was killed on 9 July 1918.
19. Taylor and Irvin, *History of the 148th Aero Squadron,* 98.
20. Matthews and Ritter, who were flying with British squadrons at the time, had recently been killed in action. Siebold and Curtis were in the 148th Aero Squadron; the others were in the 17th Aero Squadron.
21. Taylor and Irvin, *History of the 148th Aero Squadron,* 154.
22. Ibid., 157.
23. This letter has the same date as the previous letter. Possibly Springs wrote the letters at two different times and mailed them in one envelope.
24. This was probably Gen. John Salmond.
25. Kenyon and Mandel became prisoners of war, Forster was killed, and Frobisher died of wounds eight days later.
26. Actually it was Frobisher, who died from his wounds in the hospital on 10 September.
27. Taylor and Irvin, *History of the 148th Aero Squadron,* 102.
28. It was a "new" flight because so many of his men had failed to return from the previous mission.
29. Of all Springs's cryptic comments, this is the most cryptic.
30. Maj. Billy Crowe was the new squadron commander; he replaced Mick Mannock, who was killed in July.
31. The reference is to the Parisian Gaitee dancers of Paris.
32. *Fair and Warmer* was a comedy by Avery Hopwood in which Billie Carleton was acting.
33. Virginia Military Institute.
34. The phrase "according to Hoyle" refers to Edmund Hoyle (1672–1769), an English author who wrote about a variety of card games, giving the rules by which the games should be played.
35. Taylor and Irvin, *History of the 148th Aero Squadron,* 106.
36. Ibid., 161.
37. Ibid., 112.
38. Unfortunately no letter from Leroy Springs dated 26 August can be found in Springs's World War I materials.
39. According to Springs's flight log, he had credited himself with fifteen aircraft destroyed or shot down at this time.
40. Arthur Schopenhauer (1788–1860) was a philosopher who wrote extensively about what eventually became known as psychological aspects of human behavior. He died four years before Sigmund Freud was born. It is not clear exactly what Springs thought Schopenhauer was "right" about, but he may have been

thinking of Schopenhauer's comment about women, that "they are big children all their life long."

41. Taylor and Irvin, *History of the 148th Aero Squadron,* 115.
42. Taylor and Irvin, *History of the 148th Aero Squadron,* 164.
43. Ibid., 122.
44. This, which he indicates was his seventeenth aircraft shot down, is the last victory that Springs recorded in his flight log.
45. Springs is probably referring to the German insignia painted on the fabric on the sides of the fuselage.
46. Undated manuscript in Elliott Springs World War I files, South Caroliniana Library.

Chapter 8: "In Hospital," the Armistice, and After

1. Irvin, *Francis L. "Spike" Irvin's War Diary,* 19.
2. Apparently MacDill had requested that Springs transfer to the new United States–run gunnery school at St. Jean de Monts, on the west coast of France.
3. According to a summary of Springs's military record, on file at the Seeley G. Mudd Manuscript Library in Princeton, New Jersey, Springs had actually been promoted to captain on 22 August, but that information had not yet reached him.
4. Mary Williamson was Leroy Springs's secretary.
5. There is no evidence that Springs traveled to Nice, France.
6. While in Paris, Springs visited the Princeton Bureau of the American University Union and was referred to a specialist who treated him for a "slight digestive trouble," according to a letter written to Leroy Springs by Paul van Dyke, dated 11 October 1918. This letter is in the Elliott Springs files at the Seeley G. Mudd Manuscript Library, Princeton, New Jersey.
7. Lois Meredith (born 1898) was an American actress who was on the stage from 1911 until the 1920s.
8. Margaret Mayo (1882–1951), born Lillian Elizabeth Slatten, was an actress from the ages of fourteen to twenty-one, when she stopped acting to become a playwright. She formed an entertainment troupe that visited France in 1918. She was the author of the farcical comedy *Baby Mine.*
9. Morgan Harjes was an investment bank based in Paris and originally founded in 1868 by John Harjes, Eugene Winthrop, and Anthony Drexel.
10. This letter and the letter following were posted 19 October 1918 from the Folkestone Hotel in Paris. The Folkestone Hotel is located near the Paris Opera.
11. Belladonna is also known as deadly nightshade, a plant whose berries, leaves, and roots can be fatally poisonous.
12. The hospital serving American military personnel was apparently the Continental Hotel.
13. The Women's Army Auxiliary Corps (WAAC) was founded in England in 1916 to enable women to contribute to the war effort. There were four divisions: Cookery, Mechanical, Clerical, and Miscellaneous. The organization followed the military pattern, with officers and other ranks, but was not a part of the British army. Approximately nine thousand women served in France. In 1918 the organization's name was changed to Queen Mary's Army Auxiliary Corps; the organization was disbanded in 1921.

14. Keith Logan "Grid" Caldwell, from New Zealand, was a pilot in the Royal Flying Corps. He first joined 8 Squadron and then was assigned to 60 Squadron. In March 1918 he was assigned as the commander of 74 Squadron. In the incident that Springs describes, Caldwell jumped safely from his disabled aircraft just before it crashed into the ground.

15. George C. Whiting, a pilot in the 148th Aero Squadron, had been admitted to the hospital on 23 September.

16. This probably refers to the short story "The Cop and the Anthem," by the American writer O. Henry (William Sydney Porter, 1862–1910).

17. *Out to Win: The Story of America in France,* by Coningsby William Dawson (1883–1959), was published in 1918. Dawson was born in England, was educated at Oxford University, and moved to the United States. During World War I he served with the Canadian army, was wounded, and returned to the United States, where he wrote *Out to Win,* about the efforts of the American military forces in France.

18. In the United States, the Eighteenth Amendment to the U.S. Constitution, prohibiting the public sale and consumption of liquor, was proposed in December 1917, ratified in January 1919, and went into effect on 16 January 1920. Some individual states passed laws prohibiting the sale and consumption of liquor prior to 1920. The Eighteenth Amendment was repealed in 1933.

19. *Judge* magazine (published from 1881 to 1947), an imitator of *Puck* magazine, was formed by a group of writers and artists who disagreed with the policies of *Puck.* One of the better-known writers in this group was Frank Tousey, publisher of popular fiction stories known as dime novels.

20. Although dated 19 September 1918, this letter was probably written and mailed between 19 and 22 October.

21. Although this letter is dated 28 September 1918, it was probably mailed at the end of October, according to the events it describes.

22. In this section Springs is using aeronautical terms as forms of swear words. "Harry Tate," actually the name of a popular London singer, was a nickname for the RE-8 British observation aircraft that featured extensions on the upper wing to give it greater lift. The "type C" Constantine was a form of gear, and the "empennage" was the tail assembly of an aircraft.

23. A pom pom is a kind of anti-aircraft gun, and the Zeebrugge mole was a long barrier erected in the Zeebrugge harbor, held by the Germans, designed to defend against attacks by naval ships and submarines.

24. A D.F.W., Deutsche Fleugzeug Werke C.v, was an obsolescent two-seat aircraft first flown in 1916. The point of this anecdote is that the German aircrew members were using parachutes, which had not been approved for use by any pilots of the Allied air forces.

25. *Pro patria,* meaning "for country," is from Horace (a Latin phrase, it was used ironically, as Springs is using it here, by Wilfrid Owen in his poem "Dulce et Decorum Est"); *loco parentis,* meaning "acting as a parent," is a Latin legal term; and *paces somnet* perhaps means "peaceful sleep."

26. W.C.T.U. stands for Women's Christian Temperance Union; I.W.W. stands for Industrial Workers of the World; and the meaning of A.C.L. is unknown.

27. A Crossley was an automobile of British manufacture.

28. Colombey-les-Belles was a major U.S. Air Service administrative center.

29. Probably a SPAD XIII.

30. The old White place had been the residence of his grandparents, Samuel and Esther Allison White. It had not been actively used as a residence for some time.

31. In spite of Leroy Springs's admonishing remarks to his son in this (and the previous) letter, Leroy Springs could be lavish with his money when he wanted to be. An article in Ralph and Terry Kovel's "Antiques and Collecting" syndicated newspaper column dated 28 January 2007 (reprinted in the online version of the *Columbus Dispatch*) discussed a gold mesh purse that a reader had found in a barn in Pulaski, Tennessee. The purse was stamped "Tiffany & Co" and was engraved with the following words: "Lena Jones Springs, Lancaster, South Carolina." Pulaski, Tennessee, was Lena Springs's hometown. The mesh purse had eighteen sapphires and three diamonds set into the front, and the purse and an attached change purse had sapphire clasps. The Kovels estimated the value of the bag at over one thousand dollars.

32. A.P.M. stands for American Provost Marshal, military police.

33. Gene Delmont is not further identified; perhaps he was a Frenchman serving in a liaison capacity, as he is mentioned in Irvin, *Francis L. "Spike" Irvin's War Diary,* 6, 12.

34. Springs likely means psoriasis, a chronic disease that affects the skin and joints. One of its causes is alcoholism.

35. Again, there is no evidence that Springs ever visited Nice, or any other city south of Paris, on leave.

36. S.O.S. Headquarters is the Service of Supply Headquarters in Paris.

37. Gen. James G. Harbord was earlier Gen. John Pershing's chief of staff; at the end of the war he was placed in charge of movements of troops and supplies.

38. These were all South Carolina acquaintances.

39. D.S.C. stands for Distinguished Service Cross.

40. Linn Forster was killed in aerial combat.

41. Gen. Mason Patrick was at that time head of the U.S. Air Service in France; he replaced Gen. William "Billy" Mitchell.

Conclusion: Elliott Springs's Postwar Career as a Writer

1. Davis, *War Bird,* 89. The LWF initials stood for Lowe, Willard, and Fowler, the makers of LWF aircraft.

2. Ibid., 92–102.

3. Although Springs traveled to England with 150 cadets on the *Carmania* in September 1917, at Oxford University they joined 50 other aviation cadets who had previously arrived, making a total of 200 aviation cadets. Springs probably added 10 to the total number of specially autographed books published to accommodate supervisory individuals, such as MacDill and Dwyer, who were instrumental in making their training experiences a success.

4. Publication information for this edition is the same as that for the first trade edition.

5. *War Birds: Diary of an Unknown Aviator* (New York: Doran, 1926). This is the first trade edition, a large blue cloth book measuring 9.5 inches by 6.5 inches.

The title page lists no author; the only name listed is that of Clayton Knight, who drew the wonderfully detailed illustrations, some of them in color.

6. It has been reprinted nine times since its original publication in 1926, the latest occurring in 1988. Later editions were printed in England and Australia as well as in the United States.

7. Douglas, *Years of Combat*, 294.

8. Money, *Flying and Soldiering*, 85.

9. Lawrence, *Letters*, 733.

10. "Labor: Second Week," as reprinted in an online source: www.Time.com/time/magazine/article/0,9171,754421–1,00.html. The comment on Springs's literary efforts was included in an article describing Springs's response to a national textile strike.

11. Lawrence, *Letters*, 734.

12. A. W. Lawrence, ed., *Letters to T. E. Lawrence*, 2nd ed. (London: Jonathan Cape, 1964), 182.

13. One of the primary internal forms of "evidence" that Springs did not write *War Birds* is that the narrative is told in the first person, from the viewpoint of the deceased aviator. When Springs's name is mentioned, it is mentioned in third person. His name appears, like other names in the *Diary*, whenever the narrator refers to events involving the other men with whom he was training or in combat. If Springs wrote it, he referred to himself in the third person. Such an approach, writing an autobiographical account in the third person, while unusual, is not exceptional.

14. Davis, *War Bird*, 110–12.

15. *War Birds* (1927), vi. Pagination in the popular edition is the same as the trade edition.

16. Ibid., v.

17. Davis, *War Bird*, 111.

18. Ibid., 110. It has not been possible to confirm the extent to which these sources may have been used.

19. *War Birds* (1927), vi.

20. Davis, *War Bird*, 104.

21. Quoted in ibid., 112.

22. Ibid., 107.

23. This diary is among the personal papers of Elliott Springs, contained in the Special Collections section of the South Caroliniana Library.

24. A detailed comparison of passages in the Grider diaries and in *War Birds* is given in Appendix B.

25. Jacobs, *Marse John Goes to War*, 78. *Marse John* includes approximately twenty letters written by John McGavock Grider to his family from the summer of 1917 until his death in June 1918.

26. Ibid., 78.

27. Ibid., 81–82.

28. Ibid., 84.

29. In his letters home, published in Jacobs, *Marse John*, Grider excitedly describes his relationship with the London actress Billie Carleton (90, 97). It is possible

that his diary entries might have been too intimate or inappropriate for Springs to use, if in fact he had possession of the third diary.

30. Jacobs, *Marse John,* 32–33.
31. Davis, *War Bird,* 103, 110.
32. Ibid., 246–47.
33. A detailed discussion of Springs's use of materials in his letters home is found in Appendix C.
34. Many of Springs's short stories are reminiscences told by other pilots whom Springs the narrator meets in his travels. Because Springs uses this technique so often, it suggests that he, as in *War Birds,* is reluctant to be seen as the only teller of stories about the air war.
35. Pettus and Bishop, *The Springs Story,* 167.
36. *Pilots' Luck,* 21.

Bibliography

Arthur Richmond Taber: A Memorial Record Compiled by His Father. Privately
  printed, 1920. Like Elliott Springs, Taber studied at Princeton, enrolled in the
  Princeton aviation program, and traveled to England on the *Carmania* as one
  of the "Oxford group" of cadets. He died in an aircraft accident in France on 11
  February 1918.
Bishop, William Arthur. *The Courage of Early Morning: The Story of Billy Bishop.*
  Toronto: McClelland and Stewart, 1965. Biography of Canadian flying ace
  William "Billy" Bishop, written by his son. Contains information about the
  forming of the 85th Squadron, to which Springs, Grider, and Callahan belonged
  in the summer of 1918.
Bowers, Peter M. *The Curtiss JN-4.* London: Profile Publications, 1965. Detailed
  history of important early training aircraft used in the U.S. Air Service during
  World War I and after.
Clapp, Frederick M. *A History of the 17th Aero Squadron.* Nashville: Battery
  Press, 1990. Modern reprint of the original squadron history published in 1918.
  Contains essential information about squadron missions, often flown in con-
  junction with the 148th Aero Squadron.
Collins, V. Lansing. *Princeton in the World War.* Princeton, N.J.: Princeton Uni-
  versity Press, 1932. This invaluable reference work describes war-time activities
  of all Princeton men involved in World War I.
Davis, Burke. *War Bird: The Life and Times of Elliott White Springs.* Chapel Hill:
  University of North Carolina Press, 1987. Useful biography.
Doswell, Marshall, and Louise Pettus. *The Legacy: Three Men and What They
  Built; Samuel Elliott White, Leroy Springs, and Elliott White Springs.* Privately
  published, 1987. Biographical accounts of the men responsible for the early suc-
  cess of the Springs Mills.
Douglas, Sholto. *Years of Combat.* London: Collins, 1963. Douglas was squadron
  commander of No. 84 Squadron of the Royal Air Force in the summer of 1918;
  he and the other pilots of 84 knew the men in No. 85 Squadron well.
Felleman, Hazel, ed. *The Best Loved Poems of the American People.* New York:
  Doubleday, 1936. Contains a version of the poem "Willie the Weeper," to which
  Springs refers in his letters.
Grider, John McGavock. *War Birds: Diary of an Unknown Aviator.* Edited by
  Elliott White Springs. College Station: Texas A&M Press, 1988. Includes a fore-
  word by aviation historian James J. Hudson, who claims that Grider, not Elliott
  Springs, should be listed as the author.
Hohn, Marek. *Dope Girls: The Birth of the British Drug Underground.* London:
  Lawrence and Wishart, 1992. Describes Billie Carleton's unhappy involvement

with drugs leading to her death in November 1918. Carleton apparently was romantically attracted to John McGavock Grider.

Irvin, Francis L. *Francis L. "Spike" Irvin's War Diary.* Lancaster, S.C.: Tri-County Publishing Company, 1957. A companion piece to Taylor and Irvin's *History of the 148th Aero Squadron* written by that squadron's administrative sergeant.

Jacobs, Josephine Grider. *Marse John Goes to War.* Memphis: Davis Printing, 1933. Compiled by John McGavock Grider's sister. Grider's letters to his family contain much useful supplementary information about the training program and combat experiences he shared with Elliott Springs and Larry Callahan.

Laffin, John. *Swifter than Eagles: A Biography of Marshal of the Royal Air Force Sir John Maitland Salmond.* Edinburgh: William Blackwood and Sons, 1964. Salmond was the top British general in charge of the Royal Air Force in northern France in the summer and fall of 1918. The 148th and 17th Aero Squadrons were under his command.

Lawrence, T. E. *The Letters of T. E. Lawrence.* Edited by David Garnett. New York: Doubleday, Doran, 1939. In his letter to Springs, Lawrence provides an astute assessment of Springs's book.

Mauer, Mauer, ed. *The U.S. Air Service in World War I.* 4 vols. Maxwell Air Force Base, Ala.: Office of Air Force History, 1978. Volume 1, 325–339, contains an excellent account of the work performed by the 148th and 17th Aero Squadrons in support of the British army.

Money, R. R. *Flying and Soldiering.* London: Ivor Nicholson & Watson, 1936. In this excellent World War I narrative, Money comments on the picture that Springs gives of the off-duty lives of Royal Flying Corps pilots.

Munson, Kenneth. *Aircraft of World War I.* New York: Doubleday, 1968. A concise and comprehensive compilation of every important (and less than important) aircraft to fly during World War I.

Pettus, Louise, and Martha Bishop. *The Springs Story: Our First Hundred Years.* Fort Mill, S.C.: Springs Mills, 1987. An informative pictorial history of the Springs Mills from 1887 to 1987.

Pilots' Luck: Drawings by Clayton Knight. With excerpts from stories by Elliott White Springs, Roy Brown, Floyd Gibbons, and Norman S. Hall. Philadelphia: David McKay, 1929. Includes an informative foreword by Elliott Springs about flying in World War I.

Skelton, Marvin L., and George H. Williams. *Lt. Henry Clay: Sopwith Camel Ace.* Dallas: University of Texas at Dallas, 1998. Invaluable for showing the career of an aviator with similar duties as those of Elliott Springs; Clay was flight commander of C Flight, 148th Aero Squadron.

Sloan, James J., Jr. *Wings of Honor: American Airmen in World War I.* Atglen, Pa.: Schiffer Publishing, 1994. This indispensable reference book describes American aviators and flying units of World War I.

Spalding, Albert. *Rise to Follow: An Autobiography.* New York: Henry Holt, 1943. Spalding describes his experiences as adjutant to Capt. Fiorello LaGuardia in Italy in 1918.

Taylor, W. P., and F. L. Irvin. *History of the 148th Aero Squadron, Aviation Section, U.S. Army Signal Corps, AEF, BEF, 1917–1918.* Lancaster, S.C.: Tri-County

Publishing Company, 1957. This history of the 148th Aero Squadron, written by its members at war's end, is a necessary and invaluable resource.

Thayer, Lucien H. *America's First Eagles: The Official History of the U.S. Air Service, AEF (1917–1918)*. Edited by Donald Joseph McGee and Roger James Bender. Mesa, Ariz: Bender Publishing and Champlin Fighter Museum Press, 1983. Excellent early history of the role of the U.S. Air Service in World War I.

Todd, Robert M. *Sopwith Camel Fighter Ace*. Falls Church, Va.: AJAY Enterprises, 1978. Todd flew in the 17th Aero Squadron and shared in the adventures and air combats of the 148th Aero Squadron; both were assigned to support the British army.

Vaughan, David K. *An American Pilot in the Skies of France: The Diaries and Letters of Percival T. Gates, 1917–1918*. Lanham, Md.: University Press of America, 1992. Contains an account of typical American flight training program in France, in contrast to the program in which Springs trained in England.

Vaughn, George A., Jr. *War Flying in France*. Edited and annotated by Marvin Skelton. Manhattan, Kans.: Air Force Historical Foundation, 1980. Vaughn flew in the 17th Aero Squadron and amassed a victory total greater than that of Elliott Springs in less time.

War Birds: Diary of an Unknown Aviator. Edited by Elliott White Springs. Special autographed ed. New York: Doran, 1926. This original edition lacks the foreword that Springs added in later editions explaining his involvement in the story. Contains two fold-out photographs of the cadets at Oxford University and a roster of the cadets, indicating those wounded and those killed.

Wortman, Marc. *The Millionaires' Unit: The Aristocratic Flyboys Who Fought the Great War and Invented American Air Power*. New York: Public Affairs, 2006. An excellent account of the development of the Yale University aviation program prior to and during World War I and the subsequent careers of the men who completed the program.

.

Index

Italicized page numbers indicate photographs of subjects.